Studies in Eighteenth-Century Culture

VOLUME 17

Studies in Eighteenth-Century Culture

VOLUME 17

EDITED BY **John Yolton**
Rutgers University

Leslie Ellen Brown
Louisiana State University

PUBLISHED for the
AMERICAN SOCIETY FOR EIGHTEENTH-CENTURY STUDIES
by COLLEAGUES PRESS

Published 1987

Colleagues Press
Box 4007
East Lansing, Michigan 48826

Outside North America
Boydell and Brewer Ltd.
P.O. Box 9
Woodbridge, Suffolk IP12 3DF
England

First printing

Printed in the United States of America

LC 75–648277

ISBN 0–937191–04–3
ISSN 0360–2370

Editorial Policy

The editors of *Studies in Eighteenth-Century Culture* select papers of the highest quality and broadest intellectual interest in eighteenth-century studies. Papers presented at regional and national meetings of the American Society for Eighteenth-Century Studies between 1 July and 30 June must be submitted by 1 August each year to be considered for publication. Generally papers written for oral presentation require revisions and the addition of scholarly apparatus. Contributions will be judged according to the highest standards of scholarship. Papers should be written in English, but quotations in foreign languages are permissible. Papers should not exceed 20 pages, as space is limited.

For documentation and presentation, papers should follow the *Chicago Manual of Style*, 13th edition. Double-space everything, including block quotations and footnotes. Footnotes should be numbered consecutively and typed on separate sheets following the text. Submit *three* (3) copies of the paper. Photocopies of illustrations should also be submitted in triplicate. The copies of the manuscript should be accompanied by a self-addressed envelope and enough loose stamps to cover the cost of returning one copy. Send manuscripts to the current editor.

Editorial Readers for Volume Seventeen

Contents

Preface

This volume of *Studies in Eighteenth-Century Culture* is the second under the new editorial structure, the first with two editors actively involved
in the selection and editing of papers, and the first with our new publisher, Colleagues Press. These revisions and new departures mark the efforts
undertaken by the American Society for Eighteenth-Century Studies over
the past year or so to refurbish and revitalize SECC and to create a degree
of continuity from volume to volume. In keeping with the standards set
by former editor O. M. Brack, we seek to make our volumes representative of the very best papers given at both national and regional meetings
of the Society and particularly of those reflecting the interdisciplinary interests and careful scholarship of its members. Moreover, we hope that
our volumes will assist in giving wider visibility to the activities of this
relatively new but vigorous Society.

Two events of the past year are reflected in volume 17 of *Studies in
Eighteenth-Century Culture*: the geographical location of the 1986 annual meeting of the national Society in Williamsburg, Virginia, and the return
of Halley's Comet. The happy occasion of locating the ASECS meeting
in Virginia's colonial capital is reflected in two essays, those by Curtis and
Kidd. Too, the Society marked the Year of the Comet with the three
Clifford Lectures devoted to Edmond Halley and his time. For the rest,
the papers were selected from a large and varied collection which were
also originally presented at Williamsburg, as well as at meetings of the
Society's no less lively regional gatherings.

In addition to thanking our new Editorial Board and the many consul-
tants who helped us in our selection of papers, we would also like to thank
Professor Richard Peterson, the Executive Secretary of ASECS, for his
valuable assistance and support.

— THE EDITORS

Studies in Eighteenth-Century Culture

VOLUME 17

Edmond Halley when about thirty years of age painted by Thomas Murray (detail). Courtesy of the Royal Society, London.

Edmond Halley:
His Life and Scientific Achievements

N O R M A N   J.   W.   T H R O W E R

The late Sir Edward Bullard characterized Edmond Halley as "a man of prodigious versatility and most attractive personality."[1] Unfortunately, almost the only fact that most people associate with Halley is his prediction of the comet which bears his name; Comet Halley loops around the Sun every seventy-six years and then travels back beyond Neptune to begin its long return journey.[2] For most people this is a once-in-a-lifetime experience and so it attracts an enormous amount of attention; but the prediction became so important only following the appearance of the comet in 1758 after Halley had been dead for sixteen years.

This paper focusses on Edmond Halley: the man, his life and scientific achievements and not, particularly, on the comet. First the name. On the few occasions when he used his full signature as on his marriage certificate and his will, Halley wrote his first name with an "o", not a "u" — Edmond, not Edmund.[3] The surname has been even more of a problem, being pronounced "Halley" as in "valley"; "Hailey" as in "Bailey"; or "Hawley" as in "Raleigh." A researcher recently had people called up in the London telephone directory with the name and all who responded (thirteen — three refused to answer the question) said they pronounced it "Halley."[4] One respondent said he had a brother who pronounced it "Hailey"; and Colin Ronan, a prominant biographer, calls it "Hawley."[5] On the recent apparition of the comet, the scientific community arbitrarily decided to pronounce it "Halley." In Halley's lifetime the name was generally spelled "Halley," the way he spelled it himself; "Hally" was the manner in which his associate at the Royal Society, Robert Hooke, spelled it; and in the Royal Navy, in which Halley served, it was sometimes rendered in other ways including "Hawly" and "Haley."[6]

It was said of Halley that "he flourished under six crowned heads and received favors from each of them which were the pure effects of his singular merit [which was] as well known abroad, as at home."[7] Actually, he was a citizen under, or subject of, nine British rulers: two Lords Protector, five Kings, and two Queens regnant, if we count separately William III and Mary II (who predeceased her husband, after which he reigned alone). In addition, Halley had significant contact with several British consorts, and a number of foreign royal personages. Halley was born in Haggerston, about three miles northeast of St. Paul's Cathedral, London, on 29 October 1656, Old Style, or 8 November 1656, New Style. This was during the Commonwealth when Oliver Cromwell was Lord Protector of England; Oliver Cromwell was succeeded briefly by his son Richard as Lord Protector. The monarchy was restored in 1660.

Halley was less than four years of age when Charles II was crowned, 23 April 1661. It was during the reign of Charles that Halley grew from infancy to manhood. Halley's father, also Edmond Halley, was a successful merchant in the City of London who provided salt and soap for the Royal Navy. He also owned a considerable amount of rental property, much of which was destroyed in the Great Fire of London (1666), but the family business continued to flourish after this financial disaster. One of his father's apprentices taught the young Edmond Halley writing and arithmetic before he was sent to St. Paul's School. This public (that is, private) school had been founded by the Christian Humanist John Colet, a friend of Erasmus, about a century-and-a-half before Halley went there. It could already count John Milton and Samuel Pepys among its old boys, and John Churchill, later first Duke of Marlborough, was an upper classman when Halley entered St. Paul's. The High Master (as the headmaster of St. Paul's is known to this day), during most of Halley's years there, was the classical scholar, Dr. Thomas Gale, who had given up the Regius Professorship of Greek at Cambridge University to accept the position. Gale, who was later one of the Joint Secretaries of the Royal Society and Dean of York Cathedral, influenced Halley in both classical and scientific studies. Halley was elected Captain (that is, head boy) of St. Paul's.

It was while at school that Halley made his first recorded scientific observation; at the age of fifteen (in 1672) he measured the variation (declination) of the magnetic compass which, along with other similar observations, he published later in "A theory of the variation of the magnetic compass," *Philosophical Transactions* (1683). Also, while still at school, Halley accompanied the group including Sir Christopher Wren which selected the site of the Royal Observatory at Greenwich. The well-known instrument maker Joseph Moxon, whose London shop Halley frequented as a schoolboy, said that if a star were missing on a celestial chart that young Halley would soon discover the omission. Looking back on his boyhood a few years later Halley wrote:

> From my tender years I showed a marked bent toward mathematics; and when, about six years ago, [in 1672, when he was sixteen years of age] I first devoted myself to astronomy, I derived so much pleasure and delight from its study as anyone inexperienced therein could scarcely believe.[8]

Halley entered Queen's College, Oxford in 1673, and assisted the Reverend John Flamsteed, the first Astronomer Royal at Greenwich in the summertime. Halley's father provided his son with a set of instruments to enable him to continue his astronomical observations at Oxford. Halley soon mastered the mathematics then being taught at the University and wanted to do something on his own account. So, before receiving a degree, through channels, he approached King Charles II about a project for observing the southern hemisphere constellations. For this purpose Halley was given permission to travel with a friend, who would be his assistant, to the South Atlantic Island of Saint Helena, in an East India Company ship. His father provided him with a handsome allowance of three hundred pounds, three times the annual salary of Flamsteed, who also had to buy his own instruments. After about a year of observing, under very difficult conditions, Halley produced the first southern hemisphere star chart or planisphere and a catalog of telescopically determined star positions, *Catalogus stellarum Australium, sive supplementum catalogi Tychonici* (1679). This work compared with observations made over many years by a number of astronomers working in various places for the northern hemisphere. On his southern hemisphere star chart Halley named a constellation *Rober Carolinum* in honor of Charles's escape from the Battle of Worcester, in the English Civil War, by hiding in an oak tree. Upon seeing the planisphere the King gave a special order that Halley should be awarded the M.A. degree immediately, without any further requirement. The letter was dated 18 November 1678 and the degree granted 3 December of that year.

At about the same time, 30 November 1678, the young Halley, now 23 years of age, was elected Fellow of the Royal Society. He soon resigned his fellowship in order to take the paid position of Clerk to the two Secretaries, one of these being Thomas Gale. Halley was not in need of the salary which, in any case, was paid irregularly, but he wished to become more involved in the affairs of the Society. Halley became editor of the

Philosophical Transactions and embarked on a great series of publications in this journal. His articles were to number over eighty before his death in 1742. One of these articles concerned a phenomenon which he had observed on his way to and from Saint Helena, and was titled, "An historical account of the trade winds, and monsoons . . .," *Philosophical Transactions* (1686). It was illustrated by a chart showing the direction of these persistent winds which had never been mapped previously, and which has been called "the first meteorological chart."[9]

In 1679 Halley was asked to go to Danzig (Gdansk) on behalf of the Royal Society to try to resolve a dispute between Johannes Hevelius on the one side, and Robert Hooke and others at the Royal Society on the other, concerning the relative merits of instruments with open or telescopic sights. Halley performed this difficult assignment with great skill and tact, concealing his own views on the subject which differed from those of Hevelius. Early in 1681 Halley visited Paris and on May 10th called on Jean-Dominique Cassini at the Observatory where the two astronomers made observations of a comet Halley had first seen on his crossing of the Channel—the comet of 1680. Halley made a second visit to Cassini at the Paris observatory at the beginning of 1682. Halley was travelling to Italy with a friend on the Grand Tour and on his return from the Continent Halley married Mary Tooke, a daughter of a senior officer of the Exchequer. In the course of the next ten years, they had two daughters and a son. Halley set up a private observatory to continue his astronomical work at Islington, near London. It was at Islington that Halley saw the comet of 1682—the one which later was to bear his name.

He resumed his duties at the Royal Society and it was in this capacity he learned that Isaac Newton had solved some problems which had baffled Hooke and himself concerning planetary physics. In 1684 Halley visited Isaac Newton in Cambridge and urged him to publish his results, particularly on the inverse square law; Newton had lost his computations, so Halley asked him to recover them. It was through this visit and a subsequent one, and with further encouragement from Halley, that Newton produced his *Philosophiae naturalis principia mathematica*. At first an article was envisaged but it grew into a book-length manuscript which was delivered to Halley in 1686. The Royal Society had no money to pay for the publication so Halley undertook this himself. Halley referred to the *Principia* as "a divine treatise" and was anxious that Hooke (as an official at the Royal Society) should not get undeserved credit for Newton's work. Later Augustus De Morgan wrote of these events:

> But for him, [Halley] in all human probability, the work [the *Principia*] would not have been thought of, nor when thought of written, nor when written printed.[10]

The *Principia* made Newton's reputation as a scientist. Robert Grant wrote of Halley that "among all of those who have thus contributed indirectly to the progress of knowledge, there is none who exhibits such a bright example of disinterestedness and self-sacrificing zeal as the illustrious superintendent [Halley] of the first edition of the Principia."[11] Newton's own statement of the matter was that "it was through his [Halley's] solicitations that it [the *Principia*] came to be published."[12]

When King Charles II died on 6 February 1685, he was succeeded by his brother James II, for whom Halley prepared an explication of the *Principia*. Halley now came increasingly under the influence of Newton. When Newton was appointed Warden of the Mint at the Tower of London, Halley went as his deputy to the regional mint at Chester. Halley soon tired of administrative work, although he found some relief in a trip to nearby North Wales where he measured the height of Mount Snowden, using a barometer. Halley then applied for the vacant Savilian Professorship of Astronomy at Oxford but was denied this. He was believed to be a Deist, not a Trinitarian. When asked by Bishop Edward Stillingfleet if he was a Christian Halley replied, "My Lord, that is not the business I came about. I declare myself a Christian and hope to be treated as such."[13] Halley's candidacy was supported by Gale, now Dean of York Cathedral; but other churchmen who interviewed him opposed the appointment, notably Stillingfleet who called Halley "a skeptic, and a banterer of religion."[14] Flamsteed, who was jealous of Halley's growing reputation, also opposed the appointment. Newton, who was greatly in Halley's debt, nevertheless supported the successful candidate, David Gregory. During this period of his life Halley investigated and published on a wide range of topics: atoms, optics, conic sections, geo-chronology, and the silting of ports. In his investigations, he experimented with magnetic compasses, thermometers, and barometers. He invented a diving bell and made a descent in it himself. He also wrote on archaeology and on historical topics, such as the time and place of the invasion of Britain by Julius Caesar. On the basis of age and sex of all persons who had died in the city of Breslau in 1692, Halley computed a table for the value of annuities, which is the prototype of all later life insurance calculations.

Probably because of his disappointment over being denied the Oxford professorship, Halley requested that he be given a little ship to test his geomagnetic theories. Halley had been interested in magnetism since his days at St. Paul's School, and it was the subject of two of his articles in the *Philosophical Transactions*. The request for the ship was made through the Royal Society to the joint rulers King William III and Queen Mary II, who had succeeded James on his abdication in 1688. The ship, especially commissioned, was of the type known as a pink, and was named *Paramore*.[15] About this time Tsar Peter (later known as the Great) visited

Western Europe to learn shipbuilding and other crafts. When Peter came from Holland to England, Halley was asked to instruct the Tsar in the new science. Halley and the Tsar became well acquainted, and there is a story of Peter putting Halley in a wheelbarrow and pushing him through a holly hedge. We know about this because of a bill submitted by John Evelyn, in whose house Peter was living while in England. Martin Folkes, who knew Halley personally and was later President of the Royal Society, reported on the relationship of Halley and Tsar Peter:

> When Peter the Great, Emperor of Russia, came into England [1698], he sent for Mr. Halley, and found him equal to the great character he had heard of him. He asked him [Halley] many questions concerning the fleet which he [Peter] intended to build, the sciences and arts which he wished to introduce into his dominions, and a thousand other subjects which his unbounded curiosity suggested; he was so well satisfied with Mr. Halley's answers, and so pleased with his conversation, that he [Peter] admitted him [Halley] familiarly to his table, and ranked him among the number of his friends, a term which we may venture to use with respect to a prince of his character; a prince truly great, in making no distinction of men but of their merit.[16]

Peter learned of the *Paramore* and asked to be allowed to navigate her on the Thames. No request of Peter's was refused and so the Tsar of Russia became the first captain of a ship that was soon to embark on what has been called "the first sea journey undertaken for a purely scientific object."[17]

Halley was given the commission of a Captain in the Royal Navy, and he engaged in active correspondence with Josiah Burchett, the Secretary of the Royal Navy. Burchett had succeeded his master Samuel Pepys in the position after Pepys had fallen from royal favor on the accession of William and Mary. During the convulsive period "The Glorious Revolution," Halley, like other prominent men, was investigated concerning his loyalty to the new monarchs. The situation has been described as follows:

> That the grateful sense of the favours he [Halley] had received from the two preceding princes [Charles II and James II], lying always near his heart, he continued to express it with his usual warmth and openness after the Revolution: That after some time the matter reaching the ears of King William, His Majesty, upon the first news was a little alarmed, and thought the behavior of a person of so great reputation, and so conspicuous in the learned world, as Mr. Halley then was, should not be neglected; but upon a nearer enquiry, being truly informed that the warmth of . . . [Halley's] . . . zeal for the ejected prince, was the pure

effect of his gratitude, and without any mixture of particular dislike to his successor, and especially observing he [Halley] was continually employed, at his telescope, determined not to disturb his speculations; being satisfied from his character, that his close attachment to these, would effectively prevent him from pushing his affection any further at most than drinking a health.[18]

Actually, Halley was not a particularly political individual and when asked if he was for the "Hereditary Right," Halley replied: "I am for the King in Possession. If I am protected, I am content. I am sure we pay dear enough for our Protection, and why should we not have the Benefit of it?"[19] The King was correctly informed that Halley was apolitical and, in any case, consumed by his work, as indicated by Pepys, who had a very high opinion of Halley. Pepys regarded Halley as knowing more of the practice and theory of navigation than any Englishman or foreigner of the time. Pepys wrote: "Mr. Hawley, May he not be said to have the most, if not to be the first Englishman (and possibly any other) that had so much, or (it may be) any competent degree (meeting in them) of the science and practice (both) of navigation."[20]

After several delays everything was ready in the fall of 1698 and on October 20, the *Paramore* set sail with a crew of eighteen, a lieutenant and Halley as captain. Halley asked to travel in convoy with the squadron of the pirate fighter Rear Admiral John Benbow, which was on its way to the West Indies. At Portsmouth where she joined Benbow's fleet the *Paramore* fired a five-gun salute, the number merited by a rear admiral at the time. Benbow returned the same number of guns as a tribute to Halley and to science. After the *Paramore* left Benbow's fleet at Madeira, there were many adventures including being fired on by an English vessel whose captain mistook her for a pirate ship. Halley began having trouble with his lieutenant who disliked serving a captain not brought up in the navy; and he also disapproved of Halley's navigational methods. Unknown to Halley at the time, the lieutenant had earlier made an impractical proposal for the solution of the longitude problem which had been reviewed and rejected by a committee of the Board of Longitude of which Halley was a member. Halley now went to the West Indies to try to find a flag officer, possibly Benbow, to have his lieutenant court-martialled. Benbow was off fighting pirates on the North American coast so Halley returned to London in the *Paramore* for the court martial, which was held under the Presidency of Admiral Sir Cloudesley Shovell. The court martial ruled that the lieutenant was guilty only of insubordination and he was let off with a reprimand, to Halley's considerable dissatisfaction.

Halley set out again in September 1699, at his own request, without a lieutenant but with a one-armed bo'sun and a crew of twenty-two. He made daily observations including, when possible, recordings of magnetic variation. The farthest point reached by the *Paramore* was 52° 41′ South where Halley and his crew were fortunate to escape shipwreck in iceberg-infested waters. The *Paramore* returned by way of the West Indies, Bermuda and Newfoundland. Here the *Paramore* was again taken for a pirate vessel and fired on by an English ship. Halley arrived back in England 9 September 1700, having lost (on both voyages) only one crew member, a cabin boy who fell overboard during the early stages of the second voyage.

Halley had collected a great deal of scientific data on air temperature and pressure, and brought back some plant specimens which were shown at the Royal Society. More important was his information on magnetic variation. He now had 150 points of observation of this phenomenon, which he had made on the two voyages. Using these data Halley was able to construct what appears to be the earliest extant isogonic map; that is, a map where a series of lines pass through points having equal magnetic variation. This is also the first printed isoline map of any phenomenon. There are now over one hundred isoline uses identified by name. Because the isoline concept was new, Halley was asked to describe it. This he did in several paragraphs which were pasted on the side of the chart after the dedication was received by William III, Queen Mary having died before this time — on 28 December 1694. Halley's Atlantic chart was published in 1701. King William died 19 March 1702 and was succeeded by his wife's sister Anne. Halley published a world chart later in 1702. On the world chart, the isogones are extended to the Indian Ocean, using the observations of others, but not to the Pacific for which he lacked data. A poem in Latin (presumably of Halley's own composition) lauding Queen Anne is included on the map and another honoring the unknown inventor of the magnetic compass. The latter has been translated as follows:

> *To the Inventor of the Nautical Box*
> Him who first taught with magnetism to imbue
> The iron: and the ocean's watery waves
> Made clear to ships erst doubting: him who linked
> Shores, till his time far sundered, and by wind
> Brought mutual products to remotest lands:
> A thankless day, a heedless age have hid.
> No mighty name survives him, being dead
> Hope not to wrest thy fame from Stygian shades,
> Nor seek to win thy ashes honours due.
> And yet — to know within thy secret heart
> A skill surpassing common mortals, to have blest
> The life of far-off grandsons, is not this
> Itself the Elysian fields, the shining crown?[21]

The world isogonic map is dedicated to Queen Anne's consort, Prince George of Denmark.

On his return from the second Atlantic voyage Halley requested use of the *Paramore* for one more short expedition. The purpose of this was to examine the tides in the English Channel. Because of his previous success, this was speedily approved, but England was alert to the possibility of war with France, so at Torbay Halley met with Admiral of the Fleet Sir George Rooke, whose ships were guarding the Channel. Halley had to anchor many times in his observing work, but eventually he completed what he set out to do. Halley had developed a formula for computing the height of the tides in the Channel according to lunar position which is expressed on a chart he made of this phenomenon and is still used today for this purpose.[22] After his second and third voyages in the *Paramore*, Halley was awarded generous gratuities by the order of Queen Anne.

On behalf of the Queen, Halley now visited the court of the Emperor Leopold at Vienna on a secret diplomatic mission, concerning defense of Austrian ports and the head of the Adriatic Sea. The Emperor took a diamond ring from his hand and gave it to Halley. Halley also met Prince Eugene of Savoy, the Duke of Marlborough's ally in the War of the Spanish Succession. During his return journey to England, Halley visited the Crown Prince of Hanover, the future King George II of England. Following this, Halley was the successful candidate for the position of Savilian Professor of Mathematics at Oxford, in spite of the testimony of Flamsteed that Halley "now talks, swears, and drinks brandy like a sea-captain."[23] Halley was awarded an honorary doctorate by his alma mater.

At about this time in his life Halley made his well-known prognostications of the comet now named for him, which he did as he said "with immense labor." This work was published in *Astronomiae cometicae synopsis* (*A Synopsis of Cometary Astronomy*, 1705). The spectacular return of the comet of 1682 as he had predicted, after his death, has overshadowed all of Halley's other work. Halley's relations with Flamsteed deteriorated over the years because Flamsteed was reluctant to publish his observations which were very much needed. Through Newton, Halley obtained Flamsteed's observations and published them with an introduction written by Halley himself as *Historiae Coelestis* (1712). This was done with the approval of the Queen and Prince George, who paid for the work. Halley thought that, as a public servant, Flamsteed should make these data available to the scientific world. Flamsteed was furious and destroyed Halley's contribution to all of the copies of the book which he could lay his hands on except a few for his friends that were "hearty lovers of truth, that you may keep them by you as evidences of the malice of godless persons."[24]

Halley continued his observations in Oxford where he built a little observatory on the top of his house which still exists today. He became Secretary of the Royal Society in succession to Sir Hans Sloane. In 1715 Halley produced a map which perhaps best illustrates his concern with astronomical and geographical phenomena. The map shows the passage of the shadow of an eclipse over England, both the area covered and the time, to the second taken. Since this map was published before the event it depicts, it illustrates the highest attribute of science, the ability to predict. Halley published this so that the general population would not be worried by a phenomenon which had not occurred in this manner for several centuries.

Halley now proposed a precise method of determining the distance of the Earth from the Sun by Transits of Venus, which occur twice in eight years and then take over a century to recur. It was Halley's program of observations of the Transits of Venus for the years 1761 and 1769 that gave rise to Captain James Cook's first voyage to the Pacific. Halley urged that expeditions should be sent to widely separated locations on the globe to observe this phenomenon so that the distance from the Earth to the Sun, which was not known at the time, could be measured by parallax. Halley wrote:

> I strongly urge diligent searchers of the heavens (for whom when I shall have ended my days, these sights are being kept in store) to bear in mind this injunction of mine and to apply themselves actively and with all their might to making the necessary observations.[25]

His words were remembered and the observation of the Transit of Venus of 1769 was the initial reason for Cook's first Pacific Voyage (1768–1771) when, in April, 1700, the important east coast of Australia was discovered.

On Flamsteed's death, Halley became the second in the succession of Astronomers Royal at Greenwich, in 1720, being appointed by King George I. Although now well over sixty years of age, Halley refurbished the observatory and began a series of observations of the moon through all its perturbations, the saros which would take eighteen years and eleven days to complete. Characteristically, Halley, who lived to be over eighty, finished the work he had set himself. Late in life he was visited at Greenwich by Queen Caroline of Ansbach, the clever consort of King George II. The Queen wanted to improve the pay of the Astronomer Royal which had not been increased since Flamsteed took the position sixty years earlier. Halley said to the Queen:

> Pray, your Majesty, do no such thing for if the salary be increased it might become the object for emoluments to place there some unqualified needy dependent to ruin the institution.[26]

However, the Queen learned that Halley had been an officer in the navy so she arranged for him, through the King, to be given the half pension of a captain for the rest of his life. Halley received, in addition to the pension, his pay as an Oxford Professor and as the Astronomer Royal, and was never a poor man.

Halley's wife of fifty years died in 1736, and was buried in the churchyard at Lee, near Greenwich. He gave most of his property to his son, Edmond, a surgeon in the navy who, however, also predeceased him. Halley died in 1742 and was laid to rest, at his request, beside his wife. He seems to have been specifically denied a memorial in Westminster Abbey. He was particularly opposed to Archbishop Ussher's views on the date of the creation of the Earth. Halley based his objections on the salinity of the oceans which, he reasoned, would have taken much longer to become as saline as they were at that time. However, he believed in a finite Earth and, therefore, in Creation. The philosopher George Berkeley, Bishop of Cloyne, characterized Halley as "the infidel mathematician."[27] In the Royal Society Archives, there is a statement concerning the lack of a memorial to Halley in the Abbey, written long after his death by a Reverend George Turnor, in praise of Newton. It reads in part:

> Foreigners in viewing the tombs in the cloister of Westminster Abbey, after admiring the monument of Sir Isaac Newton, sometimes ask for that of his friend Edmond Halley. The reason for its not being there is one greatly to be deplored namely that being an infidel in religious matters (notwithstanding his splendid philosophical attainments) Halley is scarcely worth to be amongst those illustrious dead who repose in peace around the "Christian" Newton.[28]

This injustice was corrected on November 13, 1986, when a memorial to Halley was dedicated in the cloister of Westminster Abbey.

Halley was much admired by his contemporaries, who considered him the second of the English natural philosophers, after Newton, in an age which included Boyle, Hooke, Petty, Wren, and Sloane. He was also admired by a number of truly great scientists since that time including: Alexander von Humboldt, who applied the isoline to meterological uses, Sir George Airy, the greatest of the Victorian Astronomers Royal, and Sir Edward Bullard, who shared Halley's geomagnetical interests, and others. Interestingly, Halley has a greater reputation among scientists than among historians, even historians of science. Halley has a crater named for him on the moon (8°S and 6°W), and a permanent scientific base in Antarctica at 75° 30' S and 26° 42' W is named Halley Bay. Besides being an astronomer, mathematician, and natural philosopher, Halley is considered to be a founder of the study of dynamic meterology, of social statistics, of quantative thematic cartography, and of hydrology. In the last named field he is credited with developing the concept of the hydrological cycle through his studies of evaporation.[29] He was also an expert linguist, having learned Greek, Latin, French, German, and Arabic, the latter to advance his astronomical studies. Halley was also deeply interested in archaeology and history, and also wrote poetry. Halley's best epitaph was provided by his two daughters Catherine and Margaret. They expressed this in a formal way in the inscription on the capstone of the tomb of their parents which was later set into the wall at the Old Royal Observatory, Greenwich. The inscription reads in part:

> Under this marble peacefully rests, with his beloved wife, Edmond Halley, LLD, unquestionably the greatest astronomer of his age. But to conceive an adequate knowledge of the excellencies of this great man, the reader must have recourse to his writings, in which all of the sciences are in the most beautiful and perspicacious manner illustrated and improved. As when living he was so highly esteemed by his Countrymen, gratitude requires that his memory should be respected by posterity. To the memory of the best parents their affectionate daughters have erected this memorial in the year 1742.[30]

In spite of his own eminence, because he was an associate and contemporary of Newton, Halley in his own lifetime was a scientist in eclipse. He remains such until, every seventy-six years, Comet Halley appears in the sky and his memory is revived.

NOTES

1 Sir Edward Bullard, "Edmond Halley (1656–1741)," in *Endeavour* 15 (1956), no. 60:189.
2 On its recent apparition, Halley's comet could be observed from the Earth with binoculars from October 1985 to May 1986, with a period of about two weeks either side of the perihelion (9 February 1986) when it was not visible. It will reach aphelion in 2024, and will again be seen from the Earth in 2061.
3 *Notes and Queries*, 11th ser., 4 (1911):85 and 13th ser., 155 (1928): 24–25.
4 Nigel Calder, *The Comet is Coming; The Feverish Legacy of Mr. Halley* (New York, 1980), 44.
5 Colin A. Ronan, *Edmond Halley: Genius in Eclipse* (London and New York, 1969) and Angus Armitage, *Edmond Halley* (London, 1966) are two short modern biographies. Earlier writings on the subject include Eugene F. Mac Pike, *Correspondence and Papers of Edmond Halley* (London, 1937) and other published and unpublished work by this author on Halley. A near contemporary

account of Halley's life is contained in *Biographia Britannica*, 4 (1757): 2494–2520.

6 Norman J. W. Thrower, *The Three Voyages of Edmond Halley in the 'Paramore', 1698–1701*, Hakluyt Society, 2nd ser., vols. 156, 157 (London, 1981), 156:15.

7 Royal Society, *Collectanea Newtoniana*, compiled by Charles Turnor, 1837, vol. 4:25–27 (manuscript).

8 Quoted in Armitage, 25.

9 Sydney Chapman, "Edmond Halley as Physical Geographer and The Story of his Charts," *Occasional Notes*, Royal Astronomical Society, 9 (1941):2. This and other maps and charts by Halley are reproduced in Norman J. W. Thrower, "Edmond Halley and Thematic Geo-Cartography" in *The Terraqueous Globe*, William Andrews Clark Memorial Library, University of California, Los Angeles, 1969, and "Edmond Halley as a Thematic Geo-Cartographer," in the *Annals* of the Association of American Geographers, 59 (1969): 652–77.

10 Quoted in Ronan, 88.

11 Robert Grant, *History of Physical Astronomy* (London, 1852), 31.

12 Ronan, 86.

13 Mac Pike, 264

14 Ibid.

15 This is the way Halley spelled the name of the ship in the titles of the three journals of his voyages in her. Other spellings include "Paramour," the official designation, "Parrimore," "Parramore," etc.

16 Quoted in Mac Pike, 261.

17 Chapman, 5.

18 Mac Pike, 268–69.

19 Ibid., 269.

20 J. R. Tanner, *Samuel Pepys's Naval Minutes* (London, 1926), 420.

21 Chapman, 8–9, translated by Mrs. Chapman. Halley also wrote verses lauding Newton which were prefixed to the First Edition on the *Principia*. These were altered in later editions but Newton preferred the original form by Halley (Mac Pike, 203–7, with translation). Nautical box = magnetic compass.

22 J. Proudman, "Halley's Tidal Chart," *Geographical Journal*, 100 (1942): 174–76.

23 Quoted in Ronan, 156.

24 Derek Howse, "Newton Manuscript Documents a Celebrated Quarrel," *The Clark Newsletter*, 6 (1984): 2.

25 Quoted in Thrower, ed., *The Three Voyages*, 26.

26 Ibid., 77, n.3.

27 George Berkeley, *The Analyst or a Discourse Addressed to an Infidel Mathematician* (London, 1734).

28 Quoted in Thrower, *The Three Voyages*, 80.

29 A. K. Biswas, "Edmond Halley F.R.S. Hydrologist Extraordinary" Royal Society, *Notes and Records* 25 (1970): 47–57.

30 Quoted in Thrower, *The Three Voyages*, 79.

"Wicked Whiston" and the Scriblerians: Another Ancients-Modern Controversy

G. S. R O U S S E A U

> Who can the Comet's wond'rous Journey tell;
> Seats not unaptly deem'd the Place of Hell.
> Now burning in the Sun's immediate Beams;
> More frigid now than Greenland's frozen Streams.
> Of all God's Works, our Reason Nothing shows,
> So fitly form'd for Torments and for Woes.
>
> (quoted in Benjamin Martin, *The Young Gentleman and Lady's Philosophy*, 1756, Dialogue XV, "Of the comets")

The Scriblerians were less interested in Halley's comet, or its implications for Newtonian astronomy and celestial mechanics, than in William Whiston's prophecies based on comets.[1] The Wits had no reason to suspect Halley's mathematical authority or astronomical competence, and Halley had prudently confined himself to the field (celestial mechanics) he knew best rather than applied these physical laws to historical events. But Whiston's millenarian predictions were of another order, had more immediate social relevance than Halley's tables and periodicities: indeed his predictions provided the Wits with ready-made fuel for satire and derision. For them Whiston was a comic, if trifling, figure who became a natural butt for their Scriblerian satire, as he read significance into every motion of the stars and tremor of the earth. In time his public image was transformed into that of the worst type of "Ancient": supernaturally interpreting signs above and beneath the earth as proof that the hour of

17

apocalypse was imminent but constantly changing his mind about the day. For this ridiculous behavior the Wits enthroned him as one of the arch-dunces of the age, if not accorded a place in Pope's *Dunciad* nevertheless the explicit target of others of their satires. Newton and Halley were — in this sense — also of the party of the "Ancients," yet they were less objectionable for their more modest millenarian activities. But "wicked Whiston," as Pope eventually denounced him, was incorrigible: an arian heretic; a lapsed Cambridge professor; a social pariah; an eccentric millenarian, quack doctor, and fool-like character whose strengths could not redeem his foibles. The Scriblerian Wits assume the role of "Moderns" in adoption of this position against irrationalism and supernaturalism, Whiston and his millenarian cohorts, the Ancients; yet time was needed before the Scriblerians could assess his prophecies and penetrate through his mumbo-jumbo. The story of their response to cometary Whiston is my subject here.

Long before 1682, comets had captured the visual and literary imagination.[2] The comet's immense size, tail, blaze, and hairiness, inflamed the imagination of poets and provided them with new sources of imagery, new senses of space and magnitude, new ways to relate the supernatural to the natural world, new empires of concrete color on which to draw, as in Donne's "vagrant transitory Comets," and Milton's dozens of poetic references to comets. Long before 1682, Shakespeare had written that "Stars with trains of fire and dews of blood" reflected "disasters in the sun," and it is accurate to note that by 1600 the comet was the single most accessible image to writers succumbing to magic and superstition. As Horatio had admonished Hamlet:

> The moist star
> Under whose influence Neptune's empire stands
> Was sick almost to doomsday with eclipse

and Gloucester had forewarned his peers that "these late eclipses in the sun and moon portend no good to us. . . . We have seen the best of our times."[3] A century later the Scriblerians would have agreed with Gloucester, but as the early eighteenth century wore on, the Wits' attitude to comets gradually shifted from high seriousness to comic levity. Popular interest in comets after 1680 enhanced this transition to levity, as did increasing secularism and deism. By 1682–1683 the popular imagination was saturated with all types of astronomical speculation, as well as fantastic hypotheses regarding prior collisions of comets with the earth, cometary winters as the primary cause for the death of the legendary giants, monsters and dinosaurs, and astro-theological predictions, as in Christopher

A N
ASTROLOGICAL
A N D
THEOLOGIGAL

DISCOURSE *Upon* this prefent

Great Conjunction.

(The like whereof hath not (likely) been in fome Ages.)

Ufherd in by a

Great COMET.

And fo far, *upon* the *Heavens,* the *Planets,* and *fixed Stars*
as is a Neceffary Introduction into a Diftinct and full
knowledg of the *Principal Subject* Herein Handled.

when I Confider thy Heavens O Lord Pf. 8. 3
Look now toward Heaven and tell the Stars. Gen. 15. 5.
Lift up your Eyes on High, and behold thefe things I.a. 40. 26.

Though we may not be Star gazers, yet we muft be
Star-beholders *Caril on Job.*

LONDON,
Printed for *Langley Curtis* at the fign of Sir *Edmond-bury Godfrey*
near Fleet bridge. 1682.

Figure 1: Title page of *An Astrological and Theological Discourse* (1682). By permission of The Houghton Library, Harvard University.

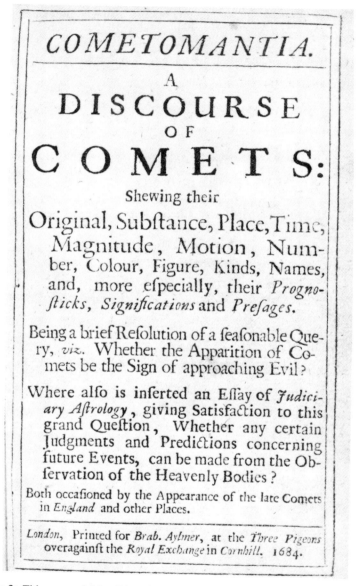

COMETOMANTIA.

A
DISCOURSE
OF
COMETS:

Shewing their

Original, Subſtance, Place, Time, Magnitude, Motion, Number, Colour, Figure, Kinds, Names, and, more eſpecially, their *Prognoſticks, Significations* and *Preſages.*

Being a brief Reſolution of a ſeaſonable Query, *viz.* Whether the Apparition of Comets be the Sign of approaching Evil?

Where alſo is inſerted an Eſſay of *Judiciary Aſtrology*, giving Satisfaction to this grand Queſtion, Whether any certain Judgments and Predictions concerning future Events, can be made from the Obſervation of the Heavenly Bodies?

Both occaſioned by the Appearance of the late Comets in *England* and other Places.

London, Printed for *Brab. Aylmer,* at the *Three Pigeons* overagainſt the *Royal Exchange* in *Cornhill.* 1684.

Figure 2: Title page of John Edwards's *Cometomantia* (1684). By permission of the William Andrews Clark Memorial Library, University of California at Los Angeles.

Nesse's astrological treatises from which prints and engravings were made.[4] In the 1680s and 90s comets elicited every type of religious response, especially supernatural ones about doomsday and the New Jerusalem.

By 1684 John Edwards, a Calvinist minister who believed that Socinianism and John Locke's philosophy had been the two worst developments of his lifetime, could write a three-hundred page treatise surveying the history of comets from the Greeks and Romans to the present time. Here Edwards explained that comets were the ultimate source of vital animal spirits that gave motion to all matter, that the Romans believed comets to be the souls of deceased heroes, and demonstrated that astrology as well as human health depended on the periodicity of comets.[5] Edwards's *Cometomantia* was not a Restoration equivalent of Eaton Barrett's best-selling Victorian book *The Comet Mania* (1857), published when Halley's comet was to return once again, but it made larger claims for comets than any book written in English before 1684. As the dire political events of 1685 evolved, and four years later, when William and Mary were crowned, prophets increasingly cited comets as prognostications and proof of these abrupt political changes. 1689 was an important year, politically as well as philosophically, noteworthy for crownings, acts of toleration, and Lockean philosophy. It also printed works and engravings noting the conjunction of astronomical, astrological, and theological realms, as in a caricature labelled "The Dutch Stockhouse of the Jesuit Father Peter: The Great Three-Horned Doctor, a great naturalist,"[6] who, as a Jesuit priest and oppressor of Protestant dissenters, collaborates with demons to enslave Protestants, and searches with these dissenters for the periodicity of Halley's comet. But nothing cometary written in English in the 1680s could rival the appearance, in 1696, of Whiston's *New Theory of the Earth*. This treatise written by a *bona fide* Newtonian who appeared to have the highest scientific credentials was ostensibly a reply to Thomas Burnet's *Sacred Theory of the Earth*, but struck some contemporary readers as outrageous and as more extravagant than Burnet.[7] Here Whiston related how the earth itself began its existence as a comet that evolved into a planet. A second comet with "little or no atmosphere" struck the Equator and set the Earth spinning. Then human sinfulness—he maintained—brought a third and punitive comet that passed in front of the orbiting earth at noon, Peking time, on Monday 2 December 2926 B.C. The tidal force cracked the earth, and the tail of the comet drenched it with water six miles deep: this was the great Noachian deluge that Whiston labelled "the Choc of a Comet."

Whiston seems to have borrowed his theory of "a Choc" directly from Halley, and his absortion may have involved plagiarism. In 1694 Halley had read two papers before the Royal Society in which he suggested as a natural cause for the Flood, the "Choc of a Comet."[8] Either Halley or the editor of the *Philosophical Transactions* suspected Whiston of plagiarism, since the editor's note concludes with a bizarre comment about Whiston's *New Theory of the Earth* having appeared a year and a half *after* Halley read his two papers. The innuendo of plagiarism from Halley appears not to have harmed Whiston immediately, not until the publication in 1708 of a second edition of *A New Theory*. The appearance of this edition coincided with the first charges of antitrinitarian heresy read into Whiston's Boyle Lectures, and proved that Halley's caution about not wanting to publish Whiston's papers postulating the comet as a cause for the flood was justified.[9] The Burnet controversy raged in the 1690s; after 1696 it took a new turn as Halley's comet and the flood were widely debated. The Scriblerians had not yet assembled, and in the 1690s Pope was still a boy, but after 1708 the Wits would have had to exist in a tunnel not to have heard the public debates about Whiston's heresy and his cometary floods. There was no need to apprize themselves: talk about Whistonism was pervasive. After the appearance of Whiston's second edition of a *New Theory of the Earth*, Whiston's notoriety spread: in 1708 he was formally charged with heresy; two years later he was banished from the Lucasian Chair at Cambridge on grounds that he was an arian. During 1708–1710 he earned a reputation as a heretic who had to be removed from university office for the protection of the Church of England. When the young Pope wrote to Cromwell that summer he referred, in verse, to "the wicked Works of Whiston," alluding to Whiston's heretical Boyle Lectures.

Throughout 1709 Whiston remained in seclusion. After his banishment from Cambridge in 1710 he claimed to be impoverished, unable to feed his children, and migrated to London. With the help of Addison and Steele he began to offer coffeehouse lectures on science and theology.[10] It is unknown to what degree they personally knew him, yet there is evidence that on several occasions in 1713–1714 Steele presided over the coffee-drinkers and introduced his speaker. At Button's, Whiston's subject was the new astronomy with an emphasis on eclipses and comets. By August 1713 Pope had heard Whiston on at least one of these occasions, as Marjorie Nicolson and I demonstrated in *This Long Disease my Life*; and on August 14, Pope wrote to John Caryll:

> You can't wonder my thoughts are scarce consistent, when I tell you how they are distracted. This minute, perhaps, I am above the stars, with a thousand systems round about me, looking forward into the vast abyss of eternity, and losing my whole comprehension in the boundless spaces

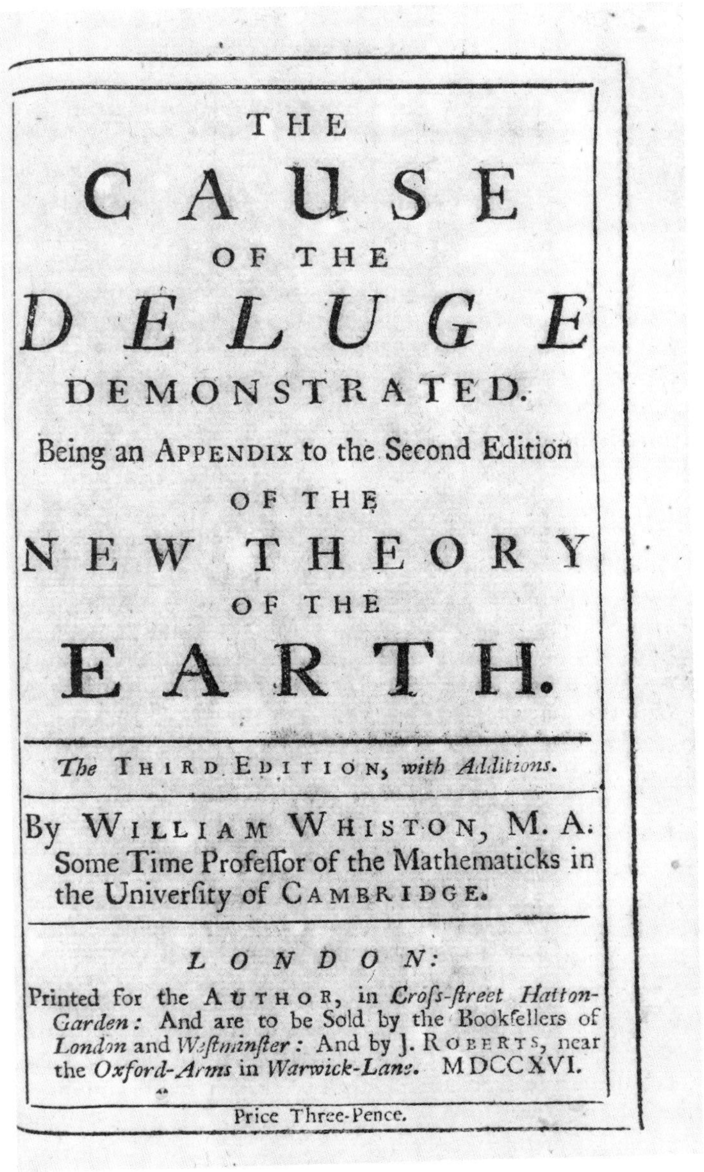

THE
CAUSE
OF THE
DELUGE
DEMONSTRATED.

Being an APPENDIX to the Second Edition

OF THE
NEW THEORY
OF THE
EARTH.

The THIRD EDITION, *with Additions.*

By WILLIAM WHISTON, M. A.
Some Time Professor of the Mathematicks in
the University of CAMBRIDGE.

LONDON:

Printed for the AUTHOR, in *Cross-street Hatton-
Garden*: And are to be Sold by the Booksellers of
London and *Westminster*: And by J. ROBERTS, near
the *Oxford-Arms* in *Warwick-Lane*. MDCCXVI.

Price Three-Pence.

Figure 3: Title page of William Whiston's *The Cause of the Deluge Demonstrated*. London, 1716.

of the extended Creation, in dialogues with W[histon] and the astronomers; the next moment I am below all trifles. . . .[11]

Pope's attitude to "wicked Whiston" was never so positive, but how did he reconcile heresy with Whiston's spellbinding performance in the coffeehouse? If Pope was transported by Whiston's coffeehouse "dialogues," as he told Caryll, especially by Whiston's "Scheme of the Solar System" based on Halley's "Table of Comets,"[12] he would be less charitable about cometary Whiston on other occasions. Just two months after Pope heard Whiston at Button's he advanced a plan to Swift to form a "Club of Scriblerus" that would study the works of the learned. From this project emerged *The Memoirs of Martinus Scriblerus* a decade later, which refers to Whiston and his comets. Yet before Martinus's memoirs saw the light of day, something happened to persuade Pope and the other Scriblerians that among the "falsely learned," cometary Whiston, unlike Halley, ranked in the front line.

Chief among these offenses (provocation of the Wits would be too strong a term) was Whiston's publication, just a single sheet, entitled *The Cause of the Deluge Demonstrated*, which appeared in February 1714 as Whiston's indicters were pressing charges against him for arian heresy.[13] Although no comet had been seen in England for almost a generation, Whiston claimed in this publication the idea of a cometary start and cometary end of the world. As a type of eighteenth-century Immanuel Velikovsky, he identified the millenarian comet as Halley's comet of 1682, and claimed that his earlier hypothesis (i.e. the flood's origination in a comet) was empirical fact. This was the same comet, he asserted, seen in 44 B.C., a year after the assassination of Julius Caesar. Most alarming, Whiston claimed, this comet was the only one listed in Halley's tables that would reduce the whole earth to flames and ashes, for it was the only one that "can come near enough to our Earth in the comets' Ascent from the Sun to cause the great Conflagration."[14]

To the Wits such certain knowledge seemed ludicrous. It was one matter for the modest and cautious Halley to compile tables and espouse hypotheses about celestial mechanics; quite another for the defrocked, dechaired, banished pauper to identify Halley's comet as the cause of a new deluge that would suddenly bring the world to an end. The Scriblerians lost no time before exposing their target: as they made grandiose plans to satirize false learning in the midsummer of 1714, they focused on Whiston and his cometary theory in an artificial letter from Martinus written "to the most amiable Lindamira" in chapter 14, expressing Whiston's fear that the "Ages must be numbred [sic], nay perhaps some Comet may vitrify this Globe on which we tred."[15] Among the "Discoveries and

MISCELLANIES.

THE
THIRD VOLUME.

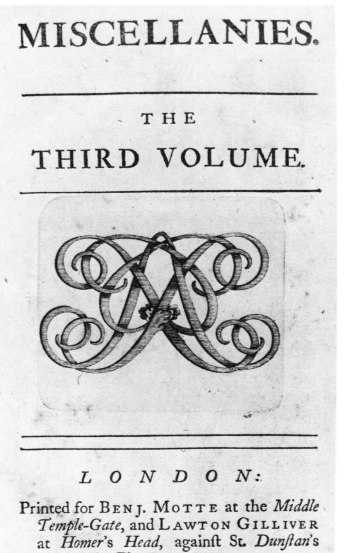

L O N D O N:

Printed for BENJ. MOTTE at the *Middle
Temple-Gate,* and LAWTON GILLIVER
at *Homer's Head,* againſt St. *Dunſtan's*
Church in *Fleetſtreet,* 1732.

Figure 4: Title page of Volume 3 of the Swift-Pope *Miscellanies.* 1732.

A True and Faithful

NARRATIVE

OF

What pass'd in LONDON *during the general Consternation of all Ranks and Degrees of Mankind;*

On Tuesday, Wednesday, Thursday, *and* Friday *last.*

13th 14th 15th & 16 Octr. 1732

by mr John Gay

 N *Tuesday* the 13th of *October*, Mr. *Whiston* held his Lecture near the *Royal Exchange*, to an Audience of Fourteen worthy Citizens, his Subscribers and constant Hearers. Besides these, there were five chance Auditors for that Night only, who had paid their Shillings a peice. I think my self oblig'd to

R   be

Figure 5: "A True and Faithful Narrative," p. 255, from Swift-Pope *Miscellanies,* Volume 3, London, 1732.

Works of the Great Scriblerus . . . written and to be written, known and unknown," is a list of "Tide-Tables, for a Comet, that is to approximate towards the Earth."[16] Martinus assembles these tide-tables in preparation for the approaching comet, which, Whiston contended, was the same one as that of 1682. His fictive tables are Scriblerian parodies of those Whiston is thought to have filched from Halley.

To the Scriblerians Whiston's theory of the millenarian deluge was derisory: all things *began* with a comet — so they shall *end* with a comet. This was the view that had to be challenged, and the astronomical events of the next three years — 1715, 1716, 1717 — provided them with plenty of ammunition. John Gay, like Pope, had heard Whiston at Button's and knew what a spellbinder he proved to his captivated audiences. Inspired by one of these occasions but not setting quill to paper for over a decade, Gay assumed the persona of a London draper named "J. Baker, Knight," who was a regular attendant at Whiston's Tuesday lectures and was probably the author of a delightful prose satire called *A True and Faithful Narrative of What passed in London during the general Consternation of all Ranks and Degrees of Mankind*, probably composed in 1731–1732 and printed anonymously in the Swift-Pope *Miscellanies*.[17]

The work is supposedly a true account of Whiston's lecture near the Royal Exchange on Tuesday October 13, 1714. Gay (assuming he was the author) fabricates a name for each of the fourteen regular auditors (tradesmen and craftsmen, not the learned), and recounts both the lecture and the course of Whiston's predictions. Millenarians, world-enders, and doomsdayers are addressed in particular: "Friends and Fellow Citizens," the narrator remembers Whiston saying prophetically, "all speculative Science is at an end; the Period of all things is at Hand; on *Friday* next this World shall be no more. Put not your confidence in me, Brethren, for tomorrow Morning, five Minutes after Five, the Truth will be Evident; in that instant the Comet shall appear. . . . As ye have heard, believe. Go hence and prepare your Wives, your Families and Friends for the universal Change."[18] Nothing more convinced the draper that Whiston believed his own prophecy than Whiston's returning "a shilling apiece to the Youths that had been disappointed of their Lecture." Then the draper describes how word of the prediction spread like fire throughout London, how initial skepticism was replaced by awesome credulity and with what consternation the dreaded comet appeared "three minutes after five." Here Gay takes a dig at Whiston for his earlier error in predicting the time of the total eclipse as two minutes *later* than it actually appeared.[19] According to the draper, the learned in London thought they were to watch an eclipse, but instead they watched a comet. Yet if Whiston proved, as an astronomer, to be exact to the minute, he was much less successful as a millenarian for, according to the narrator, the comet came and passed, "Friday came, and the People covered all the streets . . . they Drank, they Whor'd, they Swore, they L'yd."[20] If the millenarian event had demonstrated a deeper side of human nature than evidenced in normal times, London itself soon returned to normalcy, Londoners to their old habits and vices. Whiston's prediction had proved, like his apostasy, to be a fraud. He was, it now seemed, its false prophet, false apostle.

I have already suggested why Whiston was associated with the cometary end of the world in 1714 (especially in his *Cause of the Deluge Demonstrated*), even though no comet had been seen in England for some time. It remains to be shown how Whiston's unrelenting prophesies continued to irk and arouse the Scriblerians after 1714. In the year of Queen Anne's death there had been no *total* eclipse of the sun over England for 575 years. According to Halley's computations, the last total solar eclipse had occurred in 1140;[21] the last partial solar eclipse had occurred on September 13, 1699, and was barely observed in England because of inclement weather. But a total solar eclipse was more engrossing and great preparations were being made for it, not only in the Royal Society but widely among laymen and the learned and in such poems as an anonymous work called *The Eclipse* which none of the Scriblerians wrote. It was to occur on April 22, 1715, in the preparation for which Whiston was much involved. Claiming that he and Halley had predicted it would arrive in April, Whiston devised an instrument for the calculation of solar eclipses called "The Copernicus."[22] By March he was selling his Copernicus and manuals of instruction for its use in the coffeehouses; Pope and Gay may have bought one and become proficient in elliptical calculations through its use, as they both told Caryll in their letters. They and other Scriblerians eagerly awaited the total solar eclipse, especially as a millenarian event, but it came and went without excitement.

Two months after the April eclipse the second nova known to appear and disappear periodically appeared in England in June, which astronomers recognized as a reappearance of the one first described in 1686.[23] First observed on June 15, it so increased in visibility during the summer that by August it could be seen by the naked eye.[24] Many laymen considered it a comet because of its periodicity, and Whiston did nothing in the coffeehouses to disabuse them. Encouraged by Whiston, the printed ephemera that summer and autumn suggested that these continuing strange portents in the heavens were presages that would direly affect mankind. The next winter of 1716–1717 was phenomenally cold; so cold that the *Historical Register* considered the frost to be among the "most memorable occurrences and events" in English history and described how the Thames was frozen over, with whole oxen and sheep roasted on the ice.[25] All this caused the public, and especially the Scriblerians, to wonder about Whiston's role as a prophet.

On March 6 another celestial phenomenon appeared, vividly described by Halley. "This Phenomenon," he wrote in the *Philosophical Transactions*, "found all those that are skill'd in the Observation of the Heavens unprepared."[26] Calling it an aurora borealis rather than a nova or comet, Halley despaired that he would ever again see what he saw that night but he was silent about its millenarian significance. Amateurs like the Scriblerians and other laymen thought the aurora to be a comet with a spectacular tail, just as they had believed eclipses and other celestial phenomena to be comets, suggesting to what terrific degree comets then had a stranglehold on their imagination. Whiston was in the meantime feeding the popular imagination about the end of the world in the London coffeehouses and, more particularly, in Steele's Censorium: claiming that these continuing appearances in the skies were unequivocal warnings to mankind about the apocalypse and manifested divine discontent with a corrupt and sinful humanity. The newspapers brimmed with speculation that a comet had just passed or was about to pass, and even Steele's *Chit-Chat* proclaimed that "all this Degree of Light" in the skies is proof of a comet soon to collide with the earth and destroy the world we know by flames, flood and conflagration.[27]

Four days after the March 6 aurora appeared, the unsigned epilogue written for Addison's play *The Drummer* linked Pope and Whiston in transformative images suggestive of the fourth canto of *The Rape of the Lock*:

> If any Briton in this Place appears,
> A slave to Priests, or superstitious Fears,
> Let these odd Scenes reform his Brainsick Notions,
> Or BYFIELD'S[28] ready-to apply his Potions.
> Those Wits excepted, who appear'd so wise,
> To conjure Spectres from the vap'ry Skies.
> A very POPE (I'm told may be afraid,
> And tremble at the Monsters, which he made.)
> From dark mishapen Clouds* of many a Dye.
> A different Object rose to every Eye:
> And the same Vapour, as your Fancies ran,
> Appear'd a *Monarch*, or a *Warming-Pan*.
> Well has Friend WHISTON every Scene apply'd
> And drawn th' unmeaning Meteor to our Side.
> *The late *Meteor*

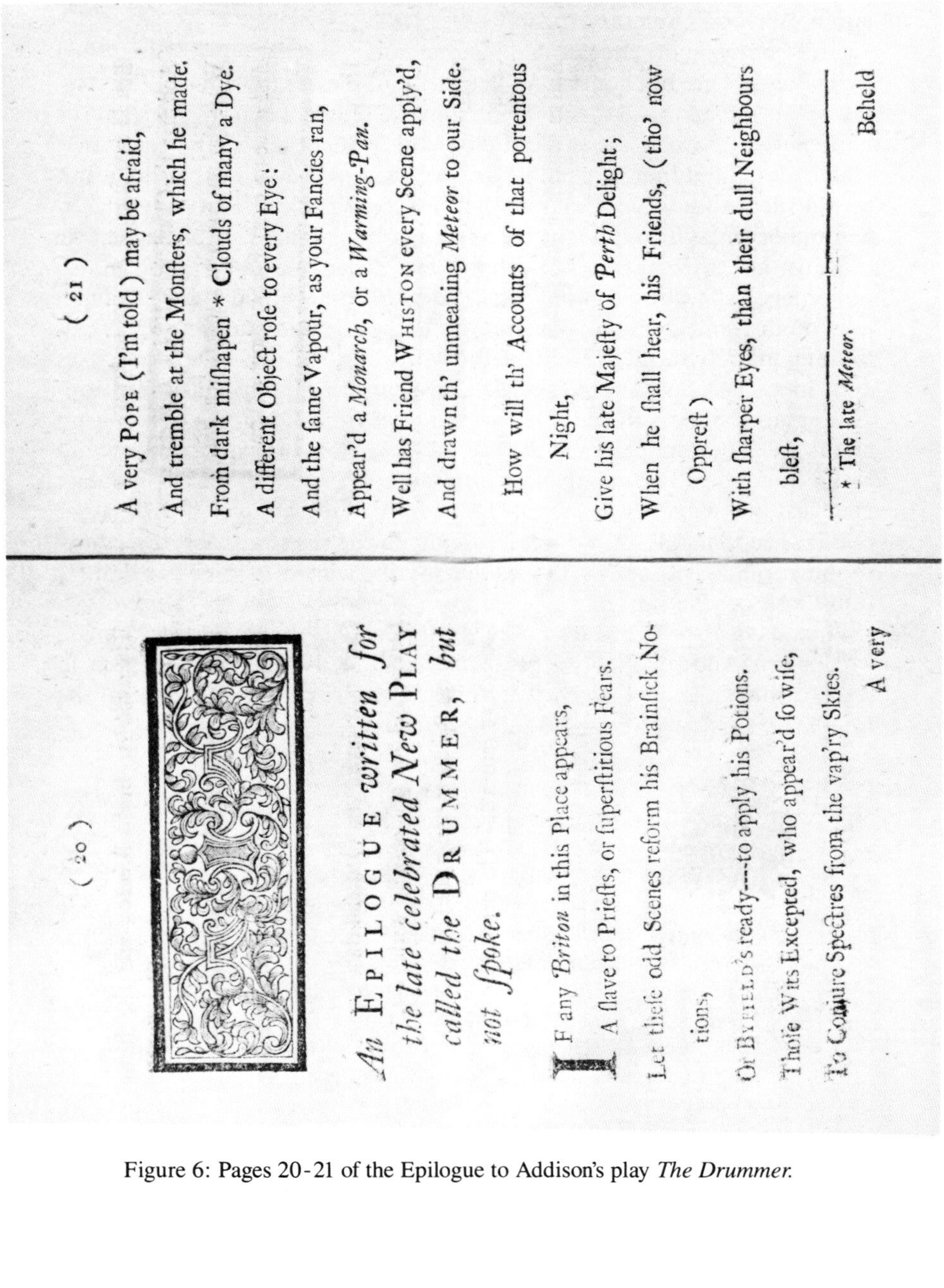

An EPILOGUE *written for the late celebrated New* PLAY *called the* DRUMMER, *but not spoke.*

IF any *Briton* in this Place appears,
A slave to Priests, or superstitious Fears.
Let these odd Scenes reform his Brainsick No-
tions,
Or BYFIELD's ready---to apply his Potions.
Those Wits Excepted, who appear'd so wise,
To Conjure Spectres from the vap'ry Skies.

A very

A very POPE (I'm told) may be afraid,
And tremble at the Monsters, which he made.
From dark mishapen * Clouds of many a Dye.
A different Object rose to every Eye:
And the same Vapour, as your Fancies ran,
Appear'd a *Monarch*, or a *Warming-Pan*.
Well has Friend WHISTON every Scene apply'd,
And drawn th' unmeaning *Meteor* to our Side.

How will th' Accounts of that portentous
Night,
Give his late Majesty of *Perth* Delight;
When he shall hear, his Friends, (tho' now
Opprest)
With sharper Eyes, than their dull Neighbours
blest,
_____
* The late *Meteor.*

Beheld

Figure 6: Pages 20-21 of the Epilogue to Addison's play *The Drummer.*

GOD's Revenge

AGAINST

PUNNING.

Shewing the miserable Fates of Persons addicted to this Crying Sin, in Court and Town.

Anifold have been the Judgments which Heav'n, from Time to Time, for the Chastisement of a Sinful People, has inflicted on whole Nations. For when the Degeneracy becomes Common, 'tis but Just the Punishment should be General : Of this kind, in our own unfortunate Country, was that destructive Pestilence, whose Mortality was so fatal, as to sweep away, if Sir *William Petty* may be believ'd, Five Millions of Christian Souls, besides Women and Jews.

Such also was that Dreadful Conflagration ensuing, in this famous Metropolis of *London,* which Consumed, according to the Computation of Sir *Samuel Morland,* 100000 Houses, not to mention Churches and Stables.

Scarce had this Unhappy Nation recover'd these Funest Disasters, when it pleased God to suffer the Abomination of Play-Houses to rise up in this Land : From hence hath an Inundation of Obscenity flow'd from the Court, and overspread the Kingdom : Even Infants disfigured the Walls of holy Temples with exorbitant Representations of the Members of Generation ; nay, no sooner had they learnt to Spell, but they had Wickedness enough to Write the Names thereof in large Capitals ; an Enormity, observ'd by Travellers, to be found in no Country but *England.*

But when Whoring and Popery were driven hence by the Happy *Revolution* ; still the Nation so greatly offended, that *Socinianism, Arianism,* and *Whistonism* triumph'd in our Streets, and were in a manner become Universal.

And yet still, after all these Visitations, it has pleased Heaven to visit us with a Contagion more Epidemical, and of consequence more Fatal : This was foretold to Us, First, By that unparallel'd Eclipse in 1714 : Secondly, By the dreadful Coruscations in the Air this present Year : And Thirdly, By the Nine Comets seen at once over *Soho-Square,* by Mrs. *Katherine Wadlington,* and Others ; a Contagion that first crept in amongst the First Quality, descended to their Footmen, and infused itself into their Ladies ; I mean, the woful Practice of P U N N I N G. This does occasion the Corruption of our Language, and therein of the Word of God translated into our Language ; which certainly every sober Christian must Tremble at.

Now such is the Enormity of this Abomination, that our very Nobles not only commit *Punning* over Tea, and in Taverns, but even on the

Lord's-

Figure 7: John Gay, *God's Revenge Against Punning.* London, 1716, p. 1.

Lord's-Day, and in the King's Chapel : Therefore to deterr Men from this evil Practice, I fhall give fome True and Dreadful Examples of God's Revenge againft *Punfters*.

The Right Honourable ———— (but it is not fafe to infert the Name of an eminent Nobleman in this Paper, yet I will venture to fay that fuch a one has been feen ; which is all we can fay, confidering the largenefs of his Sleeves :) This young Nobleman was not only a flagitious *Punfter* himfelf, but was acceffary to the Punning of others, by Confent, by Provocation, by Connivance, and by Defence of the Evil committed ; for which the Lord mercifully fpared his Neck, but as a Mark of Reprobation wryed his Nofe.

Another Nobleman of great Hopes, no lefs guilty of the fame Crime, was made the Punifher of himfelf with his own Hand, in the Lofs of 500 Pounds at Box and Dice ; whereby this unfortunate young Gentleman incurr'd the heavy Difpleafure of his Aged Grandmother.

A Third of no lefs illuftrious Extraction, for the fame Vice, was permitted to fall into the Arms of a *Dalilah*, who may one day cut off his curious Hair, and deliver him up to the *Philiftines*.

Colonel *F*———, an ancient Gentleman of grave Deportment, gave into this Sin fo early in his Youth, that whenever his Tongue endeavours to fpeak Common Senfe, he Hefitates fo as not to be underftood.

Thomas Pickle Gentleman, for the fame Crime, banifh'd to *Minorca*.

Muley Hamet, from a healthy and hopeful Officer in the Army, turn'd a miferable Invalid at *Tilbury*-Fort.

Euftace Efq ; for the Murder of much of the King's *Englifh* in *Ireland*, is quite deprived of his Reafon, and now remains a Lively Inftance of Emptinefs and Vivacity.

Poor *Daniel Button*, for the fame Offence, depriv'd of all his Wits.

One *Samuel* an *Irifhman*, for his forwatd Artempt to *Pun*, was ftunted in his Stature, and hath been vifited all his Life after with Bulls and Blunders.

George Simmons, Shoemaker at *Turnftile* in *Holborn*, was fo given to this Cuftom, and did it with fo much Succefs, that his Neighbours gave out he was a Wit. Which Report coming among his Creditors, no body would truft him ; fo that he is now a Bankrupt, and his Family in a miferable Condition.

Divers eminent Clergymen of the Univerfity of *Cambridge*, for having propagated this Vice, became great Drunkards and Tories.

A *Devonfhire* Man of Wit, for only faying, in a jefting manner, *I get Up—Pun a Horfe*, inftantly fell down, and broke his Snuff-box and Neck, and loft the Horfe.

From which Calamities, the Lord in his Merey Defend us All.
So Prayeth the Punlefs *and* Penylefs

J. Baker, *Knight.*

LONDON:

Printed for J. ROBERTS, at the *Oxford-Arms* in *Warwick-Lane.* 1716.

[Price 2 d.]

Figure 8: John Gay, *God's Revenge Against Punning*. London, 1716, p. 2.

Only a few weeks earlier Pope had described Minerva's descent in his just published translation of the *Iliad* as "like a comet," a description associated with further Jacobite prophecies of uprisings,[29] and on February 18 an article in the *Weekly Packet* had called attention to the cometary passage in the *Iliad* translation. This article commented that the cryptic message concealed in Pope's note accompanying the *Iliad* passage was not surprising in view of Pope being a Catholic himself.[30] A few weeks later, Dr. Arbuthnot tackled Whiston, who was still prophesying the end of the world in the coffeehouses, in another Scriblerian paper: a satire on the many sorts of projects with which civic authorities were deluged. This was a pamphlet addressed *To the Right Honourable The Mayor and Alderman of the City of London* and subtitled *The Humble Petition of Colliers, Cooks, Cook-Maids, Blacksmiths, Jackmakers, Braziers, and Others.*[31] Satirically claiming that a whole class of virtuosi who call themselves "Catoptrical victuallers, by gathering, breaking, folding, and bundling up the Sun-Beams, by the help of certain Glasses," planned to procure a monopoly for "cooking" in the future, and "oblige Cooks, and Cook-maids to study Opticks and Astronomy," Arbuthnot charged Whiston, among others, with participating in the scheme, just as Whiston had earlier attempted to discover the longitude. Then, early in November, yet another Scriblerian satire on Whiston appeared, originally printed on both sides of a single sheet. Sherburn and Ault both attributed it to Pope, but Nicolson and Rousseau made what still seems to me a stronger case for Gay, especially if Gay had been the author of *A True and Faithful Narrative*, since it follows as a natural sequence to that prose satire.[32]

As Swift had parodied astrological prognostications in the Bickerstaff Papers, so the Scriblerian *God's Revenge* satirized astronomical predictions, and whether one or another of the Scriblerians wrote it the satire it contains is unmistakably theirs. Looking back over the calamities of English Restoration history, Gay (if it was his) recalls the Great Plague and the Great Fire sent to chastise a sinful people. He recounts how the nation had scarcely recovered from these disasters when "other Abominations rose up in the land," which not even the abrupt political discontinuities of the 1680s could correct.[33] For "still the Nation so greatly offended, that Socinianism, Arianism, and *Whistonism* triumph'd in our Streets,"[34] and "*Whistonism*" is invoked here with such resonance that one can speculate with what frequency it was a term bandied about in the town. Yet considering the profound effect Whiston's lectures had on Pope's imagination for at least two years now, it is strange that only a year later—in 1716—Pope should return to his earlier position about the "wicked Works of Whiston" and acerbically denounce "*Whistonism*" as the natural culmination of Socinianism and Arianism. Gay, on the other hand, or possibly Swift, had already had his fun with cometary Whiston in the earlier satire, and I believe that he (Gay) was providing a sequel to the earlier work. But whether written by Gay, Swift or Pope, or some combination of the Scriblerians, the author at this point launches into an account of recent astronomical phenomena: two real, one exaggerated or invented. "And yet still, after all these Visitations [in the skies]," the satirist genially satirizes millenarian Whiston, "it has pleased Heaven to visit us with a Contagion more Epidemical, and of consequences more Fatal [i.e. namely Punning]: This was foretold to Us, By that unparallel'd Eclipse of 1714. . . . [1715].[35] Secondly, By the dreadful Coruscations in the Air this present Year [1716]: and thirdly, by the Nine Comets seen at once over Soho-Square, by Mrs. Katherine Wadlington. . . ." The eclipse and aurora we recognize, but to what do the satirist's nine comets refer? Most likely they are the author's hyperbole for other celestial phenomena that appeared during that astronomical *annus mirabilis* of 1715–1716, especially the nova that had been visible to the naked eye and which so many laymen (including all the Scriblerians) thought to be yet another comet. But the nova returned in 1716, just as the author of the 1715 article in the *Philosophical Transactions* predicted, and shone most brightly around September 10, a few weeks before *God's Revenge* appeared.[36]

God's Revenge inspired a pseudonymous "E. Parker, Philomath" to compose a series of prophecies for the New Year 1717, which appeared in December 1716 as *Mr. Joanidion Fielding. His True and Faithful Account of the Strange and Miraculous Comet Which was Seen by the Mufti at Constantinople, As appears by the Daily Courant of the Month.*[37] Whoever E. Parker was, he unequivocally attributed *God's Revenge* to Alexander Pope, whose name is included among the prophecies for 1717: "If the Pope be not Eat up by Pun-aises, for Anathema's that he never denounc'd, he shall at least be Tickled to Death, or receive a Phillip from St. Ambrose" — that is, Pope's enemy Ambrose Phillips. Whiston's name also appears in close proximity to Pope's: "Mr. Whiston's Scheme of Primitive Christianity," with its prediction of the return of the flood by collision of the earth with a comet, "shall not prevail this Year [1717]; so that it will be more for [Whiston's] Profit," the satirist's bathos continues, "to meddle only with the Inspiration of the Air-Pump at White Hall."[38] The appearance a few weeks earlier of Whiston's *Astronomical Principles of Religion*, again announcing that the earth was originally a comet and that Halley's comet of 1682 had been the cause of the great Noachian deluge, fed into Parker's aim. Parker's point of departure — "this Strange and Miraculous Comet . . . seen by the Mufti at Constantinople" — was a real comet described by the *Daily Courant* for Thursday, November 15:

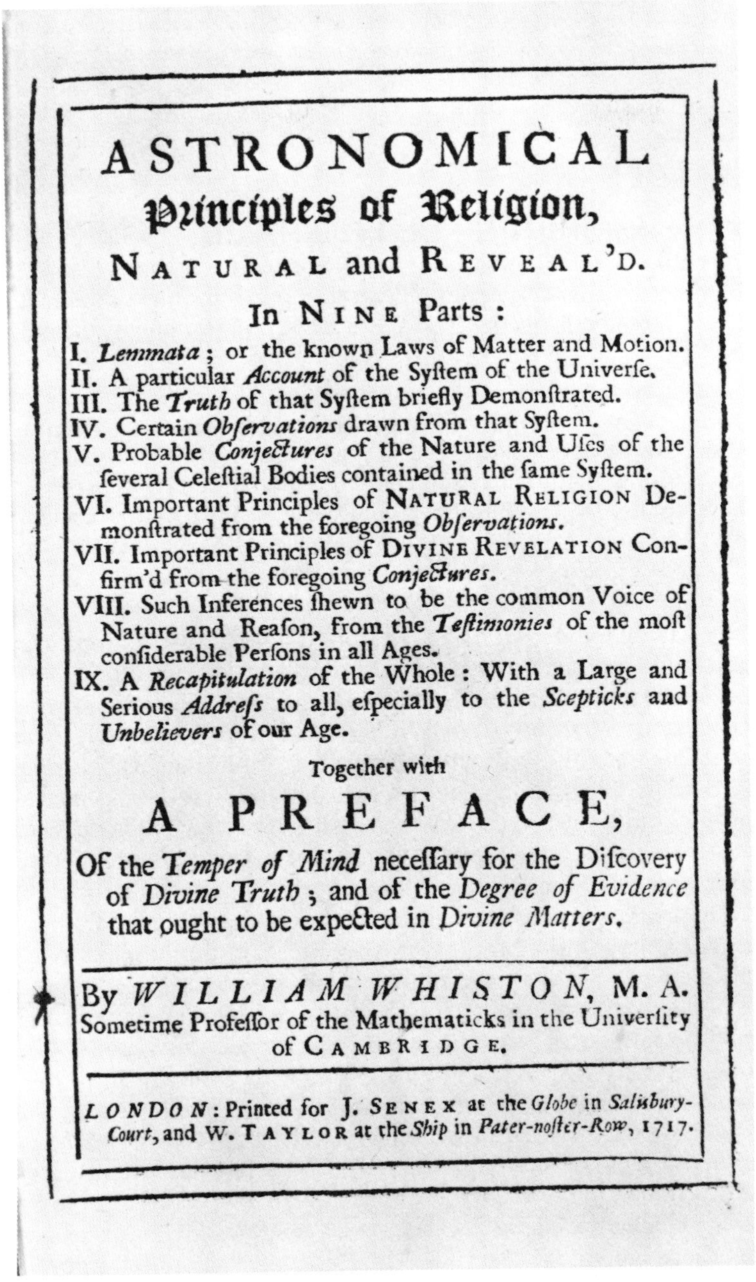

ASTRONOMICAL
Principles of Religion,
NATURAL and REVEAL'D.

In NINE Parts:

I. *Lemmata*; or the known Laws of Matter and Motion.
II. A particular *Account* of the Syftem of the Univerfe.
III. The *Truth* of that Syftem briefly Demonftrated.
IV. Certain *Obfervations* drawn from that Syftem.
V. Probable *Conjectures* of the Nature and Ufes of the feveral Celeftial Bodies contained in the fame Syftem.
VI. Important Principles of NATURAL RELIGION Demonftrated from the foregoing *Obfervations.*
VII. Important Principles of DIVINE REVELATION Confirm'd from the foregoing *Conjectures.*
VIII. Such Inferences fhewn to be the common Voice of Nature and Reafon, from the *Teftimonies* of the moft confiderable Perfons in all Ages.
IX. A *Recapitulation* of the Whole: With a Large and Serious *Addrefs* to all, efpecially to the *Scepticks* and *Unbelievers* of our Age.

Together with

A PREFACE,

Of the *Temper of Mind* neceffary for the Difcovery of *Divine Truth*; and of the *Degree of Evidence* that ought to be expected in *Divine Matters.*

By *WILLIAM WHISTON*, M. A.
Sometime Profeffor of the Mathematicks in the Univerfity of CAMBRIDGE.

LONDON: Printed for J. SENEX at the *Globe* in *Salisbury-Court*, and W. TAYLOR at the *Ship* in *Pater-nofter-Row*, 1717.

Figure 9: Title page of William Whiston's *Astronomical Principles of Religion*. 1717.

> Paris . . . They write from Malta, that an English ship arrived there from the Isles of the Archipelago and reports that there has been seen at Constantinople for eight Days, a Comet, hairy with a long Tail; which appeared soon after Sun-rising, and extended itself from North to South. This has very much frighted those People, [the Turks] who are not used to such Appearances in the Heavens.[39]

Parker visualizes the Mufti of Constantinople as he sits pensively musing on the banks of the Hellespont. His "Favorite Muse," he narrates, came to him prophetically crying out: "Behold, thou High Priest of Allah, how the Light streameth out of Darkness, and the Firmament blazeth as a Topaz."

> At this the High-Priest of Mahomet lifted his Eyes from the Ground, and lo! he beheld a palish Light, like the Crescent of the Imperial Turbant; it soon shot itself forth into the Form of a Comet, whose Body appeared two Degree Diameter; and its Tail in the Form of a Paraboloid, shot up within 20 Degrees of the Zenith; so that it appeared like the One-ey'd Polyphemus, in a Full-bottom'd Periwig.[40]

The pseudonymous Parker also recounts that consternation throughout the land continued unabated, together with various attempts to explain the mysterious comet and anticipate its possible malign or benign effects. The explanation offered by the Sannadrin, we are told, was the one that satisfied the Ottoman Emperor: for "it [the comet] only denoted the Arrival [in Constantinople] of a British Ambassadress of marvellous Beauty, with a long Train of Attendants."[41] Wortley Montagu had become Ambassador to Turkey in August 1716, three months before the pseudonymous Parker composed his delightful satire, the satirist's "British Ambassadress" being none other, of course, than Lady Mary Wortley Montagu, although the Montagus arrived in Constantinople too late to see the comet.[42] Yet even more crucial than the topical prophecy about Pope's Lady Mary, which someone as informed as John Gay would have understood in view of her relation to Pope at just this time (1716), are the references to Whiston, and I believe that they clue us in to the real author. "Mr. Joanidion Fielding" playfully writes: "[while viewing the comet] I did not see the late Coruscations, which Mr. Whiston rightly judges to be the Fire-works of Aerial Spirits. . . ."[43] A few paragraphs later: "a Friend of mine did see the Nine Comets at Mrs. Wadlington's in Soho-Square, when he was going to celebrate a Geocentrick Conjunction," adding perhaps naughtily, "I did see Mr. Halley (whom indeed I never had a good Opinion of) flying in a fiery Chariot over Greenwich-Park."[44]

This chronological survey brings us to the beginning of 1717 when Gay, or one of the other Scriblerians, had now had his fun with Whiston at least twice, in equally playful sequels. If we continued to survey the satires of the Wits in this chronological vein, and if we followed other diversions of the original Scriblerians, we would see that their fascination and vexation with cometary Whiston tapered off after 1717, as the skies became more peaceful. Furthermore, by 1717–1718 cometary Whiston himself had become old hat to Londoners who had, like Pope, actually heard him, or, like Swift, at least heard about his spell-binding coffeehouse presentations for almost a decade. But the Scriblerians, as well as Addison and Steele, were not through with cometary jests arising from their cosmic wonder and cometary imagination. A decade later Swift would, of course, make the possible collision of the comet with the earth one of the memorable events of Lemuel's travels through Laputa, about which so much Swiftiana has now been written that it would belabor the point to say anything further about it here.[45] And, looking further ahead, it may have been the recent death of Halley in 1742 that prompted Pope to compare his third group of dullards in the *New Dunciad* published in October 1743, to a comet approaching perihelion.[46] Pope's cometary wit in the *New Dunciad* cannot be traced to a single source, nor need it be since he had grown up with comets, Halleian and Whistonian, and he need not have read anything to insert them wittily into mock-epics and burlesques about "wicked Whiston." But Pope was too infirm during the winter of 1744 — his last winter — to notice that yet another comet threatened to visit England. Its imminence did not prevent Whiston, now of a great age, writing memoirs, and contemplating religious conversions, from returning to millenarian prophecies, as his *Memoirs* relate, and lesser poets than Pope and Swift from exercising their own millenarian imaginations. Even the *Gentleman's Magazine* devoted a portion of each issue in 1742–1743 to discussion of the new threatening comet, with the figure of Whiston lingering in the background and often mentioned in these accounts.[47]

By 1758 Whiston and all the Scriblerians were dead, unable to survey the town to see if Halley's comet really did return. Of course it did in 1759 and was first glimpsed near Dresden, and then widely viewed throughout Europe and America; but by now, exactly seventy-six years after the comet of 1682, comets had lost some (certainly not all) of their millenarian force. The comet glimpsed in 1758 reappeared early in the spring of 1759, and permitted Laurence Sterne, among others, who was then composing the first two books of *Tristram Shandy*, to be piqued enough to remember the cometary wit of the Scriblerians and the clever way they had identified Whiston as their favorite target. In Sterne's witty version Dr. Slop is likened to the sight of a besmirched Obadiah who is worse than "the worst of Whiston's comets."[48] Whiston is thus yoked to sentimental fiction of the 1750s but without the lengthy treatment he had received five decades earlier. During that spring of 1759 Horace Walpole played a card game at Strawberry Hill called "comets," with a pack of cards he had used seventeen years earlier in 1742.[49] The rules of the game elude me but Walpole's attitude does not: he was eager to learn whether his friend in Italy, Horace Mann, had seen or heard of the new comet, as eager to know as Madame Tussaud was in 1986 to make a waxwork model of Edmond Halley. Yet Walpole, who knew almost nothing about astronomy, doubted that the comet of 1758-1759 was Halley's comet, and as he interrogated Mann it is clear that his reason was historical rather than millenarian. Walpole had read somewhere, or heard about the events in the skies in the years immediately preceding his birth, and he wondered if another cometary *annus mirabilis* was on the way, as it had been in 1715-1716. "In short," Walpole wrote sardonically to Mann, "like pineapples and gold pheasants, these comets of Halley will grow so common as to be sold in Covent Garden market" for a shilling.[50] But during that autumn of 1759 terrific heat struck England, and as the reclusive Walpole fried in a torrid Strawberry Hill, he was not entirely willing to surrender the possibility of supernatural powers of comets. He complained, once again, to Horace Mann that all this conflagration of heat is no doubt the work of the spring's comet, and if only George II had died a few months earlier, the returning comet would have been blamed no doubt for his death too. Meanwhile, the notorious Madame Sevigny was ailing in France, and was "not well [enough]," according to Walpole, to sit up until the early hours of the morning awaiting the comet, for which purpose "she had appointed [her own personal] astronomer to bring his telescopes to the President Henault's, where a large party had gathered to view it."[51] On both sides of the Channel interest in comets was as great as ever, but no one seems to have replaced Whiston in prophesying their millenarian consequence. By the 1760s comets (but not Halley's) had come and gone for decades, some falsely called Halley's comet, others not, and the new generation of Walpole and Sterne was as eager to view comets as the Scriblerians had been. Now the ladies assumed a more active role than they had earlier in the century: all sorts of astronomical books and manuals composed at mid-century taught them how to locate comets and to plot their periodicities, and if there was no exact equivalent for females of Whiston's "Copernicus" instrument, there were nevertheless dozens of similar devices, made by Benjamin Martin and other instrument makers in anticipation of the first expected return of Halley's comet. When Caroline Herschel, for example, read her account of a new comet before the Royal Society on November 9, 1786, long after Halley's comet returned, she represented the very best of a tradition for ladies now decades old.

But despite Halley's achievement in identifying the comet of 1682 and bearing in mind the inevitable growth of astronomical knowledge during the eighteenth century, a fundamental fabric of the social domain had nevertheless altered since the Interregnum and Restoration: especially the gradual decline of superstition. When the young gentlewoman Euphrosyne and her vacationing undergraduate brother Cleonicus discuss comets in Benjamin Martin's 1755 survey of the physical sciences,[52] a question arises about the purpose of these "wondrous Bodies." Cleonicus, recollecting Whiston, answers that each comet is a type of hell—"Seats not unaptly deem'd the Place of Hell"—and cites the poetic passage found as an epigraph to this essay; but sister Euphrosyne dismisses the absurd notion that comets portend extraordinary events, raising various sensible objections to "a Plurality of Hells" and to the idea that comets possess any supernatural powers. Brother Cleonicus concurs, reminding his sister how all these superstitious ideas are "Nothing but Conjecture," the worst type of conjecture at that. But from the vantage of the more general historian today who can see beyond the gaze of Euphrosyne or Cleonicus it is unthinkable, given the climate of religious opinion before the eighteenth century, that a group of writers equivalent to the Scriblerians could have thought of deriding cometary prophecy as they did. And even the satiric author of *Hudibras*, who died just as the comet of 1680 was approaching England and as John Hill, a London physician and astrologer, was issuing an *Allarm to Europe by a late prodigious Comet seen* (1680), has Sidrophel interpret a lit-up kite flying in the sky as a supernatural omen only once:

> This Sidrophel by chance espy'd,
> And with amazement staring wide,
> Bless us! (quoth he), what dreadful wonder
> Is that, appears in heaven yonder?
> A comet, and without a beard!
> Or star that ne'er before appear'd?
> . . .
> It must be supernatural,
> Unless it be that cannon-ball,
> That shot i' th' air point-blank upright,
> Was borne to that prodigious height,
> That learn'd philosophers maintain,
> It ne'er came backwards down again.[53]

If "wicked Whiston" would have agreed with Shakespeare's superstitious Gloucester that "these late eclipses in the sun and moon portend no

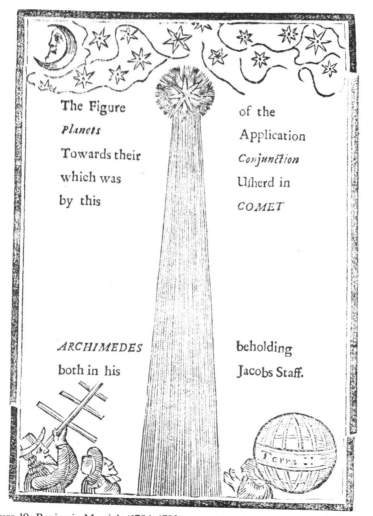

The Figure   of the
Planets   Application
Towards their   *Conjunction*
which was   Uſherd in
by this   *COMET*

ARCHIMEDES   beholding
both in his   Jacobs Staff.

Figure 10: Benjamin Martin's (1704-1782) engraving of "The Wonders of the Cometary World," marking the comet of the year 1744, but published in 1754, and reproduced here by kind permission of The Houghton Library, Harvard University.

good to us. . . . We have seen the best of our times," the more modern Scriblerians, like Euphrosyne, begged to differ. They were not erudite in matters mathematical or astronomic, but their intuition informed them that in every movement in the skies there could not be portents of imminent catastrophe. In this sense the Scriblerians were of the party of the Moderns — more discriminating, less superstitious — and eventually recognized to what degree cometary Whiston was no more prophetic than they were. For them the best of times was just beginning.

NOTES

1 For Whiston see: J. E. Force, *William Whiston Honest Newtonian* (Cambridge: Cambridge U. P., 1985); M. Farell, *William Whiston* (New York: Arno, 1981); M. H. Nicolson and G. S. Rousseau, *This Long Disease, My Life: Alexander Pope and the Sciences* (Princeton: Princeton U. P., 1968), hereafter cited as NR.

2 For the comet in literature before 1680 see: K. B. Collier, *Cosmogonies of our Fathers* (New York: Columbia U. P., 1934); J. C. Greene, *The Death of Adam* (Ames, Iowa: Iowa State U. P., 1959); Nigel Calder, *The Comet is Coming!* (New York: Viking, 1980).

3 Shakespeare, *King Lear*, 1.2.98 ff.

4 Christopher Nesse, *A True Account of this present Blasing [sic]-Star. Presenting itself to the view of the World. This August 1682*, a single- sheet folio. Nesse or Ness (1621–1705) was a non-conformist divine who wrote astrological and theological discourses about Halley's comet in 1682. His *Astrological and Theological Discourse . . . of the Great Comet* (1682, a broadside in the British Library), in which Biblical predictions are fulfilled according to the zodiac, is reproduced here.

5 John Edwards (1637–1716), *Cometomantia. A Discourse of Comets: Shewing their Original, Substance, Place, Time . . . and, more especially, their Prognosticks, Significations and Presages* (London, 1684).

6 No. 1209 in F. G. Stephens, *Catalogue of Political and Personal Satires in the British Museum. Vol. III. Part 1* (London: British Museum Publications, 1877), 738, where the cometary references in the engraving are explained.

7 The most thorough treatment of the Burnet controversy is found in M. H. Nicolson's *Mountain Gloom and Mountain Glory*; for 1689 and Locke's philosophy see John Yolton, *Perceptual Acquaintance from Descartes to Reid* (Minneapolis: U. of Minnesota Press, 1984).

8 Both papers were published thirty years later in *Phil. Trans.* 33, No. 383 (May–June 1724): 118–25; see NR, 141.

9 Halley gave as his reason: "he being sensible that he might have adventured *ultra crepidam*: and apprehensive lest by some unguarded Expression he might incur the Censure of the Sacred Order." See NR, 141.

10 James Force (ref. 1, 163) recognizes Addison's acquaintanceship with Whiston at this time but fails to explain, as we did (NR, 170–72), why Addison continued to satirize Whiston from 1713 to the late 1720s.

11 G. Sherburn (ed.), *The Correspondence of Alexander Pope*, 5 vols. (Oxford: Clarendon, 1956), 1:185.

12 NR, 145–48, 167, where the "Scheme" is described.

13 NR, 180–81.

14 Whiston, "The Cause of the Deluge Demonstrated," appended to Whiston's *Astronomical Principles of Religion* (London, 1717), 6.

15 C. Kerby-Miller (ed.), *Memoirs of . . . Martinus Scriblerus* (New Haven: Yale U. P., 1950), 149.

16 Ibid., 167.

17 As the fourth volume of the set which appeared in 1732. Authorship of the prose satire remains problematic: it has been attributed at one time or another to Gay, Swift, Pope, and Arbuthnot, all of whom have a claim; but whichever of these authors actually composed it, it clearly remains a Scriblerian project. Composition and authorship of the work has been discussed by L. D. Peterson in "Jonathan Swift and a Prose 'Day of Judgment,' " *Modern Philology* 81 (1984): 401–6. I have used the copy in the Clark Library on whose titlepage is written in an eighteenth-century hand "by Mr John Gay."

18 *A True and Faithful Narrative*, 257.

19 Ibid., 260–61.

20 Ibid., 275–76.

21 E. Halley, "Observations of the late Total Eclipse of the Sun on the 22d of April last past, made before the Royal Society," *Phil. Trans.* 19, No. 303 (March-May 1715): 245–62.

22 Whiston, *The Copernicus Explain'd: Or a Brief Account of the Nature and Use of an Universal Astronomical Instrument, For the Calculation and Exhibition of the New and Full Moon, and of the Eclipses, both Solar and Lunar: with the Places Heliocentrical and Geocentrical of all the Planets, Primary and Secondary, & c.* (London, n. d.); discussed and described in NR, 158–60.

23 E. Halley, "A Short History of the several New-Stars that have appear'd within these 150 years: with an Account of the Return of that in Collo Cygni," *Phil. Trans.* Vol. 18, No. 346 (November 1715).

24 NR, 162.

25 *Historical Register* (1716): 115.

26 *Phil. Trans.* 19, No. 347 (January-March 1716): 406.

27 See Rae Blanchard, *Richard Steele's Periodical Journalism* (Oxford: Clarendon, 1942), 261–62.

28 Timothy Byfield, a physician who had turned radical millenarian, joined Whiston, and later linked up with the French prophets from the Cevennes. The text cited here is from the copy in the Yale University Library entitled "An Epilogue written for the late celebrated New Play called the Drummer, but not spoke," and did not appear with editions of Addison's play until 1744.

29 Pope, *The Iliad of Homer*, IV., ll. 95–106.

30 Quoted in the *Weekly Packet*, 18 February 1716, section on "letters from Paris [that] tell of earthquakes and meteors in Italy, which scientists regard as portents of war."

31 *Miscellanies . . . by Dr. Arbuthnot, Mr. Pope, and Mr. Gay* (London, 1742), 3:176–80, discussed in NR, 176.

32 For date, attribution, and contents, see NR, 182–83.

33 *God's Revenge*, quoted in NR, 183.

34 NR, 183.

35 The author writes "in 1714" but the date must have been a typographical error, since neither Gay nor Pope could have made a mistake about so recent a phenomenon.

36 See note 23 above.

37 Sherburn mentions the satire in passing in his *Early Career*, 161, 182–83; C. Kerby-Miller considers it the work of the Scriblerians in *The Memoirs of Martinus Scriblerus*, 46, n. 126; NR discuss it in detail on pp. 184–86 but without coming to any conclusions about authorship.

38 NR, 185.

39 *Daily Courant*, No. 4703 (November 15, 1716): n. p.

40 NR, 185.

41 NR, 186.

42 They arrived in Adrianople, then the capital of Turkey, on March 24, 1717, and travelled to Constantinople late in May 1717; see Robert Halsband, *The Life of Lady Mary Wortley Montagu* (Oxford: Clarendon, 1956), 68–73.

43 NR, 186.

44 NR, 186.

45 Not only by M. H. Nicolson but the many studies that have appeared since her classic article, "The Scientific Background of Swift's *Voyage to Laputa*," *Annals of Science* 2 (1937): 299–334.

46 *The Dunciad*, Book IV, ll. 81–90 and the lengthy accompanying note by Pope and Warburton.

47 Signing some of the articles merely "Cometographus," the *GM* also excerpted passages about comets from Akenside's poem *Pleasures of Imagination*; commented on Cotton Mather's *Essay on Comets* (Boston, 1744); listed another anonymous millenarian work entitled *The Language of Comets, a lively Call to Repentance for National Sins* (London: J. Robinson, 1744), which some believed to have been by Whiston; and reprinted extracts about the life of Halley. A fine study of the public's anticipation of the return of Halley's comet after 1755 is found in C. B. Waff, "Comet Halley's First Expected Return: English Public Apprehensions, 1755–58," *Journal for the History of Astronomy* 17 (1986): 1–37.

48 *The Adventures of Tristram Shandy*, II, chap. 9. This passage about "Whiston's comets" is doubly interesting insofar as it contains the only use of the word "NUCLEUS" [sic] in a major novel of the period.

49 W. S. Lewis (ed.), *The Yale Edition of Horace Walpole's Correspondence*, 48 vols. (New Haven: Yale U. P., 1937–83), 18:36.

50 Ibid., 21:294. A few years earlier Mann wrote to Walpole from Italy saying that young women there distinguished themselves from older women by a come-

tary hairstyle, "so that the preceding mode a la comete is only fit for Madame Swares and such antiquated beauties" (Ibid., 20:148).

51 Ibid., 9:249 and 10:290.

52 Benjamin Martin, "Of the Comets," dialogue 15, "The Young Gentleman and Lady's Philosophy," in *General Magazine of Arts and Sciences* (London, 1755–56), 99–106. Martin's cometary views are much less supernatural than Whiston's; see, for example, his *Theory of Comets Illustrated ... and exemplified in the orbit of the comet of the year 1682, whose return is now near at hand* (London, 1757).

53 Samuel Butler, *Hudibras*, 3 vols. (London, 1819), 2:199–200.

Authorized Prophets:
Comets and Astronomers after 1759

SIMON SCHAFFER

In February 1859, on the centenary of the predicted return of Halley's Comet, the great astronomer John Herschel lectured his audience on the current theory and past history of these astonishing objects. Herschel told them that cometography was a difficult subject for popular exposition, because "there are so many things in the history of comets unexplained, and so many wild and extravagant notions in consequence floating about in the minds of even well-informed persons, that the whole subject has rather, in the public mind, that kind of dreamy indefinite interest that attaches to signs and wonders than any distinct, positive, practical bearing." Cometary transits have always displayed the troubled relationship between astronomers, theologians, natural philosophers and their public. The comet of winter and spring 1758–1759 was no exception, even if, as John Herschel himself put it, "the discovery of the periodical return of Halley's comets forms an epoch in the history of their bodies." Herschel presented this as such an epoch just because he claimed that it marked the end of a period in which comets were seen as signs and wonders. "Hitherto," he insisted, "no one has been able to assign any single point in which we should be a bit better or worse off, if there were no such thing as a comet." In common with his allies among the patricians of Victorian astronomy, Herschel saw but one sign of divine teleology in cometary transits: an opportunity for the exercise of the mathematical and physical ingenuity of astronomical theory: "*there is* a use, and a very important one, of a purely intellectual kind, which they have amply fulfilled; and who shall say that it has not been *designed* that such should be the case? They have afforded some of the sublimest and most satisfactory verifications of our astronomical theories."[1] This address represents, no doubt, a current consensus founded on the self-evidently progressive astronomical treatment of comets and their returns. The relation between bold theory and triumphant prediction, between cool reason and popular credulity, is too potent a resource to be ignored by the ideologues of science. Thus Herschel's colleague and rival, William Whewell, presented a very similar, epochal account of the events of 1758–1759 in his magisterial *History of the Inductive Sciences* (1837). "No verification of the Newtonian theory has yet been wanting," Whewell announced. "The return of Halley's Comet again in 1835, and the extreme exactitude with which it conformed to its predicted course, is a testimony of truth which must appear striking even to the most incurious respecting such matters." Herschel made an equally significant point about the 1835 recovery. Whereas in December 1758 the first observer to see the returning comet was no astronomer but a German farmer, Johann Palitzsch, in 1835 the comet was a securely professional object: "This time, the astronomers were not beaten by the farmers. Their telescopes were from day to day pointed right on the spot where it would be sure to appear — which was advertised all over the world in the almanacs; and it was caught at the earliest possible moment, and pursued till it faded away into a dim mist."[2]

Throughout the eighteenth century, comets persisted as useful resources for a wide range of earthbound practitioners. But those uses were various and do not easily fit into the historiographic straitjacket of linear progress towards rational analysis. There was no obvious division between secure cometography, derived from astronomical science, and the speculations on scriptural interpretation and imminent catastrophe which drew much public attention throughout this period. It is well known that in the 1720s Scriblerian satirists such as John Gay and Alexander Pope directed considerable wit against the apparent excesses of William Whiston's apocalyptic cometography. In the same way, as Waff has recently demonstrated, the excitement of the late 1750s also featured pamphlet wars in London about the bolder catastrophic claims of Benjamin Martin, the leading London instrument-maker and natural philosophical lecturer. Journals carried notices of supposed meetings of concerned astronomers in their "Star-Chamber" at Moorfields. But this jocularity must not be interpreted as the result of ignorant attacks on deluded popularizations of genuinely sober science. As the satirists rightly saw, very close connections did exist between the accomplishment of the return of 1759 as a proof of Newtonian cometography and the deliberate interpretation of that cometography as part of a general cosmological account of the past and future history of the world. Martin announced in his *General Magazine of Arts and*

Sciences in May 1759 that this comet was "undoubtedly the same" as that of 1682, and "as it is the first Comet which has been predicted, and has returned exactly according to that Prediction, it cannot but excite the Attention and Admiration of the Curious in general, and fill the Minds of all Astronomers with a ravishing Satisfaction, as it has, by this Return, confirmed Sir Isaac Newton's *Rationale* of the Solar System, verified the Cometarian Theory of Dr. Halley, and is the first Instance of Astronomy brought to Perfection." More authoritative astronomers agreed. The aged Lowndean professor at Cambridge, Roger Long, stoutly defended Halley's right to his posthumous triumph against foreign claimants. John Bevis, hack for Cave at the *Gentleman's Magazine*, astronomer, and Halley's editor, also worked hard during the late 1750s to show how the return confirmed the triumph of Newtonian astronomy. In so doing, he was reiterating Halley's notorious sentiment in his own *Synopsis* (1749 version) that "posterity will not forget that *it is to an Englishman that it owes this discovery*."[3] Quite apart from the contemporary English embarrassment that the recovery of the comet was at best the accomplishment of a group of French astronomers around Clairaut and Delisle, and at worst that of a Saxon peasant, the reproduction of this sentiment needed considerable interpretative labour. Furthermore, as we shall see, this was by no means the most significant enterprise of cometary debate in the 1750s. The recovery of the comet as a triumph of celestial mechanics, then, was a deliberate task set by workers in London and Paris and not the self-evident destruction of superstition by true astronomy. In this paper I examine the relationship between the careers of two astronomers of the period, Jérôme Lalande and Johann Lambert, and their interested use of the resources located in cometography. It will be argued that the comet was a resource used for profoundly differing theological, ideological and cosmological purposes. This was the object's cultural significance.

When the comet returned in 1759, Lalande was twenty-seven and already a leading figure among Parisian astronomers. Like many others of his generation, he had found a vocation in astronomy at least partly through watching the spectacular comet of 1744: "At Bourg I began to turn a curious and devoted eye to the one which astonished the world in 1744 and which seemed to instruct me that I was devoted by nature to the spectacle of heaven." In 1751 he had been sent to Berlin on the recommendation of his patron Lemonnier in order to conduct observations of the principal planets in co-ordination with those of Lacaille at the Cape, as part of a plan to estimate solar and lunar parallax. The President of the Berlin Academy, Maupertuis, had invited Lalande to Prussia to aid in major astronomical work. While there, Lalande established close links with the Berlin Academy, but the expedition itself was controversial.

Lalande took with him Lemonnier's five foot English mural quadrant, then the best instrument available in France, but was forced to defend the standard of his own work against attacks from Paris. He wrote home that "if Lacaille is more especially working for the Paris Academy, I am working for the one in Berlin of which I am a member; if he is there by order of the King, I am here for the very same reason; if he has perfect instruments, mine are just as good; he is twenty years older than me but that is not my fault, and perhaps he would be glad not to be so much older." On his return in 1752, Lalande quickly moved to distance himself from his former patron. He established his observatory at Cluny, the residence of the *doyen* of French astronomers, Delisle, professor at the Collège Royale. Under Delisle's influence Lalande gained membership of the Académie and in 1768 he succeeded to Delisle's chair at the Collège.[4] Delisle was Lemonnier's inveterate enemy, and in the late 1750s this hostility developed into a controversy over the right interpretation of the cometary return involving Lemonnier and his great follower d'Alembert, who were skeptical of the accomplishments of their contemporaries. Lalande elegantly summarized this point in his éloge of Lemonnier: "I am myself the principal result of (Lemonnier's) zeal for astronomy; I did not go to his lectures any more when I went to live with Delisle." He recalled the bitter dispute with Lemonnier: "I never ceased saying, as Diogenes to his master Antisthenes, *you will never find a rod hard enough to drive me from you.*" Because of these conflicts, the return of 1759 was an important part of a more general debate on the right way of conducting astronomy in France. According to Delisle, and others such as Lalande, Clairaut and Messier, the events of 1759 dramatized the triumph of a new celestial mechanics based on the careful calculation of cometary and planetary orbits; according to d'Alembert and his allies, these researches represented nothing more than the routine extension of the original achievement of Halley himself.[5]

Two concerns dominated the debates about the significance of the comet. The first was practical: the extreme difficulty experienced by Lalande and his colleagues in making sense of the methods of cometography allegedly found in Halley's *Synopsis*. The second was cosmological: the profound issues raised by reinterpretations of the significance of cometary returns. Lalande was very closely involved in both these issues. In June 1757 he began aiding the work of Clairaut and Mme. Lepaute on the calculation of the effects of Jupiter and Saturn on the comet's path through the space of 150 years. In October 1757, Lalande was already able to announce an estimated ephemerides for the comet, and began the preparation of a paper on the secular inequalities of the major planets. Part of the purpose of this paper was to refute the conjectures of Euler, on the possible perturbations of cometary and planetary paths due to unpredictable effects of a resisting aether. Such a resistance would send the Earth and the other planets spiralling into the Sun, and would have changed the time of the cometary return. He demonstrated that "this acceleration of the Earth should already have led to a deadly consequence for humanity, in letting us know almost the time and the manner in which it must end." Lalande repeated these results when he addressed the Académie on the occasion of the comet's return in April 1759: "This system of universal acceleration has no reality in it." He then explained the issues at length in a new edition of Halley's *Synopsis* published in the summer. Much of this work was explicitly devoted to spelling out the precise accomplishment of Lalande and his fellow astronomers during the previous two years. Lemonnier and d'Alembert continued to insist that nothing new had been added to Halley's original conjecture. Lalande answered their charges in the *Journal encyclopédique* in June 1759, telling his readers that, against the views of his critics, Clairaut and he had accomplished "the most beautiful proof which remained for us to provide for universal gravitation." Clairaut's prediction had been out by thirty days, but what was this in a space of more than 150 years? Clairaut himself complained that the encyclopedists round d'Alembert gave Halley "the glory of having done everything and said everything about the Comet."[6] Their status as proponents of new celestial mechanics hinged on this argument. At the end of his life, in August 1802, Lalande reminisced before an audience at his home town of Bourg about the significance of the return of 1759 for what he now baptized the *astronomical revolution*:

> The comet of 1759 was the first remarkable event which signaled the beginning of this happy and brilliant revolution. Halley predicted it in 1705 but the event was necessary to confirm it. . . . This comet, at the same time, provided an admirable proof of universal attraction. Its return should have been delayed by 20 months by the attractions of Jupiter and Saturn, following the results of the immense calculations which Clairaut and I made in advance and this delay was almost precisely confirmed by the observed return.[7]

Lalande's "happy and brilliant revolution"—an appropriate theme for 1802—was not a simple victory in 1759. It was hard to convince his audience that the object which appeared during winter and spring 1758–1759 was the same as that of 1682. It differed so markedly in appearance that Lalande was compelled to spend a considerable portion of his re-edition of Halley's *Synopsis* in an exegesis of the Newtonian account of the origin of cometary tails, since their variability was the only acceptable account of this dramatic transformation. "Let us therefore put away as an absurdity any reflection which might tend to produce the belief that this Comet cannot be that of 1682."[8] Furthermore, there had been an involved discussion between Delisle and his colleagues about the right way of applying Halley's prediction and method to the details of technical cometography. Newton had claimed that all cometary orbits were elliptical in autumn 1684, at least eighteen months before he had any secure evidence for the shape of any such orbits. Halley's heroic work of the 1690s, publicized at the Royal Society in 1696 and then amplified in the *Synopsis* and in successive editions of the *Principia*, had by no means been specific about any but the vaguest of indications about the return of the comets of 1680–1681 and 1682. The only method offered was the "historic" one: parabolas could be derived as approximations for each observed transit. If these parabolas were similar in orientation and direction then the transits could be provisionally attributed to the same comet, and a rough "period" derived. Inequalities in successive "periods" of suppositionally identical comets were then referred to uncomputed perturbations due to the major planets.[9]

Most of Halley's French exegetes, including Lemonnier and Delisle, had needed considerable interpretative skill to save a clear method from this set of utterances. Lalande recalled that Lemonnier had told him that as late as 1742 most French astronomers still doubted whether the perturbations of the major planets could account for the problems of Halley's approach. Lemonnier and Lacaille had a public discussion within the Académie in that year over the true author of perturbation theory and over its correct analysis. In his 1743 edition of the *Synopsis* Lemonnier complained of Comet Halley's own approach that "what was once clear has now become almost unintelligible." Lacaille and Delisle both tried to clarify this approach during the 1740s, commented on the relative merits of Bradley and Halley, and still failed to produce a French consensus on celestial mechanics, as the work by d'Alembert and Clairaut of the late 1740s on the exact application of the inverse square law in lunar theory only dramatised. Delambre, the greatest historian of this period of astronomy, commented later that "this indifference had as its principal cause the obscurity of the method and the few details given by Halley in the section of his book which would have most particularly interested calculators." In 1751 a Cambridge mathematician, Richard Dunthorne, even managed to show that Halley was utterly wrong about the identity of the comets of 1106 and 1680: in this case, at least, the "historic method" was vulnerable. Finally, as Lalande put it bluntly, by the late 1750s "the time when the Comet should appear was absolutely unknown, and, from the year 1757, everyone was waiting for it and looking for it."[10] I suggest that these comments contain a clue to one feature of the significance of 1759. Lalande joined in the competition to show that his preferred version of cometography, based on the analysis of planetary perturbation, the minimization of other physical disturbances, and the assimilation of cometography to analytical mechanics, was indeed the true inheritor of English cometography. Delisle said that Halley was "the greatest astronomer of his time as Newton was its greatest geometer." So he fought hard to persuade John Bevis to allow him, rather than Lemonnier, to edit Halley's *Tables*. The Newtonian mantle was worth winning, but the events of 1759 did not settle a secure future for a "Newtonian" analysis of other cometary paths. Thus in his autobiographical manuscript of the 1790s, *Notice de mes comètes*, Messier began his record with 1759, boasted that his observations were "so to speak the only which exist," and then noted that "in general the return of comets appears very uncertain, except the one of 1682 predicted by Halley and observed in 1759 . . . [subsequent observations] leave theories about the return of comets very uncertain." If the return was the beginning of a revolution in astronomy, as Lalande suggested, then it was a revolution born in conflict.[11]

The second trouble for cometographers in Paris in the 1750s, including Lalande, was the interpretation of the cosmological function of comets. Historians have often rashly assumed that the final propositions of the *Principia*, together with the triumph of 1759, must mark the end of comets' role as cosmic signifiers. For example, in his Lucretian ode at the start of Newton's great book, Halley wrote that "we no longer marvel at the appearances of the bearded star." But this line was excised from the ode by Richard Bentley, editor of the second edition of the *Principia* in 1713. It was replaced by Pemberton in 1726.[12] In fact, most English commentators on Newtonian cometography were keen to show the divine and cosmological significance of comets, precisely because Halley and Newton had shown how these objects could fit into a single divinely planned economy. Newton and Halley connected comets with the stability of the solar system, the scriptural history of the Earth, including the Deluge and the Apocalypse and the restoration of the matter and activity of the planets and the Sun. Newton told David Gregory in 1694 that "the Comets are destined for a use other than that of the planets"; in March 1703, Gregory also recorded that "the Comet whose Orbit Mr Newton determins may sometime impinge on the Earth," and was referred by Newton to Origen's view of the destruction of worlds. Comets were also to be viewed as beneficial: in the *Principia* Newton argued that "it is chiefly from the comets that the spirit comes . . . so much required to sustain the life of all things with us." These ideas were reproduced in Gregory's *Astronomiae physicae et geometricae synopsis* (1702) and in Pemberton's *View of Sir Isaac*

Newton's Philosophy (1728), extended and challenged in the works of sacred physics, notably those of William Whiston and John Woodward, and, of course, echoed and interpreted by Halley himself.[13]

Halley was directly responsible for the influential link between Earth history and cometary collisions. In spring 1687, while preparing the *Principia* for publication, Halley was prompted by a discussion with Robert Hooke and John Wallis to propose that the Deluge was produced by the "casual shock" of a comet. Halley's attention was recaptured by this issue after his brush with the Oxford authorities on the grounds of atheism in 1691 and his close work with Newton on comets in 1694. In December of that year he read the Royal Society a paper in which he argued that cometary collisions might have caused the Deluge, and the following week he reported that "a Person whose judgment I have great reason to respect" (presumably Isaac Newton) had warned that the scriptural Deluge might not have been cometary, but that a collision could well have reduced a former planet to the chaos from which this Earth then emerged. The publication of this paper was delayed for 30 years, but in the 1705 *Synopsis*, Halley repeated his idea that a cometary shock "is by no means impossible to come to pass," and in the extended version completed by 1717 he spelt out some of the consequences of such a clash in the context of the motion of the comet of 1680, which had approached the Earth very closely. Most famously, William Whiston adopted the hint about the 1680 comet in versions of and extracts from his *New Theory of the Earth* (1696), particularly those of 1714 and 1737, and lectured on cometary and scriptural history to large audiences until well into the 1750s. Satirical attacks and priority disputes only publicized the authority of these views. They survived the return of Comet Halley unscathed. In 1765 a Worcestershire rector, Richard Turner, catalogued the received views of cometary significance, including the restoration of activity in stars and planets, the "Habitation of the Damn'd," and "the Executioners of God's Vengence on sinful Worlds." As late as the 1790s, writers such as Adam Walker and Robert Harrington maintained the common view of a cometary cause for the Deluge.[14]

French commentators often debated the cosmological claims made by Halley and his English colleagues. In March 1742, on the occasion of the great comet of that winter, Maupertuis composed his remarkable *Lettre sur la comète*, in which the significance of comets was emphasized, their habitability discussed, and both Whiston's and Halley's theories of the Deluge examined in detail. Maupertuis's purpose was to deny divine teleology as a guarantee of cosmic stability. He rejected Newton's supposition that only the smallest comets approached the Sun lest cosmic perturbation result. Maupertuis instructed his fair correspondent that comets could "bring fatal changes to our Earth and to the whole economy of the heavens against which only habit reassures us . . . they are capable of causing us all the the catastrophes which I have just explained to you." The English cosmological versions of cometography licensed this view: "One of the greatest astronomers of the century, Gregory, has spoken of comets in a manner which re-establishes them in all that reputation of terror which they once had." Similarly, in the great *Essai de cosmologie,* published in 1750 in Berlin just before his meeting with Lalande, Maupertuis extended his criticism of Newton's feeble teleology to a general attack on the argument from design: in particular, comets could certainly crash into the planets, and the mass extinction of species and confused strata of shattered earth seemed to suggest that such collisions had happened in Earth history. In these views Maupertuis was following a similar programme to that of Buffon, whose cometary cosmogony was first presented in 1749 and then massively extended in his *Epoques de la nature* from 1778. In sections of his *Histoire naturelle* dated October 1744 and September 1745, Buffon suggested that a massive comet had detached a portion of the Sun's incandescent body and thus formed the planets, "at the time when Moses said that God divided light from darkness." Probability calculations showed the need for some such physical cause, he held, and while Whiston's hypotheses were condemned, Buffon agreed with the calculation of the English that the comet of 1680 would impinge on the Sun when it next returned in 2255. Reviewers pointed out the theological impropriety of such views, and asked whether Buffon "should be so cruel toward Whiston, Woodward and Burnet? Does he alone have the privilege of setting comets in motion?" Lalande commented approvingly on the views of Maupertuis and Buffon in summer 1773 and gave the *Epoques* an enthusiastic review in summer 1779. Like Lalande, Buffon was extremely hostile to the genre of sacred physics, especially the efforts of Whiston, Burnet and Woodward. This did not mean that the two *philosophes* were hostile to making cometary cosmologies. In the *Epoques,* composed between 1773 and 1777, for example, Buffon calculated that there must be about 500 comets in the solar system, that they had produced the solar heat "by the pressure of this great number of comets," and that cometary collisions would happen again: "It is not impossible that some day new planets will be formed in the same way."[15]

These cometary cosmologies were used in a wide range of eighteenth century discussions of many different meteorological and astronomical events. For example, the earthquake at Lisbon in 1755 fueled work on cosmological disruption: the Protestant pastor Elie Bertrand suggested that earthquakes, too, could be caused by comets, while, notoriously, both Benjamin Martin and John Wesley used the Lisbon disaster to prompt speculation that the imminent comet of 1758–1759 might also bring divine retribution. No doubt drawing on Whiston's cometary publications about the comet of 1680, and confusing this with the comet of 1682, Wesley said the returning comet would "set the Earth on fire, and burn it to a coal, if it did not likewise strike it out of its course; in which case (so far as we can judge) it must drop down directly into the Sun." The Archbishop of Canterbury, Thomas Herring, responded that "the rising and setting of the Sun is a more durable argument for religion than all the extraordinary convulsions of nature put together."[16] But Wesley's views are common amongst pietist preachers: and even though the Parisian astronomers spoke for different interests, cometary collision and significance mattered there too. Comets were too potent to be treated as meaningless wonders, rather than useful signs. Voltaire satirized the persistence of this form of astrology in a paper of June 1773 directed at Lalande and his predecessor Jacques Bernoulli: "He assured us that in truth [the comet's] wig signified nothing bad, but its pigtail was an infallible sign of the anger of heaven." Lalande's protegé Charles Messier was politic enough to record the comet of September 1793 as a "Republican" object. In February 1808 he made long notes on the great comet of 1769, first to point out the remarkable accomplishment of Friedrich Bessel in calculating a reliable ellipse with period of about 2090 years, the first success with such direct analysis, and second to baptise this object as the comet of "Napoleon the Great": "Doubtless there is no-one who is still so infatuated with judicial astrology to believe that the stars have some influence on earthly events: but this great comet, which does not resemble any others we know, which appeared at the birth of NAPOLEON THE GREAT, is an epoch remarkable enough to fix the attention of the whole world, and above all the French."[17]

However, in many ways the most significant of Messier's cometary records initiated with that of 1759 was the comet which appeared in 1770, an "extraordinary" object which as Messier put it "is that which came closest to the Earth and which has most occupied astronomers and geometers." Paris astronomers such as Pingré and du Séjour derived a period of less than six years for this nearby comet, and in 1779 the Académie offered a prize for its calculation. However, Messier and Lalande used the methods they had established in spring and summer 1759 to deduce a path for this object, a task which occupied Messier from 1770 until 1796. Lalande, moreover, made spectacular use of this object to further the project on cometary cosmology which both Maupertuis and Buffon had pursued.[18] Like them, Lalande was engaged in the construction of a cometary cosmology quite separate from astrotheology of the form recommended by English writers such as Whiston and Derham. Lalande's cosmological work explicitly broke with the assumptions of natural theology.

In his annotations on Fontenelle's *Entretiens* Lalande emphasized that the system of attraction was alone responsible for the conservation of the world, and that comets were nothing more nor less than members of the solar system. The principle of a self-sufficient cometary and planetary system was fundamental for Lalande's work in 1757–1759 and throughout his subsequent career, and inspired the crowning accomplishment of Pierre Simon Laplace. Lalande's own work on secular equations of satellites and planets extended, too, to comets and the stars. He worked hard to show that "the Sun and most of the stars are, with their own systems, in a kind of equilibrium with all the neighbouring systems." In 1757 and 1759 Lalande argued for a separation between astrotheology and celestial mechanics in the case of the possible secular accelerations of the Moon and the comets due to some aethereal resistance. Since it would send the Earth spiralling into the Sun, authorities such as Halley and Euler had tried to use this acceleration as an argument against atheist eternalism. Lalande replied that no such changes were observed, and in any case that "we are deprived of proofs which result from this for the Creation and against the eternity of the world. Purely human proofs are useless for Christian philosophers, and they will always be insufficient for the others," of whom Lalande was certainly one. In 1774 he told Voltaire that he subscribed to the Platonist doctrine of a universal geometer: the function of astronomy was the destruction of "all the superstitions of men."[19]

During the Revolution, alongside his strenuous defense of the Collège and of his colleagues, Lalande was an enthusiastic supporter of the cult of reason. Lalande was placed in charge of the Collège in September 1791, ordered its change of name in 1792, and in 1793 and 1794 recorded that it had attained its "best state" under Revolutionary administration. In February 1794 Lalande was orator at the Festival of Supreme Reason at the Pantheon. In 1796, he edited an extraordinary epic poem on the aether and the religion of rational nature composed by Martin de Bussy: Nature was an "elementary being" which "produces and organises everything by the necessary effect of the motion which is proper to it." Lalande endorsed the extreme materialism of the poem, in which the Republican virtues of reason and civic loyalty were to be reinforced by the construction of a new astral faith in the self-sustaining power of a universal active fluid. Fanatic religion and superstition would be destroyed by a better understanding of the ways in which this aether circulated through the heavens, sustained life, and even summoned into existence the greatest of human sages: "It produced Descartes, it created Newton." Lalande argued that the events of 1789 and after had made this doctrine clear: "One of the greatest benefits of the Revolution, without doubt, has been its principal object in destroying feeble prejudices and substituting for them *useful and* eternal truths." Finally, in 1803–1804, Lalande clashed with Napoleon himself on suspicion of atheism, partly because of his editorship of Meréchal's *Dictionnaire des athées*, to which he added a supplement. The supplement, and the moral testament composed at the same period, summed up the rejection of astrotheology and the role of cometography. On the one hand, Lalande confessed that "the spectacle of heaven appears to everyone to be a proof of the existence of God. I believed this at the age of nineteen: today, I see nothing there but matter and motion." On the other hand, Lalande summarized his principal astronomical achievements, including his establishment of the research programme in cosmological stability. But he also boasted that he was the "first to prove that comets could produce revolutions on Earth." Cometary cosmology and significance were not contradictory to self-sufficient celestial mechanics. Astronomers such as Lalande were proficient in the analysis of cometary motions and simultaneously argued for their human significance. He recalled that his argument for the cometary revolutions "produced an astonishing sensation." That sensation was directly connected with the comets of 1759 and 1770.[20]

Lalande's *Reflexions sur les comètes qui peuvent approcher de la Terre* was published in 1773 amidst enormous public interest and terror. The memoir dramatizes the relationship between Lalande's model of celestial mechanics and cometary significance. During the spring of 1773, Lalande and Messier were both absorbed in calculations of the perihelion and possible return of the great proximate comet of 1770. Lalande was also engaged in reading work by Buffon, Maupertuis and Voltaire which explicitly discussed the possible reality and effects of cometary collisions. In his *Elémens de la philosophie de Newton* (1738) Voltaire had already suggested that cometary collisions might occur, but that divine wisdom had arranged the universe so that this did not happen. In their challenge to this form of astrotheology, Maupertuis and Buffon had both denied that special providence occupied itself with the avoidance of such catastrophes. During March 1773, Lalande set about the calculation of the likelihood of such an event, and of its consequences. His memoir was completed for the public meeting of the Académie on April 21 and its title announced in the press. Lalande's strategy was straightforward: he began with a survey of the cometography of authorities such as Whiston and Voltaire on the relation between divine counsel and cometary collisions. He also cited Halley's celebrated speculation on the possible collision of the comet of 1680. Initially, he suggested, there seemed little basis for such reflexions. Lalande recalled that in 1769 he had refuted the claim of the London mathematics teacher and cometographer Samuel Dunn that the comet of that year would come close to Venus, and from an extended table based on the *Synopsis* he demonstrated that just eight observed comets had come within 5 degrees of the Earth at their nodes. In press, Lalande added cometary data from both Prosperin and Lambert to catalogue perihelia and nodes of over sixty comets. But there was one central consideration which made collisions possible: the career of the comet of 1682 and 1759. The principal conclusion Lalande deduced from his work with Clairaut on Halley's Comet was that cometary orbits suffered marked variations, large enough to make it impossible to rule out immense revolutions. This comet has changed its elongation from Earth by 2°10' in 76½ years:

> We cannot reject this quantity on the basis of uncertainty in the observations, because the comet of 1682 was observed for a long enough time and with sufficient care, even though it was not yet known how interesting it was to become for Astronomers in less than twenty-five years time [i.e. at the time of Halley's *Synopsis*]. This displacement of the orbits by foreign attractions is therefore very certain; it can indifferently increase or decrease according to the position of the orbits which produce it; so we can regard as *possible* the coincidence of these eight comets with our own, even at their first appearance.[21]

Unfortunately, as it turned out, Lalande's paper was not read out at the public meeting on April 21, 1773. Significantly, the Académie's time was occupied with the gift of a bust of Maupertis from his old partner La Condamine, by astronomical papers from Pingré and Le Gentil, and by Lavoisier's now celebrated paper on the calcination of metals. The effect of the rumours about Lalande's analysis was, however, startling. The news that the authoritative academician Lalande had predicted an imminent cometary collision spread throughout Paris and the provinces. The lieutenant of police demanded a public denial from Lalande, and a notice clarifying his paper was printed in the *Gazetter* on May 7. The Académie prompted Lalande to print an expanded version of his work. Lalande himself was pestered with crowds of visitors while the faithful clamoured for an archiepiscopal mass to avert the coming deluge. The announcement failed to calm these fears, precisely because of its brevity and because "everyone assumed that the astronomer's memoir must contain terrible truths, since they were being so evidently concealed." Lalande commented that "these popular clamours reached the point of terror and I believed I owed the public an explanation capable of reassuring it." By the end of May, after Lalande's essay had been printed, the terror had reached the provinces around Paris. In Normandy, especially at Evreux, acts of contrition were matched by stillbirths and public disorder. Priests preached sermons on Lalande's work, pointing out presciently that a cometary revolution could not possibly arrive until 1790 and reporting the government's view that Lalande should be reprimanded. The Académie itself played down the strife: Lalande's memoir was "merely hypothetical, and based on possibilities, but of one to 64,000, so it could not disavow the recognised principles of Astronomy" which, so it was reported, "produced an even worse effect, in confirming what he had put forward."[22]

Lalande gained little credit from this episode in May 1773: the "grand peur" he initiated highlighted the instability of stabilist celestial mechanics, and made the term "astronomical revolution" more than ambiguous. At the end of May, the *Journal encyclopédique*, never Lalande's ally since the warfare of 1759 with d'Alembert, printed a satirical poem, *Epître aux comètes*, directed against him. "Parbleu, Mesdames les comètes | Qu'est-il de commun entre nous? | Laissez en repos nos planètes | et croyez-moi, filez plus doux." The following month, the *Journal* summarized Lalande's conclusions, and suggested that given the multiplication of chances of a cometary collision with any of the planets, such a revolution was by no means impossible. The editors drew the appropriately radical conclusion: "Thus the order of celestial motions, however admirable it be, seems to contain within itself an immediate cause, natural and necessary, of the most enormous revolutions." The political message was not missed.[23] Mairobert's *Mémoires secrets pour servir à l'histoire de la République des Lettres* claimed Lalande was a publicity seeker, "known for an intriguer of the first order and a base and vile man." Both the public journals and the Académie's own *Memoires* also satirized the credulity of its own audience: "The heads of our girlfriends are uplifted and we have had a lot of trouble in calming their terrified imaginations." Fouchy wrote that the effect of the memoir highlighted the problem of explaining the meaning of the word "probable" to the public: "In using the word *impossible* in the sense of common language, we can firmly say that the encounter of a comet with the Earth is impossible and that we have nothing to fear from these stars." The academicians continued that "the people whose fear was the liveliest were the first to stop fearing, because they were the first to forget that comets existed; since it is a gift of Nature that the weakest imaginations are also the most fickle."[24]

Unsurprisingly, Voltaire exploited the occasion of Lalande's discomfiture. On June 1 he printed a substantial paper in the *Journal encyclopédique* on this subject. Voltaire pointed to three problems of contemporary cometography. First, he argued against the views of Newton and his commentators that cometary tails must be heated by proximate approaches to the Sun—since fluid, comets could not be heated above a fixed point, and so the Newtonians should "reserve this inflammatory adventure for his commentary on the *Apocalypse*." Second, and consequently, public fears were absurd: only those who "were not philosophers and, if one believes what they believe, don't have the time to become philosophers," could suffer these terrors. Public panic was traditional, and Voltaire deliberately recalled the predictions of Wesley and his ilk in the period between the Lisbon earthquake and the comet of 1759. Finally, and most damagingly, Voltaire made the now common argument that cometography was not yet a secure part of celestial mechanics. Even the great Jacques Bernoulli had been wrong about the return of the comet of 1680, though "only by 54 years and 3 days. An error so inconsiderable being regarded as nothing in the immensity of centuries by all the geometers, it is clear," joked Voltaire, "that nothing is more reasonable than expecting the end of the world for the 20th of May 1773 or some other year." Thus, he concluded, the return of comets was a reasonable but undemonstrated opinion, and those "who have predicted their returns have been taken for dupes."[25] Lalande responded to these worries in the lengthy pamphlet he published in summer 1773 and in letters to Voltaire. Lalande's pamphlet, and the debates about it in the Académie and elsewhere, show how subtle and enduring was the relation between celestial mechanics and cometary significance. This relation did not wither in 1759. In fact, the return of Halley's Comet, as it came to be interpreted, added strength to the speculative authority of the cometographers.

Most of Lalande's fullest public statement was devoted to the cosmological meaning of comets, and to their geological and historical effects. He repeated his initial estimates of the low chances of a collision, as for example that odds of 76,000 to one ruled against the Earth being a part of its orbit where it could be hit. On the other hand, he wrote in detail of the diluvial effects of a close passage — he dismissed Whiston's fantasy, but wrote poetically of the ensuing flood:

> The ravages of the Sea would be preceded by hurricanes, of which we have no conception, but which the comet and the waters would produce at once. These tempests would overturn Towns and devastate the Countryside and would be the forerunners of the final scourge of Nature. . . . Will the navy, which today forms the glory and power of Empires, yet be destined to save the human race?

Astronomical authority was cleverly deployed to write of such disasters. Details drawn from the number of observed perigee distances, now augmented by the significant analytic and philosophical achievements of Johann Lambert, sustained Lalande's cosmological conclusion that evidence from stratigraphy and cometography showed the reality of previous natural catastrophes in Earth's history, and the possibility of "that great revolution which for the human race will be the accomplishment of the centuries, the end of the world, or the beginning of a new order of things."[26]

His old enemy, Dionis du Séjour, rapidly produced a detailed analysis of the probabilities involved in Lalande's supposed scenario. It was presented to a committee of the Académie, including Laplace, d'Alembert, and Lalande himself, in August 1774. Du Séjour was a close ally of d'Alembert, and applied the approach of rational mechanics to attack Buffon's idea of cometary origin for the planets, since they would then still have a common point of intersection on their orbits. Both Euler and Pingré made the same criticism. Du Séjour also showed from hydrodynamics that the tidal effects of a close passage would be minimal, and demonstrated that the most terrifying comets (those with largest tails) were not those which had been closest to the Earth. "Thus, the comets, after having been for a long time the signs of heavenly anger, have become in the view of some speculative philosophers the agents which the Supreme Being uses to change the face of the universe." The committee was sympathetic: "The ignorant and timid vulgar, having no other reason to assure themselves against natural phenomena which are rather singular, except the example and the authority of enlightened people (*personnes éclairées*), become alarmed very easily."[27] Lalande's memoir was disturbing not for his analysis of the relation between cometography and celestial mechanics but because he had inadvertently done this publicly, thus misusing the custodial authority of the elite institutions of state. Lalande, Laplace, du Séjour and their colleagues all worked strenuously to show the secular stability of the solar system. By the late 1770s, Laplace was close to achieving this goal. But this programme went alongside the formation of a naturalistic cosmology in which comets and planets must find a role. In his essay of 1774, for example, du Séjour began to analyze the causation of the common and stable direction of planetary motion. Buffon had used this argument in his own search for a natural cause for planetary origins. Laplace and Lagrange were both to pursue crucial work on these issues of the origin of comets and of planetary motions, and the probabilities of future instabilities. In 1812–1813 the two French mathematicians published papers on the origin of comets as captured nebulae or the residues of exploded stars. Laplace integrated this account with his novel "nebular hypothesis" of the origin of the solar system first printed at the end of his *Exposition du système du monde* in 1796. He explicitly presented the cosmogonic hypothesis as a version of Buffon's work made more consistent with the truths of celestial mechanics. A rational account of astronomy and cosmology would displace superstitious astrotheology. There was thus a very close link between cosmological significance, the strategy of probability, celestial mechanics, and public welfare. This whole set of programmes linked the work of the astronomers with that of their colleagues on medical management, economic reform and the war against the charlatans.

The latter ideology has drawn more attention from recent historians. However, the construction of cometary cosmologies also played its part in the emergence of these new disciplines and interests.[28]

Within this new complex of astronomical and historical disciplines, therefore, the interpretation of cometography remained a fundamental and problematic concern. The character of that concern varied with social context: the Paris programme did not exercise a complete hegemony over European astronomers. Just as the return of 1759 did not lead to a single interpretation of cometary significance, so the work pursued by Lalande and his colleagues could not generate a single cometary cosmology. This point is amply demonstrated in the researches of Lalande's contemporary, the polymathic mathematician and natural philosopher Johann Lambert. Like Lalande, Lambert's obsession with comets began with the appearance of 1744, when he was sixteen; like Lalande, too, Lambert's career was at least partly made by his work on Halley's comet. Between 1746 and 1756 Lambert worked in Switzerland, first as secretary in Basel and then as a tutor at an aristocrat's house in Chur. He later claimed that the outline of his views on cosmology were penned in a sketch of summer 1749 at Chur. From 1756 to 1758 he went on the grand tour with his pupils, meeting the great German astronomer Tobias Mayer at Göttingen and contacting both d'Alembert and Messier in Paris in the months before the comet's return. At Göttingen, Lambert read and copied out reviews of Halley's *Synopsis*; in Paris, during the summer of 1758 when Messier and Lalande were working hard on recovering the comet, Lambert must have discussed their techniques. An unpublished study of Lambert's on "the comet which will return in 1759" involves the application of Halley's historic method to an estimate of its period. After the grand tour, Lambert left Switzerland and moved in spring 1759 to southern Germany, where he began work first on problems of optics, then of comets and cosmology. This burst of activity resulted in his *Photometria* (1760), which contains the first printed summary of this cosmology, and two crucial texts on cometography, the *Insigniores orbitae cometarum proprietates* and the *Cosmological Letters*, both of which appeared in January 1761. The former of these works, which drew principally on Euler's celestial mechanics, included a means of finding the parabolic orbit of a comet from three observations alone, although since this strategy involved an equation of the sixth degree it was wildly impracticable. Lambert also constructed an equation linking the time of the cometary path in an ellipse with one chord and two radius vectors, though, again, this proved inapplicable to practical cometography. On the other hand, his latter work, written during the summer of 1760 in an explosion of enthusiasm, outlined the details of a cosmology of the solar system and the whole stellar universe in which comets were given pride of place. It included a reprint of Halley's table of cometary orbits. Lambert's brilliant exploration of the analysis of parabolic and elliptical orbits, together with intensive lobbying and a long series of works on Leibnizian metaphysics, won him a place at the Berlin Academy in January 1765. Priority disputes with Kant on cosmology and epistemology only heightened his notoriety. For the next decade he produced a stream of papers on all branches of philosophy and mathematics, including deeply influential cometary analysis, which provided sources for future work by the German astronomers Olbers and Gauss, who defined all subsequent approaches to cometary prediction from the first decade of the next century. Their program, using Lambert's techniques, utterly changed the status of comets in astronomy and led directly to the construction of a new celestial mechanics and a new stellar astronomy in the German observatories.[29]

Lambert's mathematical and cosmological cometography was thus an important source for astronomers in the late eighteenth century. William Herschel, discoverer of the comet of 1781 which later became the planet Uranus, and the most radical cosmologist of the period, condemned Lambert's work on cosmology since it was incapable of explaining the origin and growth of cosmic structure: "The author hastily concludes ... that the comets, the planets and their satellites have *always* moved as they now move and have *always* been what they are now. This is saying a thing has *always* been what it is because I cannot account for how it *came to be* so." In 1799, Herschel was prompted to rework his observations of the heavens into a complete cosmology through a close rereading of what he held were Lambert's errors.[30] Lambert was useful for Lalande because of his ambitious estimate of the number and significance of comets in the heavens. By "making the number of comets grow as the square of the distance of their perihelia," noting that in Halley's Table 17 of the 21 comets had their perihelion distance less than that of the Earth, and that, for example, the comet of 1680 had a perihelion distance 60 times less than that of Mercury, there might be 5 million comets whose perihelion was within the known solar system. "It is very possible that there move around the Sun comets which since the deluge have hardly been once with us." This was an estimate which Lalande found it hard to resist in 1773, although he pointed out then that "I find the conjectures of M. Lambert on this great number of Comets, too vague and too hazardous, even if ingenious and sagacious." Lalande preferred to use the calculation that since 15 comets had been found since 1750, more than 300 might be orbiting the Sun, 40 of which might come close to the Earth. But Lambert's essay was seen as a "work full of imagination, spirit and knowledge."[30]

Lalande remained committed to the force of Lambert's cometography. He sponsored the research of the Toulouse astronomer Darquier, whose main concern was with the possible cometary origin of variable stars, and which culminated in his complete French translation of Lambert, published just before Darquier's death, in 1801. However, the fundamental contrast between Lalande and Lambert remained their attitude to cosmic stability. Lambert designed a universe which was finite, bounded and unchanging. The Sun is a member of an orbiting cluster of stars, and such clusters compose our galaxy. The appearance of the Milky Way was the effect of looking sideways through the disc. Such a disc, Lambert suggested, was itself composed of clusters of stars each moving round a central, massive object. Ultimately, this cosmopolitical hierarchy continued almost indefinitely, but "you will finally come to the centre of the whole world-edifice, and here I find my last body which steers around itself the whole creation. . . . There is the throne to which all systems attend like so many satellites, the capital city that issues laws to the realm of reality and keeps all in order and complete harmony, makes all a whole, bans all excess, and sets a limit to the revolt and dissolution of each fleeing part, and guides it back to its proper place."[31] Lambert's long series of centralist political analogies necessitated the exclusion of any radical change in the history of the cosmos. In this respect, as in many others, Lambert's overwhelming commitment to an ordered and rationally structured cosmos was part of a continuing debt to Leibniz and Wolff rather than the English exponents of sacred physics. Thus Lamberts's cosmology ruled out cometary collisions. The planar organisation of comets according to his law of squares was a direct consequence of this provision. "Comets and planets can . . . evade one another through entire world-epochs." For this reason, Lambert argued that true cosmology must reject the claims of Maupertuis and his allies on the mutual transmutation of comets, stars, satellites and planets. Each was a permanent and privileged category. Halley's Table was valuable, but his comments on such changes were to be ignored. Where Lalande deduced from this Table that comets were perturbed and so might conceivably collide with the planets, Lambert deduced the opposite: "The collision of celestial bodies always seemed to me to be far removed from the intentions of creation, because each small change in the path of a comet is sufficient to avoid it." Above all, Lambert was recasting the proper role of the astronomer. It is revealing that he did not claim that this reformation had already been accomplished by Halley and Newton; on the contrary, for Lambert the actually existing cometography of the eighteenth century was a degeneration from old astrology.

How could . . . a genie suggest to Copernicus the structure of the world, to Kepler its laws, and to Newton that terrible attraction and the doctrine about the cause and impact of comets, so that everything might be available for the prediction of the calamity and the inhabitants of the

Earth might see to it that instead of having all come to an end a seed for propagation might remain alive on the changed Earth!

Lambert pointed out that the accomplishment of Newtonian cometography in sacred physics and in the work of Maupertuis or Whiston meant that "comets are no longer fearful through their significance but through their effects." The scare of 1773 would prove his case: indeed, in September 1774 Lambert composed an essay "On the comets which come near to the Earth," challenging the representativeness of existing cometary records of close approaches. This essay was eventually published by the Berlin astronomers in 1799. Much earlier, in the *Cosmological Letters*, Lambert linked this argument directly with his recommendation of a new form of life for astronomers. According to Lambert, the work on comets since Newton and Halley made contemporary astronomers no better than what he called "authorized prophets." His new cosmology was designed to find a better job for cosmologists.[32]

Lambert's new cometography was intimately connected with his analysis of the condition of the life of the astronomer. Each celestial body, including each comet, was designed to be perfectly habitable by its denizens. For example, "we are created for the place which the Earth occupies." His argument against the "authorized prophets" was just this: habitability and survival was guaranteed by cosmic order, not by the predictive skill of visionary experts. "The preservation of entire celestial bodies seems to me, to say the least, more important than the preservation of such creatures that propagate their species and are reborn year after year." Worms, insects, tulips, cedars and men all had their appropriate lifespan and accommodated themselves to changing environments. Such local transience was not to be allowed for the objects of astronomy. Notably, the comets were obviously habitable, and their inhabitants must be astronomers of the proper kind. Lambert described the possible constitution of cometary shells such that they would support astronomical life: "I would give the comets considerable ground heat, and the dissolving of that liquid into vapour would serve the comets as a shield against the heat of the Sun." Since the comets constituted "the most numerous and considerable part of the solar system which is visible to us," it was obvious that their inhabitants should be superior beings: "I have made astronomers of all of them, created for the purpose of viewing the edifice of the heavens, the position of each sun, the plane and course of their planets, satellites, and comets in their whole interconnection." This was what Lambert claimed to have done himself from a more humble station. Since comets moved from system to system, the astronomers' seasons would be indefinitely longer and their lifespan and their accumulated data thus proportionately increased. "They are destined to admire the ground plan of the world-edifice, and understand in its foundation and order the series of divine counsels about its structure."[33] Lambert was not alone in speculating on cometary habitability: the "authorized prophets" in England wrote at length on the problem and the benevolent or malevolent effects of life in interplanetary space. In 1754 and 1756, the astronomy lecturer James Ferguson argued that comets were inhabited and that they must possess "Beings capable of contemplating with Wonder . . . the Beauty, Wonder and Symmetry of the Creation." Many writers, including Richard Turner, remained sympathetic to Whiston's claim that comets might be local hells. English astronomers also argued from general providence against the mutation of comets into planets: in Dunthorne's Cambridge edition of Long's *Astronomy*, it was denied that "God must cast about for a sun in decay, or take a comet out of its orbit whereof to compose a new world." Such views were commonplaces of the discourses of natural theology and cosmology. But Lambert was idiosyncratic, however, in spelling out so clearly a link between the provision for life in the cosmos and the social and moral life of those who observed that cosmos.[34]

Finally, what was the moral lesson of this life and this structure? In the last six sections of Lambert's book, added after he learnt delightedly of Mayer's detection of a series of proper motions amongst the stars, Lambert spelt this out. "The fixed stars, too, show that they are not dead masses but have their own life and motion. This is a new reason to view the order of the planets as fictitious and to conclude once and for all that the true order is the most complicated one and will never be reached by us." Lambert's analogical models of simpler languages replaced by more complex, and of interlocking geared world-systems, was itself subordinated to one universal metaphor — that of the central state and the capital, from which his astronomers were distanced forever. The central body was described as a "dark regent," and he emphasized again and again "the subordination which rules in the world." In a long analysis of "dark regents" and their dominance, Lambert indicated that fixed stars could not govern systems of fixed stars because any star would "have its own retinue of comets and planets," which, being "its very household," would preoccupy this star too much to leave it opportunity to govern systems of stars. "The supremacy must be all the more despotic, the more powerful it has to be. I therefore fall back on the idea of a body which can hold each fixed star with its whole retinue in harness." Such despotism emerged as the fundamental lesson to be learnt and taught by Lambert's new cosmologists.[35]

In this paper, I have examined the cometary cosmology of two astronomers who both took an active role in the interpretation of the return of Halley's Comet and who both worked strenuously to further the development of the celestial mechanics of cometary motion. Against the historiography which makes that return of the self-evident triumph of a single form of rational astronomy, and uses 1759 as a key marker in the destruction of cometary and cosmological significance, I have shown that both Lalande and Lambert sought to make cosmologies which gave comets fundamental roles in the universal economy which they did not perceive as contradictory with an analysis of secular stability and astronomical prediction. Their work is best seen as the expression of attempts to demarcate important roles for astronomers: as expert interpreters of the natural causes of stability and revolution, or as divinely sustained observers of a centralised and despotic world-edifice. Lalande's work was formulated within the program of the Paris academy. As we have seen, his statements on cometary collision were carefully policed by the academicians in order deliberately to preserve their role as enlightened supervisors of public instruction. In contrast, from the late 1750s, Lambert strenuously aimed to gain entry to the Berlin academy, an aim fulfilled under the aegis of Frederick II in January 1765. Throughout the 1750s and early 1760s controversy raged at Berlin between interpreters of Leibniz and of Newton. The battle did not cease with Maupertuis's death in 1759. Debates centred on Maupertuis's cosmology, on Wolff's monadology and on the relation between the measure of forces and the action of God. Protagonists on the Wolffian side included Samuel Formey, the Academy's secretary and Lambert's eulogist, and Johann Sulzer, Lambert's principal supporter in Berlin. In the same way, it was through Johann Merian, director of the Academy's literary class, that Lambert's cosmological work received publicity in a French version of 1770. The political and philosophical vision of the Academy under Frederick's autocratic control provides the local context in which to interpret Lambert's vision of a benevolently despotic world-order and its far-sighted cometographers.[36]

Such roles and practices fit the local conditions of existence of astronomers in the eighteenth-century academies; elsewhere, and at other times, astronomers pursued different ends. Thus in England cometography was part of the natural philosophy of active principles in matter and public spectacle in nature. Such a program accommodated and exploited the return of 1759—it was not transformed by that event. So in the 1740s the Scottish antiquary John Clerk, a devoted disciple of Halley and Gregory since his student days at Oxford, could seriously seek to persuade the mathematician Colin Maclaurin that it was useless expecting comets ever to return in the same path. Maclaurin's faith in Halley's methods was unshaken, but he was convinced by his observations of the comet of spring 1744 that these bodies were inhabited. In 1743 Richard Yate asked readers of the *Gentleman's Magazine*, rhetorically enough: "Who can but smile that sees the ingenious Dr. Halley employed in describing the Orbit and calculating the periodical Revolution of a meer *Ignis Fatuus* or *Jack with a Lanthorn*?" When John Winthrop lectured at Harvard in April 1759 on the return of Comet Halley, he gave an orthodox exposition of Newton's views, and also endorsed Whiston's claim about a cometary cause for the Deluge. In the 1770s, Joseph Priestley discussed the atmospheres of active electrical matter which he and his colleagues supposed existed round comets and planets alike. Priestley's correspondent, the Massachusetts lawyer Andrew Oliver, made an "artificial Comet" out of cork and golf-leaf to show how the electric fluid kept life going on these "inhabitable Worlds."[37] Herschel's "natural history of the heavens," developed in the 1780s and pursued actively for over twenty-five years, drew on just these resources. In 1795 he declared that comets would restore stellar activity by collision, but by 1808–1812 he had deduced that each comet orbited many stars, orbiting our Sun only once, and carried "unperihelioned" or active nebular matter round the cosmos. Nebulae became comets, and comets became planets. "That comets pass round other Suns than ours, is rendered probable from our knowing as yet, with certainty, the return of only one comet among the great number that have been observed." This single return was an opportunity for widely differing uses by different interpreters, and since cometography was not pacified in 1759, it is not surprising that it provided rich ideological and disciplinary resources throughout the century. This is how Lalande summed up this point in 1803, when considering the disappearance of his highly prized comet of 1770:

> So will it become necessary, after having affirmed during the eighteenth century that all comets return, to say, during the nineteenth century, that the comets don't return at all (except that of 1759)! This is why I dream of nothing but comets; I talk of nothing but comets; I recommend nothing to my correspondents but searching for comets, when I write to them that the only thing which astronomy lacks is the understanding of comets.[38]

NOTES

1 John Herschel, "On Comets," *Familiar Lectures on Scientific Subjects* (London: Strahan, 1867), 91, 117, 93. For contemporary views on the origin and significance of comets, see O. Zanotti Bianco, "Le idee di Lagrange, Laplace, Gauss e Schiaparelli sull'origine delle comete," *Memorie della Reale Academia*

delle Scienze di Torino, 2nd series, 63 (1913): 59–100, esp. pp. 61–64 for John Herschel.

2 William Whewell, *History of the Inductive Sciences* (London: Parker, 1837), 3rd edition, 1857, 2: 184; Herschel, "On Comets," 114–15.

3 For Scriblerian satire on cometography, see [John Gay], "A true and faithful narrative of what pass'd in London during the general consternation of all ranks and degrees of mankind," and [Alexander Pope], "God's revenge against punning," in Jonathan Swift and Alexander Pope, *Miscellanies, The Third Volume* (London, 1732), discussed in M. H. Nicolson, *Mountain Gloom and Mountain Glory: the Development of the Aesthetics of the Infinite* (New York: Norton, 1963), 242–49 and J. E. Force, *William Whiston, Honest Newtonian* (Cambridge: Cambridge University Press, 1985), 110–11 and 128–32. For Martin's work in the late 1750s, see Benjamin Martin, *Miscellaneous Correspondence, Containing a Variety of Subjects relative to Natural and Civil History, Geography, Mathematics, Poetry, Memoirs of monthly Occurences, Catalogues of new Books* (in *General Magazine of Arts and Sciences*, part 5 or in series of 4 volumes, 1759–1764), 3: 97–98 (May 1759) and the excellent discussion in C. Waff, "Comet Halley's First Expected Return: English Public Apprehensions, 1755–58," *Journal for the History of Astronomy* 17 (1986): 1–37. Other sources are Roger Long, *Astronomy* (Cambridge, 2 volumes, 1764), edited by Richard Dunthorne, 562; [John Bevis], "An account of the comet seen in May 1759," *Philosophical Transactions* 51 (1759): 93–94; and compare his letter in *Gentleman's Magazine* 27 (September 1757): 393–94. For discussions of the return in England, see R. Wallis, "The Glory of Gravity—Halley's Comet 1759," *Annals of Science* 41 (1984): 279–86; P. Broughton, "The first predicted return of Comet Halley," *Journal for History of Astronomy* 16 (1985): 123–33; For Martin, see J. R. Millburn, *Benjamin Martin: Author, Instrument-maker and "Country Showman"* (Leyden: Noordhof, 1976); for Bevis see R. Wallis, "John Bevis," *Notes and Records of the Royal Society* 36 (1982): 211–25; W. Ashworth, "John Bevis and his *Uranographia*," *Proceedings of the American Philosophical Society* 125 (1981): 52–73.

4 Jérôme Lalande, "Sur les derniers progrès de l'astronomie," 22 August 1802, Bibliothèque nationale MSS FF 12273 f206; Lalande to his father, 22 April 1752, Académie des Sciences, Dossier Lalande, MSS I 2289; Lalande to Maillebois, 6 May 1752, ibid., MSS I 2425. For Lalande in Berlin, see J. F. McLellan, *Science Reorganized: Scientific Societies in the Eighteenth Century* (New York: Columbia, 1985), 205 and 346 n. 23. For Lalande's career, see H. Monod-Cassidy, "Un astromome-philosophe: Jérôme de Lalande," *Studies in Voltaire and the Eighteenth Century* 56 (1967): 907–30; for work at the Collège Royale, see R. Taton, ed., *Enseignement et diffusion des sciences en France au 18e siècle* (Paris: Hermann, 1964), 275–84. Compare L. L. Bongie, "J.-J. Lalande: standard clichés and the private man," *Studies in Voltaire and the Eighteenth Century* 245 (1986): 373–402.

5 Lalande, *Bibliographie astronomique* (Paris, 1803), 824; for the argument with Lemmonier and d'Alembert, see Lemonnier, "Suite de l'apparition de la comète," *Mercure de France* (July 1759), 140–45; d'Alembert's comments are in *L'ob-*

servateur littéraire (August 1759), 181; see also R. Taton, "Clairaut de 'Le retour de la comète de Halley,'" in K. Figala and E. Berninger, eds., *Arithmos-Arrythmos: Skizzen aus der Wissenschaftsgeschichte* (Munich: Minerva, 1979), 253–74.

6 Lalande, *Bibliographie astronomique*, 677; Lalande, *Mémoires de Trévoux* (November 1757), 2850- 2863; Lalande, "Mémoire sur les équations séculaires," *Mémoires de l'Académie Royale des Sciences*, 1757 (pb. 1762), 411–70, on 413; Lalande, *Tables astronomiques de M. Halley* (Paris, 1759), 107; Lalande, *Journal encyclopédique* (June 1759), 41–50; Clairaut, *Réponse à quelque pièces la plupart anonymes dans lesquelles on a attaqué le Mémoire sur la Comète de 1682* (Paris, 1759), 7–8. For d'Alembert as opponent, see T. L. Hankins, *Jean d'Alembert: science and the Enlightenment* (Oxford: Oxford University Press, 1970) 38–41.

7 Lalande, "Sur les derniers progrès de l'astronomie," fol. 205.

8 Lalande, *Tables astronomiques*, 101–7.

9 For the work of Newton and Halley on comets, 1684–1705, the key sources are D. T. Whiteside, ed., *Mathematical Papers of Isaac Newton* (8 volumes, Cambridge: Cambridge University Press, 1967–1980), volume 6:57–61; S. P. Rigaud, *Some Account of Halley's Astronomiae cometica synopsis* (Oxford, 1835); E. F. MacPike, *Correspondence and Papers of Edmond Halley* (London: Taylor and Francis, London, 1937). There is a discussion of this work in S. Schaffer, "Newton's Comets and the Transformation of Astrology," in P. Curry, ed., *Astrology, Science and Society: Historical Essays* (London: Boydell and Brewer, 1987).

10 P. Lemonnier, *La théorie des comètes où l'on traite du progrès de cette partie de l'astronomie* (Paris, 1743), 85; J. B. Delambre, *Histoire de l'astronomie au dix-huitième siècle* (Paris, 1827), 127–28, 466–69, 673; Richard Dunthorne, "Letter concerning comets," *Philosophical Transactions* 47 (1751): 281–88; Lalande, *Tables astronomiques*, 105–8.

11 Delisle, *Lettres sur les Tables astronomiques de M. Halley* (Paris, 1749), 1: 9–10, 14 and 2:19; Delisle to Bevis, 3 December 1749, Paris Observatory MSS B10.115. For Messier, see his "Notice de mes comètes," edited by Lalande, Paris Observatory MSS C2.19, pp. 1, 7.

12 Halley's poem is discussed in W. R. Albury, "Halley's *Ode* on the *Principia* of Newton and the Epicurean revival in England," *Journal of the History of Ideas* 39 (1978): 24–43; the changes are in MacPike, *Correspondence and papers of Halley*, 204–6. For Newton and Halley on comets and matter theory, see D. C. Kubrin, "Newton and the cyclical cosmos," *Journal of the History of Ideas* 28 (1967): 325–46 and S. Schechner Genuth, "Comets, teleology and the relationship of chemistry to cosmology in Newton's thought," *Annali dell'Istituto e Museo di Storia della Scienza di Firenze* 10 (1985): 31–65. For a typical example of the interpretation of Newton as the end of astrology, see K. Thomas, *Religion and the Decline of Magic* (Harmondsworth: Penguin, 1972), 418.

13 Gregory memorandum, May 1694, in *Correspondence of Isaac Newton*, edited by H. W. Turnbull, J. F. Scott, A. R. Hall and L. Tilling, 7 volumes (Cambridge: Cambridge University Press, 1959–1977), 3: 336; Gregory memorandum,

March 1703, ibid., 4:402–3; Gregory, *Astronomiae physica et geometriae elementa* (Oxford, 1702), 481; Pemberton, *View of Sir Isaac Newton's Philosophy* (London, 1728). For sacred physics see R. S. Porter, "Creation and Credence: The Career of Earth Theories in Britain," in B. Barnes and S. Shapin, eds., *Natural Order* (London: Sage, 1979), 97–124.

14 Halley, "An account of some observations lately made at Nuremburg," *Philosophical Transactions* 16 (1687): 403–6; "Some considerations about the cause of the universal deluge" and "Some farther thoughts on the same subject," ibid., 33 (1724): 118–25; Simon Schaffer, "Halley's Atheism and the End of the World," *Notes and Records of the Royal Society* 32 (1977): 17–40. Halley's statements on cometary collisions and the comet of 1680 are in his *Synopsis of the astronomy of comets* (London, 1705), 23–24; *Astronomical tables with precepts* (London, 1752), Tttt 4. For Whiston and Halley, see Halley's comment on Whiston, 8 January 1707, Bodleian MSS Rigaud 37 fol. 89; Whiston, *New Theory of the Earth*, 2nd edition (Cambridge, 1708), 440–49; "The Cause of the Deluge Demonstrated" (1714), printed in 5th edition of *New Theory of the Earth* (London, 1737), 459–78. Whiston's cometography is unsympathetically but thoroughly summarized in S. L. Jaki, *Planets and Planetarians* (Edinburgh: Scottish Academic, 1978), 87–97, and for satirical responses to Whiston in the 1750s, see Waff, "Comet Halley's First Expected Return," 6–8. For later discussions of cometary significance, see Richard Turner, *A view of the heavens* (London, 1765), 20; Adam Walker, *An epitome of astronomy*, 13th edition (London, 1798), 36; Robert Harrington, *A new system on fire and planetary life* (London, 1796), 32.

15 Maupertuis, "Lettre sur la comète qui paroissoit en 1742," in *Oeuvres* (Lyons, 1756), 3: 209–56 (216, 225, 238, 243–48); "Essai de cosmologie," ibid., 1: 71–72; J. A. Shumaker, "Maupertuis and the History of Comets," *Scripta mathematica* 23 (1957): 97–108. For Buffon's cometography, see *Histoire naturelle, tôme premier* (Paris, 1749), 131; translated passages in John Lyon and Philip Sloan, *From Natural History to the History of Nature: Readings from Buffon and his Critics* (Notre Dame: Notre Dame, 1981), 154–55; J. Roger, ed., *Buffon: les Epoques de la Nature* (Paris: Muséum, 1962), xlix–li, 28–32. The reviews in *Bibliothèque raisonnée* (October-December 1750), 243–63 and in *Journal de Trévoux* (October 1749), 2226–45 are translated in Lyon and Sloan, *From Natural History to the History of Nature*, 225–26, 266. Lalande's review is in *Journal des savants* (July 1779), 501–3. His commentary on Buffon and Maupertuis is in *Reflexion sur les comètes qui peuvent approcher de la Terre* (Paris, 1773), 6, 19, 27, 34–36.

16 Elie Bertrand, *Mémoire pour servir à l'histoire des tremblemens de terre* (Vevey, 1756), 74–75; John Wesley, *Serious thoughts occasioned by the late earthquake at Lisbon* (1755) in *Works* (London: Wesleyan Conference Office, 1872), 11: 1–13 on p. 8; Thomas Herring to William Duncombe, 25 January 1756, in *Gentleman's Magazine* 47 (1777): 133. For comets and the Lisbon earthquake, see T. D. Kendrick, *The Lisbon Earthquake* (London: Methuen, 1956) and Waff, "Comet Halley's First Expected Return," 4–6, 15–19. Waff cites Benjamin

Martin, *The Theory of Comets Illustrated* (London, 1757), 13–14, and discusses Martin's efforts to distance himself from the comet scare.

17 Voltaire, "Lettre sur la prétendue comète," *Journal encyclopédique* 4 (June 1773): 319- 24; Messier, "Notice de mes comètes," 2, 8–9; Messier, "Grand comète qui a paru à la naissance de Napoléon-le-Grand," Académie des Sciences, dossier Messier, pp. 4–5.

18 Messier, "Notice de mes comètes," 5–6.

19 Fontenelle, *Entretiens sur la pluralité des mondes*, edited with notes by Jérôme Lalande (with his *Astronomie des dames*) (Paris, 1820), 346–47; compare his notes on Kircher in Paris Observatory MSS B5.7. For Laplace, see "Sur l'équation séculaire de la Lune," *Mémoires de l'Académie Royale des Sciences* (1786), 235–65. For Lalande on secular stability, see "Du déplacement de notre Système solaire," ibid., (1776, pb. 1779), 513–14; "Mémoire sur les équations séculaires," ibid., (1757), 413–14; Lalande, *Tables astronomiques de Halley*, 106–8. For his comments to Voltaire, see Voltaire to Lalande, 19 December 1774, Bibliothèque Victor Cousin, Paris, MSS 5 no. 57. fols. 111–12. There is a similar analysis of cometary extinction of life in d'Holbach, *Système de la nature*, (1770, edition of 1794), 6 volumes, 1:173–175 and 4:10–12. For the use of secular acceleration against eternalism see Schaffer, "Halley's atheism and the end of the world"; Leonhard Euler, "A letter concerning the gradual approach of the Earth to the Sun," *Philosophical Transactions* 46 (1749): 203–5 and "A letter concerning the contraction of the orbits of the planets," ibid., 356–59.

20 For Lalande at the Collège during the Revolution, see "Mémoire des professeurs du Collège de France," August 1793, Bibliothèque nationale, MSS Ff 12273 fols. 213–22; Journal of Lalande, Bibliothèque Victor Cousin, MSS 99, pp. 38–40. For his appearance at the Pantheon and work as radical freemason, see L. Amiable, *Le franc-maçon Jérôme Lalande* (Paris, 1889), 16. The poem of de Bussy is *L'éther ou l'Etre Suprème élèmentaire: poème philosophique et moral à priori* (Paris, 1796); Lalande's annotated edition is Bibliothèque nationale Rés Ye 3640; the citations are from pp. xii, xvi. For the clash with Napoleon, see Institut, MSS 2041 fol. 610–12; for atheism see Lalande, *Supplément au dictionnaire des athées de Sylvain Maréchal* (Paris, 1803), 26; Bongie, "Lalande," *loc. cit.* 379–385; Constance de Salm, "Eloge historique de Lalande," *Magazine encyclopédique* 2 (1820): 282–325; J. Raspail, "Les papiers de Lalande," *La Révolution française* 74 (1921): 236–54. Lalande is described as a "neo-Epicurean" in C. C. Gillispie, *Science and Polity in France at the End of the Old Régime* (Princeton: Princeton University Press, 1980), 104 n. 87.

21 Lalande, *Bibliographie astronomique*, 536–37; Voltaire, *Elémens de la philosophie de Newton* (Paris, 1738), 381; Lalande, "Memoire sur les comètes," *Mémoires de l'Académie Royale des Sciences*, 1773 (pb. 1777): 461–85, 475, 477, 480. Compare Delambre's comments in Institut, MSS 2041, fol. 97.

22 *Gazette de France*, no. 37 (7 May 1773), 162; *Mémoires secrets pour servir à l'histoire de la République des Lettres en France*, 6 (pb. 1777): 351–60 (cover-

ing May 1773); Lalande, *Reflexions sur les comètes*, iii–v; *Histoire de l'Académie Royale des Sciences*, 1773 (pb. 1777), 59–64.

23 [Dorat], "Epître aux comètes, écrite quelques jours avant la prétendue destruction des mondes," *Journal encyclopédique* 4 (1773): 492; the review of Lalande is on pp. 214–19.

24 *Mémoires secrets*, 355–56; *Histoire de l'Académie Royale des Sciences*, 1773 (pb. 1777), 62.

25 Voltaire, "Lettre sur la prétendue comète," *Journal encyclopédique* 4 (June 1773) 319–24; Voltaire to Lalande, 19 December 1774, Bibliothèque Victor Cousin, MSS 5 no. 57, fols. 111–12.

26 Lalande, *Reflexions sur les comètes*, 10–11, 25–26, 30–31, 38.

27 Lalande, *Bibliographie astronomique*, 751; Dionis du Séjour, *Essai sur les comètes en général et particuliérement sur celles qui peuvent approcher de l'orbite de la terre* (Paris, 1775), 4: xiii, 69, 72, 195–97, 344, 351. The attacks on Buffon by Euler are discussed in Roger, *Buffon: Epoques de la nature*, L; Pingré's attack is in his *Cométographie* (Paris, 1783–84), 2 volumes, 2: 152–54.

28 du Séjour, *Essai sur les comètes*, xxi; Pierre Simon Laplace, "Sur les comètes," (November 1813), in *Oeuvres complètes*, (Paris: Gauthier-Villars, 1878–1912), 13: 88–97; Joseph Louis Lagrange, "Sur l'origine des comètes," (January 1812), *Journal de physique* 74 (1812): 228–35. Lagrange and Laplace were also drawing on the work of Olbers on the asteroids and the comet: see S. L. Jaki, "Drei kosmologische Vorträge von Wilhelm Olbers," *Nachrichten der Olbers-Gesellschaft*, no. 79 (1970): 14–28. For the sources of the nebular hypothesis, see J. Merleau-Ponty, "Situation et rôle de l'hypothèse cosmogonique chez Laplace," *Revue de l'histoire des sciences* 29 (1976): 21–49 and 30 (1977): 71–72; S. L. Jaki, "The Five Forms of Laplace's Cosmology," *American Journal of Physics* 44 (1976): 4–11.

29 For Lambert's career, see R. Jacquel, *Le savant et philosophe mulhousien Jean-Henri Lambert* (Paris: Ophrys, 1977); *Colloque international et interdisciplinaire Jean-Henri Lambert* (Paris: Ophrys, 1979), 35–126; S. L. Jaki, ed., *Lambert's Cosmological Letters on the Arrangement of the World-Edifice* (Edinburgh: Scottish Academic, 1976), 1–7. For his note of 1749, see Lambert to Kant, 13 November 1765, in Kant, *Briefwechsel*, 1 (Leipzig, 1924) 38; for contacts with Messier and Mayer, see Jacquel, "Lambert et l'astronomie cométaire au 18e siècle," in *Comptes rendus du 92e Congrès National des Sociétés Savantes: Section des sciences*, 1 (Paris, 1969): 27–56. For his work on Halley see ibid., 42; for the cosmology in *Photometria*, see M. A. Hoskin, "Newton and Lambert," *Colloque Lambert*, 365–70. For his cometary methods, see J. Levy, "Lambert et la mécanique céleste: le problème des comètes," ibid., 279–84, citing Lambert, *Insigniores orbitae cometarum proprietates* (Augsburg, 1761), 124. For Lambert's place in Berlin, see P. Berger, "Lamberts Bedeutung in der Naturwissenschaft des 18. Jahrhunderts," *Centaurus* 6 (1959): 157–254; Jaki, *Lambert's Cosmological Letters*, 24–28. For his relation with Kant, see J. Lepsius, *J. H. Lambert: eine Darstellung seiner kosmologischen und philosophischen Leistungen* (Munich, 1881), 30–42. For Kant's contemporary work on cosmol-

ogy, see Simon Schaffer, "The Phoenix of Nature: Fire and Evolutionary Cosmology in Wright and Kant," *Journal for the History of Astronomy* 9 (1978): 180–200.

30 William Herschel, "Miscellaneous remarks on books &c.," Royal Astronomical Society MSS Herschel W 7/2 fol. 19ʳ; "On the direction and velocity of the motion of the Sun and Solar System" (1805), in J. L. E. Dreyer, ed., *The Collected Scientific Papers of Sir William Herschel* (London, 1912), 2:318; M. A. Hoskin, "Lambert and Herschel," *Journal for the History of Astronomy* 9 (1978): 140–42; for the perception of Uranus as a comet, see Simon Schaffer, "Uranus and the Establishment of Herschel's Astronomy," *Journal for the History of Astronomy* 12 (1981): 11–26.

31 For Lambert and Lalande, see Lalande, *Réflexions sur les comètes*, 9, 38; for Darquier, see M. E. Paloque, "Deux lettres inédites de Laplace et de Méchain à l'astronome toulousain Darquier," *Annales de l'Observatoire astronomique et météorologique de Toulouse* 12 (1936): 277–85; R. Jacquel, "L'astronome toulousain Darquier et le cosmologue mulhousien Jean-Henri Lambert,"*Comptes rendus du 96e Congrès National des Sociétés Savantes, Section des sciences*, 1 (Paris, 1974): 31–46; for the translation of Lambert, see J. Merleau-Ponty, introduction to Antoine Darquier and J. M. C. van Utenhove, *Lettres cosmologiques par J. H. Lambert* (Amsterdam, 1801, republished Paris, 1977). The hierarchy of star clusters is described in Jaki, *Lambert's cosmological Letters*, 111; the centre of the world-edifice is described ibid., p. 160.

32 Jaki, *Lambert's Cosmological Letters*, 56, 62, 63, 69, 89; Lambert,"Ueber die Kometen welche der Erde nahe vorbeigehen," *Astronomische Jahrbuch für 1802* (Berlin, 1799), 154–65; K. Bopp, "Johann Heinrich Lamberts Monatsbuch 1752-1777," *Abhandlung der Königliche Bayerische Akademie der Wissenschaften: mathematische-physische Klasse* 27 (1915): 27, no. 6 (1915): 74.

33 Jaki, *Lambert's Cosmological Letters*, 58, 66, 73, 79, 87.

34 James Ferguson, *An idea of the material universe, deduced from a survey of the solar system* (London, 1754), 26–27; Ferguson, *Astronomy explained upon Sir Isaac Newton's principles* (London, 1756), 30; William Whiston, *Astronomical Principles of Religion* (London, 1717), 156; Richard Turner, *A view of the heavens, being a short but comprehensive system of modern Astronomy* (London, 1765), 20; Long, *Astronomy*, 594. This section of Long's book was added by Richard Dunthorne and Nevil Maskelyne, the Astronomer Royal. For cometography and cosmology in England, see M. A. Hoskin, "The English Background to the Cosmology of Wright and Herschel," in W. Yourgrau and A. D. Breck, eds., *Cosmology, History and Theology* (New York: Plenum, 1977), 219–32.

35 Jaki, *Lambert's Cosmological Letters*, 161, 170, 178; Mayer's work on proper motions is printed and translated in E. Forbes, *Tobias Mayer's Opera inedita* (London: Macmillan, 1971), 109–12.

36 For the controversies at the Berlin Academy around Wolffian and Leibnizian cosmology and natural philosophy, see I. I. Polonoff, *Force, Cosmos, Monads and Other Themes of Kant's Early Thought* (Bonn: Bouvier Verlag H. Grund-

mann, 1973), chapter 3 and p. 123 n. 116 (for Kant's interest in the Berlin prize essays); R. S. Calinger, "Frederick the Great and the Berlin Academy of Sciences," *Annals of science* 24 (1968): 239–49 and McLellan, *Science Reorganized*, 68–74 (for Frederick's dominance); R. S. Calinger, "The Newtonian-Wolffian Controversy," *Journal of the History of Ideas* 30 (1969), 319–30, and Harcourt Brown, "Maupertuis philosophe: Enlightenment and the Berlin Academy," *Studies in Voltaire and the Eighteenth Century* 24 (1963): 255–69, for the philosophical controversy of the 1750s. For Lambert's supporters at the Academy, see Jaki, *Lambert's Cosmological Letters*, 1–2, 27–29.

37 Sir John Clerk to Roger Gale, 8 April 1742, in *Family remains of the Reverend William Stukeley, M.D.*, ed. W. C. Lukis for the Surtees Society (London, 1882–87), 3: 435–6; Maclaurin to Clerk, 23 March 1742 and Maclaurin to the Earl of Morton, 27 March 1744, in Stella Mills, ed., *Collected Letters of Colin Maclaurin* (Nantwich: Shiva Press, 1982) 87, 402; Colin Maclaurin, *An account of Sir Isaac Newton's philosphical discoveries* (London, 1748), 368–77; Richard Yate, "A New Theory of Comets," *Gentleman's Magazine* 13 (1743–74): 193–95; for Winthrop and his colleagues see J. C. Greene, "Some aspects of American astronomy, 1750–1815," *Isis* 45 (1954): 239–58 and M. J. Crowe, *The Extraterrestrial Life Debate 1750–1900* (Cambridge: Cambridge UP, 1986), 106–17. For Oliver and Priestley, see Priestley to Andrew Oliver, 12 February 1775, in R. E. Schofield, ed., *Scientific Autobiography of Joseph Priestley* (Cambridge, Mass.: MIT Press, 1966), 148, and Andrew Oliver, *Essay on Comets* (Salem, 1772), 18, 46, 86–87.

38 For Herschel's cometography, see "Observations of a comet," *Philosophical Transactions* 102 (1912): 115–43, Simon Schaffer, " 'The Great Laboratories of the Universe': William Herschel on Matter Theory and Planetary Life," *Journal for the History of Astronomy* 11 (1980): 81–111, on pp. 96–100, and for his pluralism see Crowe, *Extraterrestrial Life Debate*, 61–70. For Herschel's influence see, for example, Adam Walker, *A System of Familiar Philosophy* (London, 1799), 534–46: in 1758–59 the comet was mistaken and unpredictable, so "when we find such excellent astronomers and mathematicians as Dr. Halley, mistaken, I fear we must suspect that the motion of comets does not come within the sphere of calculation." The citation from Lalande is in *Bibliographie astronomique*, 850. Compare his comment in *Entretiens sur la pluralité des mondes, précédés de l'Astronomie des Dames par J. de Lalande* (Paris, 1820), 135: "This comet is the only one whose return is certain; it could be that the others will never return."

Medicine as a Key to Defining Enlightenment Issues: The Case of Julien Offray de La Mettrie

KATHLEEN WELLMAN

The role of the sciences in the development of the French Enlightenment has been a fruitful field of scholarly research.[1] The most obvious focus of attention has been the physical sciences, especially Newtonian physics, because the philosophes, overtly claiming to be "Newtons of the mind,"[2] saw themselves as both the heirs to the scientific revolution and the preeminent practitioners of the scientific method. Thus historians have noted the ways in which the philosophes, either generally or particularly, sought to apply the standards of mathematical certainty to their formulations in the social sphere.[3]

Historians who have studied the role of the natural sciences in the Enlightenment can draw less clear-cut connections between the scientific interests of the philosophes and programs for reform.[4] Philosophes like Diderot, Maupertuis, Buffon, and Holbach were particularly concerned with the philosophical ramifications of questions raised by the natural sciences. Discussions of Trembley's polyp, Swammerdam's animalcules, and the extensive documentation of monstrosities attest to their lively interest in the natural sciences. But, for the philosophes, the biological sciences raised questions and problems which defied easy resolution through programmatic statements. Perhaps it is no coincidence that those philosophes who were most involved in the natural sciences were also most sceptical about systematic reforms or that some of the most thoroughgoing explorations of the social implications of biological discoveries were cast in the guise of fiction, e.g., *D'Alembert's Dream*.

Medicine has proved to be a particularly problematic science for historians to integrate into Enlightenment reform efforts. Medical texts reveal a morass of conflicting theories and metaphysical perspectives. Medical practices are more likely to horrify than to stand as shining examples of Enlightenment. (I suspect this disheartening spectacle has made the study of medical professionalization the primary way in which historians of medicine now treat the period.) At best, it seems, the historian of eighteenth-century medicine can point to modest increases in critical acumen and professional standards or a marginally greater reliance on empirical evidence.[5]

At the same time, medicine by its very nature offered to the philosophes a clear-cut focus for their concern with the social utility of the sciences, i.e., any improvement in medicine would be immediately beneficial. There are other less obvious connections between medicine and the development of the Enlightenment: Medicine could be considered the logical heir of the scientific revolution in anatomy brought about by Vesalius and Harvey. It, like the other natural sciences, held out the hope for more thoroughgoing empirical investigations. Medicine was also one of the clearest ways to integrate man into the process of nature through comparative anatomy and physiology. In other words, through medicine one might work toward an understanding of human nature unfettered by metaphysical or theological considerations.

The question I would like to raise is whether medicine was, for the philosophes, simply the most striking example of a science which could ameliorate the human condition or whether it could and did play a more central role in formulating their concerns and programs. The case of Julien Offray de La Mettrie is a particularly illuminating perspective from which to address this issue.

La Mettrie, who was widely denounced by the philosophes[6] and is even considered an anti-philosophe by some historians,[7] might seem a strange or illegitimate example to use to suggest a connection between medicine and the philosophes. But several considerations make him an appropriate and even striking example. First of all, La Mettrie cannot be convincingly separated from the philosophes. Even those who most vehemently denounced him were either indebted to him, as Diderot was, or wrote in response to him, as Voltaire did. Though virtually all of the philosophes, regardless of their philosophical perspective, found it dangerous to be associated with his radical materialism, La Mettrie himself was eager to proclaim his adherence to the philosophes. In his last philosophical work, the *Discours préliminaire*, written in 1751 just as the philosophic movements was beginning to coalesce around the *Encyclopédie*, La Mettrie claimed to speak for the philosophes.[8] He explicitly identified his work in both medicine and philosophy with their concerns for reform and proclaimed the reformist goals of the philosophe and the physician as one and the same.

Secondly, La Mettrie was the most prominent physician among the philosophes. Although his fame or notoriety rests on his works of materialist philosophy, more than half of La Mettrie's works addressed medical issues. He studied medicine at the University of Paris. (He received his degree from the University of Reims because he could not afford the prohibitive graduation costs in Paris.) He then went to Leyden to study with Hermann Boerhaave, the most important physician of the eighteenth century. His medical practice involved a stint as an army surgeon with the *garde française* and a practice in his home town of St. Malo in Brittany.[9] His medical works include translations of the principal works of Boerhaave, an eight volume commentary on Boerhaave's physiology (lifted with substantial reworking from Albrecht von Haller), five medical treatises, and seven volumes of medical satire directed against his his medical contemporaries in Paris. La Mettrie had not only the ability to address the issues of the theory and practice but also the perspicacity to contend with diverse facets of eighteenth-century medicine. He was aware that while medical theory depended upon a body of texts, it had to reconcile its textual traditions with the demands of effective practice and clinical teaching, and that medicine was further complicated by highly charged issues of professional status. Ultimately La Mettrie is such an effective example to demonstrate the influence of medicine on the philosophes not simply because he was enmeshed in the contemporary issues of medical theory and practice and the professional disputes of his age, but also because he recast all of these issues in ways which resonate crucial concerns of the Enlightenment.

Although La Mettrie's medicine has not been throughly studied, the influence of medicine on his formation as a philosopher and a philosophe seems unmistakable. Medicine, physiological studies in particular, led him to materialism, the philosophical stance which characterizes his entire philosophical corpus. The connections between medicine and materialism in France have been traced by Ann Thomson for several of La Mettrie's medical contemporaries.[10] Her study strongly suggests that French medical materialism was, in part, a reaction against the Cartesian *bête-machine* hypothesis. And it seems clear that, as Thomson contends, the final form of La Mettrie's materialism as it appears in *L'Homme machine* is indeed part of an anti-Cartesian tradition he shares with other medical contemporaries.[11] However, the specific character of La Mettrie's materialism is even more profoundly formed by his work within the Boerhaavian corpus.

As La Mettrie worked through his translations of Boerhaave's physiological texts,[12] he developed and articulated his own epistemological perspectives through his extensive commentary on them. He vigorously applauded Boerhaave's epistemological modesty, agreeing that metaphysical questions such as the existence of First Causes, free will, and the immortal soul were not appropriate areas for scientific investigation. La Mettrie also built on Boerhaave's discussions of the physiological processes of sensation and cognition.

Boerhaave generally described physiological processes in iatrochemical or, more frequently, iatromechanical terms, but he chose to use Lockean psychology as the foundation for his explanations of sensation and cognition.[13] Locke vigorously disclaimed any intention of examining "the physical considerations of the mind . . . wherein its essence consists, or by what motion of our spirits or alterations of our bodies, we come to have any sensation by our organs or any ideas in our understanding; and whether those ideas do, in their formation, any, or all of them, depend on matter alone. . . ."[14] But some physicians, perhaps intrigued by Locke's empirical approach to philosophical questions or by the claim that his conclusions were the results of common-sense observations, were quite willing to use his descriptions of sensation as a basis of comparison or correlation with physiological processes. (These attempts may explain the wide range of eighteenth-century interpretations of Locke's *Essay*.)

Boerhaave, for example, reproduced in his physiological texts Lockean accounts of memory, imagination, reflection, etc. and then suggested the patterns of *espirits de cerveau* which might correspond to the thought process Locke described.[15] Boerhaave retreated before the materialist implications of such comparisons, claiming that the actions of nerves could not be considered as causes of the diversity of thought but were instead only "conditions established by the Adorable Author of Nature."[16] In other words, Lockean psychology offered explanations which could be considered parallel to specific descriptions of physiological processes, but Boerhaave hesitated to claim a causal connection between them.

La Mettrie was not willing to take refuge in ignorance or appeals to God's plan. He pushed Boerhaave's tentative correlations between neurological functions and Lockean descriptions of mental processes into materialism by refusing to admit immaterial causes into discussion of either physiological or psychological processes, by emphasizing all possible connections between mental and physical states, and, most importantly, by substantiating through case studies the degree to which mental states can be seen to depend on physiological processes.[17]

Boerhaavian physiology not only brought La Mettrie to materialism, it also shaped to a considerable degree the particular character of his philosophy. Recent studies of La Mettrie's philosophy have taken note of the distinctive character of his materialism particularly as explicated in *L'Homme machine*.[18] Unlike many eighteenth-century proponents of materialism,[19] La Mettrie was not dogmatic. Although he had no doubt that the universe was composed only of matter and motion, La Mettrie was loath to draw conclusions from this basic premise. (He avoids pronouncements to such a degree that debate continues about whether his materialism is at root mechanical or vitalistic.) La Mettrie also assumed that matter is essentially active and dynamic, a premise he was able to ground in the physiological evidence for muscular irritability. La Mettrie's materialism is further distinguished by its emphasis on the constitution of matter, an emphasis explicitly derived from his work in Boerhaavian physiology.

Boerhaave had confidently forged a synthesis between iatrochemical and iatromechanical theories of human physiology. He had also suggested that since medicine had become so staunchly empirical, the medical theorist could be reasonably confident in drawing analogies between the perceptible and the imperceptible. For example, according to Boerhaave, it was legitimate to make comparisons between the circulatory system and the circulation of *esprits*.[20]

But La Mettrie subjected all of these assumptions to thorough-going criticism: because medicine remained too metaphysical, analogies were unwarranted; the chemists, in particular, were too wedded to systematic explanations; and, most important to his materialism, mechanism did not take adequate account of the crucial differences between parts of machines and the parts of the human body[21] and was, therefore, an insufficient means to understand the workings of the human body. In fact the wide-ranging manifestations of any disease suggested to La Mettrie that the particular organization of matter in the individual constitution was *the* crucial factor in health and disease. The primacy of the individual constitution raised the possibility of so many variables and varieties of human response to illness and other stimuli that La Mettrie did not make dogmatic claims about how matter would act. Instead materialism entailed a medical crusade to emphasize to physicians the importance of as thorough a case study of the individual patient as possible. The medical character of La Mettrie's materialism argued for philosophic reform. Through materialism man is to be understood as a part of nature, not set apart by any metaphysical constructs like the immortal soul. Thus materialism provides a basis for understanding the diversity of human behavior and that understanding must inevitably produce tolerance for those individuals whose consitution endows them with proclivities towards the socially unacceptable. Some of these issues are treated extensively only in La Mettrie's later philosophical works but the philosophical ramifications of his materialism are evident in his commentaries on Boerhaave and the specific case studies he uses to illustrate his own treatises on disease.

These are some of the important and positive influences of Boerhaave's physiology on La Mettrie's philosophical development. But La Mettrie also presumed to criticize his teacher. He did not share Boerhaave's optimistic assessment that medical progress was assured because metaphysics had been excluded from medicine in favor of experimentalism.[22] His view of the prospects for reform was less sanguine largely because he had found his Parisian medical education, which was based on the exegesis of Aristotelian texts, to be completely useless as a basis for medical practice.[23] Repudiating his classical education as so many others did in the age of the scientific revolution, La Mettrie remarked on the occasion of his graduation that, much to his chagrin, his doctor's bonnet conferred no knowledge or ability to treat disease.[24] Although he considered the education he received from Boerhaave in Leyden to be a surer foundation for medical practice, La Mettrie criticized even Boerhaave's reformist physiological works as excessively wedded to the formulations of the iatrochemists and the iatromechanists in describing physiological processes.[25] He claimed that medicine must be rigorously critical of all received opinion and medical traditions. Medical contentions could be considered legitimate only if they were supported by empirical and clinical experiments, and ultimately medical writings must eschew metaphysical considerations to address the pragmatic concerns of the practitioner.[26]

For La Mettrie, an examination of the medical tradition led him to the epistemological perspective generally associated with the Enlightenment, i.e., a concern with and *esprit systématique* as opposed to the more rigid *esprit de système* of the seventeenth-century metaphysicians.[27] Thus he deplored the metaphysical system-making of medical schools of thought, chiding medical systematizers for having "let nature escape to embrace mere phantoms."[28] He argued that medical writings must be concerned instead with the ordered presentation of practical, empirically demonstrable case studies. His study of medicine led him to articulate a position of epistemological modesty which rejected a quest for First Causes and rigidly restricted the area of scientific inquiry to what was demonstrable and useful.

These conclusions about the epistemology most useful for medicine could also be applied to general philosophical questions. In other words, all knowledge must be directed away from systematic metaphysical investigations and towards the empirical and the useful. This epistemological perspective, reflected in La Mettrie's earliest medical works, defines, I would argue, the entire subsequent program of his philosophy.[29] But La

Mettrie does not simply *reflect* a common Enlightenment perspective. His translations of Boerhaave made him a conduit into France not only for Boerhaave's medicine, with its staunch empiricism and clinical teaching, but also for Locke's philosophy. (La Mettrie's explication of Locke's epistemology in *Histoire naturelle de l'âme* appeared the same year as Condillac's *Essai sur l'origine des connoissances humaines*.)[30] Thus his medical and philosophical writings must be recognized for their role in formulating *l'esprit systématique*.

La Mettrie was also involved in more pragmatic issues of medical practice such as the bitter pamphlet war between the doctors and the surgeons. From 1720 to 1750 the critical professional issue for French physicians was their battle to retain their privileged status against the incursions of the surgeons.[32] Within the context of these debates, La Mettrie identified a specific target for reform. He was harshly and unflinchingly critical of medicine as practiced in Paris. His critique focused on two fundamental issues: medical education and medical practice. He found contemporary medical education a bastion of ignorance because the physician refused to concern himself with the knowledge the new sciences could give him and instead persisted in the pursuit of erudition. This concern left the physician with a completely illusory basis for his practice, as he was uneducated in both the theory and the practice of medicine.[33]

La Mettrie held the corporate structure of the Parisian Faculty of Medicine responsible, in large part, for the sorry state of medical education and practice in France. He claimed that, since the Faculty had taken as its primary goal the restriction of the number of physicians to ensure that they all could earn a good living, it had in effect directed the concern of the profession away from the cure of the sick and toward an increase in social status. Thus, in addition to being ignorant, the physicians of Paris practiced society medicine. Though unconcerned with the care of patients, they were vitally concerned with increasing their wealth and social status and with preserving the privileges of their corporate order. La Mettrie attacked these privileges as indefensible since the physicians acted out of self-interest rather than from motives of public concern. Like many Enlightenment reformers, La Mettrie used privilege as a pejorative term for unwarranted and undeserved benefits, and in the doctors of Paris he found a vulnerable target.

Unlike other combatants in the pamphlet war but like many of the philosophes, La Mettrie recognized the great efficacy of a light stylistic touch under the guise of fiction. A brief discussion of one satire will give some idea of his concerns as a medical satirist. *La Faculté vengée* (1747) was successful enough to warrant republication in 1762 under the title *Les Charlatans demasqués* because, as the editor put it, "the spectacle of a doctor writing to discredit his colleagues is sure to amaze and interest Paris."[34] Within the satire, which is in the form of a play, La Mettrie presumes to eavesdrop on a meeting of the Faculty in which they call upon their patron, the devil himself, to redress their grievances: specifically, to establish their authority over the surgeons, to reaffirm the rights of the Faculty of Medicine of Paris as the only institution able to *sell* medical degrees, and finally to deal with the problem of La Mettrie. In their discussion, the doctors expose their venality, arrogance, and ignorance. For example, one doctor blithely remarks that a patient died because he prescribed fifteen doses of a medication, although the requisite amount was two, because he was thinking of a card game, *quinze*. Ultimately, the doctors remark with satisfaction that they are admirably fulfilling their role in society—population control. The devil frankly admits that he finds the doctors of Paris more despicable than most residents of hell but decides that he must continue to support those who bring him so many souls. These satires, though light in tone, were not taken lightly by the Parisian medical community. Disregarding the advice given to them by the devil in the satire to "be tranquil, laugh with the public, make it appear, if possible, that all in the satire is the opposite of what you are,"[35] the Faculty of Medicine instead had La Mettrie banished from France and his books burned.

In attacking the doctors, La Mettrie also upheld the surgeons as much better examples of the professional concerns and standards of medicine. He extolled the surgeons as "citizens so necessary in these times of war and calamity, always more useful than those who follow the false lure of Physic" [medicine].[36] He noted that, in the course of the pamphlet war, the surgeons began to argue for reforms in medical education and practice, emphasizing the empirical and the clinical as the proper foundation of medicine. They also supported crucial tenets of the new sciences, embraced epistemological modesty as a characteristic philosophical position, and asserted the necessity of practical education and the incorporation of chemistry and anatomy into medical education and practice.[37] Their sense of human knowledge as fundamentally tied to observation and experimentation connects the surgeons to the epistemology of the Enlightenment.

Although La Mettrie was the first of the philosophes to point out the ways in which the surgeons exemplified Enlightenment hopes for the progress of medicine, the encyclopedists later acknowledged them as models for the development of Enlightenment ideals.[38] For the philosophes, too, surgery rather than medicine could serve as the more persuasive model of the utilitarian benefits of medicine because the surgeons were eager to tie their goals to the broader issues of the Enlightenment, and because the Faculty of Medicine was too resistant to innovation and represented privilege, monopoly, and ignorance. Thus, for the philosophes, the physicians came to epitomize, as La Mettrie had already pointed out, striking abuses of privilege in the *ancien régime*.

By participating in a public debate and by using the popular and effective medium of satire, La Mettrie meant to increase public involvement in medical issues. Specifically he meant to goad the public into seeing that the true physician ought to be the antithesis of the spectacle of the pernicious physician his satires presented. Because medicine is vitally tied to public well-being, reform-minded citizens must concern themselves with medical reform. Because the true physician is concerned with issues of public health rather than social prestige, the public must demand that sort of physician. And since the physician can only be as good as the education he receives, the public must insist that the kind of medical education supported by the surgeons be implemented.

To drive home his point, La Mettrie took the case for enlightened medical education and practice to the public in his own medical works.[39] Each of his treatises — on small pox, dysentery, venereal disease, and preventive medicine — was written to direct information to a particular medical constituency or to the general public. Beyond the specific subject matter and purpose of these treatises, they all embodied several fundamental principles. First, medicine had to be useful, deliberately directed to the prevention and most effective treatment of disease. Second, medicine had to be reformed, and this could be accomplished by more widely disseminating medical information. Third, medical information had to be extended to the public at large so that they would be able to take better care of themselves and understand some of the issues involved in the treatment of disease. Finally and most importantly, the public had to be informed so that they could participate in medical reform. Just as his satires revealed the failings of contemporary physicians in order to provoke the public to demand better physicians, so his medical works were intended to acquaint the public with good practices and to warn them about dangerous ones. This attempt to raise public awareness of health issues can be seen as part of Enlightenment reform efforts. By making the private knowledge of the medical corporation public, La Mettrie could hope both to produce a more enlightened public and to break the Faculty of Medicine's power which was based on a monopoly on medical education. Both developments would produce an improvement in public health and undeniable social benefits.

La Mettrie's interest in medicine as the source of both his materialism and his campaign for social reform led him to engage in the contemporary discussions of just who the philosophes were, how they were to be distinguished from conventional metaphysicians, and what role they could play in reform efforts. His contribution to this discussion was a definition of the *médecin/philosophe* as the appropriate person to carry out programs of both medical and social reform because, as he said, "medicine is, without question the most useful and the most necessary of all the sciences. Physicians are the *only* philosophers who are useful to the Republic and serve the State."[40] Therefore the *médecin/philosophe* was to be the best agent of the reforms proposed by the philosophic movement. In opposition to the flagrant abuses of medicine as practiced by the Faculty of Paris, La Mettrie defended the *médecin/philosophe* as the embodiment of the knowledge offered by the new sciences and the one who sought to implement it for the benefit of the public through a concern with public health and preventive medicine. In the philosophical sphere, the *médecin/philosophe* had the task of discrediting metaphysical notions, which prevented scientific investigation into human nature. He could also use the methods of science to gauge where and how society should be reformed so as to reflect the physician's empirical understanding of man.

Medicine led La Mettrie to articulate crucial concerns of the philosophes as early as the 1740s. Within his medical writings he sought to define the philosophes and distinguish their goals and methods from those of traditional philosophers. For La Mettrie, medicine provided not only a particular focus of attack on the vested privileges of corporate order but also a paradigm of the crusade for public enlightenment and reform. His philosophical works carried out a program suggested by his medicine: his first explicated Locke in *L'Histoire naturelle de l'âme*, claiming to use Locke's "plain, historical method" to write the natural rather than the metaphysical history of the soul and suggesting that only expediency kept Locke from carrying though the materialist implications of his epistemology;[41] he then worked to establish a natural philosophy by providing empirical evidence for materialism; finally, he unflinchingly carried out the moral implications of materialism in *Discours sur le bonheur*. Moreover, his medical study underscored the critical role of the individual constitution in the treatment of disease; in his philosophical works, he saw that this unique character of the individual consitution, which made the treatment of disease vary so much from individual to individual, was an equally serious impediment to the implementation of sweeping social reform. This same issue is of vital concern to Diderot in his later works (*Rameau's Nephew* in particular).[42] Thus through his medical studies, La Mettrie was forced to acknowledge, again at an early date, the limits of Enlightenment prospects for social change. It might be suggested that medicine allowed La Mettrie to confront problems of the philosophic movement more clearly and directly than those philosophes who sought solutions to social issues within the framework of the physical sciences.

Several questions of course remain before the case of La Mettrie could be taken as exemplary of the formation of a philosophe. How many other philosophes defined their programs in response to the need for medical reform or used an epistemology grounded in medicine as a basis of philosophical discussion? There is some *prima facie* evidence that a medical formation might not be atypical of Enlightenment philosophes: there were several important medical contributors to the *Encyclopédie*. Diderot was very interested in medical issues. And medical reform was a highly-touted goal of Enlightenment.[43] But these few examples scarcely support a claim for the centrality of medicine in defining Enlightenment issues. Nevertheless, whether or not the case of La Mettrie can be taken as paradigmatic for the philosophes in general, he is indicative of fundamental affinities between the epistemology and concerns with social change of reformist physicians and philosophes. Thus a broader investigation of the overall influence of physicians in the Enlightenment might reveal that La Mettrie's perception of the affinities between their reform interests and intellectual concerns and those of philosophes was accurate and that medicine played a significant or perhaps even fundamental role in the development of some of the philosophes and their notions of social reform.

However, the question for historians cannot simply be how many philosophes followed La Mettrie's path through medicine to Enlightenment or how many physicians were involved in the Enlightenment, but rather the more complicated question of the influence of La Mettrie's medically structured materialism. Medicine is not simply a convenient way to connect La Mettrie to the movement we call the Enlightenment but rather the ultimate form of La Mettrie's contribution to the philosophy of the period. La Mettrie's concern with medical issues introduced crucial elements to the Enlightenment. His role in the development of an *esprit systématique* has already been noted. La Mettrie's translations of Boerhaave not only led him to adopt Lockean psychology as the best framework within which to discuss brain functions but also to make the easy transition from Locke to materialism and to emphasize the physiological evidence for this step. And, finally, his philosophical works made the implications of materialism explicit. Once these issues had been raised the philosophic movement at large could not evade them, no matter how hard some philosophes tried to distance themselves from the radical implications of La Mettrie's philosophy. To assess the ultimate influence of medicine in defining philosophical issues, the medical roots of French materialism in the eighteenth century must be more consistently acknowledged and attempts must be made to separate protestations against materialism, whether genuine or motivated by caution, from the legacy bequeathed by La Mettrie of medicine based on empirical studies, epistemology grounded in physiology, and social reform understood and limited by medical insights.

NOTES

1 See for example Roger Hahn, *The Anatomy of a Scientific Institution: The Paris Academy of Sciences 1666–1803* (Berkeley: University of California Press, 1971); Thomas Hankins, *Jean D'Alembert. Science and the Enlightenment* (Oxford: Oxford University Press, 1970); René Taton, ed., *L'Organisation et diffusion des sciences en France* (Paris: Hermann, 1964); Sergio Moravia, *La Scienza dell'uomo nel settecento* (Bari: Laterza, 1970).

2 Peter Gay, *The Enlightenment: An Interpretation*, Vol. 2, *The Science of Freedom* (New York: W. W. Norton & Co., 1969), 174–85.

3 Charles Gillispie, *The Edge of Objectivity: An Essay in the History of Scientific Ideas* (Princeton: Princeton University Press, 1960); Henry Guerlac, "Where the Statue Stood: Divergent Loyalties to Newton in the Eighteenth Century," in Earl Wasserman, ed., *Aspects of the Eighteenth Century* (Baltimore: John Hopkins Univ. Press, 1965) 317–34. Leonard Marsak, "Bernard de Fontenelle: The Idea of Science in the French Enlightenment," *Transactions of the American Philosophical Society* 49 pt. 7 (December, 1959); Ruth Murdoch, "Newton and the French Muse," *Journal of the History of Ideas* 19 (June 1958): 323–34; Keith M. Baker, *Condorcet: From Natural Philosophy to Social Mathematics* (Chicago: University of Chicago, 1975).

4 See for example Jean Ehrard, *L'Idée de la nature en France à l'aube des lumières* (Paris: Flammarion, 1970); Georges Gusdorff, *Dieu, la nature, l'homme au siècle des lumières* (Paris: Payot, 1972); Philip Ritterbush, *Overtures to Biology: The Speculations of Eighteenth Century Naturists* (New Haven: Yale University Press, 1964); Jacques Roger, *Les sciences de la vie dans la pensée française du XVIII⁰ siècle* (Paris: Armand Colin, 1963).

5 Lester S. King, *The Medical World of the Eighteenth Century* (Chicago: University of Chicago Press, 1958) and *The Philosophy of Medicine: The Early Eighteenth Century* (Cambridge: Harvard University Press, 1978); *The Road to Medical Enlightenment, 1650–1695* (New York: American Elsevier, 1970); Toby Gelfand, *Professionalizing Modern Medicine* (Westport, Conn.: Greenwood Press, 1980); "Empiricism and 18th Century Surgery," *Bulletin of the History of Medicine* 44 (January-February, 1970): 40–53.

6 Diderot's harsh indictment is often cited. He said of La Mettrie: "Dissolute, impudent, a buffoon, a flatterer; made for life at court and the favor of nobles. He died as he should have, a victim of his own imtemperance and his folly. He killed himself by ignorance of the art he professed." In "Essai sur les règnes de Claude et de Néron," in *Oeuvres complètes de Diderot* (Paris: Garnier, 1875–77) 3:2.

7 Giuseppe A. Roggerone, *Controilluminismo: Saggio su La Mettrie e Helvetius* (Lecce: Milella, 1975).

8 This argument is developed in chapter nine of my dissertation, "Julien Offray de La Mettrie: Medicine in the Service of Philosophy," Unpublished Ph.D. dissertation, University of Chicago, 1983, pp. 302–27. I disagree with the argu-

ment developed by Ann Thomson in her critical edition of the *Discours préliminaire* in which she claims that La Mettrie's notion of the philosophe is not well-developed and that the seventeenth-century *libertin* tradition is the best context in which to place him. See Ann Thomson, *Materialism and Society in the Mid-Eighteenth Century: La Mettrie's "Discours Préliminaire"* (Geneva: Droz, 1981), 90–107.

9 Standard biographical sources on La Mettrie are: Pierre Lémee, *Julien Offray de la Mettrie, Saint Malo 1709– Berlin 1751, médecin, philosophe, polémiste, sa vie et son oeuvre* (Mortain: Editions Mortainais, 1954); Raymond Boissier, *La Mettrie: Médecin, pamphlétaire et philosophe* (Paris: Société d'édition "Les Belles Lettres," 1931).

10 Thomson, *Materialism and Society*, 23–30.

11 Aram Vartanian argues that in *L'Homme machine* La Mettrie changed his fundamental philosophical allegiance from Locke to Descartes in *La Mettrie's "L'Homme machine,"* (Princeton: Princeton University Press, 1960), 43 ff.

12 Hermann Boerhaave, *Aphorismes sur la connoissance et la cure des maladies*, trans. Julien Offray de La Mettrie (Paris: Chez Huart, Braisson, Durand, 1745); *Institutions de medicine*, trans. Julien Offray de La Mettrie, 2 volumes (Paris: Chez Huart, 1740); *Traité de la matière médicale pour servir à la composition des remèdes indiqués dans les Aphorismes par M. Hermann Boerhaave, auquel on a ajouté des opérations chymiques du même auteur*, trans. Julien Offray de La Mettrie (Paris: Chez Huart, 1739).

13 While it seems unlikely that Boerhaave met Locke (Locke's exile in Holland ended four years before Boerhaave assumed his first university position), there are several ways he could have come in contact with Locke's ideas. First, the University of Leyden seems to have been particularly receptive to new ideas. It was the gateway to the rest of Europe for Cartesianism, Newtonianism, and Lockeanism. See Hélène Metzger, *Les Doctrines chimiques en France au début du XVIIe à la fin du XVIIIe siècle* (Paris: Presses Universitaires de France, 1923). Secondly, Locke spent part of his exile at the University of Leyden working with professors who were Boerhaave's immediate predecessors. Third, Locke and Boerhaave were both concerned to promulgate the medical ideas of Thomas Sydenham. See the following for discussions of the medical character of Locke's philosophy: François Duchesneau, *L'Empiricisme de Locke* (The Hague: Nijhoff, 1973); Kenneth Dewhurst, *John Locke (1632–1704) Physician and Philosopher: A Medical Biography* (London: The Wellcome Historical Medical Library, 1963)

14 John Locke, *An Essay Concerning Human Understanding*. Edited with introduction by Peter H. Nidditch. (Oxford: Clarendon Press, 1975) 1:43.

15 Herman Boerhaave, *Institutions de médecine*, nos. 571, 573–80.

16 Ibid., no. 580.

17 *Institutions de médecine de M. Hermann Boerhaave traduites de Latin en français par M. de La Mettrie et avec un commentaire par M. de La Mettrie*. Second edition. 8 volumes (Paris, 1743–50).

18 Thomson, 39–46 and Vartanian, 13–40, 59–90.

19 John Yolton, *Thinking Matter: Materialism in Eighteenth-Century Britain* (Minneapolis: University of Minnesota Press, 1983); Robert Schofield, *Mechanism and Materialism: British Philosophy in the Age of Reason* (Princeton: Princeton University Press, 1970).

20 Boerhaave, *Institutions de médecine*, nos. 570–80.

21 Wellman, "Medicine in the Service of Philosophy," 109–42.

22 La Mettrie, *Institutions de médecine*. 1:10.

23 La Mettrie, *Ouvrage de Penelope, ou Machiavel en médecine*, 3 vols., (Berlin, 1748–1750) 120–24.

24 Ibid., 123.

25 Important sources on iatromechanism and iatrochemistry are: Marie Boas, "The Establishment of the Mechanical Philosophy," *Osiris* 10 (1952): 412–541; Robert Le Noble, *Mersenne ou la naissance du méchanisme* (Paris: Vrin, 1943); Allen G. Debus, *The Chemical Philosophy: Paracelsian Science and Medicine in the 16th and 17th Centuries*, 2 vols. (New York: Science History Publications, 1977); "The Paracelsians and the Chemists: The Chemical Dilemma in Renaissance Medicine," *Clio Medica* 7 (September, 1972): 185–99; *The Chemical Dream of the Renaissance* (Indianapolis: Bobbs-Merrill, 1972); "Fire Analysis and the Elements in the 16th and 17th Centuries," *Annals of Science* 23 (January 1967): 127–47; Robert Multhauf, *The Origins of Chemistry* (New York: Watts, 1966).

26 La Mettrie, *Institutions de médecine*, 2:3.

27 For a fuller elaboration of this distinction see Ernst Cassirer, *The Philosophy of the Enlightenment* (Boston: Beacon Press, 1954), 93–120.

28 La Mettrie, *Ouvrage de Pénélope*, 284.

29 See discussion on page 84.

30 Etienne Bonnet de Condillac, *Essay on the Origins of Human Knowledge*, ed. Robert G. Weynat (Gainesville, Florida: Scholars' Facsimiles and Reprints, 1971).

31 For discussion of the medical practice in the eighteenth century see Paul Delauney, *Le Monde medical parisien au XVIIIᵉ siècles* (Paris: Rousset, 1906); *La Vie medicale du XVIIIᵉ siècle* (Paris: Editions Hachette, 1935); Toby Gelfand, *Professionalizing Modern Medicine*.

32 Julien Offray de La Mettrie, *La Faculte vengée, comédie en trois actes par M***, docteur régent de la Faculté de Paris* (Paris: Quillau, 1747); *Les Charlatans demasqués, ou Pluton vengeur de la société de médecine, comédie ironique en trois actes en prose* (Paris-Geneve: Aux despens de la Companie, 1762); *Saint Cosme vengé* (Strasbourg: Chez Doulseker et Pocke, 1744); *Ouvrage de Pénélope, ou Machiavel en médecine* 3 vols. (Berlin, 1748–50).

33 La Mettrie, *Ouvrage de Pénélope*, 1: unpaginated preface.

34 La Mettrie, *Les Charlatans demasqués*, iv.

35 La Mettrie, *La Faculté vengée*, 176.

36 La Mettrie, *Saint Cosme vengé*, 68.

37 La Mettrie thoroughly discusses this issue in two chapters entitled "De la Preeminence de la médecine ou la chirurgie," and "Des Chirurgiens médecins," in *Ouvrage de Pénélope* 2:217–41.

38 Toby Gelfand, *Professionalizing Modern Medicine*, 9–13; William Coleman, "Health and Hygiene in the *Encyclopédie*: A Medical Doctrine for the Bourgeoisie," *Journal of the History of Medicine* 29 (1974): 399–421.

39 Julien Offray de La Mettrie, *Lettres de M.D.L.M. docteur en médecine sur l'art de conserver la santé et de prolonger la vie* (Paris: Chez Prault, 1738); *Memoire sur la dyssentérie* (Leyden: Elie Luzac,, 1750); *Oeuvres de médecine de M. de La Mettrie* (Berlin: Fromery, 1751); *Système de Hermann Boerhaave sur les maladies vénériennes traduit en français par M. de La M. Avec des notes et un dissertation du traducteur sur l'origine, la nature, et la cure de ces maladies* (Paris, 1735); *Traité de la petite vérole avec la manière de guerir de cette maladie* (Paris: Chez Huart, 1740).

40 La Mettrie, *Politique du médecin de Machiavel*, xx.

41 La Mettrie, "Traité de L'âme," in *Oeuvres philosophiques*, 2d ed. 2 vols. (Berlin, 1774) 1:51–183.

42 Denis Diderot, *Rameau's Nephew and Other works*. Translated by Jacques Barzun. Edited with an introduction by Ralph H. Brown. (Indianapolis: Bobbs-Merrill, 1964).

43 Diderot said of medicine: "It is very hard to think cogently about metaphysics or ethics without being an anatomist, a naturalist, a physiologist, and a physician." This passage is quoted in Arthur Wilson, *Diderot* (New York: Oxford University Press, 1957), 93. Diderot also sought contributions from twenty physicians to the Encyclopedia. Voltaire carried on campaigns for medical reform and was particularly involved in the campaign for inoculation.

From Curiosité to Utilité:
The Automaton in
Eighteenth-Century France

REED BENHAMOU

In 1738, the curious Parisian with three *livres* in his pocket could join his fellows at the Hôtel de Longueville to hear a concert of flute music performed by an automaton. If by April of that year 7,500 had parted with a sum equal to the weekly wage of a young *ouvrière*,[1] it was because (as the Duc du Luynes noted in his diary), the spectacle centered on "une machine digne de curiosité."[2] Less restrained, the newspapers of the day exhausted superlatives in praising the invention. To the *Mercure de France*, it was "un Phénomene de Méchanique, le plus singulier et en même-temps le plus agréable qu'on ait peut-être encore vû."[3] Prévost's *Pour et contre* labelled it "le plus merveilleux morceau de mécanique qui ait paru jusqu'aujourd'hui."[4] And Desfontaines, in his *Observations*, found it to be "un chef d'oeuvre de Mécanique, un prodige de génie, un miracle de l'art"; almost breathless with anticipation, he asked of the flautist's inventor, Jacques Vaucanson, "Que n'a-t-on pas lieu d'en attendre?"[5]

He had not long to find out. Within two years, Vaucanson's *flûteur* was once again on the concert circuit, this time accompanied by a more ambitious mechanical musician which played the fife and drum — at the same time; and a duck which took grain from the hand, swallowed it, and then excreted it, as Vaucanson told Desfontaines, in a visibly changed form and from an end opposite to that from which it went in.[6] (This aspect of the duck has received perhaps more attention than it deserves considering that, in 1811, an automaton in the form of a life-sized elephant could produce the same effect if given 24 hours notice.)[7]

Vaucanson who, despite his claim to the Académie Royale des Sciences, had constructed these automata as much to make money as to demonstrate "les solides principes de mécanique," sold his trio of performers in 1743; and turned to the invention of industrial equipment, including the loom which is generally, and wrongly, attributed to Jacquard.[8] Their new owners continued to exhibit them; but the market began almost immediately to fill with a variety of talking heads, singing birds, moving pictures, fortune tellers, chess masters, harpsichord players, artists, and scribes.[9] Contemplation of this wealth of self-powered devices can lead us in a number of different directions, all illustrative of eighteenth century life. The scatological has already been treated. The scurrilous, satirical, literary, philosophical, mechanical, and cultural remain.

The Scurrilous and Satirical

Vaucanson's first automaton, modeled after the statue by Coysevox which then embellished the Tuileries gardens, was a life-sized flautist in the shape of a faun; it produced music through the action of artificial lungs, a mechanical tongue, and articulated fingers. One could even, the Duc du Luynes reported, provide it with another flute: it would still play.[10] It was perhaps a tribute to the dexterity with which Vaucanson was able to endow his *flûteur*, in combination with the faun's goatish reputation, that inspired the anonymous author of the *Epître à Monsieur de Vaucanson* to the first of the following verses. Desfontaines' own reputation appears to have inspired the second.

> Génie en miracles fertiles
> C'est peu de te faire admirer
> Pour rendre ton art plus utile
> Permets que j'ose t'inspirer
> Cher Vaucanson, tout le beau sexe
> Veut que je t'implore aujourd'hui
> Un Sathyre avec son annexe.
> . . .
> Plus d'un galant abbé qui tremble
> Voyant que l'automate aura
> Toutes les qualités ensemble
> De plus jamais ne parlera
> Et discrètement portera
> Un grand attribut qui ressemble
> A celui du Dieu des Jardins.

(The *Epître* was aptly credited to the Librairie Le Fouineur.)[11]

The pamphleteer Chevrier also employed Vaucanson's genius to satirical effect in "Le Colporteur," an anecdote in which he described the sale of a courtesan's possessions. These were said to include "un corps à ressort, que le célèbre Vaucanson avait imaginé pour porter, par la force d'un cabestan, les peaux éloignées à la poitrine, et en former un sein charmant qui trompait les yeux même des connaisseurs."[12]

Nobody's fool, however, was Mme du Deffand, who analyzed her house guests in a letter to Horace Walpole: "J'admirais hier au soir la nombreuse compagnie qui était chez moi: hommes et femmes me paraissaient des machines à ressort, qui allaient, venaient, parlaient, riaient, sans penser, sans refléchir, sans sentir, chacun jouait son rôle par habitude. . . ." In this letter of October 10, 1766, Mme du Deffand seems to echo La Bruyère, who, in his "Caractères" of 1688, had said, "Le sot est automate, il est machine, il est ressort, le poids l'emporte, le fait mouvoir et toujours, et dans le même sens, et avec la même égalité; il est fixé et déterminé par sa nature et j'ose dire par son espèce."[13]

The Literary and Philosophical

Given the number and intricacy of the automatons produced in the eighteenth century, and the deeper issues of human purpose and nature to which they give rise, their relative absence from the literature and philosophy of the time is disconcerting. It was, however, the nineteenth and early twentieth centuries that integrated automatons into literature; the twentieth, reacting to the impact of automatic machinery upon workers and, perhaps, to a generalized *angst*, that ponders them in philosophical terms.[14] For the Age of Reason, automatons were, as we shall see, potentially useful illustrations of human function; and, as we have seen, useful metaphors for human foolishness.

Still, they did find their way into certain minor works of eighteenth-century literature. The satirical poetry already cited may be included in this category, as might Restif de la Bretonne's *Les Contemporaines, ou Aventures des plus jolies femmes de l'âge present* (1785), which mentioned Vaucanson's *flûteur*; or Mme de Genlis's moral tale, "Alphonse et Dalinde," which borrowed the characters of two automatons created by the Swiss craftsmen Jacquet-Droz and Leschot, exhibited in Paris in 1783. Here, too, we might place the ponderous alexandrines of Delille's *Epître à M. Laurent, chevalier de l'ordre de Saint Michel, à l'occasion d'un Bras artificiel qu'il a fait pour un Soldat Invalide* (1761).

"Literature" might also be sufficiently broad a category to encompass the use of automatons and automatic devices in the theater. The architect Servandoni, for example, created a series of *spectacles* for the Easter seasons of 1738, '39, and '40. The last of these, which adapted the *Aenide* to mechanical theater, was praised by Prévost for combining "tout ce qu'il y avoit de plus grand dans l'Architecture, dans la Peinture, dans la Perspective, et dans le jeu mécanique de Machines." Prévost had also applauded Servandoni's first offering, a reproduction of Saint Peter's in Rome; but the *Amusements littéraires* had been restrained: "Ce spectacle était d'une nature à attirer un monde infini et n'a attiré presque personne. C'est ce qui a donné lieu à un Plaisant de fabriquer une prétendue Bulle sous le nom du fameux Pancrace Pellegrin, Patriarche de l'Opéra, par laquelle on accorde des Indulgences plénières á ceux qui vont visiter cette représentation d'Eglise."[15]

Marmontel, who had commissioned an automatic asp from Vaucanson for *Cléopâtre*, was even less lucky with his public — and, perhaps, with the asp, which moved and hissed in a highly realistic fashion. When asked his opinion of the play after one of its (few) performances, a spectator referred obliquely to the asp's sound effect, saying that he was "de l'avis de l'aspic." Another wrote:

> A la pièce de Cléopâtre
> Où fut l'aspic de Vaucanson
> Tout fut sifflé à l'unisson ...
> Et le souffleur, oyant cela
> Croyant encore souffler, siffla ...

while a third translated his own reaction into pseudo-patois:

> Mais quand j'avons plus fait la hue
> C'est quand Cléopâtre est mordue.
> Qu'javons vu grouilles un serpent
> Qu'elle a tiré for proprement
> Du bleu mitan d'un plat d'asperges
> On n'rit que d'ça dans not'auberge

Stung, Marmontel confided to his *Mémoires* that "la surprise que causoit ce petit chef-d'oeuvre de l'art faisoit diversion au véritable intérêt du moment. J'ai préféré depuis un dénouement plus simple."[16]

As in literature, so in philosophy: the automaton's role is limited. It is moreover — and it is important to emphasize this — a straightforward role. Eminently reasonable, the *philosophes* ascribed no mystic significance to these mechanical devices, even when they employed them to describe the mysteries of a mechanical universe. The nineteenth century sometimes ascribed to the eighteenth a religious superstition in so far as automatons were concerned;[17] and twentieth century thinkers might "emphasize the unity of the animate and inanimate, the organic and inorganic," or ponder "man's never-ending struggle to . . . become as one of the gods himself, by transcending both matter and himself."[18]

Such attitudes are anachronistic in the eighteenth-century context. Fontenelle might praise the work of the *père* Sébastien by saying that his mechanisms for a *tableau mouvant* took up so little space that he imitated "d'assez près le méchanicien de la nature dans les animaux, dont une des plus surprenantes merveilles est le peu d'espace qu'occupent un grand nombre de machines ou d'organes qui produisent de grands effets."[19] La Mettrie might consider "toute la matière organisée comme une machine très perfectionnée, douée d'un principal moteur qui seul la différencie de celles construites par les hommes."[20] Voltaire might characterize Vaucanson as the "rival de Prométhée" who took "le feu des cieux pour animer les corps."[21] Conversely, Ange Goudar could grumble, "je défie à M. de Vocanson [sic] et à tous les machinistes de la terre ensemble de faire un visage postiche qui rende les passions parce que pour exprimer les passions de l'âme, il faut une âme."[22] None confused the (super)natural with the artificial, nor the creation of *anatomies mouvantes*— working models of physiological functions—with the creation of life. *Anatomies mouvantes* and similar devices may be seen as expressions of mechanism, however; and they also illustrate the link between *curiosité* and *utilité*, a point more fully discussed later.

The Mechanical and Cultural

However intricate their actions, all automatons constructed prior to our own, electronic era utilized a mechanical vocabulary little changed from Classical times. Their power, derived from springs, reservoirs of water or steam, or pendulums, was distributed by a variety of means, most of which are contained in Desfontaines' description of the inner structure of the *flûteur*: "Que de roües, que de poulies, que de leviers, que de vis, que de lames, que de soûpapes, que de pivots, que de soufflets, que de réservoirs, que de fils, que de cordes, que de chaînes, que de tuyaux, que de cylindres!"[23] But if the makers of eighteenth-century automatons did not expand the mechanical repertoire, they did perfect and refine it. The *écrivain*, the charming android by the Jacquet-Droz that still operates at the Historical Museum of Neuchâtel, by no means the most complex of its kind, dips its pen in ink, blows an (invisible) speck of dust from its paper, and can be programmed to write any phrase not exceeding forty characters. There is even evidence that at one time it could write under dictation, letters probably being relayed from a kind of keyboard.[24] In its body, about the size of a two-year-old child, are lodged two interacting systems, one controlling the direction and pressure of the various strokes and the other controlling the selection of the letters. Even greater feats of miniaturization were possible: highly realistic sounds and movements were programmed into the bird-shaped automatons dear to the eighteenth century; the bodies were frequently no more than fifteen centimeters from head to tail.[25]

Once set in motion, automatons could be stopped and restarted, but they were not capable (as are electronic devices) of modifying their mode of operation in reaction to outside circumstance. Any redirection — which was certainly possible through, for example, the exchange of one cam for another — had to come from outside the device, from its operator or "prime mover." It may well be this obvious dependence of the automaton on an outside force that both reinforced eighteenth-century belief in a clockwork universe and kept its *philosophes* from confusing man-made and divinely created machinery.

The audience for automatons was, however, largely indifferent to philosophical overtones. What it demanded was a high degree of realism, an appeal to both the senses and the intellect, and mechanical perfection. Critics could be severe. The Duc du Luynes, for example, regretted that in Vaucanson's *flûteur*, "la bouche demeure toujours ouverte. Il y a cependant un mouvement réel dans la lévre supérieure, mais ce n'est que dans les deux côtés."[26] The remarkable talking head constructed by the *abbé* Mical was largely ignored by the public because, as a contemporary put it, "dans un pays où il faut plaire même en démontrant le quarré de hypoténuse," Mical's invention "n'est que savante & ne flatte pas nos sens en aucune manière."[27] Audience reaction was, thus, carefully measured. As a subscriber wrote to the *Journal de Genève* on June 6, 1789, "on éprouve un sentiment agréable à l'aspect d'un chef-d'oeuvre de méchanique dont l'exécution est parfaite; ce sentiment devient un plaisir vif lorsque l'imitation de quelques-unes des facultés humaines a été l'objet du travail de l'Artiste & qu'il a réussi. . . . Mais c'est sur-tout lorsque l'Artiste a su émouvoir plusieurs sens à la fois . . . que le plaisir du spectateur approche du transport. . . ."

It will be noted that the writer of this passage referred consistently to *artistes*. The *Notice de l'Almanach sous verre*, a periodical which announced a broad range of events in the physical and applied sciences, commonly referred to inventors as *mécaniciens*, although it occasionally dubbed one an *artiste* or even an *artiste mécanicien*. Fontenelle, it may be remembered, used *mécanicien* in his eulogy of the *père* Sébastien, while Ange Goudar defied the *machinistes* to create a device that could express emotion. These terms were by no means interchangeable. As their contexts make clear, *mécanicien* was the most prestigious, being applied to those affiliated with the courts of Europe (*Notices*) or even to the deity (Fontenelle); *artiste* was given to those whose *artifice* was of exceptional quality; *machiniste* was patronizing, when not pejorative.

Inherent in these terms is the disdain for the artisan, if not for his products, characteristic of the educated classes in eighteenth-century France. In 1680, Richelet's *Dictionnaire français* had noted that what was *mécanique* was "bas, vilain et peu digne d'une personne honnête et libéral"; in 1777, Sabatier de Castres' *Dictionnaire des origines* distinguished between a *machiniste* and a *mécanicien*, saying that the former was "un homme adroit . . . sans aucun principe et aucune régle de mouvement." The attitude, at least as old as classical Greece,[28] was unaffected by the attention given the mechanical acts by the *Encyclopédie* or the *Descriptions des arts et métiers* reluctantly pursued by the Académie Royale des Sciences. Vaucanson, who felt the need to "parvenir," reacted by stressing the principles upon which his work was based, and by doing little of it himself. The *père* Sébastien followed suit; like Vaucanson, he developed designs which were given to others to execute. The *abbé* Mical, on the other hand, was known to have "travaillé de ses mains tous les détails de son ouvrage."[29] Perhaps it is only coincidence that it was the *abbé* who had the greatest difficulty in attracting an audience; but such involvement was deemed excessive by certain academicians: "On peut inventer des chefs-d'oeuvre en mécanique sans avoir fait exécuter ou agir une seule machine," Condorcet said, "comme on peut trouver des méthodes de calculer les mouvements d'un astre qu'on n'a jamais vu." Despite his attempts to distance himself from machinery, Vaucanson could not agree. "Il est beaucoup plus aisé de faire des observations météorologiques, des démonstrations sur la glace, sur l'aimant, sur l'élétricité, que d'inventer et de composer une bonne machine," he wrote in 1765, adding "celui qui a inventé le rouet à filer la laine . . . ne serait regardé par les Académiciens . . . que comme un artiste et serait méprisé comme un faiseur de machines. Il y aurait cependant de quoi bien humilier ces messieurs s'ils faisaient réflexion que ce seul mécanicien a procuré plus de bien aux hommes que n'en ont procuré tous les géométres et tous les physiciens . . . dans leur compagnie!"[30]

From Curiosité *to* Utilité

According to De Jaucourt, who defined *curiosité* for the *Encyclopédie*, the only aspect of this quality "digne de l'homme [est] le désir qui l'anime à étendre ses connoissances, soit pour élever son esprit aux grandes vérités, soit pour se rendre utile à ses concitoyens."[31] The second of the parallel phrases introduced by *soit* explicitly acknowledged the link between *curiosité* and *utilité* implicit in many of the inventions and devices produced by eighteenth-century *mécaniciens*. Before passing to the curiosity of the practioner, however, we should recognize the lighter face of the curiosity of the spectator.

In Condorcet's words, eighteenth-century France was "un monde . . . avide de nouveauté"[32]; and this thirst was slaked in a variety of ways, some of which did indeed lead to broader knowledge. The public lectures that went on throughout the century, such as those on physics given by the *abbé* Nollet, are an example; Vaucanson's demonstrations of the workings of his automatons are another. Visitors to the Hôtel de Longuevile were made aware of the interaction of wires, pulleys, levers, gears, and valves, and the explanation almost certainly added to the delight of audiences watching the lips and fingers of a wood-and-papier-mâché construction manipulate a flute, or the beak of a copper-clad duck shake grain into a gullet Vaucanson described as a small chemical laboratory.[33] Here, there was the requisite appeal to both the intellect and the senses, the *agréable* joined to the *utile*.

The spectator's *curiosité* in such an instance is relatively superficial, a kind of mental tickle to watch things work. The curiosity of the *mécanicien* is of a different order, however. At its lowest level, it's a desire to make things function; at its higher, it uses simulation to understand — and even discover — phenomena. As investigators in this area have put it, "from observation of the world we derive enough information to construct a model — then from this model we infer further properties of the world."[35]

In his letter to Desfontaines, Vaucanson made it clear that he did indeed intend to model natural phenomena. The mechanism that moved the wings of his duck, for example, was based not on that of past automatons, such as the rooster crowning the Strasbourg clock, but on the anatomy of a living animal. "Je ne crois pas que les Anatomistes ayent rien à désirer sur la construction de ses aîles," he said. "On a imité, os par os, toutes les éminences qu'ils appellent apophyses." And, naming those bones, he told how each moved at its respective joint.[35]

The second stage of modeling — discovery of other phenomena — is well represented in the fife-and-drum player. Vaucanson had thought, for example, that the sound of each note would be determined solely by the position of the fingers on the holes and the amount of air blown through the pipe. In testing the quality of the music, however, he learned that notes were also affected by the speed and agility of the tongue, and by the preceding tone. In the end, he had developed, and demonstrated, a theory of the instrument; and, because the mechanical tongue of his automaton was capable of greater speed and flexibility than any human tongue, he created what "can be regarded as a competence model" against which human players could be judged.[36]

The intellectual aspects of the *mécanicien*'s curiosity went largely unrecognized in the eighteenth century, even by those who, like Prévost and Diderot, indulged in ecstacies of wonder at mechanical complexity. Desfontaines came closest. Reporting on the *flûteur*, he admired the way in which its cords and chains moved the arms and fingers "de la même maniere que dans l'homme vivant"; then added, "c'est sans doute la connoissance de l'homme . . . qui a guidé l'Auteur dans sa Mécanique. *Mais pour l'exécution il lui a fallu d'autres lumieres. L'imagination peut à peine se representer de pareils efforts: comment a-t'elle pû les produire?*"[37]

The mode of thought that baffled Desfontaines is temporo-spatial rather than sequential, pictorial rather than verbal. It has lately come to be characterized, and even prized, as right-brained activity; but the eighteenth century exalted left-brained, sequential thinking. The products of the hand were, to it, largely unrelated to the products of the mind; and they gained legitimacy only in so far as they engaged the minds of others. In general, this did not happen on any sustained basis; and the products of the practitioner's *curiosité* were simply objects of curiosity to the public.[38]

There was also doubt about their utility. When William Coxe, chaplain to the Duke of Marlborough, saw the three Jacquet-Droz automatons in 1777, for example, he reported, "These are certainly wonderful inventions . . . but still they are mere toys, and surely an unworthy waste of great genius. . . ."[39]

It might be thought that providing delight was a worthy use of genius; but even in a world that liked to be amused, Coxe's attitude was neither uncommon nor altogether unjustified. Some makers of automatons produced devices fulfilling the same social needs today met by whoopee cushions and Chinese fingerstalls. Lavocat, *mécanicien* to the court of Brussels, seems to have specialized in this area. Four of his peculiar inventions came on the market in 1779–80: a chair which folded its arms over its user, trapping its victim in place; a pocket which closed on any hand inserted in it; a room which locked as soon as anyone took food from a center table; and, finally, a vehicle that moved with no visible guidance, its driver being hidden inside. (Lavocat evidently assumed its user would so indulge himself for extended periods, since sanitary arrangements were thoughtfully placed beneath the seat.) Lavocat could be practical as well as a practical joker, however. He devised a self-propelling chair for the infirm, just as a German surgeon developed a chair imitating the amble of a horse, "à l'usage des hypocondriaques & des femmes attaquées de vapeurs hystériques."[40]

Several eighteenth-century *mécaniciens* turned their attention to the needs of the sick or disabled, their products revealing how *utilité* may be served by *curiosité*. Nowhere is this more evident than in the advances made in prosthetic devices.

Articulated, artificial limbs had been made at least as early as the sixteenth century, their limited flexibility dependent on iron gears and levers controlled by an undamaged hand. Among the earliest existing designs are those by Ambroise Paré, dating from around 1560, which like most such devices were given to clockmakers and goldsmiths for execution. Obviously, none was cheap: in 1587, a Swiss clockmaker contracted to make for 20 *écus d'or* an iron hand, the fingers of which flexed either together or serially.[41]

A startling advance was made in the late seventeenth or early eighteenth century, when the *père* Sébastien, *mécanicien* (engineer) to the court of France, undertook to make prostheses for a Swede who had lost both arms above the elbow. Understandably, success was limited; but the device did permit its user to lift his hand to his head, and remove and replace his hat.[42]

It is not clear what material the *père* Sebastien specified for his invention; but the arm by Kriegseissen, submitted to the Académie Royale in 1732, was made of copper. Designed for persons whose elbow joints were intact, the device operated with pulleys and cords, attached to the outside of the casing and providing flexibility to the fingers and thumb.[43]

Around 1760, a *mécanicien* named Laurent appears to have combined the approaches of the *père* Sébastien and Kriegseissen. The device he made for a double amputee included an elbow joint and was evidently commanded internally. (Because of a badly fractured shoulder, only one prosthesis could be fitted). Its wearer was said to be able to move the arm "à sa volonté" and to write "très-lisiblement." Laurent's skill, lauded in Delille's ponderous *Epître*, earned him a knighthood in the Order of Saint Michel.[44]

Further improvements in these necessary devices were made by Henri Jacquet-Droz and his associate, J.-F. Leschot, who frequently turned from the production of automatons for this work, where their experience in miniaturization and programming was of enormous benefit. An arm made by Leschot in 1792 combined materials frequently used in androids —

leather, cork, parchment, and papier-mâché on a steel frame—to bring the weight down to only 480 grams. Hands made by Jacquet-Droz in 1775 were admired by Vaucanson, who is reputed to have said to the twenty-two-year-old inventor, "Jeune homme, vous débutez où je voudrais finir."[45]

Vaucanson's reference was to the *anatomie mouvante* to which he had given intermittent attention over the years. His interest was in no way unique. Models of human organs were used in Antiquity (as findings at Pompeii in the eighteenth century, and Ras-Shamra-Ugarit in the twentieth attest) and in the Renaissance (Leonardo being credited with glass and plaster models of the aorta which demonstrated the rush of blood occasioned by the opening and closing of valves in the heart).[46]

Interest was renewed in the seventeeth century, however, as greater attention was given to the study of medicine; and by the eighteenth century, a number of artisans—among them Mlle Bihéron, famed for wax gynecological models—specialized in this area. The purpose of such models was, obviously, didactic: the difficulty in obtaining and preserving human remains made them a desirable, even necessary adjunct to lectures on medicine and anatomy.

But while the *anatomie mouvante* was a teaching device, it was also a problem "ligne de curiosité" (to borrow the phrase used by the Duc du Luynes about Vaucanson's *flûteur*). To develop a model that replicated vital human functions would increase medical competence; but it would also allow the serious *mécanicien* the opportunity to explore, and perhaps even solve, complex physico-technical problems. In an age largely convinced that the human body was an exceptionally intricate machine, the challenge of replicating that machinery was irresistible. (It should be underscored here, as it was above, that there was no tendency to confuse the creation of such a machine with the creation of life; and little tendency to use such a machine to ponder the nature of man.)

A solution to the problem was reported as early as December 20, 1677, when the *Journal des Savants* excerpted an article from the *Journal d'Allemagne* entitled, "Machine surprenante de l'homme artificiel du sieur Reyselius"; but this machine, which supposedly demonstrated "au doight & à l'oeil la circulation du sang" and "le mouvement naturel des poumons" is almost certainly apochryphal. (It should be remembered that another story excerpted from the German periodical reported a sixteen-year pregnancy; the fetus, dead in the eighth year, was said to have been in a state of perfect preservation when the mother was autopsied).

Vaucanson was keenly interested by *anatomies mouvantes* because, as he told the Académie des Beaux-Arts de Lyon in 1741, "l'on pourra par le moyen de cet automate faire des expériences sur les fonctions animales et en tirer des inductions pour connaître les différents états de la santé des hommes afin de remédier à ses maux. Cette ingénieuse machine . . . pourra servir enfin à faire des démonstrations dans un cours d'anatomie." His interest was shared by the surgeon Claude Nicolas Le Cat, and a rivalry in this arcane area grew up between the two men. Neither succeeded, of course, although an associate of Vaucanson reported, in 1762, that he had seen in Vaucanson's studio "un automate à cirulation du sang." In an age in which blood-letting was basic to medical practice, this capability was considered the most important. It was also the most difficult to achieve because of the twin difficulties of finding and processing sufficient quantities of rubber to simulate the circulatory system with tubing of varying diameter. The plan proposed by Louis XVI, to set up a processing plant in Guyana, was slowed by a reluctant bureaucracy; and eventually Vaucanson turned away in disgust.[47]

Concurrent with the interest in *anatomies mouvantes* was an interest in developing a machine to reproduce human speech. Once again, the model was seen as a way of understanding physical process — the respective roles of the glottis and the vocal cords being then the subject of much debate — and Vaucanson was urged by both camps to develop an automaton that could settle the controversy. There is no evidence that Vaucanson attempted such a machine, but others did so. C.-G. Kratzenstein received the prize offered by the Imperical Academy of Saint Petersburg in 1779 for a machine capable of producing the five vowels. Kratzenstein's invention, which employed a series of bent pipes, was less accomplished a speaker than the talking head of the *abbé* Mical, exhibited as early as 1778. This, if reports can be believed, stated clearly "Le Roi fait le bonheur de ses peuples et le bonheur de ses peuples fait celui du Roi." The *abbé*'s technology remains a mystery. Better known is the "voice box" constructed by the Baron von Kempelen which used a bellows and speaker modeled on human and oral and nasal cavities; with it, the Baron could form not only syllables but Latin phrases such as *Romanorum imperator semper Augustus*.[48]

To continue to catalog these products of eighteenth-century *curiosité* would be exhausting without in any way being exhaustive. Suffice it to say that while many provided only an ephemeral amusement, others explored areas that put theory to the test of experience. Technological and scientific developments have invalidated many of the results; but they have done nothing to diminish the light they shed on the science and culture that inspired them and to which they responded. As Jean-Paul Zimmermann has said, "Gardons-nous de les mépriser: ils ont fait l'admiration des cours, ils ont offert une matière aux méditations de quelques esprits attentifs, ils représentent enfin le caractère propre, l'*idée* d'une civilisation, d'une culture originales."[49] It is neither clear nor important whether he was speaking of automatons or of the *mécaniciens* who made them.

NOTES

1 The attendance figures and wage comparison are given by André Doyon and Lucien Liaigre, *Jacques Vaucanson: Mécanicien de génie* (Paris: PUF, 1966), 33–34. They add (61) that attendance dropped to between 150 and 200 persons in the first seven weeks of 1739, while gate receipts fell from 22,418 *livres* to 577.

2 L. Dussieux and E. Soulié, eds., *Mémoires du Duc du Luynes sur la cour de Louis XV (1735–1758)*, 17 vols. (Paris: Firmin Didot, 1860–65), 2:103.

3 *Mercure de France*, April 1738, 738.

4 Quoted by Marie-Rose de Labriolle, "Le *Pour et contre* et son temps, I," *Studies on Voltaire and the Eighteenth Century* 34 (1965):255; the author cites *Pour et contre* 14:213.

5 Pierre François Guyot Desfontaines, "Lettre CLXXX," *Observations sur les écrits modernes* 12 (1738):338 and 341–2.

6 Jacques Vaucanson, "Lettre CCCXLV," *Observations sur les écrits modernes* 23 (1741):347–48. Doyon and Liaigre quote (125–26) Christophe Frédéric Nicolaï (*Chronique à travers l'Allemagne et la Suisse*, 1768), who casts doubt upon the authenticity of the duck's digestion: "Le fait est que dans le postérieur du canard, une masse est préparée qui ressemble aux aliments digérés et qui est expulsée au moment voulu par le mécanisme."

7 *Notice de l'Almanach sous verre* 44 (1811):34.

8 Quoted by Doyon and Liaigre, 72; 205–53, 293–318, and 383–419 discuss Vaucanson's inventions for industry.

9 For a general description of these devices, see Alfred Chapuis and Edmond Droz, *Les Automates: Figures artificielles d'hommes et d'animaux* (Neuchâtel: Du Griffon, 1949; English translation by Alex Reid, 1958).

10 Dussieux and Soulié, 2:13.

11 *Mémoires secrets (1742–1744)*, quoted by Doyon and Liaigre, 54–5. Desfontaines' difficulties are recorded in the *Archives de la Bastille*, ed. F. Ravaisson, 19 vols. (Paris, 1866–1904), 10:812, 10:918, and 12:463.

12 Jean Sablière, *De l'automate à l'automatisation* (Paris: Gauthier-Villars, 1966), 44.

13 Quoted by Alfred Chapuis, *Les Automates dans les oeuvres d'imagination* (Neuchâtel: Du Griffon, 1947), 49–50.

14 For an overview of the automaton in literature see the work just cited. Jean-Claude Beaune's *L'Automate et ses mobiles* (Paris: Flammarion, 1980) is an example of contemporary philosophical speculation.

15 Quoted and discussed by De Labriolle, 255–56.

16 Quoted (in order) by Alfred Chapuis and Edouard Gélis, *Le Monde des automates*, 2 vols. (Paris, 1928), 2:153; Eliane Maingot, *Les Automates* (Paris:

Hachette, 1959), 34; Doyon and Liaigre, 225; Maurice Tourneux, ed., *Mémoires de Marmontel*, 4 vols. (Geneva: Slatkine Reprints, 1967), 1:247.

17 See for example the otherwise unimaginative *Journal suisse d'horlogerie* 19 (1895):263–64, which tells its audience of watchmakers that one of their number had been accused of sorcery in the eighteenth century because of the perfection of his automatons.

18 John Cohen, *Human Robots in Myth and Science* (London: George Allen & Unwin, 1966), 7.

19 Bernard Le Bovier de Fontenelle, *Eloges des académiciens de l'Académie royale des sciences morts depuis l'an 1699*, 2nd ed., 2 vols. (Paris: Libraires Associés, 1766), 2:341.

20 Alfred Chapuis, *Automates, machines automatiques et machinisme* (Geneva: Publications Techniques, 1928), 35.

21 Quoted by Alfred Chapuis, "Des statues mouvantes de l'ancienne Egypte aux machine électroniques: les automates," *Atomes* (August 1951), 263.

22 Quoted by Doyon and Liaigre, 56, note.

23 Desfontaines, 338–39.

24 *Journal suisse d'horlogerie* 31 (1907):412–15 and 42 (1918):262.

25 Pierre Devaux, *Automates et automatisme* (Paris: PUF, 1948), 19–20 and 23–26.

26 Dussieux and Soulié, 2:103.

27 François Metra, *Correspondance secrète, politique & littéraire . . .*, 18 vols. (London: John Adamson, 1787–90), 16:339–40.

28 Richelet quoted by Pierre-Maxime Schuhl, *Machinisme et philosophie* (Paris: Félix Alcan, 1938), 22, who also discusses (1–33) Greek and European attitudes toward the mechanical arts. Sabatier de Castres quoted by Doyon and Liaigre, 39, note.

29 Doyon and Liaigre, 28, 72, and 79; Fontenelle, 2:337–38; information on the *abbé* Mical, reprinted from the *Journal de Paris* (May 1, 1778), is found in Emile Campardon, *Les Spectacles de la foire . . .*, 2 vols. (Paris: Berger-Levrault, 1877), 2:428–29.

30 Quoted by Doyon and Liaigre, 220 and 423.

31 "Curiosité," *Encyclopédie . . .*, 17 vols. (Paris: Le Breton, 1751–65), 4:578. Contemporary views of the *utile* are presented by Jean Sgard, "La Presse provinciale et ses lumières," in *La Presse provinciale au XVIIIe siècle* (Grenoble: Université de Grenoble, 1983); see, for example, 52, which quotes the editor of the *Affiches d'Angers* (1775): "se rendre utile à ses concitoyens est . . . le premier de nos devoirs."

32 Quoted by Doyon and Liaigre, 40.

33 Vaucanson, "Lettre CCCXLV," 348.

34 David M. Fryer and John C. Marshall, "The Motives of Jacques de Vaucanson," *Technology and Culture* 20 (1979):262–63.

35 Vaucanson, "Lettre CCCXLV," 348.

36 Fryer and Marshall, 262.

37 Desfontaines, "Lettre CLXXX," 341–42; italics added.

38 In *Drawing on the Right Side of the Brain* (Los Angeles: J. P. Tarcher, 1979), Betty Edwards has assembled a bibliography (203–05) on this phenomenon.

Work by Roger W. Sperry of the California Institute of Technology is considered seminal.

39 William Coxe, *Sketches of the Natural, Civil, and Political State of Swisserland* . . ., 2nd ed. (London: J. Dodsley, 1780), 283.

40 *Notice de l'Almanach sous verre* 12 (1779):63–64, and 13 (1780):104. The vehicles were probably powered by internal cranks (cf. Gallon, *Machines et inventions approuvées par l'Académie royale des sciences* . . ., 7 vols. [Paris, 1735–77], 5:171–73, for comparable chairs by Maillard). In Lavocat's defense, it should be noted that he was following an old tradition among automaton-makers, as victims of the water-powered machines of the Renaissance might attest.

41 Joseph-François Malgaigne, ed., *Oeuvres complètes d'Ambroise Paré*, 3 vols. (Paris: J.-B. Baillière, 1840–41), 2:615–21; Anthony Babel, *Histoire corporative de l'horlogerie* . . . (Geneva: Jullien & Georg, 1916), 49–50.

42 Fontenelle, 2:337–38.

43 Gallon, 6:384.

44 Jacques Delille, *Epître à M. Laurent* . . ., 2nd ed. (London, 1761).

45 Chapuis and Gélis, *Le Monde des automates*, 313; Charles Perregaux and F.-Louis Perrot, *Les Jacquet-Droz et Leschot* (Neuchâtel: Attinger, 1916), 165–67; quotation in François Faessler, S. Guye and Edmond Droz, *Pierre Jacquet-Droz et son temps* (La Chaux-de-Fonds: Comité des Fêtes, c. 1971), 74.

46 Doyon and Liaigre, 110–114.

47 Doyon and Liaigre, 148 and 151. Rubber was known in France as early as 1730, but the chemistry and technology needed to process it were not developed until the early 1760s.

48 Chapuis and Droz, 329–21; see also Campardon, 2:428–29, and Doyon and Liaigre, 162–74.

49 Quoted by Faessler, Guye and Droz, 152.

"A Visible History of Art": The Forms and Preoccupations of the Early Museum

P A U L   H O L D E N G R Ä B E R

As the unquestioned exemplarity and educative value which the classical text provided to the fortunate few spread during the eighteenth century to a larger class of readers, the common reader, "l'honnête homme" of the eighteenth century (as Robert Darnton has portrayed him), read Rousseau, not "in order to enjoy literature but to cope with life."[1] And thus, as Darnton writes, "Rousseauistic readers fell in love, married, and raised children by steeping themselves in print."[2] The work of Rousseau fulfils, in an exemplary manner, one of the ideals always assigned to literature, but more personal and widespread during the enlightenment: to educate. Rousseau's correspondence shows that many readers felt that their lives had been transformed by the reading of *La Nouvelle Héloise*, felt, afterwards, that it had made them, in the words of an anonymous admirer, better people.[3]

While the widening educative function of books during the century was only one aspect of their value, while one could read in order to learn to enjoy literature as well as to cope with life, the museum, as it came into being in the second part of the eighteenth century, had as its founding principle a primarily educative role.[4] In material terms, the progressive idea of generalized education, which had expressed itself in the seventeenth century with the opening of libraries to the public, expressed itself now in the construction of separate buildings devoted solely to the arts. There had already been, during the second half of the eighteenth century, several building competitions for the Prix de Rome, set by the Académie Royale d'Architecture (later to be renamed "Ecole des Beaux Arts"),

107

competitions which had the museum as their theme. Many of the architectural drawings that resulted would not have been suited to practical needs and were, in the words of Helmut Seling, "innocent of utility,"[5] not giving, for instance, the slightest indication of how they were to display works, much more infatuated by their intended symbolic value as Temples of Art. Dominique Poulot has pointed out that "the idea of the museum during the enlightenment had first been that of a monumental building."[6] Museums were monuments like any other monument. Only in 1814 would clear indications be given in the drawings of the Ecole Nationale des Beaux-Arts competitions as to where paintings and sculptures should be housed in these projected institutions, indications which gave these drawings the specificity they had lacked. But the early competitions do point to a public concern in the second half of the eighteenth century with the creation of a new space for displaying works. Whether it was, for example, the Museum Fridericianum at Cassel built by Simon Louis du Ry between 1769 and 1779, or the Museum Pio-Clementino built by Michelangelo Simonetti and continued by Giuseppe Camporesi from 1773 to 1786, these buildings belonged to the Goethe era, "the great period of *Bildung* with its faith in the educational, elevating power of the arts in the widest sense — including, that is, the *beaux arts* as well as what comes under a faculty of arts."[7]

The eighteenth century extended the pedagogical model for reading to seeing itself, to the kind of seeing that took place in these new spaces built to promote a wider visibility of the work of art. The belief that one could learn, in an orderly way, from seeing led the museum to be formed in such a way that it could serve as a tool for instruction. This belief in the inherent pedagogic power of the eye did not have its origins in the eighteenth century. The museum's seemingly systematic materialization of ideas about learning had a long past. During the sixteenth century, the Jesuits had developed elaborate methods of visual education. Images and engravings were the necessary complement to the written text. By looking at them on the walls of the schools or in the "text"-books, scrupulously divided by subject (history, mythology, science . . .), one could learn much faster than by simply listening to a discursive lesson in a classroom. As Father Richomme wrote in 1597, "Through their colors and lineaments, at a glance [the images] implant in our minds the knowledge of many things that would not reach us through the ear for a long time."[8]

The emergence of the Galeries Historiques in the sixteenth century showed another form of belief in the power of the eye and was, as such, a forerunner of the museum. The Galeries Historiques were primarily portrait galleries representing important figures from the past. The first such collection, assembled around 1520, was that of the Italian humanist, Paul Jove. The collection was made up of the portraits of 240 illustrious men of the past, every portrait having the same dimensions.[9] As Philippe Ariès comments, "The portraits of Jove do not constitute an art gallery, but they are a museum of history."[10] From then on, history was something that could be illustrated. Jean Adhémar has shown how, beginning in the seventeenth century, the French royal tutors taught history to the future kings by showing them portraits. Thus, the walls of Louis XIII's bedroom are lined with the "portraits of his predecessors. . . . He enquires who they are, what they are doing. He is told, and thus he learns the history of France."[11] A century later, around 1715, Saint-Simon writes that for the future Louis XV (then age five), he proposes "an education through the eyes" in which he will "line a whole gallery with the portraits of illustrious men from Louis XI to Henri IV."[12]

Such royal tutelage by visual instruction was, during the eighteenth century, only part of the broadening and stabilization of larger principles of orderly visual instruction, which occurred at the same time that the foundations of the museum were more firmly established and that reading became the popular pastime of a general public. The *Lesen* revolution and the *Sehen* revolution went hand in hand (not surprisingly, as the dissemination of the printed text had taught comfort with a visual reading, rather than with the old aural hearing.)[13] The museum was a palace constructed, first, to honor the infinite mobility of the eye (which can see all it is shown), and next, to domesticate the eye's relentless movement. This domestication was to be accomplished by the training that a rigid and methodological organization could offer to both eye and mind: its success or failure meant the success or failure of the museum itself, insofar as the museum was identified as a pedagogical tool.

The pedagogical museum (with its chronological and geographical methods of displaying objects), intrinsically a construction grounded in an idea of history, arose in this form, and as a public and national institution, during the eighteenth century. But, although it had new concerns, it had, in part, emerged from the tradition of the gallery and cabinet. Most of these earlier collecting ventures, *gabinetto, cabinet, closet, Kammer,* and *Kabinett* "were all varieties of the same thing: a small room for displaying curiosities, *objets d'art*, books and lesser pictures, arranged regardless of interior decoration, the collection itself forming the decorative scheme";[14] another form "was a long room [derived] from the *grande salle* of French medieval chateaux."[15] In his 1727 *Museographia*, the first museological work ever published, C. F. Neickelius classified one of the varieties of *Kabinetten*, the "Raritaten-Kabinett," as a "Schatz-Raritaeten-Naturalien-Kunst-Vernunft-Kammer," or, "chamber of treasures-rarities-objects-of-nature-of-art-and-reason,"[16] a denomination which exemplifies the rambling form of the cabinet.

The accumulation, the cacophonic abundance that resided within these collections, should not be interpreted as a lack of organization, shared by the seventeenth and early eighteenth centuries, which then yielded to a sudden discovery of order in the later part of the eighteenth century. The episteme of the seventeenth and early eighteenth centuries, which perfectly expresses itself in the exotic accumulations of the cabinet and gallery, was based, as Bernard Deloche notes, simply on a differently ordered vision of man and his works: one did not expect to gain from these spaces a better knowledge of art as a whole, but a pleasing reflection of reality, half natural, half the product of human art.[17] The cabinet and gallery, in which the eye was perpetually distracted by the baroque ideal of a pleasing variety, came to seem lacking in linearity, disorderly to those who had fully interiorized newer ideals of linearity in classification.[18] History expresses itself in the museum through space, through a well-directed space. The methods devised to make it a historical-educational institution would concentrate on the most minute details of organization, seeking to make museum-going an arrowed experience.

Christian Von Mechel, a friend of Winckelmann, suggested in 1779 that the reorganization of the Belvedere Museum in Vienna should result in an arrangement that was "as far as possible a visible history of art."[19] This "visible history," such as it was, was organized around the unifying principle of the school of painting (a principle on which, later, the organization of the Louvre would be based). In 1793 Alexandre Lenoir opened, in a thirteenth-century convent of the Petits-Augustins in Paris, the Musée des Monuments Français. The objects displayed were principally medieval French monuments that Lenoir had been able to rescue from the threat of destruction by the revolutionaries. Lenoir's zeal for preservation is best expressed by his own words in the forward to the catalogue of "his" museum:

> I was entrusted with gathering, in the Petits-Augustins, the monuments threatened with destruction. Animated by a true love of art, I did more than that. I gathered together all the monuments which misguided fury had mutilated or destroyed. I shall pass over the difficulties, the annoyances, the obstacles, and even dangers which I had to overcome in order to assemble some five hundred monuments of the French monarchy, to put them in order, to restore, classify, describe, and reproduce them by means of engravings.[20]

The objects displayed were ordered "within an overall chronological framework" that was "without precedent."[21] Chronology was already implicit, if in a loose way, in the idea of ordering paintings according to schools in Von Mechel's "visible history of art." But now, in Lenoir's museum (fourteen years after Von Mechel's reordering of the Belvedere Museum), objects were, in a general chronology, to be distributed according to century which, as Stephen Bann describes in an essay appropriately entitled "The Poetics of the Museum," "extended over five separate rooms. The history of France was illustrated in clear paradigmatic form from the thirteenth century until the age of Louis XIV."[22] Every century, for Lenoir, could be reduced to one adjective: "the naive art of the thirteenth century"; "the sumptuous art of the seventeenth century."[23] One room, though, was devoted to "monuments of all centuries." This was the "Introductory Room," a "preface to the great work," as Lenoir writes, which, "at a glance is able to present the general scheme of our chronological order."[24] This presentation gave visitors, for the first time, the opportunity to "experience the notion of the 'century' as a unifying principle."[25]

Whether organization was according to school or to century or to the other didactic principles current, the variety of organizational preoccupations all suggest that the museum was envisioned as a historical institution: it was organized according to a certain idea of history, of the past. The choice of a method is never an innocent matter; particular ideological preoccupations always inform the method chosen for cutting up, dividing, classifying the past's productions. Even though both systems are historical, the effect of a classification by school is very different for the viewer from that of one by century. Two sets of the same objects, each organized according to only one of these two different modes of division that arose in the eighteenth century, would have told two very different stories about what the past had been.

There were, from the start, severe resistances to the form chosen for this new institution, resistances to the museum's way of displaying objects in a linear sequence. In 1785 a Viennese nobleman named Joseph Von Rittershausen, responding to Von Mechel's attempt at a rational ordering of the Belvedere, exclaimed, "If you want a history of art you can go to a museum but the sensitive man should be kept away from it."[26] The tension between Von Rittershausen's and Von Mechel's positions is that between the amateur and the professional; it is the tension between the dilettante (in the original sense of the word, from *delectare*, to delight in) and the specialist (a version of the scholar new to the eighteenth century), who classifies, assigns a position to each artist and each painting. Von Mechel was quite clear: the large public collections, he wrote, "are intended for instruction more than for fleeting pleasure. . . . [They] are like a rich library in which those eager to learn find works of all kinds and all periods."[27]

The museum, a modern totalizing collecting venture, is not to be a place of *délices*, as the gallery and cabinet had been. For "fleeting pleasure" is an aristocratic occupation contrary to the democratic ideal of the museum. The old form of involvement that the aristocracy had with art must be substituted by something solid such as education, because pleasure or delight do not fit into a society in which the work ethic, transmuted into "accomplishment" or "betterment," is supreme. But the debate between Von Mechel and Von Rittershausen is more than just one of choice between rationalism and hedonism, for both are ways of making sense of the works of the past. It is a debate between two different forms of knowledge or, in Foucault's more modest terms, between the old and the "new way of connecting things."[28] The opposition between Von Rittershausen's position and Von Mechel's is the same opposition Bernard Groetheuysen finds "between the *orbis pictus* of the Renaissance, animated by the spirit of an adventurous knowledge, and the encyclopedism of the eighteenth century, based on a learning of appropriation."[29]

The museum in the eighteenth century was deeply tied to the encyclopedia, fully a child of the encyclopedic spirit of division, naming, classifying.[30] It is not an accident that the museum and the book were so firmly linked in the minds of the first formulators of the museum, that Von Mechel spoke of the museum as a "rich library," or that Lenoir spoke of his ordering as "a book opened for instruction."[31] From its primeval origin in the Greek *mouseion*, the museum (though in a radically different form) was already an encyclopedic place of learning; by the seventeenth century, the identification of museum and encyclopedia was embedded in language, the words frequently used interchangeably. Numerous books with the word "museum" in the title were published, all of them purporting to offer the entire body of knowledge on a given subject (for instance, the *Museum Metallicum* of Aldrovandi of Bologna, the naturalist and collector.) When the museum, during its formative years in the second part of the eighteenth century, followed as a paradigm the encyclopedia's systematic method of organization, it also took on the role the encyclopedia had assigned itself as a heuristic tool for investigation. The museum was struck by the same urge for classification as the encyclopedia. Fragmenting the world in its classifications and subclassifications, it held forth a totality, an organic whole subsuming any residual fragmentation.

Ephraim Chambers believed that the advantage he had over his predecessors was that his *Cyclopaedia*, by its method of organization, by the mere fact that it was organized at all, had, in his words, the "advantage of a continued discourse."[32] This totality of knowledge came forth, within the economy of the encyclopedia, through cross references. Von Mechel's idea of having paintings set in such a way that they would provide a "visible history of art" was based, similarly, on the idea that the collection might now have "the advantage of a continued discourse." The museum, through that conception, became synonymous with the "history of art," which the museum itself brought into being. "History of art" recognized in the museum, as Hubert Damisch writes, "its methodological and fetishized form."[33] "History of art," that is to say the museum, provided a seemingly natural-neutral text for the objects thus displayed, and the objects were no longer ends in themselves, but objects of discourse. This text had the advantage of continuity, identified with the continuity and directiveness of history itself. Cross references in the encyclopedia were analogous to the ordering of the rooms and paintings in the museum.

By basing itself (if indirectly) on the model of the encyclopedia's universal project, both through its objects and discourse, the museum succeeded in displaying and refracting the whole of past history; and history, like the paintings hung in the museum, entered the realm of the public. As the possession of the people, history no longer spoke solely of the prince or court. It had come to belong to everyone, as had the knowledge incorporated in the encyclopedia, which was not only an offering to the community, but also the product of a communal effort. The rationalizing enterprise of the museum gave the people a reified image of their own splendor, gave them a visible history from infancy to adulthood. It gave them this history on a number of levels. It offered them a history of the human race, in which history became world history. The museum also suggested, as a definitive historical unit, the century, in all its compactness, virility, and monumentality ("le siècle de Louis XIV," for instance).

Most clearly of all, the museum offered a national history, for instance in the idea of French or German schools of painting, the history of nations in combat in the seemingly innocent realm of art (where the museum becomes a tool for legitimizing xenophobic nationalism and serves as the basis of a nation's proof of power). Lenoir's museum, for instance, was constructed on the model of progressive chronology, one century surpassing another, showing the evolution of the human spirit, which meant the French spirit. The culmination of the museum was to be "the nineteenth-century room, or, the room of the heroic feats of the Emperor, Napoleon the Great,"[34] which was to illustrate (or be synonymous with) the nineteenth century. Lenoir shows his affinity with the French historiographers of the seventeenth century, whose task it was to celebrate the King and his Court.[35] Napoleon, in his expeditions, contributed to the riches of Lenoir's museum, and Lenoir repaid him by celebrating his victories. Lenoir's ultimate intention was, through his museum, to make a "veritable *Monumental History of the French Monarchy.*"[36] If such museums took the monarchy as their subject, the artists themselves were the subjects (servants) of that monarchy in the process of being transformed into the subject of the more general pedagogical system of Art History. As Damisch writes, the museum portrays art as "the collective product of a mass of many partial workers."[37] The artists themselves are felt to belong to the nation: "A great man is a national property," wrote the Abbé Grégoire at the 1792 Convention.[38] These workers are consequently transformed into mere members of an overall mechanism supported by the museum itself. Each artist thus appears as nothing more than a link in the chain, and each painting has very little to say if it is not set into and validated by the new-born discipline of Art History.

What was to come out of this disciplined approach to art when, as Adorno wrote, "Venus becomes a document," when "art becomes a matter of education and information,"[39] when every artist is inscribed within the general economy of a history of art? Was the museum perceived as having taken the right turn when it adopted the fragmenting and totalizing model the encyclopedia had to offer? Many, over the centuries that followed, felt that the museum failed, even in its own terms, even with all the methods it employed for organizing works, whether according to school, century, or other conceptions. Even in terms of organization, where the museum believed itself to be most successful, it has been seen to be inadequate. Throughout its two centuries, it has called forth strong reactions, from Von Rittershausen's aesthetical position, warning the sensitive man against the museum, to Valéry's critique, on both aesthetic and rational grounds, of the museum's "abuse of space." For Valéry, the museum is a "home of incoherency" built by a society which is neither "voluptuous nor reasonable"; it demands of us the same gaze for all things, and yet (he continues), a cold confusion reigns among the sculptures," a "tumult of frozen creatures each of which demands in vain the non-existence of all the others," "disorder strangely organized."[40] By demanding the same undifferentiated (indifferent) gaze for each painting, it achieves "an invisibility, an insensible sameness" which is "nothing but *disorder* in its perfect state."[41] From Von Rittershausen to Valéry, there is an implicit and recurrent understanding that it is impossible for the museum to serve both the needs of art and those of history.

NOTES

1 Robert Darnton, "Readers Respond to Rousseau: The Fabrication of Romantic Sensitivity," in *The Great Cat Massacre* (New York: Vintage Books, 1985), 241.

2 Ibid., 251.

3 In March of 1761, a reader of *La Nouvelle Héloise* wrote to Rousseau: "I feel myself to be better since I have read your novel, which I hope, is not one." *Correspondance Complète de Jean-Jacques Rousseau*, ed. R. A. Leigh (Genève: Institut et Musée Voltaire, 1969), 257. Cited in Darnton, *Great Cat Massacre*, 248.

4 Historians of the museum such as Christiane Aulanier, *Histoire du Palais du Musée du Louvre* (Paris: Editions des Musées Nationaux, 1969); Alma S. Wittlin, *The Museum: Its History and Its Task in Education* (London: Routledge & Kegan Paul, 1949); Germain Bazin, *Le Temps des Musées* (Liège: Desoie, 1967); Volker Plagemann, *Das deutsche Kunstmuseum, 1790–1870* (München: Prestel Verlag, 1967); and J. Mordaunt Crook, *The British Museum; A Case-History in Architectural Politics* (London: Penguin Books, 1972) have focused primarily on the biographies of the museum founders and their particular museums, or the political and art historical problems inherent in the institution, largely ignoring its relation to larger cultural problems and its fundamental orientation and preoccupations. A great deal of work has been done on contemporaneous and interrelated institutions, most notably that of Michel Foucault, for instance in his work on medical perception (*The Birth of the Clinic*, 1963) or on prisons (*Discipline and Punish*, 1975); the museum influenced many of the terms of such explorations, but there has been, as yet, no "archaeology" of the museum itself and its impact.

5 Helmut Seling, "The Genesis of the Museum," *Architectural Review* 141, no. 840 (February 1967): 106. For a history of the Académie Royale d'Architecture, the Ecole des Beaux-Arts and the role played by the Grand Prix de Rome d'Architecture, see Donald Drew Egbert, *The Beaux Arts Tradition in French Architecture* (Princeton: Princeton University Press, 1980).

6 Dominique Poulot, "Les Musées à la Gloire de l'Empire: notes pour une recherche," *Gazette des Beaux-Arts* 98, no. 1352 (September 1981). All translations are mine unless otherwise noted. See also Nikolaus Pevsner, *A History of Building Types* (London: Thames and Hudson, 1976).

7 Seling, "Genesis of the Museum," 104.

8 Quoted in Jean Adhémar, "L'Enseignement par l'Image," *Gazette des Beaux-Arts* 97, no. 1345 (February 1981): 53. For the history of Jesuitic education in France, see François de Dainville, *Les Jésuites et l'Education de la Société Moderne, la naissance de l'humanisme moderne* (Paris: Beauchesne, 1940). On alterations in the visualism and spatialism of the sixteenth century, see Walter J. Ong, *Ramus, Method, and the Decay of Dialogue* (Cambridge, Mass.: Harvard Univ. Press, 1958), 314–18; and "Space and Intellect in Renaissance Symbolism," *Explorations*, no. 4 (1954): 95–100.

9 Jean Adhémar, *Frère André Thévet, grand voyageur et cosmographe des Rois de France au XVI siècle* (Paris: Editions Franciscaines, 1947), 59.

10 Philippe Ariès, *Le Temps de l'Histoire* (Paris: Seuil, 1986), 160.

11 Adhémar, "l'Enseignement par l'Image," 54.

12 Quoted in Jean Adhémar, "L'Education Visuelle des Fils de France et l'Origine du Musée de Versailles," *La Revue des Arts* 1 (March 1956): 31.

13 The emphatic visualism of the eighteenth century has been widely discussed. See, for instance, Lawrence Lipking, *The Ordering of the Arts in Eighteenth-Century England* (Princeton: Princeton Univ. Press, 1970), 23–37; and Jean H. Hagstrum, *The Sister Arts* (Chicago: Univ. of Chicago Press, 1958), 130. On the link between print and visualism, see Elizabeth Eisenstein, *The Printing Press as an Agent of Change* (Cambridge: Cambridge Univ. Press, 1979), 231–36 and 252–68; and Walter J. Ong, *Orality and Literacy* (London: Methuen, 1982), 120–29.

14 Crook, *British Museum*, 24.

15 Ibid., 26. On the cabinets of curiosities, see J. von Schlosser, *Die Kunst-und Wunderkammer der Spätrenaissance* (Leipzig, 1908).

16 Caspar Friedrich Neickelius, *Museographia* (Leipzig, 1727), 409.

17 Bernard Deloche, *Museologica: Contradictions et logique de musée* (Paris: Librairie philosophique J. Vrin, 1985), 86.

18 One of the signs of these newer ideals of linearity, as Krzysztof Pomian notes, is the enthusiasm for natural history which replaces the baroque cabinet's emphasis on rarity: "The physiognomy of the cabinets changes in consequence." Pomian, "La Culture de la curiosité," in *Scienze credenze occulte livelli di cultura* (Florence: Leo S. Olschki, 1982), 539. On classification in natural history, see H. Daudin, *De Linné à Jussieu: Méthode de classification et idée de série en botanique et en zoologie (1740–1790)* (Paris: Félix Alcan, 1926); and Daudin, *Cuvier et Lamarck: Les classes zoologiques et l'idée de série animale (1790–1830)* (Paris: Félix Alcan, 1926).

19 Christian Von Mechel, *Catalogue des tableaux de la galerie impériale et royale de Vienne* (Bâle, 1784), xv.

20 Alexandre Lenoir, *Musée Imperial des Monumens Français: Histoire des arts en France et description chronologique* (Paris, 1810), Avant-Propos, ii. I have used, in part, the translation in Lorenz Eitner, *Neoclassicism and Romanticism 1750–1850* (Prentice Hall, 1970) 2:6. On Lenoir, see Louis Courajod, *Alexandre Lenoir, son journal et le Musée des Monuments Français*, 3 Vols. (Paris: H. Champion, 1878–1887). Lenoir's description of his own activity (order, restore, classify, describe, reproduce, and above all save from destruction because of his "love of art") could provide a model for the clinical portrait Bernard Deloche gives of the task of the curator ("conservateur" in French). The curator's and the museum's first task is to acquire, as Deloche writes in a chapter entitled "Obsessio neurotica": the "conservateur is first of all a collector, for the museum is born from the collection which the institution has not forgotten." He continues, "the conservateur does not collect for himself, does not acquire for himself, but is the museum's delegate for constituting a collective patrimony. He nevertheless has lost none of the obsessional preoccupations of the collector" (*Museologica*, 25). Thus, the curator, in Deloche's view, sublimates and mediates his desire for possession by possessing for the museum rather than for himself. The curator, in his desire for accumulation, demonstrates a "neurotic and regressive behavior. On the one hand, he invests in objects that which he cannot live in human relationships, for the object alone restitutes to him the docile image of himself; on the other hand, as a collector he confuses time and death."

21 Stephen Bann, "Historical Text and Historical Object: Poetics of the Musée de Cluny," *Lotus International*, no. 35 (1982), 39; reprinted in Bann, *The Clothing of Clio* (Cambridge: Cambridge Univ. Press, 1984) as "Poetics of the Museum: Lenoir and Du Sommerard" (in a revised version).

22 Ibid., 39.

23 Alexandre Lenoir, *Description historique et chronologique des monumens de sculpture reunis au Musée des Monumens Français* (Paris, 1797), Avant-Propos, ii.

24 Lenoir, *Musée des Monumens Français*, 154. Lenoir's phrasing suggests his identification of the museum with the book. For plans of the museum, see M. M. Réville and Lavallée, *Vues pittoresques et perspectives des salles du Musée des Monumens Français* (Paris, 1816); and M. J. E. Biet and M. M. Normand, *Souvenirs du Musée des Monumens Français* (Paris, 1821–26).

25 Bann, "Historical Text and Historical Object," 39.

26 Quoted in Bazin, *Temps des Musées*, 159.

27 Von Mechel, *Catalogue des tableaux*, xv.

28 "What came surreptitiously into being between the age of the theatre and that of the catalogue was not the desire for knowledge, but a new way of connecting things both to the eye and to discourse. A new way of making history." Michel Foucault, *The Order of Things* (London: Tavistock Publications, 1970), 131.

29 Quoted in Roland Barthes, "The Plates of the Encyclopedia," *New Critical Essays*, trans. Richard Howard (New York: Hill and Wang, 1980), 27.

30 Louis Marin writes that the museum is the "rationalized illustration of the encyclopedia." Marin, "Fragments d'histoires de musées," *Cahiers du Musée national d'art moderne*, no. 17/18 [*L'Oeuvre et son accrochage*] (March 1986), 16.

31 Von Mechel, *Catalogue des tableaux*, Préface; Lenoir, *Musée Impérial*, 154.

32 Ephraim Chambers, *Cyclopaedia, or an Universal Dictionary of Arts and Sciences* (London, 1728), Preface.

33 Hubert Damisch, "The Museum Device: Notes on Institutional Changes," *Lotus International*, no. 35 (1982) 2, 11.

34 Lenoir, *Musée Impérial*, xi.

35 For the role of the historiographers of the King, see Orest Ranum, *Artisans of Glory: Writers and Historical Thought in Seventeenth-Century France* (Chapel Hill: Univ. of North Carolina Press, 1980).

36 Lenoir, *Musée Impérial*, 154.

37 Damisch, "Museum Device," 14.

38 Abbé Henri Grégoire, *Rapport sur les destructions opérées par le vandalisme, et sur les moyens de le réprimer* (Paris, 1793), 16.

39 T. W. Adorno, "Valéry Proust Museum," *Prisms* (New York: Schocken Books, 1967), 177.

40 Paul Valéry: "Le Problème des Musées," *Oeuvres* (Paris, Gallimard, 1960), 2:1290–91. I have used, in part, the translation of David Paul, "The Problem of Museums" in *Degas Manet Morisot*, Vol. 12, *Collected Works of Paul Valéry*, (New York: Pantheon-Bollingen Series 45, 1960): 202–4.

41 Paul Valéry, "La Crise de l'Esprit," *Oeuvres* (Paris: Gallimard, 1957) 1:991.

Chinese Export Porcelain in Eighteenth-Century Tidewater Virginia

JULIA B. CURTIS

Chinese export porcelain constitutes one of the largest groups of artifacts recovered from archeological sites in Southeastern Virginia and is present on nearly all colonial sites so far dug in the James River basin. The artifact, the Chinese exportware shard, or whole vessel with a history of Virginia ownership, is a physical manifestation of numerous facets of eighteenth-century society. Its presence in Virginia is eloquent testimony to a pattern of world trade as intricate as the complex intellectual network of the Enlightenment. The presence of eighteenth-century Chinese porcelain shards at colonial sites in Virginia bespeaks the growing gentility of colonial society, a gentility evinced in the decoration of the colonials' houses and the growing popularity of such social ceremonies as tea and coffee drinking. The increasing use of Chinese porcelain, reflected in contemporary inventories and in Virginia's archeological collections, attests to the growing affluence of Virginians in the eighteenth-century.

The quality of Chinese exportware that came to Virginia is a manifestation of Virginia's status as a British colony and the status of even its wealthiest citizens as provincials. Conversely, however, the types of wares found on Virginia's colonial sites were common to other international markets, such as those of Holland and Sweden. The survival of eighteenth-century inventories, the existence of hundreds of collections of eighteenth-century exportware in Europe and America, and the discovery of Dutch and Swedish wrecks carrying Chinese export porcelain make it possible to analyze the thousands of exportware shards in Eastern Virginia's archeological collections from a socio-economic as well as an art-historical perspective.

119

The presence of such large quantities of Chinese porcelain in Virginia has amazed both Chinese ceramicists and students of American social history. Its transmigration to colonial Virginia is directly related to the growth of trade between China and Europe and to the craze for oriental trade goods, or "china-mania," which the China trade generated in Europe. The craze specifically for Chinese porcelain arose first in Holland, then, in the late seventeenth century, in England. The Virginians, as provincial citizens of the British Empire, adopted the enthusiasm only after it was firmly established in London.

A number of excellent works describe the origins of the China trade which ignited the European craze for Chinese porcelain,[1] but the specific cause of the "china-mania" that affected colonial Virginia lies in the foundation of the Dutch and English East India companies in the seventeenth century. In 1600, Queen Elizabeth I granted a group of English merchants a charter to trade with the East, and in 1602, the Dutch monarch chartered a similar company. Both companies were founded to supply Holland and England respectively with spices at a profit to the company stockholders. The two companies were often competitors in the same Far Eastern markets and on numerous occasions fought each other for territory. In 1623, for example, the Dutch massacred all the natives and Englishmen at the British factory, or warehouse, at Amboyna in the Moluccas, or Spice Islands. While the principal goods in which the two East India companies traded remained the same for two hundred years, their importance to the trade changed markedly over those two centuries. Until the mid-seventeenth century, spices were the most valuable homebound cargo, but by 1700, Chinese and Indian textiles had displaced spices as the most valuable trade commodities. Although the Dutch began buying teas in bulk from the Chinese in 1637, according to T. Volker, tea and coffee became the most significant areas of growth in the eighteenth-century, by which time spices had become a relatively minor commodity of trade. From 1600 to 1800, porcelain remained a relatively minor commodity when rated by value, although not necessarily by bulk. But whereas the Dutch brought porcelain to Holland in generally ever-increasing quantities throughout the seventeenth century, the British, until the 1680s confined the bulk of their porcelain trade to the area east of the Persian Gulf.[2]

During much of the seventeenth century, England was an economic and cultural backwater, with a relatively small market for any kind of luxury items, including Chinese porcelain. Holland, on the other hand, was enormously rich and had a large middle and upper class living extremely well off the proceeds of the country's world-wide empire of trade. The Dutch were enthralled by Chinese exportware. In 1602, Dutch seamen captured the Portugese carrack, the *San Jago*, with a sizable cargo of porcelain, which was sold at auction in Middleburg. In 1603, the *Santa Catherina*, another Portugese merchantman, was captured and its contents sold in Amsterdam. Never had so much Chinese porcelain reached Northern Europe, and it created an enormous stir, particularly amongst the French and the Dutch. During the first half of the seventeenth century, the Dutch imported Chinese porcelain literally by the ton.[3] Chinese porcelain figured prominently in seventeenth century Dutch still-lifes and inventories.[4] Dutch inventories and current excavations in Amsterdam reveal that the Dutch used Chinese porcelain for eating and drinking as well as for decoration. The Dutch also appear to have brought Chinese exportware to Virginia in the first half of the seventeenth century.

I have argued elsewhere[5] the circumstantial case for Dutch transportation of the early seventeenth-century Chinese porcelain found at Virginia sites, so I shall allude only briefly to my arguments. First, the records at the India Office Library indicate clearly that the British East India Company was not bringing any appreciable amount of porcelain to London, from whence it was later transshipped to America, until the 1680s. Even then they had some trouble selling the wares. The Dutch, on the other hand, were bringing tens of thousands of pieces to Holland from about 1610 on. Furthermore, most of the types of Chinese exportware found on early seventeenth-century Virginia sites are identical to wares excavated from two Dutch East Indiamen, the *Witte Leeuw*, sunk in 1612, and the *Banda*, sunk in 1615.[6] Finally, Dutch traders were a significant presence in the Chesapeake Bay from the 1620s on. In 1619, a Dutch ship brought the first Blacks to Virginia, and in the 1620s and 1630s, Dutch boats plied the Chesapeake in search of tobacco. Between the 1640s and 1660, when they were excluded from trade in Virginia by the Navigation Acts, Dutch merchants established permanent factories in Norfolk and elsewhere in the Chesapeake in order to facilitate their trade in tobacco.[7] These traders probably supplied the Virginia colonists with their earliest Chinese porcelain, apparently sporadically and in small quantities.

Virginians enjoyed a modest amount of Chinese porcelain in the seventeenth century, mostly in the form of bowls of various sizes. After about 1715, however, the amount of Chinese porcelain began to increase markedly, as a rising standard of living gentrified tidewater Virginians and encouraged the drinking of tea, coffee and chocolate. The Chinese porcelain that came to tidewater Virginia in the eighteenth century undoubtedly came from London.

English enthusiasm for things Chinese apparently took a great leap forward with the arrival of Charles II's Portuguese bride, Catherine of Braganza, who appeared in England in 1662 with an equipage of oriental objects, including lacquered furniture and tea, which caused amazement amongst the upper classes. But according to Hugh Honour, tea had probably entered England through Holland in the 1650s; in 1658, Thomas Rugge wrote that the "excellent and by all Physicians, approved, China drink, called by Chineans Tcha, by other nations Tay, alias Tee, is sold at the Sultaness Head Coffee House, . . . by the Royal Exchange, London."[8] So by the restoration of Charles II in 1660, two drinks which would generate an enormous demand for Chinese porcelain were being imbibed in London, and "china-mania" had taken root among the upper classes in England.

Although the East India Company records mention little Chinese porcelain imported to England before the 1680s, there is evidence of interest in the porcelain earlier in the seventeenth century among the very affluent. Charles I had sixty-five pieces of "purselaine" at Somerset House. An early example of interest specifically in Chinese ceramics is illustrated in a 1644 inventory at Tart Hall, cited by Peter Thornton, which contained glass, basketwork and brassware in addition to Chinese porcelain, in a manner similar to the cabinets of curiosities at Dresden and elsewhere on the continent. By 1678, the Dutchess of Cleveland must have amassed a "large" collection of Oriental porcelain, because in that year she sent it to Paris to be sold.[9] A recently published catalogue of Chinese and Japanese ceramics at Burghley House, near Stamford, based on an inventory of 1688 and a will of 1691, indicates that at least one major English country house had assembled a collection something like Queen Mary II's before Mary moved from Holland to England.[10]

Daniel Defoe credited Queen Mary II with bringing "in the Custom or Humour . . . of furnishing houses with China-ware, which increased to a strange degree afterwards, piling their China upon the tops of Cabinets, Scrutores, and every Chimney-Piece. . . ."[11] Mary's interest in Chinese porcelain was evident while she was still in Holland. Nicodemus Tessin described her audience chamber at Honelaarskijk as being "richly decorated with Chinese work and pictures. . . . The chimney was full of precious porcelain, part standing half inside it, and so fitted together that one piece supported another." Celia Fiennes, the aristocratic late seventeenth-century traveler, found Queen Mary's Water Gallery at Hampton Court "decked with China," but Mary's collection at Kensington Palace particularly impressed the English aristocracy.[12] It is in part to Mary's enthusiasm for Chinese ceramics, which originated in Holland, that the English owed their China-mania. The beginning of Mary's reign coincided with a marked increase in the importation into England of tea and coffee. By the 1690s, these two trends combined to create a vastly increased demand for the products of the Chinese potter in both table and ornamental wares, and the British East India Company attempted to meet this demand.

The records of the Honorable East India Company are voluminous but the sales records are very spotty and exist only from 1694 to 1722. Nevertheless, when combined with records of Company orders issued to its supercargoes, or purchasing agents on the ships, an excellent overview of the types of Chinese exportwares brought to the West can be ascertained. As K. N. Chaudhuri, historian of the Honorable East India Company, has observed, the importation of Chinese exportware to London was directly related to the growing custom of drinking tea, coffee, and to a lesser extent, chocolate, in England and the colonies.[13] Nevertheless, during the years for which records of auctions exist, a trend is discernible away from a variety of wares, particularly decorative "rollwagens" (tall, slender vases), large covered jars, and figures, to the plainer wares for table and tea and coffee drinking. Thus, by 1720, when Virginians began to increase their importation of Chinese porcelain in which to consume the new beverages, the Honorable East India Company had switched to a policy of bringing in enormous quantities of "ordinary wares" to meet the growing demand in England, Ireland and the colonies.

In 1704, for example, the East India Company offered a wide variety of objects for sale, wider than it offered a decade later. At a sale of the *Union's* cargo in 1704, merchants could buy a lot of seventy Dutchmen sitting, twelve Men on Sea Monsters, "21 ditto broke," sixty-five pulpitts with Paderies, three images with golden bellies and black faces, three Devils, and ten "fine hubble-bubble (houkas) at 61 shillings. At the same sales, utilitarian wares predominated, but even those staples of the trade, tea, coffee and chocolate cups, were scalloped, ribbed, octagonal, square and came in all sorts of color combinations, such as rouge de fer and gold, cream and red, and black with gold rims.[14]

By 1712, the *Dispatch Books* of the East India Company reveal that the standardization which characterized the Company's porcelain purchases in the eighteenth century had begun. The Company's order for that year consisted chiefly of two sorts of wares: dinner services and beverage sets. These included 40,000 chocolate cups with handles, 110,000 tea cups with saucers, 6,000 tea pots, 10,000 milk jugs, and 2,000 sets of small sugar bowls, two to a set. The Company charged the supercargoes, its emissaries to China, not to buy "large pieces such as Jars, Beakers or great dishes or bowls . . ."; by 1712 they were no longer fashionable.[15]

The trend towards standardization continued. A surviving sales catalogue of 1721 offered blue and white coffee cups in groups of 10,000 divided into five lots, 77,336 blue and white tea cups and saucers divided into twenty-seven lots.[16] The pulpits with or without paderies, small boys on toads, the large ladies with odd hands, and other figures listed in the 1704 sales are missing from the lists in 1721. This standardization occurred at the very moment when tidewater Virginia began importing Chinese exportware in bulk. Given the nature of the East India Company's imports, it is small wonder that the earlier eighteenth-century wares found in Virginia are more various and variously decorated than the later eighteenth-century wares. Furthermore, it is not surprising that, at most of the colony's eighteenth-century sites, a monotonous array of utilitarian forms decorated with underglaze blue, and later, polychrome glazes, confronts the student of Virginia's artifacts.

Further research is necessary before the entire network of eighteenth-century trade between China, London and Virginia can be spelled out. By mid-century, however, it is clear that dinner wares and tea services were available in Norfolk at stores run by merchants who also imported English and possibly Dutch wares. In the *Virginia Gazette* of July 25, 1766, the Norfolk merchants Balfour and Barraud advertized "china bowls of all sorts, plates, dishes, chocolate cups and saucers, coffee and tea cups and saucers, tea and milk pots, mugs etc.," as well as earthenware, delft, Dutch tiles and "English China [porcelain] of all types. . . ." Chinese porcelain has been found at plantations on both sides of the James such as Shirley, Flowerdew Hundred and Mt. Pleasant. Surviving letter and account books may indicate whether their owners could also have purchased Chinese porcelain in the stores that sprang up at Cabin Point and other tobacco inspection stations on the James after the establishment of these stations in the 1730s.[18]

Historians have graphically depicted the rigors of life in seventeenth-century Virginia, with its high mortality rate, the prevalence of earthbound, or post, buildings, as opposed to buildings with a stone or brick foundation, and the planters' susceptibility to the vicissitudes of tobacco prices.[19] Despite a depression in tobacco prices which began in the late seventeenth century and lasted into the 1740s, Virginians' standard of living began to improve within the first three decades of the eighteenth-century.[20] The 1730s saw the beginning of a building boomlet that was responsible for so many of the well-built houses on the banks of the James and York Rivers and in the town of Williamsburg. These houses are a symbol of the gentrification of colonial Virginia about which Richard Bushman writes so eloquently.

Bushman makes a most articulate case for studying the American colonial in the context of Anglo-American culture. He points out that American colonial centers responded to cultural innovation at about the same rate as did provincial English cities. "Dancing masters, theatre companies, and wig makers showed up in Williamsburg and Philadelphia about the same time as they did in Bristol and Lincoln."[21] The Governor's Palace in Williamsburg, built between 1709 and 1714, was a major landmark in Williamsburg's establishment as the new capitol of the colony, but the Palace also evokes the hundreds of small manor houses built between about 1690 and 1740 that still inhabit the English countryside and country towns.[22] Houses such as these, which we in Virginia think are very grand until compared with large English country houses, became the seats of the fabled Virginia gentry, and because of the nature of the plantation system, these houses became the center of the planters' cultural lives. In these houses, as in their English counterparts, the Virginia upper and middle classes gathered their neighbors and extended family to take part in a growing number of social ceremonies which displayed the social graces, wit and learning of the participants. Chinese porcelain provided the Virginia gentry with the implements to carry out these social ceremonies.

Before discussing the material evidence of these eighteenth-century social ceremonies in diaries and inventories, it is necessary to allude to what the archeologists call "food ways." A look at contemporary diaries and inventories very quickly persuades the reader that eating and drinking were no longer something done to sustain life but had become highly involved and also routine social events. The taking of a large meal some time between noon and dark, and the drinking of wine, tea, coffee and chocolate were all occasions which encouraged the attendance of guests outside the immediate family. Furthermore, these social events took up a great deal of time. An hour's immersion in the London diary of William Byrd II,[23] owner of Westover, will convince you that after Byrd read his Greek and Hebrew and did his exercises, his day was filled with a progress from a meal to a coffee house, where he often took chocolate, to a tea, and to a punch party at night. Even at his plantation in Virginia and in Williamsburg, he was constantly entertaining or being entertained at dinner and afterwards at tea or coffee and still later at supper, with wine and/or punch, and once in a while, coffee following.

A study of Byrd's three extant diaries—dating from 1709 to 1712, 1717 to 1721, and 1739 to 1741—tells us much about the uses to which Chinese porcelain could have been put in eighteenth-century Virginia.[24] In the earliest diary, dated 1709 to 1712, exportware was probably little used for drinking tea; the references to tea are generally medicinal. When Byrd's neighbor, Col. Benjamin Harrison, of Berkeley plantation, was dying, Byrd sent him some tea, which "he drank a great deal of. . . ." The following day, Byrd gave him "tea with ten drops of spirits of saffron," but despite this treatment, Harrison died.[25] In the years covered by the first two diaries, Byrd generally had boiled milk for breakfast, although by 1717, he would sometimes drink chocolate.[26] By 1739, when the last diary commences, Byrd almost always drank tea, or less frequently, coffee, every morning.[27] In London, tea was also drunk, especially with ladies, after dinner, which was eaten some time after noon.[28] But upon returning from London in 1720, Byrd usually served coffee, not tea, to guests after dinner at Westover. It was not until 1739, the period of his last diary entry, that we know Byrd routinely served tea to visitors who came in the afternoon and coffee to guests after dinner.[29] By the 1720s, we have seen from London sales records, tea and coffee services were being sent to the West from China, and tea and coffee cups and saucers constitute probably the biggest single source of shards at archeological digs in the James River basin.

Finally, another noticeable change in Byrd's drinking and entertaining habits is the increasing frequency with which he drank punch after the 1720s. One can find numerous references to drinking punch in the middle years, 1717 to 1721, particularly in August, 1720, and Byrd even gave it to his slaves on occasion.[30] In the later years, he apparently drank punch chiefly in Williamsburg. On May 2, 1740, for example, Byrd dined at three o'clock at Wetherburn's Tavern and, as he put it, "entertained the Governor. I ate boiled tongue. After dinner we drank arrack punch till 6 and then walked."[31] The several punch bowls listed in the inventories of the period attest to the popularity of punch in mid-eighteenth-century Virginia. Arthur Allen III, of Bacon's Castle, Surry Co., died possessed of two glass punch bowls in 1728.[32] Colonel John Allen, of Claremont Manor, in Surry County, had a silver punch ladle and probably five Chinese export and three earthenware punch bowls when he died in 1742.[33] The sixteen "china bowls" listed in the Raleigh Tavern inventory of 1771 are probably punch bowls too; directly following their listing is a listing of two silver punch ladles and two silver punch strainers.[34]

The survey of inventories from various counties written from 1728 to 1775 indicates that the trends discernible in Byrd's diary are also seen in other households and taverns. Tea equipages and coffee and chocolate pots and cups figure prominently in colonial Virginia households, attesting to the Virginians' improving standard of living and increasing gentrification.

Eighteenth-century inventories from Surry and York Counties illustrate the complexity of tea, coffee, chocolate, and punch consumption as a socioeconomic phenomenon. Drinking punch was relatively simple. The inventories list punch bowls which, when small, could be drunk from directly. Otherwise, punch required glasses, which most of the affluent households surveyed would have contained, and a punch ladle and perhaps a strainer.[35] Only the bowl might have been of Chinese porcelain. But tea, coffee and chocolate drinking required numerous objects to do it properly, many of which were of export porcelain.

Tea was the most complicated of the three beverages to consume and has left us the largest group of shards. Several inventories abbreviate the tea equipage by referring to "1 set of China and board," as in Peyton Randolph's inventory of 1775, or to a "tea table and furniture," such as was found in the hall and the room above the chamber at Bacon's Castle, in Surry County, in 1728.[36] But such brief references give a simplistic idea of the implements necessary to the eighteenth-century tea ceremony in colonial Virginia. Affluent households often contained tea tables; Arthur Allen III, of Surry County, possessed two Dutch tea tables at his death in 1728. Inventories listed tea boards, usually mahogany, but occasionally japanned, as at the Peyton Randolph house in Williamsburg in 1775.[37]

The tea was often kept in cannisters, as in two japanned tea chests and cannisters found in the little middle room at the Governor's Palace in 1770. Tea kettles were often listed in the kitchen, sometimes with trivets. They were often copper but Governor Botetourt owned one Dutch lead boiler with tea kettle and four Dutch lead coffee pots and lamps. Henry Wetherburn died in 1760 owning both a silver tea kettle and tea pot. Tea pots came in all sorts of materials and are occasionally listed as having a tea pot stand. The majority of tea pots listed were not of Chinese export porcelain; they were often of metal.[38]

The inventories list tea bowls and saucers, in those days without handles, but the inventories imply that sometimes tea and coffee cups shared the same saucer. The Raleigh Tavern inventory of 1771 lists "44 china saucers, 17 cups, 11 china coffee cups." A few of the armorial services still extant illustrate this practice.[39] Tea services almost always had a "slop basin," or waste bowl, and generally a sugar dish, a milk pot, and, at Wetherburn's Tavern in 1760, "a spoon and tong stand." One plate was occasionally listed with the rest of the vessels mentioned.[40] However, there was no mention of anything being served with tea in Byrd's diary.[41] In eighteenth-century Virginia, the tea itself appears to have been the focus of the ceremony. Tea spoons are mentioned in inventories of more affluent households and sugar tongs as well.[42]

Coffee and chocolate were less complicated beverages to administer than tea but required coffee and chocolate mills for grinding. Governor Botetourt had on hand 21 1/2 pounds of "India coffee" at his death in 1770. Coffee and chocolate pots also came in metal as well as almost every kind of ceramic; Raleigh Tavern had two tin coffee pots in 1771, and Governor Botetourt had eleven Staffordshire coffee pots as well as other ceramic and metal pots.[43] The ceramics listed in the inventories are often reflected in the shards.

The present state of our knowledge makes it difficult to generalize about the degree to which the possession of tea, coffee and chocolate sets filtered down the economic ladder. In her study of Yorktown inventories between 1730 and 1750, Mary Beaudry points out that the value of estates listing some semblance of a tea equipage ranged from £23 to over £2000. Of the thirty-four estates listed in Beaudry's appendix, nine were valued between £100 and £300, and ten between £300 and £600. The fact that rudimentary tea services were found in three York County estates valued at under £90 would seem to indicate that, as Beaudry puts it, "the social significance of tea-drinking caused those other than the very wealthy to strive" to obtain the equipment for this genteel ceremony. Beaudry further hypothesizes that the fact "that there is no [economic] cut-off point at which the amount of total estate value may be correlated with ownership of so-called status goods . . . is indicative of a community in which there existed no firm distinctions between social strata."[44] If Virginians had the money to buy goods associated with an affluent lifestyle, they simply bought them and used them.

Beaudry's conclusions are borne out in large part by the archeological remains in Yorktown, Williamsburg and Jamestown. Tea and coffee wares and Chinese porcelain are found on widely distributed sites. It could be argued, however, that the three towns were largely inhabited by wealthy planters in season and by merchants the year round. Furthermore, most of the rural sites dug in tidewater Virginia had been the plantations of the gentry, so their archeological remains are hardly typical of the poor farmers who made up the bulk of Virginia's population. Scholars must do much more work on the inventories of this group and archeologists dig more sites associated with men of modest means before we can hypothesize about the implications of the inventories and the shards for the poorer classes of eighteenth-century tidewater Virginia.

One point the inventories make clear: the possession of Chinese export porcelain was widely diffused among affluent Virginians. Of the thirty-four households listed in Beaudry's appendix, twenty-two owned some Chinese export porcelain.[45] In 1728, Arthur Allen III had eight china cups and one china plate with his tea table and furniture in the hall at Bacon's Castle in Surry County. By 1742, his relative John Allen died possessed of nine china plates, seventeen china dishes, as well as six chocolate cups, nine tea cups and a "set of china" not enumerated.[46] The 1760 inventory of Wetherburn's Tavern indicates that a Chinese export porcelain tea service and five china bowls were in use at the tavern. At neighboring Raleigh Tavern, the biggest single listing in the 1771 inventory is for 122 china plates, but the tavern also boasted large numbers of china tea and coffee cups and other sundry pieces of chinese porcelain. In 1775, Peyton Randolph's house in Williamsburg contained eight dozen "red and white china plates" and "22 ditto"(i.e., red and white dishes,) as well as "a Sett of Ornamental China" and sundry other pieces of exportware.[47] Thus the Virginia inventories reflect the trend revealed by the sales records of the East India Company, that utilitarian table wares formed the bulk of the British porcelain trade by the 1720s. The shards found in Virginia also reflect this pattern of importation and use.

A study of the eighteenth-century Chinese export porcelain shards and whole vessels found in the James River basin indicates that, in general, the tablewares of the Virginia gentry were markedly inferior to the dinner and tea services of the English and continental upper classes. The difference in quality reflects the Virginians' status as provincials. Furthermore, the provincial quality of Virginians' porcelain is borne out by the fact that it resembles closely the types of wares common to, for example, the Swedish and Dutch markets of the mid-eighteenth-century. The dating of these eighteenth-century tablewares was greatly advanced in 1974 with David S. Howard's publication of *Chinese Armorial Porcelain*, in which he illustrates pieces from over 3000 armorial services that he groups by borders and dates by studying the coats of arms on the exportware services illustrated. Howard's almost infallible method enables us to date with some precision the eighteenth-century shards in the James River basin.[48]

The sales records of the India Office indicate that the Chinese exportware produced in the early eighteenth century was more variously decorated than the later wares; this fact is reflected in the decoration of the shards found on Virginia's eighteenth century sites. Furthermore, the general level of quality of the porcelain was quite high through the 1720s, the paste, or body, quite free of impurities and a bluish-white, and the glaze very glassy and relatively thin, so that it bonded very well with the body of the vessel. The cobalt used was generally quite pure and produced a bright, deep blue, in marked contrast to the later blue and white wares, on which the blue can be quite ink-like or, conversely, very faded. The painters sometimes took the trouble to modulate the tone of the blue, creating shadings, as they have on these shards from saucers depicting two male Chinese figures found at Flowerdew Hundred, near Hopwell. (Illus. 1) The man on the left is probably an attendant; he lacks the formal garb, including waistband, of the man on the right. Early wares were sometimes molded, like a small saucer decorated with flowers and tendrils found by Noel-Hume in Williamsburg in a 1705 context,[49] or ribbed, like the bowl shard decorated with a vigorously painted lotus scroll and vine pattern from Flowerdew. (Illus. 2) The earlier wares sometimes had a decorative design called *an hua*, or secret design, carved on them. A tea bowl and saucer from Flowerdew Hundred with blue and white border has a small abstract floral design, (Illus. 3) whereas a milk jug or bottle from Governor's Land, west of Jamestown, with diaper borders, has a larger lotus-like design decorating its rounded sides. Blue and white wares sometimes had a brown, or cafe au lait glaze on the outside, but could also have a soft celadon green glaze, as does the tea bowl with a landscape in underglaze blue on the bottom of the bowl. (Illus. 4)

By about 1690, imari ware, decorated with underglaze blue and overglaze iron red and gold, had become popular in Europe, and is frequently found on sites in this area. A plate rim from Jamestown, painted in an asymetrical design with vigorous rococo swirls, is very similar to those found at King Carter's Corotomen, which burned in 1725. (Illus. 5) Finally, a unique piece in the James River basin dates from this period. The famille verte shards found at Jamestown probably made up a cache-pot, or round-sided flowerpot, and are incised with a very well-carved lotus flower and spear petal pattern. Some of the decoration is in underglaze blue, and the blue bands contain a border of iron-red flowers, green leaves and black dots characteristic of the famille verte, or green family, palette prevalent around the turn of the century. The combination of underglaze blue and famille verte died out shortly after 1700.

With the advent of the 1730s, the amount of exportware dispatched to Europe began to increase markedly and the quality to vary considerably. By the beginning of the eighteenth century, the body even of exportwares was relatively free of imperfections and the potting is almost uniformly excellent, unlike seventeenth century wares. Until about 1760, the great difference in contemporary wares relates to the quality of the painting, not the potting. Shards resembling a complete teabowl decorated with large petals containing a peony spray and a landscape with a lake, a pagoda and a mountain in the distance, are found on numerous local sites; hundreds, if not thousands, must have been used in tidewater Virginia. The suggestive brushwork and the use of a very few strokes to depict the flowers and landscape bespeak the speed with which it was painted. (Illus. 6) A punch bowl, probably made c. 1735, and found at Newtown, near Norfolk, now known as Pleasant Point, is an extreme example of speedy painting. (Illus. 7) The figures are depicted with four lines and a blob for the man's torso and arm, the mountains by a long stroke and a blob, and the pine trees by a few horizontal brushstrokes crossed by vertical strokes. A blue and white saucer from Jamestown, decorated with graceful storks amid flowers and trees carefully outlined and without any wash, is an example of pencil drawing from the 1740s. A small teapot of blue and white decoration found at the Drummond site on Kingsmill Plantation, east of Jamestown, is a superb example of the potter's art. (Illus. 8)[50] The tea pot is made of a soft paste porcelain, a slightly different clay from the normal exportwares, which absorbs the cobalt blue differently and thus allows for very precise brushwork. It is very similar to tea wares made for A. J. Sichterman, an officer of the Dutch East India Company from Groningen, the Netherlands, about 1745.[51]

By the mid–1720s, a new range of colors became available to the Chinese potters, called famille rose, or the pink family. It almost certainly derived from a European technique of enameling on metal; the glaze, a translucent pink, is composed of gold and tin oxide. It is painted onto the body of the piece which has already been glazed at 1300 degrees centigrade, like the blue and white porcelain; it is thus on the overglaze and the piece must be fired a second time at a lower temperature. As Margaret Medley has observed, "the stability of the [rose family's] enamel pastes permitted delicate shading of tones in a wide variety of colour combinations. Minute details could be picked out in different colours without fear of these running [during firing,] so that the birds and flowers, for instance, could be painted with a marvelous attention to detail rivaling that of the European miniaturist."[52] Extremely little famille rose of that quality found its way to Virginia.

Nevertheless, the famille rose porcelain found on tidewater Virginia sites is not without interest. A famille rose bowl, made about 1735 and decorated with deep red and yellow flowers and a deep pink diaper border interrupted by floral cartouches, is now the property of the Association for the Preservation of Virginia Antiquities, but has a history of descent in the family of the minister who baptized Pocahontas. (Illus. 9) Large shards from a nine-inch plate found at the College of William and Mary are painted with an undulating iron-red border of cloud collars and a central landscape containing cherry-trees picked out in heavy pink overglaze. On these and similar wares, the use of the famille rose enamels is quite carefully confined but heavily applied. Another later, c. 1745 example, perhaps more typical of famille rose, is a punchbowl decorated with heavily enameled peonies and large green leaves on brown branches from Jamestown. (Illus. 10)

A variation of the famille rose palette, composed of black outline filled in with faint grey wash and modulated pink or orange overglaze, sometimes with bits of gold added, was made particularly successfully between about 1730 and 1750 and occasionally appears on eastern Virginia sites. The shards from a saucer from Jamestown provide an example of the intricacy of detail possible using this glaze; the saucer, decorated in gold and faint touches of iron-red, is not of the first quality but nonetheless attractive and well-painted. (Illus. 11) Imari remained a popular ware in this period. Numerous pieces were found during the excavations of Wetherburn's Tavern. A partial dinner plate from Kingsmill Plantation is a particularly well-preserved example of the ware and conveys a sense of why it was popular in Europe and in Virginia. (Illus. 12)

Blue and white exportware continued to be popular in the middle decades of the eighteenth century. A coffee cup from Jamestown is decorated with the ubiquitous giant peony, a carefully executed latticework fence
and bamboo. (Illus. 13) This motif is used continuously through the 1770s
with varying quality of painting. A blue and white teabowl from Kingsmill with cafe au lait exterior is painted very hastily, with single blobs of
blue depicting the leaves and a few brushstrokes shading the petals of the
peony. (Illus. 14) The shards of the coffee cup and saucer from Jamestown
dating about 1765 are decorated with a landscape style frequently encountered on shards from eastern Virginia sites, with willow trees, plum blos-
soms depicted by circles, large houses and tiny sailboats, all drawn with
few and heavy brushstrokes typical of the later cruder blue and white
wares. (Illus. 15) Finally, the general decline in the quality of painting
on blue and white wares can be seen in the painting on the large platter
dating to about 1775 or 1780 from the Whittle House in Norfolk. The
platter has what is often referred to as a Fitzhugh border, taken from a
service made for Thomas Fitzhugh, an officer of the Honorable East Indian Company, about 1780. (Illus. 16) The Fitzhugh pattern generated
very little interest in Great Britain but was to become enormously popular in the new republic after the American Revolution.

Although Chinese export porcelain with blue and white decoration make
up a majority of the shards found on local sites, a few of the polychrome
overglazed exportwares dating from after 1760 deserve mention. A partial
service in the Collection of Colonial Williamsburg Foundation, decorated
with spear border, large famille rose peonies and exotic birds with peacocks'
tails on a rock, is like intact pieces with a history of local ownership in
the Williamsburg area and shards from Jamestown and Williamsburg. A
punchbowl from Wetherburn's Tavern is decorated with a gold chain border
and the increasingly whispy floral sprays that characterize post–1760s polychrome wares. The Chinese lady on shards from Claremont Manor, in Surry
County, is typical of shards found on numerous plantation sites along the
James, including Shirley, and is a basically simple pattern inexpensively
produced. (Illus. 17) The polychrome ware found on later eighteenth-century
sites is often decorated with a typical floral pattern not unlike that found
on a service made about 1770 for a member of the Grigby family (Illus.
20), the flowers rendered with six or eight quick brush strokes of pink, two
green leaves, the piece covered with a thick greyish glaze. Many examples
can also be found in local archeological collections of porcelain shards decorated with the simple band and star or chain borders found on exportware
made about the time of the American Revolution.[53]

The nature of the Chinese exportware found on colonial sites in the

James River basin reveals the provincial status of its owners when compared with wares made for the families of the English upper classes. A few examples must suffice. The nicely painted bowl in the collection of the Association for the Preservation of Virginia Antiquities, with a history of Virginia ownership, is a worthy example of the ware (Illus. 9) but nowhere near as fine as the extremely thinly potted and exquisitely painted tea bowl and saucer made for a member of the Dutch Reverhorst family about 1745. (Illus. 18) An excellent example of the difference between the quality of armorial wares and regular tablewares can be seen in a comparison of the two blue and white plates with inner and outer diaper borders and floral cartouches at the rim. (Illus. 19) The plate on the right was made for a member of the Leuthellier family; it is decorated with a well-painted parrot, the family crest, and the inner border contains exquisitely executed cartouches of a scholar on a terrace gazing at his garden. The plate on the left is identical to many shards found here, including a rim shard from Gloucestertown of virtually identical ware. The brushwork on the armorial plate is considerably finer, the brush strokes more numerous, and the glaze thinner than on the non-armorial plate, whose brushwork is blurred by a thicker glaze. The Chinese imari service made for the English Horsemonden family with Virginia connections—the first Mrs. William Byrd II was a Horsemonden—is in marked contrast to most of the imari wares found in Virginia.[54] The chocolate pot, cups and saucers with the arms of Grigby impaling Bird of about 1770 to 1780 (Illus. 20) are more carefully painted than most of the later wares found on colonial tidewater sites, including a respectably painted punchbowl of about the same date found at Wetherburn's Tavern. The archeological collections of Williamsburg and environs are not, however, totally devoid of armorial porcelain; shards of plates from the service of Lord Dunmore, Virginia's Governor between 1771 and 1775, have been found on several sites in Williamsburg. (Illus. 21)

A comparison of the Virginia shards with the wares found on three eighteenth century wrecks reveals that, despite its relatively mediocre quality, the exportware in Virginia was comparable to the common tablewares imported for the Swedish and Dutch markets in the eighteenth century. A blue and white eight-inch plate with bamboo borders is one of the most prevalent border types from the 1740s found on tidewater Virginia sites (Illus. 21); such wares were also found on the *Hollandia*, an East Indiaman sunk in the mid-1740s, and on the *Goteborg*, sunk near Gothenburg, Sweden, in 1745. To judge from photographs of the *Goteborg's* cargo, it carried a great many wares like those found here.[55]

The recent discovery of a Dutch East Indiaman sunk about 1750 in the

South China Sea has vastly enlarged the comparative scope of the study of mid-eighteenth century Chinese export. The wreck was excavated by Michael Hatcher, a salvage diver based in Singapore, who brought up the ship's bell, dated 1747, with about fifty European stoneware jugs and about forty wine bottles, as well as 126 Chinese gold ingots. The artifacts recovered, as well as the nature of the cargo, have led Christian Jorg, Chief Curator of the Groninger Museum in Groningen, to conclude that Hatcher had found the *Geldermalsen*, a Dutch East Indiaman sunk in 1752.[56] Hatcher salvaged over 162,000 vessels which were sold in Amsterdam in April, 1986.[57]

The recovery of wares from the *Geldermalsen* has provided thousands of intact examples of Chinese porcelain wares identical to hundreds of shards found in the James River basin. At Kingsmill alone, at least five sets of shards identical or very similar to wares from the *Geldermalsen* have been unearthed. The earlier-mentioned tea bowl with cafe au lait glaze on the reverse has the same center scene as dozens salvaged from the wreck, with a giant peony, a large rock and a weeping willow. (Illus. 14) The rim and part of the bottom of an octagonal plate from Kingsmill are similar to a partial set of octagonal plates and platters raised from the *Geldermalsen*, with similar floral cartouches on the rim and a pine tree in the center scene. The plates from the *Geldermalsen* are somewhat simpler, lacking an outer border and having a simpler border on the cavetto. (Illus. 22)[59] A saucer from the same site with sketchy diaper border, skeletal tree branches and a mountain or rock rendered by a quick outline filled in with wash is very much like dozens of tea bowls and saucers from the Dutch East Indiaman. (Illus. 23)[60] A dinner plate found at Kingsmill is of almost identical pattern to dozens from the *Geldermalsen*, with three groups of flowers on the rim, a diaper border with floral cartouches on the cavetto, and chrysanthemums in the center. The example from Virginia is slightly better painted, with lotus leaves carefully rendered with outline and shaded blue wash in the center scene. (Illus. 24)[61] A plate found at Wetherburn's Tavern has a pattern similar to that on tea bowls from the wreck, with sketchy diaper border and a stiffly painted bamboo.[62] These examples are but a few of the possibly hundreds of parallels between the wares in Virginia archeological collections and those salvaged from the South China Sea by Michael Hatcher.

The massed ranks of exportware excavated from the *Geldermalsen* (Illus. 25) provide students of eighteenth-century social history and material culture with a graphic example of the implications of the China trade for western Europe and for Virginia. The increasing availability of Chinese ceremonies during the eighteenth century provided the Virginia colonists with the vessels from which to drink the new and popular beverages, tea, coffee, chocolate and punch. The rising popularity of these beverages occurred at a time when Virginians were experiencing a rising standard of living, and the increasing supply of both the ceramics and the beverages provided the colonists with an outlet for their increasing affluence. Finally, the confluence of these two trends encouraged the gentry and "middling classes" to indulge in the social ceremonies reaching them, as provincials, only after such ceremonies had been established in London. The beauty, availability and durability of Chinese export porcelain makes it one of the most interesting material remains of the complex society that contributed so much to the origins of revolutionary America.

NOTES

1 See, for example, Alice Baldwin Beer, *Trade Goods: A Study of Indian Chintz* (Washington, D. C.: Smithsonian Institution Press, 1970); Ralph Davis, *The Rise of the English Shipping Industry* (London: Macmillan, 1962); Holden Furber, *Rival Empires of Trade* (Minneapolis: University of Minnesota Press, 1976.)

2 T. Volker, *Porcelain and the Dutch East India Company* (Leiden: E. J. Brill, 1970), 48. See also, C. R. Boxer, *The Dutch Seaborne Empire 1600–1800* (New York: Alfred A. Knopf, 1965) and K. N. Chaudhuri, *The Trading World of Asia and the English East India Company, 1660–1760* (Cambridge: Cambridge University Press, 1978) for the rise of the Dutch and English East Indian companies. For shorter accounts, see Christine van der Pijl-Ketel, ed., *The Ceramic Load of the Witte Leeuw* (Amsterdam, Rijksmuseum, n.d.) and Jean Sutton, *Lords of the East: The East India Company and Its Ships* (London: Conway Maritime Press, 1981)

3 For an excellent short account of the Dutch trade in Chinese porcelain see C. J. A. Jorg, *Porcelain and the Dutch China Trade*, (The Hague: Martinus Nijhoff, 1982), 91–140.

4 A. I. Spriggs, "Oriental Porcelain in Western Paintings," *Transactions of the Oriental Ceramic Society* 36 (1964–66). Information on seventeenth-century Dutch inventories obtained by oral communication from Christian J. A. Jorg, Senior Curator, Groninger Museum, Groningen, Netherlands.

5 Julia B. Curtis, "Chinese Ceramics and the Dutch Connection in Early Seventeenth Century Virginia," *Vereniging van Vrienden der Asiatische Kunst*, 15 (1985): 6–13.

6 Julia B. Curtis, "Chinese Ceramics and the Dutch Connection in Early Seventeenth Century Virginia," 6–8. See also, J. Dumas, *Fortunes de Mer* (Paris: Atlas Films, S. A., 1981).

7 John R. Pagan, "Dutch Maritime and Commercial Activity in Mid-Seventeenth Century Virginia," *Virginia Magazine of History and Biography* 90 (1982): 485–501.

8 Hugh Honour, *Chinoiserie: The Vision of Cathay* (New York: E. P. Dutton and Company, Incorporated, 1961), 51.

9 Cited in Linda Schulsky, "Queen Mary's Collection of Porcelain and Delft and Its Display at Kensington Palace Based Upon an Analysis of the Inventory Taken in 1697" (Unpublished Master's thesis, Cooper-Hewitt Museum and Parsons School of Design, 1986), 7, 13–14.

10 See Gordon Lang, *Exhibition of Chinese and Japanese Export Porcelain at Burghley House* (Highfields, Brighton, Sussex: Manor Park Press, [1985?])

11 Quoted in Schulsky, 13.

12 Quoted in Arthur Lane, "Queen Mary II's Porcelain Collection at Hampton Court," *Transactions of the Oriental Ceramic Society*, 1949–50, 25, and Schulsky, 14–15.

13 K. N. Chaudhuri, 406.

14 India Office Library, *Home Miscellaneous Series*, 12: 30–67, 186–223. See pp. 62–65 and 220–21 for types of figures.

15 Quoted in Chaudhuri, 408.

16 India Office Library, *Home Miscellaneous Series*, 14: 196–205.

17 Quoted in Ivor Noel-Hume, *Pottery and Porcelain in Colonial Williamsburg's Archeological Collection* (Williamsburg: Colonial Williamsburg Foundation, 1969), 11.

18 James H. Soltow, *The Economic Role of Williamsburg* (Williamsburg: Colonial Williamsburg, Incorporated, 1965), 15, 48–63.

19 Edmund S. Morgan, *American Slavery, American Freedom: The Ordeal of Colonial Virginia* (New York: Norton, 1975), 158–95, 215–34; Cary Carson et al., "Impermanent Architecture in the Southern American Colonies," *Winterthur Portfolio* 16 (Summer-Autumn 1981): 135–96.

20 Alan Kulikoff, "The Economic Growth of the Eighteenth Century Chesapeake Colonies," *Journal of Economic History* 29 (March 1979): 279–80, 284, 286.

21 Richard L. Bushman, "American High-Style and Vernacular Cultures," *Colonial British America*, Jack P. Greene and J. R. Pole, eds. (Baltimore: John Hopkins University Press, 1984), 366.

22 Bushman, 349, 357–58.

23 Louis B. Wright and Marion Tinling, eds., *William Byrd of Virginia: The London Diary (1717–1721) and Other Writings* (New York: Oxford University Press, 1958.)

24 Louis B. Wright and Marion Tinling, eds., The *Secret Diary of William Byrd of Westover, 1709–1712*, (Richmond: Dietz Press, 1941), hereafter cited as Wright and Tinling, *London Diary*; Maude H. Woodfin and Marion Tinling, eds., *Another Secret Diary of William Byrd of Westover, 1739–1741*, (Richmond: Dietz Press, 1942), hereafter cited as Woodfin and Tinling, *Another Secret Diary*. Other printed diaries consulted yielded little information on changes in habits of consuming tea, coffee, punch and chocolate.

25 Wright and Tinling, *London Diary, 1709–1712*, 160–63.

26 See, for example, Wright and Tinling, *London Diary, 1709–1712*, 76, 106, 115, 127, 273, 325, 483; Wright and Tinling, *Another Secret Diary*, 88, 102, 149, 287, 359, 437, 523.

27 Woodfin and Tinling, *Another Secret Diary, 1739–1741*, 5, 47, 53, 147, 177.

28 See, for example, Wright and Tinling, *London Diary*, 60, 78, 79.

29 See, for example, Woodfin and Tinling, *Another Secret Diary 1739–1741*, 33–38, 46–47, 51, 61, 67, 70–73, 84, 165, 182.

30 See, for example, Wright and Tinling, *London Diary*, 386, 412, 423, 435–43, 456, 528, 466.

31 Woodfin and Tinling, *Another Secret Diary, 1739–1741*, 63. See also 165.

32 Surry County Records, *Deed Book, 1715–1730*, Part 3, 807–10.

33 Surry County Records, *Will Book, 1738–1754*, 438–44.

34 Graham Hood, ed., *Inventories of Four Eighteenth Century Houses in the Historic Area of Williamsburg* (Williamsburg: Colonial Williamsburg Foundation, n.d.), 20. Hereafter cited as Graham Hood, *Inventories*.

35 See, for example, Surry County Records, *Deed Book, 1715–1730*, Part 3, "A True and Perfect Inventory . . . of the Estate of Mr. Arthur Allen, Deceased . . . ," 807–10.

36 Graham Hood, *Inventories*, 24; Surry County Records, *Deed Book, 1715–1730*, Part 3, 807–10.

37 Graham Hood, *Inventories*, 20, 24–25. Governor Botetourt had a tea board of silver or plated silver. *Inventories*, 7.

38 Graham Hood, *Inventories*, 6, 7, 21, 29. See also Surry County Records, *Will Book, 1738–1754*, 438–44.

39 See, for example, David S. Howard, *Chinese Armorial Porcelain* (London: Faber and Faber, 1974), 255 (Arms of Husbands, c. 1730), 292 (Arms of Haggard, c. 1732).

40 See, for example, Surry County Records, *Deed Book 1715–1730*, Part 3, 807–10.

41 See, for example, Woodfin and Tinling, *Another Secret Diary, 1739–1741*, 12.

42 Surry County Records, *Will Book, 1738–1754*, pp. 438–39, 541–42; Graham Hood, *Inventories*, 29.

43 Graham Hood, *Inventories*, 6, 9, 22.

44 Mary C. Beaudry, "Ceramics in York County, Virginia, Inventories, 1730–1750: The Tea Service." Paper presented at the Eighth Annual Conference of the Society for Historical Archeology, January 9, 1975, Appendix 3 and p. 6. Hereafter cited as Mary Beaudry, "Ceramics in York County."

45 Mary Beaudry, "Ceramics in York County," Appendix 3.

46 Surry County Records, *Deed Book, 1715–1730*, 807–10; *Will Book, 1738–1754*, 438–44.

47 Graham Hood, *Inventories*, 28, 20–21, 24–25.

48 David S. Howard, *Chinese Armorial Porcelain* (London: Faber and Faber, 1974).

49 Oral communication, Ivor Noel-Hume.

50 I am indebted for much of the information on the shards from the collection of the Virginia Historic Landmarks Commission to Merry Outlaw and Bly Bogley Straub. See also William M. Kelso, *Kingsmill Plantation, 1619–1800* (Orlando: Academic Press, 1984.)

51 C. J. A. Jorg, *Oosterse Keramiek uit Groninger Kollekties* (Groningen: Wolters Noordhoff Grafische Bedrijven, 1982), 64–65.

52 Margaret Medley, *The Chinese Potter* (New York: Scribner's, 1976), 246–47.

53 See, for example, Geoffrey A. Godden, *Oriental Export Market Porcelain* (London: Granada Publishing, 1979), 287, 289, 290.

54 Geoffrey A. Godden, 210. A plate from this service is in the collection of the Colonial Williamsburg Foundation.

55 Stig Roth, *Chinese Ceramics Imported by the Swedish East India Company* (Goteburg: Gothenburg Historical Museum, 1965), 12.

56 C. J. A. Jorg, *The Geldermalsen: History and Porcelain* (Groningen: Kemper, 1986.)

57 Christie's, Amsterdam, *The Nanking Cargo, Chinese Export Porcelain and Gold, European Glass and Stoneware*, 28 April–2 May 1986.

58 C. J. A. Jorg, *The Geldermalsen*, Illus. 47, 66.

59 C. J. A. Jorg, *The Geldermalsen*, Illus. 44, 64.

60 C. J. A. Jorg, *The Geldermalsen*, Illus. 49, 66.

61 C. J. A. Jorg, *The Geldermalsen*, Illus. 61, 74.

62 C. J. A. Jorg, *The Geldermalsen*, Illus. 48, 66.

LIST OF ILLUSTRATIONS

1. Southside Historic Sites Incorporated.
2. Southside Historic Sites Incorporated.
3. Southside Historic Sites Incorporated.
4. Virginia Historic Landmarks Commission.
5. Colonial National Historic Park — Jamestown.
6. Author's Collection.
7. Virginia Historic Landmarks Commission.
8. Virginia Historic Landmarks Commission.
9. Collection of the Association for the Preservation of Virginia Antiquities.
10. Colonial National Historic Park — Jamestown.
11. Colonial National Historic Park — Jamestown.
12. Virginia Historic Landmarks Commission.
13. Colonial National Historic Park — Jamestown.
14. Virginia Historic Landmarks Commission.
15. Colonial National Historic Park — Jamestown.
16. Virginia Historic Landmarks Commission.
17. Claremont Manor.
18. Private Collection.
19. Author's Collection.
20. Private Collection.
21. Author's Collection.
22. Virginia Historic Landmarks Commission.
23. Virginia Historic Landmarks Commission.
24. Virginia Historic Landmarks Commission.
25. Collection of Colonial Williamsburg Foundation. Dinner service from the *Geldermalsen*.

Anglo-Irish Attitudes: Changing Perceptions of National Identity Among the Protestant Ascendancy in Ireland, ca. 1690–1750 [1]

DAVID HAYTON

As a colonial ruling *élite* in close geographical proximity to the "mother country," the Protestant squirearchy of eighteenth- and nineteenth-century Ireland were in a peculiar predicament, pulled in different directions by opposing loyalties. Even the Irish patriotism of the later eighteenth century is compromised by its narrow confessional basis, and its detachment from the mainstream of Gaelic Irish culture. From time to time historians have sought to resolve the apparent contradiction between the extravagant outbursts of Irish national feeling which issued from the Ascendancy and the underlying exclusiveness and Anglocentrism which eventually turned the Protestant "political nation" towards union with Great Britain in order to stave off a threat of Catholic republicanism. One concept, developed by the late Gerald Simms and enshrined in the pseudo-official *New History of Ireland* being published under the auspices of the Royal Irish Academy, derives from an analogy between the patriotism of the Ascendancy and that of eighteenth-century colonial America, locating the Protestant sense of Irishness in a growing consciousness of separate political and, more important, economic interests from those of England.[2] The term "colonial nationalism," originally coined to describe movements for greater autonomy in the dominions of the late nineteenth- and early twentieth-century British Empire, is itself an anachronism.[3] What it fails to take into account in an eighteenth-century context is the evidence of contemporary perceptions of nationality among the Protestant Irish. After all, the Ascendancy did not view itself as a "colonial" class but as "the Irish nation"; and on this ground George Boyce has advanced a counter-interpretation of Protestant patriotism which presses for its acceptance at something nearer face value. "Anglo-Irish political thinking," he writes, "held no brief for the idea that they were colonists, or that Ireland was in any respect like Virginia or Maryland."[4] This empirical, anti-reductionist approach, seeking to understand the mentality of the Ascendancy on its own terms, has considerable attractions, but as a line of argument it is not quite as straightforward as at first it might appear. For in the *early* eighteenth century Irish Protestants did not have a clear and unqualified perception of their Irish nationality. They did not all refer to themselves as Irish all of the time, and their notions of who exactly comprised "the Irish people" were in the process of transmutation from an acceptance of a Catholic "nation" to a belief in a Protestant one.

Evidence pertaining to "perceptions of national identity" is scattered across a great variety of source materials, and conclusions always run the risk of being impressionistic. What is more, the fragments must be set firmly in context, both in terms of author and circumstances. The hazards of dragging out of context *obiter dicta* of such individual, not to say idiosyncratic, commentators as Swift or Berkeley are glaring. To underline the point, I will only offer one further example, that of the Irish-born radical pamphleteer John Toland, from whose published writings and private correspondence might be gleaned a variety of conflicting interpretations of national self-awareness. In the late 1690s and very early 1700s for instance, as a *protégé* of Sir Robert Clayton, the governor of the Irish Society, and of Robert Harley, one of the leaders of the English Country Party, both of whom were embroiled in conflicts of interest with the Irish Parliament, Toland was sympathetic to, and may have defended, the claims of the English legislature for constitutional superiority over the Irish; in the late 1710s and early 1720s, when personal and political fortunes had changed, and he had found a new patron, he took the opposite view.[5] In his political writings for an English public he occasionally masqueraded as an Englishman, or even as a Briton, but when travelling on the Continent, and in need of hospitality from fellow Irishmen, he was prepared to allow that Ireland was his "native land."[6] But even if evidence of this kind were outweighed by a stock of unequivocal and objective statements of national allegiance, it would still be impracticable to impose a precise measurement on the developments this paper is intended to describe. What is happening is not a sudden, blinding mass-conversion, but a gradual and piecemeal shift in understanding.

This shift in the self-image of the Ascendancy was towards an affirmation of Irishness. It began, I would argue, in the aftermath of the "Glorious Revolution" of 1688, had gathered considerable momentum by the time of the Wood's Halfpence imbroglio in the 1720s, and was more or less complete by the middle of the eighteenth century. In the 1690s Anglo-Irish Protestants, whether Irish-bred, Irish-born or Irish-based, tended to think of themselves first and foremost as the representatives of the "English interest" in Ireland, in contrast to the "Irish interest" of the native Catholics and the Scottish interest of the Presbyterians in Ulster. By the 1720s, however, the term "English interest" had acquired a quite different political usage, denoting those in the Irish administration and Irish parliament who, on issues like Wood's Halfpence, supported English government at all costs. Correspondingly, in this terminology, it was the "patriot" opposition in the Dublin Parliament which now constituted the "Irish interest." Robert Molesworth, a patriot *eminence grise*, could be praised by an admirer as "the best of friends to poor Ireland's rights," while a heartfelt panegyric on another of rhe country's parliamentary defenders, Dublin alderman John Stoyte, called upon "Irish druids" to join in the lament.[7] A similar raising of patriotic consciousness can be found in literary circles. Whereas writers like Farquhar and Steele carelessly ridiculed their fellow Irishmen, the playwright William Philips, grandson of the Ulster plantation servitor Sir Thomas, contributed to the patriot cause in 1722 an allegorical denunciation of English and Hanoverian exploitation, *Hibernia Freed*, in which the heroes were Gaelic chieftains and high-kings.[8] The emphasis is already swinging away from the English origins of the Ascendancy. To borrow a term from the philologists, we seem to be witnessing the supersession of a national identity best labelled "Hiberno-English" by one that is more appropriately expressed as "Anglo-Irish."

In telescoping this process I have undoubtedly made the emergence of a dominant sense of Irishness appear more rapid and smoother than it actually was. For there were formidable obstacles to be surmounted before an Irish Protestant could happily call himself an Irishman. The first was the habit of referring to the Irish Catholics (and, to add to the confusion, the "Old English" Catholics, the pre-Reformation settlers, as well as the Gaels) as "the Irish" *tout court*. The Jacobite army in the war of 1689–1691 was invariably "the Irish army," in Protestant commentaries, while the agent for the Irish estates of the Wentworth family was one of many to claim afterwards that he had been "a great sufferer by the Irish in the late troubles."[9] In 1699 "several of the Irish," that is to say Catholic ex-Jacobites, were arrested in County Clare for returning from France without the requisite royal license, and a newspaper announcement of festivities on 1 July (old style) explained that this was "the anniversary of the overthrow of the Irish, at the Boyne."[10] The usage was naturally frequent in Protestant sermons commemorating the outbreak of the rebellion of 1641. A Church of Ireland bishop, St. George Ashe, preached a typical homily in 1712, identifying the Catholics as "the natives of our kingdom" and drawing the contrast between Irish papists and English Protestants, between "the Irish" in Ireland and the English interest there.[11] It was an attitude fostered by the persistence of the plantation principle. Schemes of colonization continued to be devised into the eighteenth century, as landlords bent on the improvement of their estates or the maintenance of the reformed religion sought to attract Protestant tenants, whether English or refugees from Europe like the Huguenots and Palatines.[12]

No less of a deterrent to an assumption of Irish nationality, at least at the beginning of this period, was the changing image of the Irishman in late seventeenth- and early eighteenth-century England. Restoration comedy had extended the former simplistic stereotype of the ferocious savage and, with the aid of a best-selling jestbook, *Bogg-Witticisms*, had popularized the idea of "Teague" as a richly humorous character, ridiculous and contemptible where once he had been a blood-curdling monster.[13] "Irish" became a byword for anything inferior, and Protestants in Ireland conceded that their country was now despised in England. And what was worse, the stage Irishman was now no longer drawn more or less exclusively from the lower orders. The Irish gentleman, a down-at-heel army officer much given to bragging, duelling and chasing widows, was becoming a familiar literary figure. Sir Ulick MacKilligut and his ilk usually bore recognizably "native Irish" names, and were intended in many cases to represent the ruined Catholic "pretended jontleman," as one dramatist put it, and not the "real gentlemen of Ireland."[14] But at the same time there was nothing in the characterization that was necessarily denominational, and often the satire was designed to include the Protestant gentry within its scope. English Country Party polemics over the question of the resumption of the Irish forfeited estates in 1699–1703, which were directed specifically against the complaining "poor Protestant purchasers" in Ireland, those Anglo-Irish squires who had bought or leased lands from the original grantees and who were now to be dispossessed, made great play with the conventions of anti-Irish humour, labelling their opponents as "some Irish folks," and attributing to them "typically" Irish bulls and blunders.[15] It was presumably this constant derision, as much as the Catholic connotations of the word "Irish," which made the first Duke of Ormonde "devilishly nettled" to be called an Irishman, when, as the world knew full well, he had been born in London.[16] Lord Abercorn was clear that what he resented was his countrymen being "made the subject of jests by the worst part of our neighbours."[17] Paradoxically, though, as Abercorn's comment perhaps implies, the effect on an Irish Protestant of having his Irishness rammed down his throat by English humorists may in the long run have produced a patriotic reaction. By 1731 an Irishman had been moved to reply in print to the "reflections" to which his compatriots were being subjected; and when some ten years later Sir Charles Hanbury Williams penned a few witty verses on the exploits of a "Milesian" fortune-hunter he raised a storm of Irish indignation and was for a time hounded out of London society, to take his refuge, as Horace Walpole said, in a foreign embassy.[18]

For a time, and it is particularly noticeable in the reigns of King William III and Queen Anne, two concepts of Irish nationality were current among Anglican Protestants in Ireland, one defining only the indigenous Gaelic and Catholic Irish as "the Irish" and the Protestants as "the English interest"; the other regarding all the inhabitants of the island as "Irish" and on occasion going so far as to talk of the Protestants as the true Irish nation. It was possible for even someone like Molesworth to think of himself as English in some ways and Irish in others; for the historian Sir Richard Cox to aim his history of *Hibernia Anglicana* at "the inhabitants" of the country, or elsewhere to write that he had "behaved himself like a true Englishman, which . . . is not inconsistent with a tender affection for my native country"; and for Lord Abercorn to regret the absence of "English" tenantry on his property to offset the presence of the "Irish" while he saw the Protestants not just as "the inhabitants of Ireland" but as "the whole nation."[19] The same confusion vitiated political theorizing. Henry Maxwell's *Essay upon an Union of Ireland with England* (1704) talked of Ireland on the one hand as a "colony" or "province" of England and on the other as a "nation" or "kingdom" in its own right. Undoubtedly some distinction should be drawn between those Irishmen of comparatively more recent vintage, from seventeenth-century planter families, and those whose connexion with the country went back many more generations. The former (including all but one of the examples cited above) were more likely to be conscious of their "colonial" origins. Similarly one might contrast those semi-absentees (like Molesworth) who maintained establishments on both sides of the Irish Sea, with others whose sole residence was in Ireland. But the practice of thinking in two ways about nationality was widespread among Protestants and almost habitual. Even when Swift calculatingly addressed his fourth "Drapier's Letter" to "the whole people of Ireland" he slipped back into using "the Irish" to refer to the Catholics and "the true English people of Ireland" for the Protestants, describing the arch-patriot William Molyneux, of all people, as "an English gentleman born here."[20] Of course, Swift was in one sense arguing for the rights of Irish Protestants as Englishmen who just happened to be domiciled on the "wrong" side of the water. A clearer instance of the coexistence in the Ascendancy mind of the two concepts of Irish nationality comes from a poem by a Church of Ireland rector, Edmund Arwaker, written in 1694. Recalling the Jacobite war, Arwaker at first tells how "Hibernia that unhappy land, her empress Albion durst withstand, and strove to wrest the sceptre from her hand." However, when the war is over we find that Hibernia has been subjected not to Albion but to "her sovereign," and now "pleased with the blessings of his gentle reign," she can "sing her liberty regained, which, if unconquered, she had ne'er obtained."[21] In other words, we start with the notion of a Gaelic Ireland struggling to throw off the domination of England, and end with a quite different scenario, William, King of Ireland, saving the Protestant kingdom from the tyrant James.

To accept the idea of a Protestant Hibernia required that something be done about the Catholics, whose presence in the background threatened to spoil this idealized picture. Their claim to be more Irish than the Anglo-Irish had to be dealt with. The most radical solution is to be found in William Molyneux's celebrated *Case of Ireland*, a simple denial of their separate, special status. It was, Molyneux wrote, "manifest that the greatest body of the present people of Ireland, are the progeny of the English and Britons [i.e. Welsh], that from time to time have come over to this kingdom, and there remaining a mere handful of the ancient Irish at this time, I may say, not one in a thousand."[22] The Protestants, therefore, as the propertied class, constituted the political nation, "the people," in the same way that the propertied class did in England. It was not, however, necessary to go this far in order to relegate the native Irish from their place as "the Irish, properly so called." The means more readily at hand was a systematic denigration of their character and way of life, all aspects of which were represented as primitive, barbaric and squalid. Without the good example set by the Protestants among them, it was said, the Catholic peasantry would "let all run into its original wilderness, and live like cannibals one upon another, or like their native wolves, from whom they are now but one degree removed."[23] The impression of barbarism and near-bestiality thus built up is reflected in the adjectives commonly chosen to distinguish the Catholic "natives": the "wild Irish," the "mere Irish," and the significantly ambiguous "natural Irish." The effect was to make the ordinary peasant appear less than human, and to make it easier for the Protestant gentleman to appropriate his nationality.

In overcoming the several obstacles to their developing national awareness, early eighteenth-century Irish Protestants also made particular use of two elements in the symbolism of Irish nationality: St. Patrick as the country's patron saint; and Hibernia as her classical personification. St. Patrick's Day was celebrated by Protestants as well as Catholics with great enthusiasm. Swift on one occasion encountered crowds of expatriate Irishmen parading in the Mall with crosses about their persons, while in 1698 there was a report that King William himself had "done the Irishmen the honour to wear the cross in his hat."[24] It is not difficult to see how the saint could have meant so much to the Protestants. Contemporary Anglican theology, imbued with the influence of patristic scholarship, emphasized the desirability of returning to the practices of the "primitive" church. Moreover, one of the principal themes in sixteenth- and seventeenth-century Irish historiography had been the Protestant effort to demonstrate the purity and independence from Rome of early Christianity in Ireland.[25] St. Patrick might appear, therefore, as the founding father of Irish Protestantism. Similarly "Hibernia" provided Protestant Ireland with a national symbol reaching beyond association with the Gaelic world to a remote and idealized classical past. In her sororal relationship with Brittania, she also expressed perfectly the common Protestant view of Anglo-Irish relations, an alliance of equals, whether it be elder and younger sibling or, as Swift represented it in the unpublished "Story of the Injured Lady," of bride and suitor. "Hibernia," "Hibernian" and such derivations as "Hibernicus" were common currency in early eighteenth-century patriot literature, and in polite correspondence, where, for example, Lord Orrery might acknowledge that the beauty of the Irish countryside had "turned me into a Hibernian."[26] It may not be too far-fetched to suggest that this phraseology had the additional attraction of enabling an Anglo-Irishman to avoid having to call himself "Irish." I would not wish to press the point, for clearly a great deal can be ascribed to mere literary convention; but in the light of what has been said about the changing English stereotype of the Irishman, it does seem that there are occasions when the devising of circumlocutions of this sort becomes almost obsessive. A patriot poem of 1780, proclaiming the decline of old England and the rise of a new Irish nation, shows a particularly fertile invention. Ireland is "Hibernia," "Ierne," "this green isle"; its maidens are "daughters of the Hibernian soil," "virgins of the Atlantic shore," "daughters of the Atlantic plain." Nothing, and no one, is ever "Irish."[27]

One might ask why the notion of Britishness, as an umbrella national identity, did not offer the early eighteenth-century Irish Protestant an intellectual and semantic escape-route from dilemmas over national allegiance. The answer is simple: for most Anglo-Irishmen the overpowering difficulty with the term "British" was that it implied a community of interest with the Ulster Scots, who were indeed sometimes referred to as "the British interest."[28] Antagonism between Church of Ireland Protestants and Presbyterians was one of the driving forces in early eighteenth-century Irish politics, producing bitter party divisions in Queen Anne's reign between Whigs, who favoured some degree of toleration for Protestant Dissenters and a united front against the threat of popery, and

Tories and High Churchmen who took the opposite view, that the graver danger to the establishment in Church and state came from the Presbyterians.[29] *Some Queries upon the Demand of the Presbyterians to Have the Sacramental Test Repealed*, published in 1733, demanded to know "whether the Scottish Ulster Presbyterian farmers, tradesmen and cottagers ... be not a more knavish, wicked, thievish race than even the natural Irish of the other three provinces."[30] Prior to the 1740s, when the designation "Briton" does begin to occur a trifle more frequently, there are only rare instances of Anglo-Irish Protestants calling themselves "British" or talking of a "British interest" in Ireland, and these either date from times of crisis for the Protestant community in Ireland, or appear in the work of writers expounding the theme of Protestant unity.[31]

There are undoubtedly some elements in the picture of the developing national identity of early eighteenth-century Irish Protestants which would justify a theory of "colonial nationalism," or at least something like it. A sense of Irish nationality could be acquired by the Anglo-Irishman not just by breeding or birth, but by the mere fact of residence in the country. Transplanted Englishmen, such as the Church of Ireland Primate Thomas Lindsay, a stalwart of the "patriot" party in the Irish House of Lords in George I's reign, could in due course become staunch upholders of the "Irish interest." An Irishman observed in 1702 that "had we a new set [of office-holders] taken out of London, that had no knowledge or engagements in Ireland, yet in seven years they would carry a grudge in their hearts against the oppressions of England; and as their interest in Irish ground increased, so would their aversion to the place they left."[32] The coincidence of peaks of anti-English sentiment with periods of acute financial insecurity, in the late 1690s and early 1700s say, or the late 1740s and early 1750s, suggests a direct link between national feeling and economic self-interest on the part of gentlemen whose rents were exceedingly slow in coming in. So too does the history of the patriotic agitation in the Irish Parliament in the 1720s. A constitutional grievance, the 1720 English Declaratory Act, which denied the Irish House of Lords its appellate jurisdiction and asserted the right of the English Parliament to legislate for Ireland, elicited not a whimper of protest in succeeding sessions of the Irish Parliament. But against Wood's Halfpence those same "patriot" M.P.s and peers were vociferous to a fault.

A case could also be made, though less forcefully, that many of the manifestations of Protestant Irishness in the first half of the eighteenth century parallelled nothing so closely as English provincial self-consciousness. Englishmen had, after all, been accustomed for generations to think of their county as their "country." Thus the annual feasts organized for Irish Protestants in London, to follow sermons com-

memorating 1641, have their counterparts in similar festivals of local patriotism held in the metropolis for Wiltshiremen, Suffolk men, Cumbrians
or North country men in general.[33] It might even be argued that the pride
the Anglo-Irish were coming to display in their capital city and their institutions, from their Parliament, with its imposing new accommodation,
to the race-course at the Curragh, "our Newmarket,"[34] differed in scale
rather than essence from the civic pride of the populace of English provincial cities like Bristol, Norwich and York. In Ireland, however, the distinction between civic and national pride is harder to make. As the national
capital, Dublin had a symbolic importance; and most of its institutions,
university, King's Inns, above all Parliament, were to some degree national
institutions. Outside Dublin, there is evidence of a certain amount of
localist sentiment with which a more truly "national" feeling might be effectively contrasted. In politics, for example, regional loyalties sometimes
helped give rise to factions based on county or provincial groupings. Speaker Conolly, himself an Ulsterman, was said to have found his chief support among the "Northern Members," while his great rival for the
leadership of the Irish Whig party, Lord Chancellor Midleton, commanded
a "Cork squadron" from his native county.[35] But as Professor Oliver
MacDonagh has observed, localism did not take a powerful hold on the
emotions of the Anglo-Irish: "In the minds of the planters of the Willia-
mite era, Ireland was . . . undifferentiated internally."[36] In part this was
because the very Irishness of the Anglo-Irish was in itself a kind of localism, with Protestant Ireland a "petite patrie" in the greater English cultural and political empire.

Yet there were important ways in which Anglo-Irish patriotism did
represent a more distinctive sense of national identity. By the 1750s the
Anglo-Irish had succeeded not only in developing a perception of separate
economic and political interests, but in rooting themselves in the Irish past.
We have seen how William Molyneux attempted to write Gaelic Ireland
out of existence, so to speak, so that he could begin the history of the
seventeenth-century Irish nation with the Norman invader, Strongbow,
and identify his fellow Protestants with the Anglo-Norman constitutional heritage. The same effect was achieved through the denigration of contemporary Gaelic Ireland and the elaboration for the Anglo-Irish of a
national symbolism of their own. But at the same time, Protestant anti-
quarians and historians, including two Church of Ireland bishops, William Nicolson of Derry and Francis Hutchinson of Down and Connor,
were discovering in the Gaelic past a civilization comparable to that of
the ancient Greeks, or so it was claimed. Their findings and the work of
Catholic scholars were being presented to an English-speaking audience
in Ireland, and often the subscription lists for these histories were largely

composed of Protestant gentlemen. What has been diagnosed as "a more positive attitude" to the Gaelic past, and even to the Gaelic present, is already apparent in Protestant Ireland in the 1740s. *The Ancient and Present State of the County Down*, published in 1744, the first fruit of the Dublin-based Physico-Historical Society and its schemes for a systematic local history of Ireland, was specifically concerned to refute current English calumnies against the "native Irish" and to vindicate their culture and customs from the charge of barbarism.[37] Shortly afterwards we find the Dublin apothecary Charles Lucas, the *enfant terrible* of Irish politics, and the author of some traditional anti-papist invective, adopting a historical perspective which enables him to sympathize with the wrongs the native Irish have suffered. At one stage he is even prepared to deny one of the great principles of Protestant Irish political theory, that the frequency of rebellions in the kingdom had been due solely to the innate perfidiousness and bloodthirstiness of the natives. Instead, he blames "the oppressions, instigation, evil influence and connivance of the English."[38]

Of course the period from ca. 1745 to ca. 1790, which in retrospect might be looked upon as the golden age of Protestant patriotism, was also the zenith of Protestant self-confidence, after the demise of Jacobitism and before the rise of the republican and Catholic Emancipation movements. Anglo-Irish attitudes in the early nineteenth century are doubtless much more complex, with the returning motif of ambivalence. Nonetheless, by 1750 the Anglo-Irish had succeeded in creating a brand of "nationalism" that in spirit was far from "colonial." This was one aspect of a maturing political culture: the same underlying process that is reflected in such apparently diverse concurrent phenomena as the growth of a lively domestic "Grub Street" press, and the erection of the grandiose public architecture for which Georgian Dublin is famed. And at a time when, we are told, the ruling *élites* of Scotland and Wales were fast abandoning their native culture and institutions in a keen pursuit of Anglicization,[39] in Ireland at least, this trend in English "internal colonialism" was being put into reverse.

NOTES

1 In its original form, this paper was delivered at the Annual Meeting of the American Society for Eighteenth-Century Studies at Williamsburg in March 1986. I should like to thank those present for their comments.

2 J. G. Simms, *Colonial Nationalism 1698–1776: Molyneux's "The Case of Ireland ... Stated"* (Cork: Mercier Press, 1976); *A New History of Ireland, Vol. IV:*

Eighteenth-Century Ireland 1691–1800, eds. T. W. Moody and W. E. Vaughan (Oxford: Clarendon Press, 1986), esp. J. L. McCracken, "Protestant Ascendancy and the Rise of Colonial Nationalism, 1714–60" (104–22), and R. B. McDowell, "Colonial Nationalism and the Winning of Parliamentary Independence, 1760–82" (196–235).

3 R. Jebb, *Studies in Colonial Nationalism* (London: E. Arnold, 1905).

4 D. G. Boyce, *Nationalism in Ireland* (London: Croom Helm, 1982), 106–8.

5 *The Miscellaneous Works of . . . John Toland . . .* (2 vols., London, 1747), 1:liii–liv; 2:318–22, 459–63; E. Ludlow, *A Voyce from the Watch Tower. Part V: 1660–1662*, ed. A. B. Worden (Camden 4th ser., London: Royal Historical Society, 1978), 42; P. Kelly, "A Pamphlet Attributed to John Toland and an Unpublished Reply by Archbishop William King," *Topoi* 4 (1985): 81–90; Toland, *The Art of Governing by Partys* (1701), 105–6; G. Carabelli, *Tolandiana . . .* (Florence: Nova Italia, 1975), 219, 223–24; J. G. Simms, "John Toland (1670–1722), a Donegal Heretic," *Irish Historical Studies* 16 (1968–9): 315; J. B. Duke-Evans, "The Political Theory and Practice of the English Commonwealthsmen 1695–1725" (Oxford University D. Phil. thesis, 1980), 213–15, 217–18, 220, 228–29.

6 Toland, *Works*, 2:349, 381, 405, 407–9, 429, 459, 466.

7 *A Funeral Elegy on the . . . Death of Robert Vis[count] Molesworth . . . By M. B.* [1725]; *An Elegy on the . . . Death of Alderman J[ohn] S[toyte]* (Dublin, 1728), 12, 25.

8 G. C. Duggan, *The Stage Irishman: A History of the Irish Play and Stage Characters* (Dublin: Talbot Press, 1937), 168, 220–22, 239–41; Farquhar, *The Recruiting Officer*, ed. M. Shugrue (London: E. Arnold, 1965), 14; *The Spectator*, ed. D. F. Bond, 5 vols., (Oxford: Clarendon Press, 1965), 1:87–88, 2:217, 598, 4:104; W. Philips, *Hibernia Freed* (London, 1722). I hope to publish an account of Philips's career and writings.

9 British Library, Additional MS. 22192, f. 11.

10 *Flying Post*, 16–18 Nov. 1699; *Post Boy*, 8–11 July 1699.

11 St. G. Ashe, *A Sermon Preached to the Protestants of Ireland, Now in London, at the Parish Church of St. Clement Dane, October 23, 1712* (London, 1712), 5–7, 20–22.

12 C. O[tway], *Sketches in Erris and Tyrawley* (Dublin, 1841), pp. 347–48 *et seq.*; D. L. Savory, "The Huguenot-Palatine Settlements in the Counties of Limerick, Kerry and Tipperary," *Proceedings of the Huguenot Society of London* 17 (1947–52): 127–29; Grace L. Lee, *The Huguenot Settlements in Ireland* (London: Longmans, 1936); L. M. Cullen, *The Emergence of Modern Ireland 1600–1900* (London: Batsford, 1981), 37–38, 77–78.

13 See Duggan, *Stage Irishman*, passim; J. O. Bartley, "Bulls and Bog Witticisms," *Irish Book Lover* 30 (1946–8): 59–62.

14 Duggan, *Stage Irishman*, 274–75.

15 J. Trenchard, *A Letter from a Soldier* (London, 1702), 16, 20; *The Several Addresses of Some Irish Folks* (London, n.d.), 4.

16 "Letters of Richard Thompson to His Brother Henry," ed. J. J. Cartwright, *Camden Miscellany VIII* (Camden Society, new ser., 1883), 31–33.

17 Public Record Office of Northern Ireland, T.2541/I.K./1/5 (Abercorn MSS.), Abercorn to Edward Southwell, 19 Dec. 1713.

18 *A Modest Argument, Pro and Con, Enquiring into the Cause Why Base and Mean Actions Should Be Committed by the Irish in Particular, More than Any Other Nation* (London, 1731); *The Works of the Right Honourable Sir Charles Hanbury Williams*, 3 vols. (London, 1822), 1:91–3; Horace Walpole, *Memoirs of King George II*, ed. J. Brooke, 3 vols. (New Haven: Yale U.P., 1985), 1: 138; See also A. P. W. Malcomson, *The Pursuit of the Heiress: Aristocratic Marriage in Ireland 1750–1820* (Belfast: Ulster Historical Foundation, 1982), 29. Of course, it might equally well be argued that an enhanced sense of Irishness made Anglo-Irishmen more sensitive; i.e. that the egg preceded the chicken.

19 Historical Manuscripts Commission, *Various Collections*, 8:284; *Calendar of State Papers, Domestic*, 1699–1700, 36; Duke-Evans, "English Commonwealthsmen," 213–15; J. C. Beckett, *Confrontations: Studies in Irish History* (London: Faber, 1972), 11; Brit. Lib., Add. MS. 29589, f. 310; P.R.O. Northern Ireland, T.2541/F.A. 1/1/9 (Abercorn MSS.), Abercorn to R. Plumer, 15 Oct. 1717; T.2541/I.K./1/5, same to Edward Southwell, 19 Dec. 1713.

20 Swift, *The Drapier's Letters*, ed. H. Davis (Oxford: Clarendon Press, 1935), 79, 81, 85.

21 E. Arwaker, *An Elegy on His Excellency Lieutenant-General Tolmach* (London, 1694), 5–6.

22 W. Molyneux, *The Case of Ireland ... Stated* (London, 1698; repr. Dublin: Cadenus Press, 1977, as "Irish Writings from the Age of Swift," V), 34–35.

23 *Some Account of the Irish ...* (London, 1753), esp. 33–34.

24 Swift, *Journal to Stella*, ed. H. Williams, 2 vols. (Oxford: B. Blackwell, 1948), 2:640; Folger Shakespeare Library, L.C.2751, Newdigate newsletter, 18 Mar. 1697 [-8].

25 Jacqueline R. Hill, " 'There Was an Englishman, an Irishman and a Scotsman ...': Perceptions of Irish History, 1690–1790" (forthcoming). I am very grateful to Dr. Hill for allowing me to read this article in advance of publication, for several illuminating discussions on its subject-matter, and, not least, for scrutinizing an early draft of the present paper.

26 *Hibernicus' Letters*, 2 vols. (London, 1729); Lord Orrery in 1747, quoted in Constantia Maxwell, *The Stranger in Ireland* (London: J. Cape, 1954), 154.

27 *The Contrast: Or a Comparison between the Characters of the English and Irish in the Year 1780* (Dublin, 1780).

28 *Reasons Why the Bill to Prevent the Growth of Schism ... Should Not Be Extended to Ireland* (Brit. Lib., Dept. of Printed Bks., 516. m. 18 [71]), a broadsheet dating from 1714, explained to an English audience that Protestant Dissenters in Ireland were principally to be found in the province of Ulster, "where the strength of the British interest lies." See also [D. Defoe], *The Parallel: Or Persecution of Protestants the Shortest Way to Prevent the Growth of Popery in Ireland* (Dublin, 1705), 24–25.

29 D. W. Hayton, "Ireland and the English Ministers, 1707–16" (Oxford Univ. D.Phil. thesis, 1975), 2–5, 30–39, 104–108, 120–148.

30 For amusing evidence of the depth of animosity even a decade later, see *The Wouns o' the Kirk of Scotland* (Dublin, 1743).

31 Trinity College, Dublin., MS. 1.6.13, ff. 189–90, James Bonnell to Rev. John Strype, 18 Oct. 1692 (I owe this reference to Mr. J. I. McGuire); J. Stearne, *A Sermon on the Prayer of Moses* (Dublin, 1695), 9. See above, n. 29.

32 Quoted in W. E. H. Lecky, *A History of Ireland in the Eighteenth Century*, new edn., 5 vols. (London, 1892), 1:401.

33 *Daily Courant*, 19 Oct. 1713; Hist. MSS. Comm., *Townshend MSS.*, p. 130; "The Wiltshire Society," *Wiltshire Notes and Queries* 2 (1896–9):35; G. Holmes, *British Politics in the Age of Anne* (London: Macmillan, 1967), 301; J. D. Marshall, "Cumberland and Westmorland Societies in London, 1734–1914," *Transactions of the Cumberland and Westmorland Antiquarian Archaeological Society* 84 (1984):239; *The London Diaries of William Nicolson, Bishop of Carlisle 1702–1718*, eds. C. Jones and G. Holmes (Oxford: Clarendon Press, 1985), 6, 330.

34 *The Letters of Joseph Addison*, ed. W. Graham (Oxford: Clarendon Press, 1941), 149.

35 Hayton, "Ireland and the English Ministers," 113.

36 O. MacDonagh, *States of Mind: A Study of Anglo–Irish Conflict 1780–1980* (London: G. Allen & Unwin, 1983), 15–16.

37 Ann De Valera, "Antiquarian and Historical Investigations in Ireland in the Eighteenth Century" (Univ. Coll. Dublin, M.A. thesis, 1978), Chapters 1–2.

38 S. Murphy, "Charles Lucas and the Dublin Election of 1748–1749," *Parliamentary History* 2 (1983): 94, 96.

39 M. Hechter, *Internal Colonialism: The Celtic Fringe in British National Development 1536–1966* (London: Routledge & K. Paul, 1975), 109–19; P. Jenkins, *The Making of a Ruling Class: The Glamorgan Gentry 1640–1790* (Cambridge: Cambridge U.P., 1983), 209–10, 213–14.

From "the French and Dutch are more sober, frugal and industrious" to the "nobler" position: Attitudes of the Prince of Wales toward a General Naturalization and a Popular Monarchy, 1757-1760

JOHN L. BULLION

During the years 1757–1760, as the earl of Bute contemplated how to prepare the future George III for his destiny as king, he decided that his royal pupil must understand the causes of, and the best solution for, a situation that many contemporaries believed to be the principal danger to the future expansion of British commerce: the high cost of labor in Britain. Accordingly, he assigned the relevant literature, indicated his own preferences among the competing theories, and required the prince to write essays on this and related subjects.[1] In all but one of these essays, George argued that the expense of labor was directly related to the weight of taxation on the "necessaries" of the poor, such as candles, soap, malt liquor for brewing beer, and the leather and skins necessary for making shoes and clothes. Such taxes raised the price of these necessities of life, and were "in their own nature severe and offensive, because they fall heavy on the poorest of the people who cannot indemnify themselves but by raising the price of their labor." They were also "contrary to sound politics, as the price of manufactures rise[s] with the price of labor." The end result of this process was obvious. "The sale of our manufactures . . . must diminish by every such aggravation of the price of them, as the cheapest [goods] at foreign markets are generally preferred to the best." Any decline in trade was harmful to Britain, for "our national profits sympathize with our foreign sales." And "what is of more importance than all the rest," the prince concluded, "these [taxes] give a rigid and oppressive air to government, which becomes odious from the minute it appears to be so."[2] Thus they "ought to be removed entirely, or reduced to very moderate [duties]."[3]

In one essay, however, which he wrote in 1757, and titled "On Industry in Great Britain," George questioned the significance of these opinions. Without denying that taxes on necessities raised wages, he claimed that they were a minor cause of the high price British manufacturers paid for work. And without discarding his conviction that the burden of taxation on the poor should be lightened, he proposed other, more radical cures for the heavy expense of labor. Thus, a description of "On Industry in Great Britain" permits scholars to know the full range of ideas and policy alternatives that Bute and the prince seriously considered.[4] Moreover, an understanding of the reasons why they finally rejected the policies espoused in that essay gives an insight into the political strategy Bute and George developed during the 1750s for governing Britain.

I

The prince began "On Industry in Great Britain" by referring to general principles. "The number of inhabitants, and particularly of laboring people, provided they are employed," he asserted, "is the real wealth and strength of a state." On the other hand, "an idle and debauched populace [is] one of the greatest grievances a commercial state can labor under." Such an unproductive populace diminished a state's commerce, and "without commerce, no country can grow rich." "What is worse," a country without commerce "can never be secure against the encroachments of ambitious neighbors." And, as George recognized, the fact that Britain was an island would not preserve her security should she lose her trade. "An island without foreign commerce," he pointed out, "can have but an indifferent navy, [and] consequently cannot protect itself."

Having established to his satisfaction the premier importance of productive laborers to commerce, and of commerce to the state, the prince briefly sketched the development of manufacturing in Europe and in England. In his account, he emphasized two factors. One was the decisions governments made about trade and manufacturing, for the prince was certain that intelligent political leadership could overcome many obstacles. The other was the national characters of the various peoples of Europe. "Queen Elizabeth," for example, "with the assistance of able ministers and the wisdom of Parliament, carried the superiority of both [commerce and manufacturing] to an amazing height." Among other decisions, the encouragement they gave to highly skilled, "naturally industrious" Flemish workers to immigrate to England helped make English manufacturers "the best and most perfect in Europe." As the trade in these goods flourished, the navy "soon became the terror of the world." But when the quality of English leadership declined, the Dutch and the French began to enjoy the advantage in trade. In part, this was due to wise decisions in those countries, but it owed even more to the fact that "the French and Dutch are more sober, frugal, and industrious than the English." In the prince's opinion, an understanding of this difference in national character was crucial to any grasp of the success and failure in a nation's commerce, and central to any plans for meaningful change.

George's commitment to this concept may be clearly seen in his explanation of why France, "by underselling the English, have got the greatest part of [the] Turkish, Italian, and Spanish trades." As he noted, "Postlethwayt gives the national debt, and the continuation of taxes, as the cause of this."[5] "Perhaps he may be right in part," the prince conceded, "but undoubtedly the national debt is not the principal source of the high price of labor." Rather, that was "the general disposition of the manufacturers to idleness and debauchery." What caused the general disposition to idleness? Because the number of laborers in Britain was relatively small compared to other countries, and because they could be confident of finding employment whenever they wanted it, they could choose when, how much, and how efficiently they worked. What they decided depended on the price of basic necessities. "When provisions are cheap," according to the prince, "they work less." "When they are dear, they work better and more constantly, [and] therefore their work is cheaper." But the poor were not merely idle, they were also debauched by a taste for things beyond their station in life, the result of "the manner of living" they enjoyed in Britain. "If the poor will give up superfluities, and pay taxes only on their necessaries," the prince calculated that their taxes "will not amount to a thirty-sixth part of what they earn." In contrast, the Dutch paid six times more in taxes on necessities. Thus it did not surprise George to learn that "the necessaries the poor ought to consume are not dearer in England than in France and Holland." The crucial difference was not taxes, but habits of consumption. "When wheat is very dear, the French poor eat but little bread and content themselves with roots, while our manufacturers cry out they are starving unless they can eat the finest bread in as great quantities as when wheat is very cheap." This "indulgence in unnecessary things" was not confined to the finest bread, either. The prince believed the taste for luxuries "is carried to a very extraordinary height in this kingdom, for the manufacturing populace consume brandy, gin, tea, sugar, foreign fruit, strong beer, printed linens, snuff, tobacco, etc." While they had "these superfluities," George concluded, "no one can think the price of labor too low." He pointed to the example of "one little manufacturing town in the west of England, of about three thousand inhabitants, [where] excise [duties are] paid for two thousand hogshead on strong beer, beside what is spent in spirituous liquors." To the prince, this was "a strong proof of exorbitant wages." Moreover, there was other proof that "our manufacturing poor instead of being the strength and riches of the state, are become a burden to it." Presumably because many were unwilling to work, "the poor rate [has] increased within the last century from £700,000 to £2,500,000 *per annum.*" But even more to the point, the relative scarcity of productive labor enabled those who did work to command higher wages and thus both to feed and to stimulate further their extraordinary appetite for luxuries. Thus the high cost of labor in Britain, though affected to a certain extent by taxes, was in fact largely due to the scarcity of labor and to the way of life of the poor there. Lowering the cost of labor would therefore require more than lowering taxes.

According to the prince, one course of action in particular would both increase the numbers of the laboring poor and improve their moral and economic behavior. Borrowing from Elizabeth's example, he argued that "the most expeditious means of increasing the number of people, of keeping down the price of labor, of enforcing industry, and of improving our manufacturers, is by a general naturalization" of foreign Protestants. By "general naturalization" George meant permitting foreigners to become subjects merely by swearing the appropriate oaths to the government and taking communion in any Protestant church, rather than restricting naturalization to each individual immigrant who had the time, money, and connections to obtain a private Act of Parliament. Removing this restriction would, he was sure, encourage many foreign Protestants to immigrant to Britain.[6] These people, who were accustomed to hard work, low wages, and a less luxurious manner of living, would by their numbers and industriousness compel native Britons to work harder and cheaper. Thus "the gentry, the clergy, and the farmers would be benefitted by the improvement of their lands." English manufactured goods "would be improved and rendered cheaper, which would increase foreign trade," which in turn would increase "the number of ships and sailors thus employed [which are] the means of a large navy." A general naturalization would also, the prince predicted, induce "many rich men," already attracted by "the excellence or our constitution," to settle in Britain, and by their wealth improve the resources of the nation.

But as obvious as the benefits of a general naturalization law were to the prince, he was well aware that others "violently opposed" it. So he proposed, "if this remedy cannot be adopted, the example of the Dutch ought to be followed," and laborers compelled "to work moderately six days in the week." "This would," George believed, "be equal to an increase of one-third of [the] manufacturing people, [and] some think it would amount to above twenty millions more *per annum* in commodities than are now produced." He advised supplementing this policy by using "every means . . . to oblige the poor [who were not working] to work six days in the week," which would produce "an addition of ten millions worth of commodities *per annum*." He concluded by insisting that without a general naturalization, "the only method of preventing the French and Dutch from underselling us is to establish a good policy by which the poor would be kept to work, and less given to luxury, idleness, and debauchery." George was not sanguine about the ease with which establishing that good policy could be achieved. As he commented, "Making laws to answer this object [is] difficult." Still, he obviously felt that the benefits of success would justify the effort.

After making these bold proposals for lowering the price of labor, the prince ended "On Industry in Great Britain" in a less controversial fashion, by listing nine "general commercial maxims [which] are invariable unless from a great change of circumstances." Most of these stressed the interdependence of the commercial and landed interest, and the crucial importance of maintaining a favorable balance of trade, both with foreign nations and with colonies. Unsurprisingly, he noted that "the prosperity of our trade depends very much on the encouragement given to our manufactures, or laws made relative thereto." It also, he observed, "depends upon the judicious manner of laying and collecting our taxes, and upon the ease, readiness, freedom and cheapness of exportation." This observation did not contradict his basic position in the essay. He had not insisted that taxation played no role in establishing wages; rather he argued it was a comparatively less important factor. George concluded his list with this maxim: "the prosperity, strength, riches, and even the well-being of this kingdom depends on our being able to sell our native produce and manufactures as cheap, and as good in quality, in foreign markets as any other commercial state." No doubt the prince's acknowledgement of this truth strengthened his conviction that the cost of labor had to be lowered, either by a general naturalization or by a stricter regulation of laboring people.

II

The source for the prince's ideas and reforms in "On Industry in Great Britain" is obvious. All of the ideas expressed in this essay—the stinging critique of the "manner of living " of Britain's manufacturers, the effect of their habits on the price of labor, the insistence that that cost must be lowered or trade would suffer, the unfavorable comparison of English with European laborers, the citation of examples from the Tudor era, the various advantages of encouraging immigration, and the plans for compelling the poor to work more regularly and constantly—had been used by those who favored a general naturalization in Parliament and in pamphlets for many years.[7] In particular, "On Industry in Great Britain" bears the marks of its author's familiarity with the arguments and proposals of one of the ablest and most outspoken proponents of that policy, Josiah Tucker.[8] These ideas were not, of course, original with either Tucker or other supporters of relaxing the laws governing naturalization. During the seventeenth and the first half of the eighteenth centuries, most who theorized about the economic roles of the poor posited a direct relationship between the cost of labor and the volume of trade, stressed the necessity of providing regular, constant employment for the poor and requiring them to work , and enlivened their arguments with "frequent blasts against 'idleness.'"[9] Those who favored a general naturalization adopted these doctrines enthusiastically. They justified encouraging immigration by referring to them as undeniable descriptions of present reality and irrefutable prescriptions for future policy. As they did so, they ignored or discounted the ideas of men such as Daniel Defoe, who had questioned the prevailing views by arguing instead that high wages did not necessarily hinder productivity or stagnate trade, and that idleness was often the result of an absence of incentives for laborers.[10] Even Tucker, whose subtle and powerful mind was attracted by the objections Defoe and, later, David Hume raised against the assumption that a growing trade required low wages, submerged his interest in their arguments whenever he advocated a general naturalization.[11] Thus the prince and Bute were left unexposed to any views which challenged the orthodoxies of the seventeenth and early eighteenth centuries' economic thought when they read tracts espousing that policy.

Unquestionably, when George wrote "On Industry in Great Britain," he and his tutor were convinced by Tucker's arguments, and persuaded of the wisdom of his solutions. Bute did not design his asssignments merely to acquaint his pupil with the various positions on public issues. Rather, the aim of his pedagogy was to teach the prince whatever Bute believed was the correct position. What cannot be known with certainty is which argument, or consideration, moved first the tutor, then the student, to champion the cause of a general naturalization. Probably its supporters' emphasis on the moral shortcomings of the poor played an important part in that decision. Bute referred to the people of Britain as "prostituted" in 1756, and added that they did not have "as strong an aversion to vice, corruption, and arbitrary power" as the young prince. The future king, he averred, would have to bring liberty and virtue to them.[12] George accepted his mission willingly, vowing to Bute that he would not accept the throne unless he could reasonably hope to make Britain "again famous for being the residence of true piety and virtue."[13] To men convinced that Britons were not virtuous enough, and committed to replacing vice with virtue, an argument that stressed the economic significance of "the general disposition of the manufacturers to idleness and debauchery" must have seemed persuasive, and remedies that promised to change that disposition equally so.

Whatever the reasons why arguments in favor of a general naturalization and policing the poor's activities at and away from work impressed Bute and the prince, certainly they were not blind to the unpopularity of these policies and the political difficulties of implementing them. Removing restrictions on naturalization had been "violently opposed," as George noted, and successfully as well. Despite the full support of the Whig oligarchy and the ministries of the day, naturalization bills failed in the House of Commons in 1746–1747, 1748, and 1751. Opponents of those measures argued that the true cause of high wages was high taxes on the poor's necessities, predicted that a general naturalization would tempt only "some inconsiderate foreigners, especially Germans . . . not celebrated either for their sobriety or abstemiousness," and concluded that the policy would enrage the people without producing the desired effect.[14] These points were as popular in the country as in the House. In 1751, a Bristol crowd celebrated the defeat of a naturalization bill by burning an effigy of Josiah Tucker.[15] Three years later, after the repeal of the Jewish Naturalization Act of 1753, another crowd in the same city chanted during the parliamentary elections, "No general naturalization! No Jews! No French bottlemakers! No lowering wages of laboring men to 4*d*. a day and garlic!"[16]

Comparing the reactions of Tucker and Bute to these events is instructive. Popular and parliamentary opposition to his theories and proposals did not keep Tucker from continuing to espouse both a general naturalization and a stricter regulation of the poor. It did, however, cause him to reconsider his role as an instructor to the prince. The bishop of Norwich, who served as preceptor to the prince from 1751 to 1753, had asked Tucker "to put into the hands of his royal pupil such a treatise as would convey both clear and comprehensive ideas on the subject of natural commerce," and be free from "the narrow conceptions of ignorant or the sinister views of crafty and designing men." Tucker began to work "with all imaginable alacrity," but never completed the treatise. The furious opposition to his ideas by "the herd of mock patriots" in Parliament and by the people, inflamed "by misrepresentations and false alarms," convinced him that publishing such a work under the royal patronage "might disserve [the prince] in the eyes of others," because "of the many jealousies to which it was liable and the cavils which might be raised against it."[17] To be sure, neither Bute nor George anticipated publishing "On Industry in Great Britain." Still, nothing in that essay reveals any apprehensions about the effect of the identification of the prince with Tucker's analysis of and remedies for the high price of labor on his subjects' attitudes toward him. Nor is there any hint that the widespread opposition to these ideas should deter the prince from encouraging another attempt to relax restrictions on naturalization and, if that again failed, from trying to compel the people to lead more industrious and less luxurious lives. The point of "On Industry in Great Britain" is clear: the new king should advocate these reforms, despite their unpopularity. Such was the position of Bute and the prince in 1757.

III

It was not their position for long. In every other essay he wrote before succeeding to the throne that touched on the cost of labor in Britain, beginning with "On methods to be used in writing a history of revenues and taxes after the Revolution" in 1758, George stressed that the remedy for high wages was lowering taxes on the poor's necessities.[18] He never again argued in favor of a general naturalization of Protestants or a stricter regulation of the poor. The explanations he used to justify the wisdom of reducing taxes disclose why he and Bute came to endorse a policy they had regarded as essentially ineffectual in 1757.

Just as they had done when the prince wrote "On Industry in Great Britain," the two men appropriated basic arguments and conclusions from other sources, in this case from prevailing contemporary views on taxes and their effects. Since the excise crisis of the early 1730s, the opposition viewpoint of that era that taxes on necessities were harmful to the poor and to trade had become an axiom of taxation policy. Proponents of that orthodoxy emphasized in their arguments that these duties inevitably and quickly raised wages and thus increased prices of manufactured goods.[19] Bute and George, who had earlier been impressed by the questions Tucker raised about this portrayal of the relationship between taxes and wages, now referred to that relationship as an undeniable fact of economic life. Significantly, however, the two men went beyond this justification for lowering taxes. They added to it an argument that was uniquely their own, one which they believed to be more compelling than compassionate, fiscal, or commercial considerations. "Of more importance than all the rest, these [taxes on necessities] gave a rigid and oppressive air to government, which becomes odious from the minute it appears to be so."[20] Since the composition of "Industry in Great Britain," Bute and the prince had become concerned with popular appearances, perceptions, and opinions. They had concluded that if the new king's subjects perceived him and his government to be oppressive, they would detest the monarch and his ministers. This concern was one reason why the two men worried during the summer of 1758 about the ability of their ally, William Pitt, to resist pressure to send British troops to Germany. "If this unhappy measure should be taken," the prince predicted, "we shall be drawn deeper in a continent war than ever." Because he believed continental involvement was as unpopular with his subjects as it was at Leicester House, he feared that Pitt's implication in such a policy would mean "when I mount the throne, I shall not be able to form a ministry who can have the opinion of the people."[21] That same concern with popular opinion explained his *volte-face* on the primary cause of and best remedy for the high cost of labor in Britain. Had Bute and the prince been persuaded by purely intellectual arguments that "On Industry in Great Britain" was incorrect, the prince would have written an essay similar to it in form and subject, exposing how those doctrines misrepresented and misinterpreted reality. I have found no such essay. Political reality, as they saw it, not intellectual reconsideration, convinced them to elevate the reduction of taxes to a much more important role than George assigned it in 1757, and to discard his earlier recommendations.[22] The two men had realized that the prince could not espouse a general naturalization or a regulation of the poor's lives without forfeiting the good opinion of his people. That was a price they were unwilling to pay.

Why not? Bute and George wanted to win and retain the affections of the people beause they had come to believe that "the nation's confidence [and] the people's love" would be necessary both to preserve Britain's place in the world and to accomplish the political, fiscal, and moral reforms they thought should be made.[23] This belief can only have been strengthened by George's growing disenchantment during 1758 with politicians in general—all of whom he felt were greatly deficient to Bute in integrity and ability—and with "the great orator" Pitt in particular, who by late 1758 was acting an "infamous and ungrateful part."[24] In contrast, the prince's opinions of his subjects improved as time passed. Not only did he never repeat the unfavorable comparison he made between them and European laborers in "On Industry in Great Britain," but he even criticized "the odious doctrine that the poor were mere beasts of burdens and should be treated accordingly, as in France and Holland; that the harder they labored and the less they received, the less time and money they would have to idle away, and the more governable they would be found." The "nobler" position, according to him, recognized the differences between Britons and "continental slaves." Moreover, he concluded that "in subduing the ill qualities of the poor, we might subdue their good ones too; and that if once tamed to the degree desired at home, they might become in the same degree spiritless and unserviceable abroad."[25] With these words, the prince implicitly rejected one of the reforms he proposed in "On Industry in Great Britain." He still wanted to restore virtue in his kingdom, but he now believed that the prerequisite for this was not the regulation of the poor, but winning the people's confidence and support. To accomplish that goal, Bute and he started to consider how to make him a popular monarch, beginning with his first official remarks as George III[26]

IV

What, then, is the historical significance of "On Industry in Great Britain?" If it resulted in nothing, not even another essay on the subject, should it be regarded only as interesting juvenilia, an exception that proves the rule? I think not. That Bute and the prince would even temporarily endorse policies that had been violently opposed and would be difficult to implement reveals their genuine concern about the future of British trade and manufacturing, and their firm conviction that measures had to be taken to lower the high cost of labor. Moreover, the reason why this essay was unique is significant in itself. The ending of harsh criticism of the poor, and the discarding of thoughts about supporting legislation providing for a general naturalization of foreign Protestants and compelling the poor to work harder and lead more virtuous and frugal lives, are important indications of how committed George and Bute became to making sure he would be perceived as the "much-vaunted and long-awaited 'patriot king.'" Scholars have only recently begun to appreciate how carefully George III and Bute worked to make the new king popular during the days immediately after his accession.[27] The abandonment during 1758 of the controversial policies the prince endorsed in "On Industry in Great Britain" in favor of a commitment to the more popular doctrine that reducing or repealing taxes on the poor's necessities would lower the cost of labor indicates that the two men were preparing to pursue that goal well before October 1760.

NOTES

1 Bute's pedagogical methods are best described in John Brooke, *King George III* (London: Constable, 1972), 107–108. The prince himself commented that he prepared for his essays by reading "the history of the time, journals, debates, political pamphlets, and manuscript collections." "On methods to be used in writing a history of revenues and taxes after the Revolution," [1758], Royal Archives, Additional Georgian Manuscripts, 32/1225. (Hereafter manuscripts from this source will be cited as RA, Add. I should like to acknowledge the gracious permission of Her Majesty Queen Elizabeth II to publish material from the Royal Archives.) This essay may be dated by the reference to the current national debt, which corresponds to the debt for 1758. Many of George's essays may be dated by using this method; others can be assigned approximate dates because he wrote his essays on historical periods in chronological order. The twelve essays by him that discuss the cost of labor may be found in RA, Add. 32/259–261, 1087–449, and 1531–696.

2 "Account of sessions of Parliament and taxes raised during the reign of William and Mary up to 1694," [1759–1760], RA, Add. 32/1403. The prince's convictions that English laborers were paid more than their counterparts in Europe, and that French manufactured goods cost less than British products, were shared by virtually all of his contemporaries. How accurate were these beliefs? Calculating wages and prices for the eighteenth century is extremely difficult, owing to the paucity of data covering extended periods of time and all regions and countries, and to the questionable accuracy of most contemporary statistics. Still, careful analysts of eighteenth-century economies believe that British labor commanded a higher price and enjoyed a better standard of living than European workers did. Scholars also have discovered that after 1750 the proportion of British domestic goods sold in Europe declined, and Britons were compelled to make up the differences by seeking and developing markets elsewhere. These historians tend to explain this by referring to European tariffs, rather than to the cheaper labor there. Whatever the explanation, however, it seems clear British manufacturers were being undersold in European markets. Finally, Ralph Davis has convincingly argued that the establishment of linen and silk industries in Britain during the 1700s was the result of the passage of protective tariffs. Without that legislation, British manufacturers would have been unable to compete with French producers of those goods in British markets. In conclusion, contemporary perceptions about wages in Britain and about the prices of manufactured goods there and abroad were most likely correct. See Phyllis Deane, *The First Industrial Revolution* (Cambridge: Cambridge University Press, 1965), 55–56, 142–43; Phyllis Deane and W. A. Cole, *British Economic Growth, 1688–1959: Trends and Structures* (Cambridge: Cambridge University Press, 1969), 18–22, 82–88; and Ralph Davis, "The Rise of Protection in England, 1689–1786," *Economic History Review*, 2nd. ser., (1966), 316.

3 "On methods to be used in writing a history of revenues and taxes after the Revolution," [1758], RA, Add. 32/1228. For a full discussion of George's ideas

about taxation, see John L. Bullion, "'To know this is the true essential business of a king': The Prince of Wales and the Study of Public Finance, 1775–1760," *Albion* 18 (1986): 429–54.

4 "On Industry in Great Britain," [1757], RA, Add. 32/259–261. For the date, see note 5. Quotations in section I are from this source.

5 A comparison of passages in the prince's essay with Malachy Postlethwayt, *Britain's Commercial Interest Explained and Improved*, 2 vols. (London: D. Browne, 1757), 1: 11–14, 43–51, reveals that he borrowed from it when he wrote "On Industry in Great Britain."

6 The prince did not define "general naturalization" in "On Industry in Great Britain," but he clearly used the term in the same way the supporters of a bill for naturalizing foreign Protestants in 1748 did. See "Arguments in support of the bill for naturalizing foreign Protestants," 4 February 1748, in T. C. Hansard, ed., *The Parliamentary History of England, from the Earliest Period of the Year 1803*, Ser. 1, 41 vols. (London: Longman, 1806–1820), 14: 137–40.

7 A convenient contemporary source for these arguments is ibid. For good surveys of opinion for and against a general naturalization, see Thomas W. Perry, *Public Opinion, Propaganda, and Politics in Eighteenth-Century England: A Study of the Jew Bill of 1753*, Harvard Historical Monographs 51 (Cambridge, Mass.: Harvard University Press, 1962): 31–44 and 72–89; and W. George Shelton, *Dean Tucker and Eighteenth-Century Economic and Political Thought* (New York: St. Martin's, 1981), 70–87.

8 Compare "On Industry in Great Britain" with Josiah Tucker, *A Brief Essay on the Advantages and Disadvantages which respectively attend France and Great Britain, with Regard to Trade*, third edition (London: T. Trye, 1753), iv, 14, 36–38, 53–54n, and 65–84.

9 D. C. Coleman, "Labour in the English Economy of the Seventeenth Century," *Economic History Review*, 2nd. Ser., 8 (1955–56): 280–281. Coleman's essay is usefully elaborated upon in Joyce Oldham Appleby, *Economic Thought and Ideology in Seventeenth-Century England* (Princeton, N. J.: Princeton University Press, 1978), 73–98, 129–157. For the period 1700–1750, see A. W. Coats, "Changing Attitudes to Labour in the Mid-Eighteenth Century," *Economic History Review*, 2nd. Ser., 11 (1958–59): 35–36.

10 For the views of those who dissented from orthodoxy, see ibid., 35–37; and Richard C. Wiles, "The Theory of Wages in Later English Mercantilism," *Economic History Review*, 2nd. Ser., 21 (1968): 113–26.

11 At times during the 1750s, Tucker argued publicly that "there was no necessary reason why high wages should act as an obstacle to continuous economic expansion." In other pamphlets, however, he urged the reduction of wages, and bitterly criticized English labor's idleness and immorality. Coats, "Changing Attitudes," *Economic History Review*, 2nd. Ser., 11 (1958–59): 51; see also Wiles, "Theory of Wages," ibid., 21 (1968): 124–26. Tucker espoused the latter positions whenever he argued for a general naturalization. When analyzing why he did so, scholars would be best advised to eschew attempts to reconcile Tucker's various positions on wages during the 1750s, and rather remember Coats's wise warning: "In considering the activities of propagandists it is easy

to underrate the extent to which established doctrines are adapted or distorted to suit the needs of a particular interest group." A. W. Coats, "Economic Thought and Poor Law Policy in the Eighteenth Century," ibid., 13 (1960–61): 40.

12 The earl of Bute to Gilbert Elliot, 16 August 1756, quoted in James Lee McKelvey, *George III and Lord Bute: The Leicester House Years* (Durham, N. C.: Duke University Press, 1973), 42–43.

13 The prince to Bute, [early June 1757?], in Romney Sedgwick, ed., *Letters from George III to Lord Bute, 1756–1766* (London: Macmillan, 1939), 6.

14 See "Arguments against the bill for naturalizing foreign Protestants," 4 February 1748, Hansard, ed., *Parliamentary History* 14: 141–47. The quotation is from 145.

15 Shelton, *Dean Tucker*, 70.

16 Quoted in Linda Colley, *In Defiance of Oligarchy: The Tory Party, 1714–1760* (Cambridge: Cambridge University Press, 1982), 155.

17 Josiah Tucker, *Four tracts together with two sermons on political and commercial subjects* (Gloucester: R. Raikes, 1774), ix–xi.

18 "On methods to be used in writing a history of revenues and taxes after the Revolution," [1758], RA, Add. 32/1220–1232.

19 See William Kennedy, *English Taxation 1640–1799: An Essay on Policy and Opinion* (London: G. Bell, 1913), 104–23. It is difficult to measure to what extent these arguments were correct. Most contemporaries simply assumed the arguments correctly depicted reality, without ever testing their accuracy by looking for an increase in wages and prices after the imposition of a duty on a specific necessity. Among modern scholars, how much taxes on necessities affected trade and industry in eighteenth-century England is a matter of controversy. All would agree, however, that the impact was less immediate and dramatic than eighteenth-century observers believed. For a discussion of the difficulties of determining these effects, see William J. Hausman and John L. Neufeld, "Excise Anatomized: the Political Economy of Walpole's 1733 Tax Scheme," *The Journal of European Economic History* 10 (1981): 131–32, 141–43.

20 "Account of sessions of Parliament and taxes raised during the reign of William and Mary up to 1694," [1759–1760], RA, Add. 32/1403.

21 The prince to Bute, [ca. 2 July 1758], in Sedgwick, ed., *Letters from George III to Bute*, 11.

22 This decision was more a change in emphasis than a change of opinion. In "On Industry in Great Britain," the prince had acknowledged that heavy taxes and the tastes and vices of manufacturers both contributed to high wages in Britain. So did Postlethwayt and Tucker. The former supported a more liberal naturalization policy; the latter was certain "our trade is greatly burdened by the *nature* of *most of our taxes, and the manner of collecting them*." (Postlethwayt, *Britain's Commercial interest*, 2: 532–33; Tucker, *Brief Essay*, 38.) What divided opinion in the pages of pamphlets and essays was which was the more important. In the political world, one of the options had been foreclosed.

23 The prince's essay on the British political system, quoted in Brooke, *George III*, 121–22.

24 The prince to Bute, [ca. 2 July 1758], [? December 1758], and [? December 1758], in Sedgwick, ed., *Letters From George III to Bute*, 11 and 17–19.

25 "Account of sessions of Parliament and taxes raised during the reign of William and Mary up to 1694," [1759–1760], RA, Add. 32/1409. As Coats noted in "Changing Attitudes," *Economic History Review*, 2nd Ser., 11 (1958–59): 35–51, from the 1750s to the publication of *The Wealth of Nations*, more sympathetic attitudes toward laborers came to predominate in economic thought. Particularly toward the end of that period, theorists began to argue that depressing wages would encourage idleness, because the laborer would have no incentive to work. Higher wages, conversely, would stimulate him to greater productivity. Moreover, they asserted that the English worker's taste for luxuries (re-defined in their writings as "comforts" and "conveniences") would operate as a powerful and beneficial incentive as well. The prince certainly became more sympathetic to laborers in his later essays, but there are no indications in them that he did so because of these, or any, economic considerations. On the crucial question of the level of wages, George continued to advocate keeping it as low as possible. Political motives, not new theories about economic activity, explained his change of heart.

26 See Earl Fitzmaurice, *Life of William, Earl of Shelburne, Afterwards First Marquess of Landsdowne*, 2 vols. (London: Macmillan, 1912), 1: 33.

27 See John Brewer, *Party Ideology and Popular Politics at the Accession of George III* (Cambridge: Cambridge University Press, 1976), 47–48 and 101–102; the quotation is from 101.

Blackstone's Commentaries
as Constitutive Rhetoric

JEFFREY SMITTEN*

There is a persistent image of Blackstone as a reactionary apologist for
the legal status quo in eighteenth-century England. In this view, Blackstone is said to be an ideologue, blind to historical change and closed to
any way of thinking but his own. Jeremy Bentham sees him as a "bum-
bling antiquarian," slavishly devoted to an outmoded constitution.[1] Sir
Ernest Barker sees him less as an antiquarian than as a hidebound squire:
"He sat in Parliament from a rotten borough: he required a bottle of port
before him when he was writing (so the story runs) 'that he might be in-
vigorated and supported in the fatigue of his great work': he had a cor-
pulency of body, accentuated by an unhappy aversion from exercise; and
his belief, as one might expect on the basis of such data, was a happy
but heavy belief in the divine right of whatever is."[2] Daniel J. Boorstin
grants Blackstone higher intellectual purpose but still claims that for him
the English law is immune from time, change, and criticism: "The whole
of the English law was a unified natural phenomenon like the rest of God's
works. And to criticize the shape of the law would be like criticizing the
shape of a tree."[3] Nor does Blackstone seem to have fared better at the
hand of more recent, fashionable critics. Duncan Kennedy uses a combination of deconstruction, phenomenology, and Marxism to argue that
Blackstone draws indiscriminately on past and present to produce a fundamentally incoherent legal system manifesting his desire "to legitimate
the legal status quo of the England of his day."[4] One might think that
Kennedy's analysis simply reflects the general irreverence of Critical Legal Studies,[5] but the notion that Blackstone blindly defends the status
quo is hardly novel.

There are, however, important exceptions to this notion. Some biographers have discussed Blackstone's support for specific legal innovations, thus questioning the interpretation of him as mere apologist ignorant of the flow of history.[6] For them, he is not an enemy to reform but "an advocate of moderate reform based on experience."[7] Lurking in the idea of experience, perhaps, are the seeds of a more sympathetic, more comprehensive understanding of Blackstone's approach to legal thinking. To enhance this understanding let us consider the most significant exception, the one giving us the best lead toward understanding Blackstone's mode of thought: the common-law tradition described by J. G. A. Pocock.

Through the seventeenth century and into the eighteenth students of the common law moved toward a complex historical interpretation of the feudal past. One late fruit of this movement was the historical thought of Burke, which, Pocock claims, stems from the common-law tradition that "conceived the law of England as custom and custom as perpetual adaptation."[8] Although Pocock does not discuss the *Commentaries* in detail as an embodiment of this tradition, his characterization of Burke's ideas, as I will suggest (albeit from a different perspective), could readily describe Blackstone's leading themes. "Burke's essential ideas," writes Pocock,

> are that institutions are the products of history; that history consists in an unceasing process, in which the generations are partners and in which men perpetually adapt themselves to new needs and new situations; that existing institutions are the fruits of this process and, whether because they represent the latest adjustment or because they have been retained through many adaptations, embody the wisdom of more men, in a higher state of refinement, than the individual intellect can hope to equal or exceed; and that political wisdom lies in participating in this process—which can be identified with order and nature—not in attempting to reconstruct institutions on *a priori* lines.[9]

Far from entailing a blind defense of the status quo, the tradition of common-law thought rests on the complex humanist idea of adaptation, the recognition that, on the one hand, the collective wisdom of the past is greater than the individual intellect operating in the present; but that, on the other, the heritage of the past must be accommodated to the new needs and situations of the present. There is an incessant tension, though not a polar opposition, between past and present: the two differ from each other yet are united by powerful bonds of historical continuity. Blackstone, the great defender of the common law, is obviously one of the inheritors of this intellectual tradition.

My purpose, then, is to show that Blackstone's approach to the law, like Burke's, rests on adaptation. But I wish to define Blackstone's approach, not through an analysis of the tradition of common-law thought, but by placing the *Commentaries* in a different context, examining it in terms of a rhetorical concept rather than in terms of legal history and institutions. I have two motives for this recontextualizing. One is that Pocock has described the common-law tradition so well that little would be accomplished by simply adding someone like Blackstone to it — unless one had new information about his sources and predecessors. Since I am not a specialist in legal history, such an analysis is beyond my ability. My other motive is perhaps better: by attending to the rhetorical basis of the *Commentaries*, we may be able to formulate in a new, more general, and more fundamental way the mode of legal thinking at work in the text, thus presenting a stronger challenge to the view of Blackstone as mere defender of the status quo. To make this challenge it will be necessary to open up a previously undiscussed aspect of the *Commentaries*: its function as — to use James Boyd White's term — constitutive rhetoric. Before turning to the *Commentaries* let us try to define this rhetorical concept.

In his stimulating recent study, White claims that the law ought to be conceived as a rhetorical activity.[10] Constitutive rhetoric is his term for the way in which a language — including legal arguments and decisions — can create a shared community of value and meaning. Without a common language, an agreed upon set of terms in which to comprehend events, there can be no community, culture, or civilization. Constitutive rhetoric, accordingly, is what holds people together in a community. As White puts it, "The establishment of comprehensible relations and shared meanings, the making of the kind of community that enables people to say 'we' about what they do and to claim consistent meanings for it — all this at the deepest level involves persuasion as well as education, and is the province of what I call constitutive rhetoric" (37–38). The law, a major element of this constitutive rhetoric, is especially important because it "is a way in which the community defines itself, not once and for all, but over and over, and in the process it educates itself about its own character and the nature of the world" (225). To conceive of the law, then, in terms of constitutive rhetoric is to place it in a longstanding humanist tradition radically opposed to two other common traditions of defining the law.[11] One of these is the concept of law as authority, a set of unquestionable commands compelling certain kinds of behavior; the other is bureaucratic, the law seen as a systematic set of rules for managing various social institutions (29–31). In opposition to these traditions, to see the law as constitutive rhetoric means to see it not as an objective structure but as a process, a conversation: the law "works by establishing roles and relations and voices, positions from which one may speak, and giving us as speakers the materials and methods of a discourse. It is this discourse working within the social context of its own creation, this *language* in the fullest sense of the term, that is the law" (98). In this definition, the law is not a fixed, immutable structure but rather a process of hearing arguments and of establishing relationship between opposed viewpoints.

If the law is understood as constitutive rhetoric, then justice under the law, White maintains, becomes not a matter of authority or logical consistency but of character and community:

> The heart of what we mean by justice resides in questions of character and relationship and community — in who we are to each other — for this is what determines the meaning of what is done. If these things are got right, the material manifestations — the rules, the results — will take care of themselves; if they are not got right, the rules and results will be wrong, and this is true in the family, in the custody hearing, in the sentencing proceeding, in the ordinary trial, in national political arrangements, and in international relations. Talk about justice is at its heart talk about character and relations. (134)

The law in this definition is not a fixed set of rules, and justice is not a matter of making rules consistent with each other or with desired ends. Justice, as White sees it, is an attitude toward others, the desire and ability to engage contrary views sincerely. He makes this point strongly when discussing judicial decision-making:

> The ideal would be a judge who put his (or her) fundamental attitudes and methods to the test of sincere engagement with arguments the other way. We could ask, does this judge see the case before him as the occasion for printing out an ideology, for displaying technical skill, or as presenting a real difficulty, calling for real thought? The ideal judge would show that he had listened to the side he voted against and that he had felt the pull of the arguments both ways. The law that was made that way would comprise two opposing voices, those of the parties, in a work made by another, by the judge who had listened to both and had faced the conflict between them in an honest way. In this sense the judge's most important work is the definition of his own voice, the character he makes for himself as he works through a case. (47)

The excellence of a judicial decision lies not in its outcome but in how that outcome is reached. When the judge has worked through the case with all possible attention, openness, and sincerity, justice has been done. A community has been created in which arguments are posed in relation to each other, conflicts faced squarely, and a decision made in full recognition of "the radical uncertainty in which we live" (24). The legal process, in White's eyes, can do no more.

Blackstone also sees the law as constitutive rhetoric. Although we will see that Blackstone is not so much concerned with weighing competing arguments as with weighing rules against circumstances and past against present (adaptation), his intention, like White's, is clearly to show that law is a matter of "character and relationship and community," not of an abstract, conceptual system. On the one hand, he presents this view of the law in his general precepts. Especially important in this regard is the opening lecture, "On the Study of the Law." Here Blackstone explicitly lays down the ideal of mind and character that his students should reach, and he defines the place of this ideal in the practice of the law. On the other, Blackstone in his subsequent lectures works to establish his own *ethos* as a speaker. Thus, his lectures on the history of the law do not map out a system so much as illustrate the sort of character involved in sound legal thinking. As he works through various problems in history and definition, Blackstone shows his students how — not what — to think when confronting issues in an uncertain world. He does so by showing how the law is bound up in a situation and how it changes over time. Although we will discern limits to Blackstone's openness, the basic thrust of his thinking — and the foundation of his success — is clear. He is not an apologist defending an abstract system of rules fixed for all time; instead, he is a humanist, fully aware of the important role of character, relationship, and community in the unending process of adapting the law. He would, in short, agree with his fellow humanist Vico that "it is . . . impossible to assess human affairs by the inflexible standard of abstract right; we must rather gauge them by the pliant Lesbic rule, which does not conform bodies to itself, but adapts itself to their contours."[12]

Let us begin by establishing Blackstone's view of his audience and his purpose in relation to that audience. Whom does he take to be his auditors and what kind of legal thinkers does he think they can become? One seemingly irrelevant aspect of this definition receives unexpectedly heavy emphasis at the start: the social status of the audience. He comments early in his introductory lecture: "For I think it is an undeniable position, that a competent knowledge of the law of that society, in which he live, is the proper accomplishment of every gentleman and scholar; an highly useful, I had almost said essential, part of liberal and polite education."[13] One of Blackstone's major concerns, in other words, is with the social quality of the profession, a concern of legal reformers in England since the sixteenth century.[14] For "our gentlemen of independent estates and fortunes, the most useful as well as considerable body of men in the nation" (1:7), mastery of the law is essential to both the private management of their property and their public conduct of affairs should they serve on the bench or in Parliament. The law is not seen as a career in itself but as a necessary adjunct to the maintenance of English society. But even when Blackstone accepts the possibility that his auditors will go on to practice law, he worries that current conditions in the Inns of Court are not such as to attract "young nobility and gentry" to the professional study of the law (1:25); and he deplores apprenticeship as destructive of any liberal (i.e., gentlemanly) habit of mind (1:31–32). How, then, are we to understand Blackstone's preoccupation with the social quality of the law, and what is its relevance to constitutive rhetoric?

This concern, though abhorrent to many of his critics from Bentham on, does not represent mere social snobbery, nor a reactionary desire to return to an earlier, more comfortable era, nor a thoughtless defense of the status quo. Rather, as John Barrell has suggested concerning the later eighteenth century generally, Blackstone's linking of law and social class is designed to ensure an impartial comprehensiveness of vision in an age of social fragmentation.[15] Moreover, in terms of our analysis, such vision is fundamental to the law conceived as constitutive rhetoric. Blackstone consistently opposes the law conceived as a collection of isolated, self-contained technicalities to the law conceived as a liberal, communal spirit virtually inherent in the upper class. Guardianship of the law

> can no where be so properly reposed as in the noble hands where our excellent constitution has placed it: and therefore placed it, because, from the independence of their fortune and the dignity of their station, they are presumed to employ that leisure which is the consequence of both, in attaining a more extensive knowledge of the laws than persons of inferior rank: and because the founders of our polity relied upon that delicacy of sentiment, so peculiar to noble birth; which, as on the one hand it will prevent either interest or affection from interfering in questions of right, so on the other it will bind a peer in honour, an obligation which the law esteems equal to another's oath, to be master of those points upon which it is his birthright to decide. (1:12; see also 1:6–7, 9–10; 4:436)

Such a comprehensive, impartial outlook is essential to the proper making of the law. As we have seen, White argues that the law expresses in a single language the antagonistic positions found in the community. The law's great achievement is to bring opposed views into relationship with one another; and the key to this achievement is judicial character, the impartiality that allows careful attention to both sides of a question. By the same token, Blackstone seeks, along with many others in the later eighteenth century, a social group capable of this kind of impartiality. Hence, he argues that the landed class is not only *de facto* the ruling class but also the class, by virtue of its long history and traditions, most likely to possess impartial comprehensiveness of vision. This group has the leisure to attain "extensive knowledge of the laws," the great significance of which we will note shortly, and it has a long tradition of impartial decision-making ("delicacy of sentiment"). Given these qualities of character, one necessary prerequisite for the making of just laws is fulfilled: the capacity to attend openly and sincerely to opposing views. This is not an exclusively social function, but for Blackstone it is certainly socially conditioned. In the history and traditions of the landed class, Blackstone can locate the essential quality of mind necessary to the law conceived as constitutive rhetoric.

But, although Blackstone is very much concerned with the social basis of the law, he is equally, if not more, concerned with its intellectual basis. Perhaps Blackstone's most persistent theme is that legal study should enlarge and expand, not narrow and concentrate, the mind. The great danger, in his estimation, is that the lawyer will become trapped by the system of laws so that he is cut off from the rhetorical interchange that should shape the law. In particular, he singles out the legal apprenticeship system:

> The evident want of some assistance in the rudiments of legal knowledge, has given birth to a practice, which, if ever it had grown to be general, must have proved of extremely pernicious consequences: I mean the custom, by some so very warmly recommended, to drop all liberal education, as of no use to lawyers; and to place them, in it's [sic] stead, at the desk of some skilful attorney; in order to initiate them early in all the depths of practice, and render them more dextrous in the mechanical part of business. . . . If practice be the whole he is taught, practice must also be the whole he will ever know: if he be uninstructed in the elements and first principles upon which the rule of practice is founded, the least variation from established precedents will totally distract and bewilder him: *ita lex scripta est* is the utmost his knowledge will arrive at; he must never aspire to form, and seldom expect to comprehend, any arguments drawn *a priori* from the spirit of the laws and the natural foundations of justice. (1:31–32)

A lawyer whose sole conception of the law is *ita lex scripta est* will never be able to adapt the law to changing human needs and situations. For such a lawyer, the law is a fixed system, because he completely lacks discretion, the ability to test conclusions against facts. The quality of mind that Blackstone admires, however, rests upon openness, the ability to get beyond the rigid letter of the law to its underlying—adaptable—spirit.

Legal study, accordingly, will not be confined to mastering an abstract system of rules but will touch upon all the social, moral, and intellectual resources involved in legal thinking. Blackstone presents a strong case for the liberality of the law against those who would exclude it from the university as mere mechanical training:

> [T]hat a science, which distinguishes the criterions of right and wrong; which teaches to establish the one, and prevent, punish, or redress the other; which employs in it's [sic] theory the noblest faculties of the soul, and exerts in it's practice the cardinal virtues of the heart; a science, which is universal in it's use and extent, accommodated to each individual, yet comprehending the whole community; that a science like this should ever have been deemed unnecessary to be studied in an university, is a matter of astonishment and concern. Surely, if it were not before an object of academical knowledge, it was high time to make it one; and to those who can doubt the propriety of it's reception among us (if any such there be) we may return an answer in their own way; that ethics are confessedly a branch of academical learning, and Aristotle *himself has said*, speaking of the laws of his own country, that jurisprudence or the knowledge of those laws is the principal and most perfect branch of ethics. (1:27)

Legal thinking draws upon the whole range of knowledge we have about human behavior, both academic and experiential. Since study of the law is so closely tied to practical knowledge of human affairs, one of the great dangers Blackstone foresees for the student is social isolation. We have just noted Blackstone's distaste for the apprenticeship system, and in imagery reminiscent of Sprat and Swift he condemns the isolation imposed on the student by this process: "He is expected to sequester himself from the world, and by a tedious lonely process to extract the theory of law from a mass of undigested learning. . . . How little therefore is it to be wondered at . . . that so many persons of moderate capacity confuse themselves at first setting out, and continue ever dark and puzzled during the remainder of their lives!" (1:31). Cut off from the varied resources of legal thought, the student will be unable to think beyond the code of laws; he will not have the extensive knowledge that will enable him to hear arguments openly or to adapt laws to changing circumstances.

Hence, Blackstone suggests a course of study that will give the student the knowledge he needs truly to understand the law code, not simply to manipulate it. Prior to studying the law, "perusal and imitation of the purest classical writers" (particularly historians and orators) is highly recommended together with mathematics to sharpen logic and science to provide an expanded context for understanding nature and art. To these areas should be added study of natural and Roman law. Then, after the student has completed his course of study, he should still delay entering practice:

> If, at the conclusion, or during the acquisition of these accomplishments, he will afford himself here a year or two's farther leisure, to lay the foundation of his future labours in a solid scientifical method, without thirsting too early to attend that practice which it is impossible he should rightly comprehend, he will afterwards proceed with the greatest ease, and will unfold the most intricate points with an intuitive rapidity and clearness. (1:33–34)

The goal of such an educational regimen is the development of discretion, knowledge of human affairs that is almost intuitive and that is prior to any particular system of laws. Such discretion is what White means by "character" when he argues that "the deepest judicial excellence is an excellence of attitude and character" (47). These are qualities that cannot be found in a law code; rather, they are prior to the code and constitute the spirit with which the code is to be understood and applied. Without discretion the judge or lawyer is a slave to the code; with it, he can adapt the code to changing circumstances, putting (again to cite White) his "fundamental attitudes and methods to the test of sincere engagement with arguments the other way" (47).

Perhaps the most telling indication of Blackstone's rhetorical conception of the law is the place he gives to equity. In many ways, equity is the endpoint of all Blackstone's instruction. During his career he followed Lord Mansfield in making a controversial attempt to join the rule of law with equity, indicating the great importance the concept of equity had for him.[16] He argues at length (3:429–42) that courts of law and of equity do not differ in the way they must interpret the law but only with respect to matters of administration and jurisdiction. That is, the difference in his eyes is formal, not substantive, and he urges "for the sake of certainty, peace, and justice, that each court would as far as possible follow the other" (3:441; see also 4:423). In this context it is hardly surprising that Blackstone calls equity "the soul and spirit of all law" (3:429). If we can understand the nature of equity for Blackstone, we will have grasped one of the central precepts of legal thinking for him, a precept that is tied inextricably to constitutive rhetoric.

Blackstone refers to equity in two seemingly contradictory ways: as the system of procedures appropriate to the court of equity and as a principle of reasonable interpretation of the law.[17] In the former sense, equity is "a laboured connected system, governed by established rules, and bound down by precedents" (3:432); in the latter, it is simply "synonymous to justice" and to "the true sense and sound interpretation of the rule" (3:429). Clearly, it is the second sense of reasonable interpretation that most concerns us here. Near the end of his introductory discussion of the nature of laws in general, Blackstone lays down five means of interpreting the will of a legislator (1:59–62), the last of which is the basis of equity. Blackstone writes: "The most universal and effectual way of discovering the true meaning of a law, when the words are dubious, is by considering the reason and spirit of it; or the cause which moved the legislator to enact it" (1:61). From this principle equity takes its rise, since the rigid application of a law in all future cases ignores changing circumstances, or as Blackstone puts it: "There should be somewhere a power vested of excepting those circumstances which (had they been foreseen) the legislator himself would have excepted" (1:61). A law will be just only if it is adaptable and adapted to changing situations; similarly, a law is unjust if it presumes to cover all future situations without exception. Given this notion of equity, it follows that it cannot be fixed in a code of laws: equity can only operate in terms of the particular circumstances of each case and not in terms of fixed rules. Again, as Blackstone states: "Equity, thus depending, essentially, upon the particular circumstances of each individual case, there can be no established rules and fixed precepts of equity laid down, without destroying it's [sic] very essence, and reducing it to a positive law" (1:61–62). Equity, in other words, depends upon discretion, the ability to weigh paricular circumstances against general prescriptions. It is this ability, as we have seen, that lies at the heart of the law conceived as constitutive rhetoric.

It is one thing to argue for the law as constitutive rhetoric in precept and another to demonstrate that concept in practice. If Blackstone's lectures are to be successful, he will have to show his students how to think about the law by creating a pattern of thought, a voice, which embodies discretion. In his introductory lecture, Blackstone describes how the student should approach legal history by tracing the laws back to their Anglo-Saxon, Roman, or feudal origins. Then,

> these primary rules and fundamental principles should be weighed and compared with the precepts of the law of nature, and the practice of other countries; should be explained by reasons, illustrated by examples, and confirmed by undoubted authorities; their history should be deduced, their changes and revolutions observed, and it should be shewn how far they are connected with, or have at any time been affected by, the civil transactions of the kingdom. (1:36)

Blackstone implies that the history of the law is to be conceived as a conversation, as engagement between various legal codes and traditions. The history of law is in a profound sense a composition, a heterogeneous collection of materials that is nonetheless capable of being comprehended by a single speaker. In so attempting to grasp this material, the speaker must convey his awareness of the limits of his understanding, acknowledging that he, too, is limited by time and place in an uncertain, changing world. It is such an approach that we should expect to see illustrated in the body of the *Commentaries.*

But if we turn to the lectures with this notion of constitutive rhetoric in mind, we may at first be disappointed and puzzled; for there is little overt sense of Blackstone confronting opposing arguments. For all his good sense and tact in evoking historical parallels, analogies, and precedents, Blackstone does not create a dialectic, nor does the reader (or auditor) observe him struggling with arguments that pull him in contrary directions. All appears seamless and harmonious, even as he explains exceptions and qualifications.

Take, for example, his treatment of homicide (book 4, chapter 14). The general organization of the chapter is an orderly, systematic classification of the types and subtypes of homicide. In making his classification, he points to authorities, comparisons, and precedents, placing contemporary English law in a broad historical and metaphysical context but at the same time seeming to emphasize coordination, not conflict, between contrary ideas. The discussion of "excusable homicide" (4:182–88) is typical. Blackstone indicates two types of excusable homicide: that by misadventure (*per infortunium*) and that in self-defense (*se defendendo*). With regard to the former, he invokes historical parallels and precedents, drawing upon shooting accidents, boxing, and cock-throwing as well as Roman law on the moderate chastisement of servants, medieval jousts, and the public games of the Greeks and Romans. With regard to the latter, Blackstone distinguishes homicide *se defendendo* from manslaughter by referring not only to English law but also to Roman law and to the law of nature. The upshot of these varied references, however, is not a dialectic but rather a harmony. Blackstone cites them not as being in opposition to the principles and traditions he accepts but as illustrating and confirming them. He insists, for example, that when the English law holds that some guilt attaches even to "excusable homicide," it is not peculiar in that regard but is in concord with Jewish, Roman, Greek, and feudal legal thought. Given such harmony, one is inclined to agree with Boorstin that this is "another example of the kind of coordination of apparently contrary ideas which Blackstone effected in his attempt to make a rational system of English law."[18]

However, closer inspection of the lectures discloses that beneath this harmonious surface lies a sense of the law as being bound up in a situation. In other words, Blackstone may show his students how various legal traditions support and confirm one another, but that sense of harmony never displaces his view of the law as something adapted to a situation. This view of the law demands that Blackstone be able to weigh rules against circumstances, to exercise that discretion essential to justice. Consider the discussion of "deliberate and wilful *murder*" (4:194–204). Blackstone defines a number of general conditions that are necessary to constitute deliberate murder, but he is always aware of how those general conditions are tied to and affected by concrete circumstances. The law, that is, is not merely prior to a given situation but is weighed against it. This principle is not stated directly, but it clearly emerges from the way in which Blackstone handles his illustrations.[19] To choose a single example, one general condition is that the murder victim be "*a reasonable creature in being, and under the king's peace*" (4:198). Blackstone's illustrations immediately begin to suggest that the important aspect of the law is its application. He first cites some limit cases: "to kill an alien, a Jew, or an outlaw, who are under the king's peace of protection, is as much murder as to kill the most regular born Englishman; except he be an alien-enemy" (4:198). These limits are not absolute, but merely exemplary, functioning as topics for legal argument tied to the immediate situation. They provoke questions of definition and application, not a search for metaphysical justification. Similarly, he distinguishes between killing a child in the womb, which "is now no murder," and having it die after birth as a result of injuries received prior to birth, which is murder. Because Blackstone merely accepts the distinction, its thrust is toward application in a given situation, not toward metaphysical analysis or justification. For Blackstone, it is more important that we be able to talk about a situation than that we have an explicitly justified system resting on all its metaphysical postulates. Finally, he discusses the law covering murder of bastard children. It requires that there be one witness if the child is born dead, else the mother may be tried for murder. Blackstone concludes that this law "savours pretty strongly of severity," even though it is similar to laws of other European nations. Accordingly, he closes this section by noting how English courts have modified the application of this severe law by admitting presumptive evidence that the child was born alive. Thus, although the law is a continuous principle, it is also adaptable to a situation. Blackstone may not feel the pull of opposing arguments, but he exercises openness and flexibility in the application of general principles. This is the art of the lawyer and judge — one that involves character and community.

There is another — complementary — dimension to Blackstone's lectures that we must consider. Though he may suggest that the law is bound up in a situation, he still may not have a well-developed sense of how the law changes over time. As a legal historian, he must not only weigh laws against circumstances, but he must also show how the laws have been shaped over the years. In particular, as White argues, the good historian, like the judge, must "make sense of competing views" and not simply present a single view of the past (115). Yet a glaring instance of failure in this regard is Blackstone's treatment of Norman law. For Blackstone, the Norman lawyers embodied all that is pernicious in legal practice: pedantry, solitude, and authoritarianism. Both the divinity and the law of the Norman conquerors were

> frittered into logical distinctions, and drawn out into metaphysical subtleties, with a skill most amazingly artificial; but which serves no other purpose, than to shew the vast powers of the human intellect, however vainly or preposterously employed. Hence law in particular, which (being intended for universal reception) ought to be a plain rule of action, became a science of the greatest intricacy. (4:410)

The result of this approach and system was a "complete and well concerted ... scheme of servility" (4:413). Thus, as Pocock has said, Blackstone sees Norman feudal law as an intrusion into the field of native English law.[20] It is an excrescence that, in Blackstone's eyes, the English courts have worked for centuries to clean away, returning the nation to its native state of liberty. Blackstone fails to see how the Norman law contributed vitally to the historical development of English law, how it, too, became a part of the total composition of the law. Here appears to be an instance of Blackstone as ideologue, viewing English law as a single system and ignoring competing views.

This failure cannot be explained away, but it can be comprehended and placed in perspective. Because Blackstone is not open to the contribution of Norman law, it does not follow that he had no sense of historical change in the law. Indeed, precisely because he conceives of the law as constitutive rhetoric, he must reject a system founded, in his view, on the totally opposite premises of technical dexterity and metaphysical justification. Norman law is the antithesis of English law, and it is therefore difficult to include the one within the other. In this opposition, Blackstone juxtaposes two radically different, incompatible legal traditions.

With this qualification noted, we should expect nonetheless to find in the *Commentaries* a definite sense of historical change in the law. And, indeed, Blackstone is aware of the constant process of historical change so that he weighs present against past as he did rules against circumstances. This point is made clearly in the discussion of tenures, among the most historically oriented chapters of the *Commentaries* (book 2, chapters 4–6).

The general relationship of the three chapters shows his awareness of the problem of change, for he divides the topic into chapters on the feudal system, the system of ancient tenures, and modern tenures. At the beginning of chapter 4, he suggests that the past must be measured against present, writing that his ensuing discussion of the historical foundations of modern tenures will be both entertaining and useful, "as in viewing the majestic ruins of Rome or Athens, of Balbec or Palmyra, it administers both pleasure and instruction to compare them with the draughts of the same edifices, in their pristine proportion and splendor" (2:44). Later, he remarks that it is only by referring to the older system that we can "explain any seeming, or real, difficulties, that may arise in our present mode of tenure" (2:78). He concludes the three-chapter discussion of tenures by recalling the interconnection of the various historical manifestations of law: "Thus have we taken a compendious view of the principal and fundamental points of the doctrine of tenures, both antient and modern, in which we cannot but remark the mutual connexion and dependence that all of them have upon each other" (2:101). Blackstone wants his audience to perceive change in the law and yet to remain open to the past by constantly juxtaposing past and present. Blackstone presents the law of tenures not as a system completed by history but as one in process of change.

Moreover, Blackstone not only demonstrates awareness of change but also suggests that the English law is a composition of disparate materials, thus indicating his openness to competing views. He does so by defending the common law as the embodiment of the true spirit of the English community (see 1:17), not as a fixed structure or code. It is this spirit that permits the continuing adaptation of the law in the midst of historical change. To make his defense, Blackstone connects the common law of tenures with individual liberty on the basis of a distinction between the feudalism of the "northern or Celtic nations" (2:45) and that of the Norman invaders (2:48). The former he characterizes as a "plan of simplicity and liberty, equally beneficial to both lord and tenant, and prudently calculated for their mutual protection and defence" (2:58), the latter as a "complicated " and "extensive" "slavery" (2:76) maintained by "the art and finesse of the Norman lawyers" (2:52). The original feudal plan was based on mutual defense, so that community members protected each other's individual property as well as that of the whole community (2:46); and Blackstone finds it "reasonable" to believe that the early Saxons in England had the rudiments of such a plan (2:48), though conforming more to the idea of a national militia than to a military system (1:397). This plan incorporated within it a sense of the inherent rights of the individual that were not in any way granted from the crown (2:52; 4:413). But under the Normans this plan degenerated, so that a scheme for raising a "national militia" became merely a tyrannical means of raising money for the crown (2:75–76). Under the reforms of Charles II, these mercenary abuses were abolished, leaving only tenures such as free and common socage, which Blackstone terms "relicks of Saxon liberty" (2:81). Thus, the abiding spirit in the common law of tenures is individual liberty, which subsisted over time and in different legal forms. Although Blackstone's grasp of these changes in only partial, he nonetheless clearly recognizes that the law entails not just the mastery of a code but the ability to adapt the laws to a perpetually changing situation.

If one were to pick out the single image that best represents Blackstone's conception of the law, a prime candidate would be the famous comparison of the law to a Gothic castle:

> We inherit an old Gothic castle, erected in the days of chivalry, but fitted up for a modern inhabitant. The moated ramparts, the embattled towers, and the trophied halls, are magnificent and venerable, but useless. The inferior apartments, now converted into rooms of conveniences, are chearful and commodious though their approaches are winding and difficult. (3:268)

Here Blackstone captures, in his own terms, some of the leading motifs of the law seen as constitutive rhetoric. Foremost among these is a sense of the law as a composition created over time. The final result is a kind of harmony—the castle is magnificent on the outside and comfortable on the inside—but there is no doubt about the heterogeneity of the materials added at different times. Each age has built for its own purpose (and will continue to do so), though ultimately contributing to a single whole. Although Blackstone may not recognize the contribution of all the builders of the English law, he nonetheless clearly avoids the twin pitfalls of rigid antiquarianism and doctrinaire modernism, both of which would in effect maintain the consistency of a single legal system.[21] For Blackstone, adaptation of the law to changing historical circumstances is the essence of the art of the lawyer and judge. Discretion—a matter of character and relationship and community (to echo White)—is the most important element in the making of the law, for it is the means by which the law may be adapted to an uncertain, changing world. By so conceiving of the law as a form of constitutive rhetoric, Blackstone is not a blind apologist for the status quo but rather a humanist in the tradition of Cicero, Vico, Burke and Gadamer. Accordingly, one of Blackstone's major purposes in the *Commentaries* is to show his auditors and readers how to think about the law as a part of a changing human community.

NOTES

*This paper was originally presented to the seminar on "Blackstone and His Heritage" at the 1986 meeting of ASECS in Williamsburg. I would like to thank Rebecca Tate for reading and commenting on an earlier version of this paper.

1 The phrase belongs to Martin Shapiro, "William Blackstone," *International Encyclopedia of Social Science* (New York: Macmillian, 1968), 2:82.

2 *Essays on Government*, 2d ed. (Oxford: Clarendon Press, 1951), 126.

3 *The Mysterious Science of the Law: An Essay on Blackstone's "Commentaries"* (Cambridge: Harvard University Press, 1941), 122.

4 "The Structure of Blackstone's *Commentaries*," *Buffalo Law Review* 28 (1979): 211.

5 See Louis Menand, "Radicalism for Yuppies," *New Republic*, 17 March 1986, 20–23.

6 See, for example, Harold G. Hanbury, "Blackstone as a Judge," *American Journal of Legal History* 3 (1959): 1–27 and "Blackstone in Retrospect," *Law Quarterly Review* 66 (1950): 218–47; Sir W. S. Holdsworth, "Some Aspects of Blackstone and His *Commentaries*," *Cambridge Law Journal* 4 (1932): 261–85; David A. Lockmiller, *Sir William Blackstone* (1938; rpt. Gloucester: Peter Smith, 1970), 128–31; Julian S. Waterman, "Mansfield and Blackstone's *Commentaries*," *University of Chicago Law Review* 1 (1933): 549–71.

7 Lockmiller, *Blackstone*, 167.

8 *The Ancient Constitution and the Feudal Law: A Study of English Historical Thought in the Seventeenth Century* (Cambridge: Cambridge University Press, 1957), 243.

9 Ibid., 242.

10 *Heracles' Bow: Essays on the Rhetoric and Poetics of Law* (Madison: University of Wisconsin Press, 1985). Hereafter cited in the text.

11 Some sense of the long humanist tradition behind White's concept may be found in Ernesto Grassi, *Rhetoric as Philosophy: The Humanist Tradition* (University Park: Pennsylvania State Univeristy Press, 1980). An important eighteenth-century formulation of constitutive rhetoric is Vico's 1709 lecture, *De nostri temporis studiorum ratione*, translated as *On the Study Method of Our Time*, trans. Elio Gianturco (Indianapolis: Bobbs-Merrill, 1965). The philosophical implications of the ideas underlying constitutive rhetoric are explored most profoundly by Hans-Georg Gadamer, *Truth and Method* (New York: Seabury Press, 1975). The book originally appeared in 1960. Especially pertinent are the discussions of the *sensus communis* (19–29) and historicism (153–341).

12 *On the Study Method of Our Time*, 34. Vico alludes to the *Nicomachean Ethics* 5.10.

13 *Commentaries on the Laws of England*, 4 vols. (1765–69; rpt. Chicago: University of Chicago Press, 1979), 1:5–6. Hereafter cited in the text by volume and page.

14 Paul Lucas, "Blackstone and the Reform of the Legal Profession," *English Historical Review* 77 (1962): 456–89.

15 *English Literature in History, 1730–80: An Equal, Wide Survey* (New York: St. Martin's Press, 1983), 17–50.

16 Sir W. S. Holdsworth, "Blackstone's Treatment of Equity," *Harvard Law Review* 43 (1930): 6–32. It should be noted that the manuscript of Blackstone's lectures dating from 1761–62 contains only a relatively sketchy treatment of equity. Only after he came under Mansfield's influence did he apparently expand the discussion for the printed version. See ibid., 11–12.

17 Ibid., 1–6.

18 *Mysterious Science*, 136.

19 Some sense of the difference between Blackstone's approach and that of other legal traditions emerges if one compares the *Commentaries* with a work such as Pufendorf's *De jure naturae et gentium* (1672). The latter is concerned to establish the logical consistency and authority of a system, with constant reference to scholarly, metaphysical, and theological precedents. There is little sense, in Pufendorf, of the application of the law to a specific historical situation. (See, for example, book 3, chapter 1, on injuries, one of the sections closest in subject matter to Blackstone on homicide.) In Blackstone the law is constantly situated with respect to circumstance and history.

20 *Ancient Constitution*, 244.

21 This is not to deny Blackstone's antiquarian and political interests. After all, he was a member of the Antiquarian Society, and he wrote studies of historical antiquities along with some in literary history. He was also very interested in architectural history. See Lockmiller, *Blackstone*, 62, 75–83. Politically he is easily situated in a long line of polemical defenders of the English constitution. See, for example, Gerald L. Belcher, "Commonwealth Ideas in the Political Thought of the Defenders of the Eighteenth-Century English Constitution," *Eighteenth-Century Life* 3 (1976): 63–69. As Shapiro (82) has pointed out, Blackstone's convenience as a target to some extent accounts for the caricature of him as antiquarian-apologist.

Women, Publishers, and Money, 1790–1820

JAN FERGUS
JANICE FARRAR THADDEUS

At the end of the eighteenth century, a woman who considered herself genteel had few options if she wanted or needed to make money. Working-class women could procure jobs as servants or shop assistants; the work was ill-paid and constricting, but it was available. Those in the middling classes who desired larger incomes were generally barred from the sort of employment where such incomes were feasible. Of the few professions open to women, acting was the most lucrative, but it was self-promoting and flamboyant – and hence morally suspect. Writing alone offered the promise of decent wages without demanding a lengthy apprenticeship or even a remarkable genius – and a writer's gentility might survive relatively undamaged. Perhaps the rush of women into print during the last half of the century can be traced to such considerations. Whatever the reasons, as Judith P. Stanton has shown, the number of published women writers increased dramatically – by about fifty percent per decade – in the second half of the century, with fiction and poetry the favored genres.[1] Money became the subject as well as the object of many of these women, who often created what Edward Copeland has called "fictions of employment." Writers for the Minerva Press, such as Agnes Maria Bennett, whose father was a grocer, depicted employment as a practical and necessary means of support, whereas the more genteel authors viewed earned money with a certain unmistakable distaste.[2] In Frances Burney's *Wanderer* (1814), for instance, Juliet Granville suffers a complicated mixture of satisfaction and distress when she is first paid for her needlework:

> There is a something indefinable, which stands between spirit and delicacy, that makes the first reception of money in detail, by those not brought up to gain it, embarrassing and painful.[3]

Burney's fictional character never quite resolves her relationship to her earnings, but Burney herself eventually learned how to negotiate with her publisher. And Burney was not unique. Archival records show that many of the other women who chose to enter the profession of authorship at the end of the eighteenth century were also able to deal firmly and successfully with their publishers.

Because partial publishing records have survived, we have been able to study in detail portions of the careers of two women writers at the end of the eighteenth century and the beginning of the nineteenth: Mary Darby Robinson (1758–1800) and Amelia Alderson Opie (1769–1853). Robinson published five works with Hookham and Carpenter, who were essentially fashionable booksellers producing as a sideline a few titles each year.[4] The Hookham records, previously unknown to scholars, provide a rare view of transactions between authors and small publishers in the 1790s. Because Thomas Hookham and James Carpenter engaged in a lawsuit after the dissolution of their partnership in 1798, the records survive among the Chancery Masters' Lists in the Public Record Office (C104/75/1–3). They consist of two large ledger books labelled F and G and one small "Petty Ledger" labelled F. All three ledgers document credit purchases between 1791 and 1798 by individual customers, usually other booksellers or members of the aristocracy and gentry residing in London. Some pages of ledgers F and G also include information about the printing, publishing, and sale of various Hookham publications. Hookham's accounts with Robinson are especially well documented and revealing.[5] In mid-career Robinson switched from Hookham to the house of Longman, a large company which sold only to the trade, and the move to the larger house entailed a more profitable relationship between author and publisher, as the archives indicate. Opie's thirty-year association with Longman was also profitable, but subject to stresses, as reflected in her publisher's letters to her.[6] As writers, both women developed middling to strong contemporary reputations in a variety of genres, and their lives are comparable in that both were born in prosperous circumstances,[7] yet both came to depend on their professional income.

At this period there were four chief methods by which authors published their works, and Robinson and Opie between them employed all four.[8] The available schemes were: subscription, fee for limited copyright, profit-sharing, and publishing on "commission" (whereby the author assumed responsibility for repaying the capital if the book did not make a profit).[9] The modern system of royalty payments, by which the author receives a percentage of the list price, was not yet practiced, or at least not widely practiced. We found no instance of it in either set of records.

Subscription could be the most lucrative method, but it was demeaning, especially for women, since it required direct solicitation for payment. The run-of-the-mill beginning author would use this method to test the waters — publishing proposals and carefully gauging the response. Even after all this careful preparation, subscription publication might be only minimally profitable. Hookham and Carpenter author Emily Clark, for instance, who dedicated her book "by permission to His Royal Highness the Prince of Wales," and further styled herself as "grand-daughter of the late Colonel Frederick, son of Theodore, King of Corsica," got £43.01.0 in subscriptions for her two-volume novel *Ianthé* (1798), and 229 copies sold in addition, but she seems ultimately to have made only about a pound from Hookham (G/137, 126).[10]

The blanket fee for limited copyright, which became possible after *de jure* perpetual copyright was struck down by the House of Lords in 1774, seems to have been the most prestigious if not the most lucrative system of payment. Longman gauged this fee — and gauged it very accurately, on the whole — by the number of copies printed, price, and anticipated speed of sale.[11] Hookham and Carpenter, on the other hand, hardly ever bought copyrights. Perhaps they knew that their sense of the market was not finely tuned enough. When they bought the pseudonymous Matilda Fitz John's four-volume novel *Joan!!!* in 1796 they paid £63, printed 750 copies, sold 509, and lost £9.19.2 (G/122). Predicting sales was certainly important, but in any case the market was small. At Hookham a cautious author might print as few as 500 copies, though orders of 750 were more usual. At Longman in the 1790s, print orders for unknown authors were almost invariably for 750 copies (25 Feb. 1815, I/99/70). The amounts paid for subsequent works depended somewhat on previous sales. Anna Maria Porter was offered only fifty guineas per volume for her *Don Sebastian*, since the sale of her *Poems* was "considerably short of the expenses of the work," 650 copies remaining of the 1000 printed (19 Jan. 1814, Longman I/98/121). On the other hand, Longman was willing to offer £1000 in 1815 to Ann Radcliffe for a book-length poem, sight unseen. Their prose was oily, sliding into the third person: "If they take the liberty to request to be favd with the perusal of the whole of the Poem, it is only to complete their expected gratification" (27 Feb. 1815, I/99/189, draft). Evidently this strategy was unsuccessful, since Radcliffe never published any poetry with Longman.

With an untried author, Longman preferred profit-sharing. To Harriet Hughes regarding her three-volume novel *She Thinks for Herself*, Longman offered to "be at the entire expence of publishing the work, & divide the clear profits with the author," with a printing of "500 or 750 copies" (18 Nov. 1812, I/97/377). They also suggested profit-sharing to Elizabeth Hamilton when she approached them about publishing her school-texts, with the further statement that if educational institutions appeared to be adopting the texts, they would name a copyright fee (6 Feb. and 1 March 1815, I/99/73,97). Profit-sharing eliminated all risk for the author. The publisher assumed the responsibility for deciding what to print and reprint, and absorbed any losses. If there were profits, these were equally shared between author and publisher. However, it could be more profitable for the author to gamble by publishing on commission.

In an 1811 letter to Lady Impey, who was inquiring on behalf of her thirty-one-year-old son, Longman explained the fourth option: publishing "on account of the author." If Longman assumed the risk and shared the profits, and the edition sold out, the Impeys stood to gain the munificent sum of £22.3.0; if the author assumed the risk and the publisher charged a 10% commission (a kind of modern royalty in reverse), the author would gain half again as much, or £33.0.0 (15 Feb. 1811, I/97/23).

This was the set of options faced by Mary Darby Robinson (1758–1800) when she first began to cast about for ways to support her profligate husband and their child in the 1770s. Writing was not her only source of income. She had taken to acting, excelling so memorably that she was known as "Perdita" Robinson. Although she left the stage in 1780 during her brief liaison with the Prince of Wales, she eventually secured £500 per year in honor of their affair. Gillray's cartoon "The Thunderer," published 20 August 1782, most succinctly summarizes Robinson's notorious reputation at that time.[12] In Gillray's rendering, Robinson's lover, Lieutenant Colonel Banastre Tarleton, has vanquished his headless three-plumed rival Prince George, and she is enticing him to "Alamode Beef, hot every Night — " at the sign of the "Whirligig." To have her image, thus sexually impaled, published throughout fashionable London must have caused unimaginable torment to the genteelly nurtured Robinson. At her death she was working on an autobiography whose chief purpose was to explain why she had succumbed to the Prince. Not long after she began the relationship with Tarleton, she was stricken with an arthritic condition which crippled her for life. How did she handle this predicament? Laetitia Hawkins tells us — though not kindly:

> She then took up a new life in London, became literary, brought up her daughter literary, and expressed without qualification her rage when her works were not urged forward beyond all others.[13]

Figure 1: Gillray, "The Thunderer."

She was literary, but did she make money?

Robinson attempted to control her own career, and she made many publishing decisions herself. But even so her earliest literary efforts — poems in subscription volumes and periodicals, and the two-volume novel *Vancenza; or, The Dangers of Credulity* (1792) — apparently brought her no satisfactory income. In 1794 she switched from her current publisher[14] to Hookham, who delivered her novel *The Widow* to the booksellers on February 13th. In July she received £21, which for someone in her position did not go far. "Let common sense judge how I can subsist upon £500 a year, when my carriage (a necessary expense) alone costs me £200," she wrote a friend on 4 October 1794. "My mental labours have failed through the dishonest conduct of my publishers. My works have sold handsomely but the profits have been theirs."[15] Hookham and Carpenter do not seem to have cheated Robinson, but their records are difficult to read. She or a surrogate seems to have stopped by at the shop (which was nearby) on the average of once a week — to have presentation copies of her own works bound, to buy a book or periodical — and presumably to inquire into her current sales. Although Robinson liked to live elegantly, she also watched her pennies. In fact, at one point the records carefully note that she received a credit of 4/11 when overcharged 1 *d.* apiece for the binding of fifty-nine copies of *The Sicilian Lover* (G/12). So far as we can tell, this is the only instance of "dishonest conduct," and it occurred in 1796. Still, Robinson's financial position did not improve. With Hookham over a two-and-a-half-year period she published "on account of the author" three novels, a play, and a sonnet sequence. In spite of the fact that in 1796 Robinson was the best-selling single author at Hookham,[16] she cleared over her four-and-a-half year relationship with them less than £10.[17]

The reason for this sad outcome was not that Hookham cheated Robinson, nor that she disbursed money extravagantly, but that she misjudged the market. In 1794, she had printed 1500 copies of *The Widow* — at least twice as many as an unknown author would have chanced — and for the first five months it sold briskly, right past the break-even point, which was about a third of the edition. But in 1796, her best year, Robinson made two errors, one of them fatal. She published her tragedy *The Sicilian Lover* — for which, incidentally, she had not secured a production — and it did not sell. Four months after publication, only thirty-two copies had been bought. Because *The Sicilian Lover* fell dead from the press, she owed more than £22. This was unfortunate, but not overwhelming. Her fatal mistake was that when *Angelina* sold right through the first edition — which she had judiciously limited to 750 copies — she rushed to print a second edition, and the book almost instantly stalled. Jane Austen was to experience a similar disaster with the second edition of *Mansfield Park*, but her loss was offset by profits on *Emma*.[18] Robinson, however, immediately fell into debt, and deeply so. Since she had earlier drawn some of her profits, she now owed £133.13.1, and she was never able to pay it back—or at any rate she never did pay it back. Hookham and Carpenter themselves, as we have already noted, were not always good judges of the market, and Robinson was probably not receiving good advice.

It's not clear what impulse caused Robinson to shift in 1797 from Hookham to Longman, but she certainly made the proper choice. At Longman she no longer had to bother with all the petty details of managing her own costs. She simply accepted the copyright money and let Longman take care of the rest. For the last three years of her life, she averaged about £150 per year.[19] She certainly did not match her £500 pension, but she was at last keeping her profits. Evidently she needed this money, needed it so much that she took advances, steadily; this sort of borrowing was rare at Longman. One gets the sense that the larger organization treated her with more consideration than the smaller one had done. Certainly the relationship was more dignified and professional, with fewer exchanges of small amounts of cash. But the Prince of Wales fell behind on his payments, and Robinson's furious efforts to support herself by her writing were insufficient. Her reputation was growing, and she was well known in the highest literary circles, exchanging poems with Coleridge. Longman's confidence was reflected in their print order of 1250 instead of 1000 for her last book. According to her daughter, although eventually "she had voluntarily relinquished those comforts and elegancies to which she had been accustomed," she died in debt.[20] As she said of her writer-heroine in her last novel, "All that her honourable, her incessant industry could procure, was insufficient for the purposes of attaining a permanent independence."[21]

Like Robinson, Amelia Opie moved in fashionable circles for part of her life and overdrew her accounts with her publishers, even though she enjoyed a sizeable income from other sources. Nonetheless, both her life and her career were more prosperous than Robinson's. Opie remained respectable despite a youthful flirtation with William Godwin and his set.[22] Her childless marriage to the rather uncouth painter John Opie left her with about £10,000 when he died in 1807, a sum which could have brought her an income of as much as £500 a year.[23] She lived in London and Norwich for more than forty-five years after his death and continued to publish tales until she formally became a Quaker in 1825, remaining so until her death in 1853.[24] Unlike Robinson, who depended on her income from writing in her last years, Opie relinquished hers. A Quaker could not publish fiction: after 1825, Opie published only one book of heavily didactic tales and a volume of poetry.[25] Even without

Quakerism, Opie might have chosen to retire from her profession at about this time because her popularity had considerably declined.

During more than thirty years as a writer of poetry and didactic domestic fiction, Opie was reasonably successful. From eleven novels and three books of poetry published by Longman between 1804 and 1834, she earned at least £4280.[26] These profits amount to about a third of Maria Edgeworth's earnings during approximately the same period, and almost exactly as much as Burney received from her four novels.[27] During her most profitable period, between 1804 and 1820, Opie obtained an average of more than £200 a year, although wide variations appear in yearly receipts, from nothing in 1807 to nearly £500 in 1818.[28] At this time, she was a moderately popular author by her publisher's own definition. Longman generally printed 2000 copies of any new work by Opie, midway between the 1000 copies said to be printed of "the generality of books" and the 3000 for "some of the popular novelists of the present day" (25 Feb. 1815, I/99/70). Few novelists were "popular" in this sense — perhaps only Walter Scott among Longman's authors. Novels by writers such as Jane Porter and Jane West, like Opie's, were printed in initial runs of 2000 at this time.[29] As a rule, the 2000 copies of Opie's works were distributed as a first and a false second edition, allowing both the firm and the author to obtain the prestige of a reprinting without the expense.

More than 70 percent of Opie's earnings came from sharing her profits equally with Longman. The firm apparently offered her a copyright fee only when she produced four-volume works. They bought the copyright of three novels at £100 or guineas a volume: *Simple Tales* (1806; £400), *New Tales* (1818; £420), and *Tales of the Heart* (1820; £400). On the whole, profit-sharing brought Opie more money than sale of copyright. She made over £300 a volume by profit-sharing on her most popular works and at least £100 a volume on every other publication that appeared between 1801 and 1825, although often only after many years had passed.[30] She could have earned more if she had published her most popular works on commission — 40 to 50 percent more *if* the work sold out. But the risk was very great, as Robinson discovered. By profit-sharing, however, Opie ran no risks. The only disadvantage of the system — also a disadvantage of publishing on commission — lay in having to wait at least a year from publication to distribution of profits.[31]

Despite particularly good earnings from profit-sharing between 1813-1816,[32] Opie seems to have run into debt within ten years after her husband's death, as copies of letters to her from Owen Rees, a Longman partner, indicate. His tone modulates from early friendliness and banter — though somewhat patronizing — to irritation and finally distance, as Opie's manuscripts become overdue, her accounts are overdrawn, and her sales dwindle. On the whole, however, the letters show a remarkable willingness on the part of the firm to accommodate Opie — and a corresponding determination on her part to obtain the best terms possible.

Hints of financial distress began to appear in February 1814, when Opie inquired whether the firm would buy the copyright of *Father and Daughter*; they declined:

> The sale of the work has of late been so slow that we could not make you such an offer for the copyright as we apprehend would in any way meet your ideas: indeed it would be in your interest to retain the property & continue to publish as hitherto. (8 Feb. 1814, I/98/132)

Rees did not ignore her need for money, however. A letter dated the following November enclosed as a gift a bank note for £100, "As we find a little money would be convenient to you at Christmas . . . as a testimony of the uniform satisfaction we have experienced in our Literary intercourse with you" (25 Nov. 1814, I/99/38). "Satisfaction" from "Literary intercourse" was, curiously, a more delicate phrase than the one Rees deleted, which alluded to profit: it contained an acknowledgment "that we have not been unprofitable publishers of your work."[33] Opie was understandably perplexed by Rees's patronizing delicacy and wondered whether the £100 was an advance on profits. He replied that it was "a *present*, which we thought justly due to you" and offered "such advances as you may desire" on the publication of her new work. He continued:

> That your writing may not be unduly hurried, we add that we value your share of the Bills & Copyrights in our hands at £200, at which sum we shall at any time be ready to purchase them. In short we wish to accommodate you in any way that you would require." (24 Jan. 1815, I/99/62)

Wisely, Opie did not accept this offer, whatever her current need. These copyrights brought her £134 in 1815, another £200 by 1820, and a further £200 before 1838, more than double Longman's offer, but over a substantial period. The firm's willingness to accommodate Opie clearly had limits.

When eight months later Opie requested an advance without depositing a manuscript, Rees's reply was a curt two sentences of irritable acquiescence: "You may draw upon us for any sum not exceeding £100 — We were in hopes you would have spared us till the publication of your new work" (13 Sept. 1815, I/99/128). Over a year later, after her next work, *Valentine's Eve*, had finally appeared, Rees sent Opie £60, with a note indicating that this sum increased her debt to the firm to more than £217 (6 Dec. 1816, I/100/39). Since Opie's earnings during the three previous years had approached £900, not including the gift of £100, this degree of debt is remarkable. A six-year gap in the correspondence now occurs, during which time Longman bought the copyrights of *New Tales* and *Tales of the Heart* at fairly generous prices. By 1821, however, the firm was not willing to purchase Opie's next novel, *Madeline*, and Rees's tone had become somewhat more formal and distant:

> We have returned your MS herewith, agreeably to your request. Should you decide to have it published, we will with pleasure undertake it on the plan of dividing the profits of each edition with you as in the case of the *"Father and Daughter."*
>
> Our Literary friend, to whose perusal we submitted the work, is of opinion that the journal form renders the work less attractive. (6 Nov. 1821, I/101/181)

Rees no longer seems to read the manuscript himself, farming it out to a "Literary friend." Only 1500 copies of *Madeline* were printed, and they were remaindered eleven years later. Opie's popularity had declined; her kind of didacticism was no longer in demand. The two-volume *Madeline* did not do very well—her share of the profit came to almost exactly £200. Her biographer is certainly wrong to accept Mary Russell Mitford's report that the copyright of Opie's next novel would have been bought for £1000 had she not converted to Quakerism and declined to complete it.[34] Her few remaining publications were neither as popular nor as profitable as her earlier work.

The Hookham and Longman archives provide, then, detailed information hitherto not readily available about the conditions that affected women's attempts to make money from writing at the turn of the century. First, although Opie and Robinson were dramatically different from one another in their public reputations as women—and in their private lives—what strikes us most forcibly is how similar their monetary position was. Both of them had an outside income of approximately £500 a year, both made for at least a portion of their careers enough money to support a moderately genteel single woman at the time,[35] and yet both fell into debt. This indebtedness evidently occurred partly because Robinson and Opie lived fashionable lives in London, and partly because their ability to sell their works was limited. Writers of poetry and fiction depended on a buying public that remained fixed in size. Robinson's books were never printed in editions larger than 1500, and sold even less. Just one of Opie's fictional works achieved a total printing of more than 3000 copies, and only two others reached 3000.[36] By the evidence of the Longman records, most fiction then, as now, sold much less than history or even anthologies. By contrast, a hackneyed collection like the *Elegant Extracts* would ordinarily have a press run of 5000 or more.[37]

Given this limited audience, a woman's choice of publisher was especially significant. Although the four methods of publication did not vary, publishers seem to have differed in which of these methods they preferred to make available to writers. Robinson found Longman a far more profitable publisher than Hookham because Longman was willing to purchase her copyrights. The combination of profit-sharing and copyright-buying that Longman offered Opie worked to her advantage. Austen would have made more money if she had published by profit-sharing the four novels that appeared during her lifetime. Her combination of selling copyright and publishing for herself produced the measly grand total of less than £700.[38]

At the end of the eighteenth century, women believed that they were working in an atmosphere that did not condone their money-making activities. Much of the current rhetoric supported this belief. In 1794, for instance, the *Critical Review* accused Robinson of writing her poems for "calls more pressing than the impulse of genius or the desire of fame."[39] Distaste for this sort of patronizing reproach may have encouraged many women — as shown in the Hookham ledgers, the Longman letters, and elsewhere — to use men as fronts when negotiating money matters. The most famous case is Burney's brother Charles, who negotiated *Camilla* into a copyright of £1000 plus subscriptions of an approximately equal amount. In fact, however, Hookham and Longman do not actually seem to have discriminated against women writers. As far as we can determine, the two publishers offered both men and women similar terms for similar work. Possibly for this reason, we find some evidence that, increasingly, women were negotiating for themselves. After Charles Burney's death, Burney herself wrote a sharp third-person letter to Longman, objecting to their assertion that sales of *The Wanderer* had stalled and requiring half-yearly notice of its progress.[40] In the Hookham and Longman records, many women published under their own names and conducted their own business transactions.[41] As mentioned earlier, Lady Impey actually managed her son's negotiations. Accompanying this new professionalism among women, we occasionally detect at Longman the remains of an avuncular, supportive attitude in relationships with women in general. We have found no indication in the archives that any male writer of this period was permitted to remain in debt as Robinson and Opie did. Since the debts were quite substantial, Hookham's failure to arrest Robinson for her two-year-old unpaid note and Longman's willingness to accommodate both Opie and Robinson with sizeable advances suggest that, if anything, some women writers could be quite adroit in converting their publishers' patronizing impulses into financial support.

NOTES

1 Judith P. Stanton, "Statistical Profile of Women Writing from 1660 to 1800," forthcoming in *Eighteenth-Century Women and the Arts*, ed. Frederick M. Keener and Susan E. Lorsch.

2 Edward Copeland, "Employment and the Novel," forthcoming in *Studies in Philology*.

3 *The Wanderer*, 5 vols. (London: Longman, 1814), 3:175.

4 We are grateful to Ruthe Battestin for her help in locating the Hookham records. Subsequent references will appear in parentheses in the text; citations will include the letter and page number of the appropriate ledger.

5 During the 1790s, Hookham also published novels by Ann Radcliffe and Clara Reeve, but unfortunately no records of these transactions have survived.

6 The records of the House of Longman are much more extensive and varied than the Hookham records. The firm, still extant, has deposited its archives at the University of Reading, and most have recently become available on mirofilm (*Archives of the House of Longman* [Cambridge, Eng.: Chadwyck-Healey Inc.]). The records include copies of the firm's letters to authors and other publishers from 1810 on, as well as information about printing costs (from 1794) and sales of works published on commission and by profit-sharing (from 1803). Because Longman sold only to the trade, the archives contain only a few records of individual purchases (for instance, when an author asked for a Longman publication and had it charged against his own publishing account).

7 Opie's father was a physician and Robinson's a merchant. Eventually, John Darby lost his fortune and deserted his wife, while James Alderson retained both, and as a result of these differing circumstances Robinson married unwisely at fifteen, and Opie married well at twenty-nine.

8 There is no up-to-date general book on the subject of book-publishing in the eighteenth century. The standard work is Frank A. Mumby and Ian Norrie, *Publishing and Bookselling, Part I: From the Earliest Times to 1870*, 5th ed. (London: Cape, 1974), but this date is deceptive, since the latest scholarship is not incorporated into the text. Terry Belanger discusses methods of publication in "Publishers and Writers in Eighteenth-Century England" (*Books and Their Readers in Eighteenth-Century England*, ed. Isabel Rivers [New York: St. Martin's Press, 1982], 5–25) and includes a helpful bibliography. However, he emphasizes that authors often provided their own capital in advance, as a subsidy, which was not the case in either the Hookham or Longman establishments. Profit-sharing, which Belanger mentions as rare in the 1790's (6), had become common enough by 1807 for Longman to set up a special "divide" ledger. And, on at least one occasion, Hookham did use profit-sharing—on the second edition of Mrs. Marriott's anonymously published *The Minstrel*, 3 vols., printed in 1794 (F/702). The first mention we have found of profit-sharing is in a fictional account, the letter from Henry Davis to Jonathan Dustwich which prefaces *Humphry Clinker*.

9 The "commission" system was so called because the bookseller took a commission (usually 10, but sometimes 7.5 percent on the wholesale price). In addition, at Hookham trade customers took a free copy for every twenty-five ordered.

10 Clark lists in the front of her book more than 250 copies sold by subscription, but only a third of these are mentioned in the Hookham records. She might have delivered the rest of the books herself, and if she did, she would have gleaned about £90 more, but the records do not note that the author received any copies. The Robinson records clearly indicate how many copies went to the author. Actually, in the end, Clark owed Hookham £7.11.9, but she had spent £8.1.8 on her miscellaneous account with the firm, so that she may be said ultimately to have gained that £1.

11 In 1814, Owen Rees of Longman estimated that Opie's seventh edition of *Father and Daughter* would last "about five years" and he was precisely right: Longman Letter Books, transcribed by Michael Bott (I/98/132, 8 February 1814, hereafter cited by number in the text).

12 Conventional portraits of Robinson and a few satirical prints can be found in Wallace Collection Monograph I: John Ingamells, *Mrs. Robinson and Her Portraits* (London: The Trustees of the Wallace Collection, 1978).

13 Laetitia Hawkins, *Memoirs, Anecdotes, Facts, and Opinions*, 3 vols. (London: Longman, 1824), 2:33–34. Hawkins appreciates Robinson's difficulties. She says in the course of her account that Robinson's husband turned down "Employment in writing" when he was imprisoned for debt, whereas, "in this depth of misery, his wife was eminently meritorious; she had her child to attend to, she did all the work of their apartments, she even scoured the stairs, and accepted the writing and the pay which he had refused" (25).

14 Robinson had used a variety of publishers, including C. Parker, T. Becket, J. Bell, and J. Evans and T. Becket. Bell had published *Vancenza* for her. In September, 1800, just before her death, she had a poem published by Laurie & Whittle.

15 John Taylor, *Records of My Life* (1832), quoted in Robert D. Bass, *The Green Dragoon, the Lives of Banastre Tarleton and Mary Robinson* (New York: Holt, 1957), 344.

16 For instance, 172 of the 277 books sold by Hookham in 1796 to G. G. J. and J. Robinson, booksellers on Paternoster Row, were by Mary Robinson (G/2).

17 Robinson's account is noted in the Hookham Ledgers F/699, F/711, G/12, G/28, and G/142. Many items are mentioned twice, as if a clerk had hurriedly made notes which later needed to be rationalized. Between 29 January 1794 and 1 June 1798, when her books were remaindered, Robinson withdrew approximately £84 in cash and £23 in items which might be called personal expenses. She also spent £16.11.0 having presentation or subscription copies of her books bound. Some of her disbursements and also some of her earnings may not have appeared on the Hookham accounts. There are no expenses for advertising, and she certainly did advertise, placing the ads very carefully at judicious intervals, and changing the wording when appropriate (for instance, there are advertisements for *The Widow* in 1794 in *The Morning Chronicle*

on 10, 14, 18 Feb., and again on 12 March, and in *The Morning Post* on 12 Feb., 17 Feb., 26 Feb., 4 March, and 12 March. On 12 March, Robinson's daughter's novel was also published, and the ads appear together). Advertising costs, when noted by Hookham, seem to have run as high as £7–£13 per book. In addition, Robinson took at least 150 copies of her various books to dispose of herself.

18 See Jane Aiken Hodge, *Only a Novel: The Double Life of Jane Austen* (New York: Coward, McCann & Geoghegan, 1972), 124. Hodge is wrong to state that the second edition of *Mansfield Park* "finally cleared £118 18s. 4d." (125); in fact, the John Murray ledgers make clear that overall the novel lost £63.9.11. This sum represents the difference between £182.8.3, the initial loss on the novel, and the nearly £119 that was realized in three years of slow sales followed by the remaindering of most of the edition.

19 Robinson's advances and fees for copyright, together with the Longman costs for printing, paper, advertising, etc., appear in the Longman Impression Books I/140/43, 44, 64 and I/141/32. With Longman, Robinson published: *Walsingham* (1797), 4 vols., 1000 copies printed, £150 copyright; *The False Friend* (1799), 4 vols., 1000 copies, £150; *The Natural Daughter* (1799), 2 vols., 1000 copies, £60; and *Lyrical Tales* (1800), 1 vol., 1250 copies, £63; she had also begun collecting subscriptions for her poems and written a pseudonymous book on "the Cruelties of Mental Subordination" which she later had produced under her own name. In addition, she published numerous poems in various periodicals. How much money she gained from these periodical publications cannot be determined.

20 Mary Elizabeth Robinson, ed., *Memoirs of the Late Mrs. Robinson, written by herself* (London: Hunt and Clarke, 1826), 144.

21 *The Natural Daughter* (London: Longman, 1799), 2: 69–70.

22 Margaret Eliot Magregor, *Amelia Alderson Opie: Worldling and Friend* (Menasha, Wisconsin: The Collegiate Press, 1933), 19–22.

23 Ada Earland, *John Opie and his Circle* (London: Hutchinson, 1911), 236.

24 Magregor, 87.

25 Magregor lists also a number of essays and poems that appeared in various periodicals, 132–34.

26 Opie's yearly earnings on each of her works, along with information on size of editions, selling prices, speed of sale, and so forth, are entered in Longman I/1/77, 112 (Joint Commission and Divide Ledger, 1803–07); I/2/76, 78, 79, 80, 102, 150, 227, 276, 291, 300 (Divide Ledger, 1807–28); I/3/82, 91, 110, 124, 138, 146, 171, 214, 246, 262, 345 (Divide Ledger, 1828–67); and I/4/259–62 (Divide Ledger 1828–67). See also microfilm Longman Archives, reels 1 and 2. Additional information, including data on sales of copyright, is entered in the Impression Books, 1801–12 (I/141/122; I/142/53, 107, 176, 179, 207, 218; I/143/74, 104, 187; also on reels 37–38) and in Copyright Ledgers 2 and 3, 1800–29 (reel 51/76, 101–102). When compiled, the figures indicate that Opie's earnings (in five-year segments) came to: 1804–05, £357.4.5½ (and possibly another £122, estimated profits between 1801–03; see footnote 26); 1806–10,

£745.5.11 3/4; 1811–15, £990.15.4; 1816–20, £1331.0.11; 1821–25, £504.4.5; 1826–30, £133.11.1; 1831–38, £119.7.4; total £4181.10.4¼, plus a gift of £100 in 1814.

Opie may have received some other profits from the writing not published by Longman mentioned in note 25. Before her association with the firm, she also published anonymously *The Dangers of Coquetry* (2 vols., 1790).

27 For Edgeworth's earnings, see Marilyn Butler, *Maria Edgeworth* (Oxford: Clarendon Press, 1972), 492: she reprints a list that Edgeworth made in 1842, indicating receipts of £11,062.8.10 overall. Burney apparently made a total of approximately £4280 from her novels. She eventually received £30 for *Evelina* (Edward A. Bloom, "Introduction," *Evelina* [London: Oxford Univ. Press, 1982], xi); £250 for *Cecilia* (Joyce Hemlow, *Fanny Burney* [Oxford: Clarendon Press, 1958], 148); about £2000 for *Camilla*, of which £1000 came from the sale of the copyright (Edward A. and Lillian D. Bloom, "Introduction," *Camilla* [London: Oxford Univ. Press, 1983], xx, xix); and about £2000 for the first and second editions of *The Wanderer* (Hemlow, 337).

28 In 1818, Opie sold the copyright of her *New Tales* for £420. The additional £70.10.11 earned came from her half profits on the year's sales of *Father and Daughter* (7th ed.), *Poems* (6th ed.), *Temper* (3rd ed.), and *Valentine's Eve*.

29 According to the Longman Copyright Ledger, 1800–17, reel 51/92–93, 2000 copies were printed of Porter's *The Scottish Chiefs* (5 vols., 1810). The Longman Impression Books show that West's *The Loyalists* (3 vols., 1812) also received an initial printing of 2000 (I/143/188). On the whole, these records indicate that Opie commanded higher prices per volume for her novels than either of these fairly popular writers. Porter received £315 for the copyright of *The Scottish Chiefs* and West £210 for *The Loyalists*, less than Opie's £400 for the copyright of *Simple Tales* in 1806. All of these women, however, were receiving more than the minimum of £50 a volume demanded by Charlotte Smith in the 1790s in her correspondence with Cadell and Davies; see Judith P. Stanton, "Charlotte Smith's 'Literary Business,' " to appear in the first volume of *The Age of Johnson*, ed. Paul Korshin. Stanton is also editing Smith's correspondence.

30 The Longman archives indicate that Opie received a total of £296.17.11½ for the fourth through the ninth editions (including part of the third) of *Father and Daughter* (1801). The first edition consisted of 750 copies; if the second and third editions consisted of 1000 each, as did the fourth, fifth, and eighth, Opie must have made about £77 additional for the first two editions and part of the third. Similarly, she made £356.3.6¾ from the third through the sixth editions of her *Poems* (1802), including part of the second edition. If the first and second editions consisted of 750 and 1000 copies respectively, then Opie's total earnings for this work would have been increased by another £45. These earnings compared favorably with the £100 that Edgeworth obtained for the copyright of *Castle Rackrent* (1800), a work almost contemporaneous with Opie's *Father and Daughter* that also went through several editions.

Apart from the receipts already mentioned, Opie earned £335.12.2¼ for *Adeline Mowbray*, 3 vols. (1804), by the time the last of 2500 copies printed altogether was sold in 1823; for *The Warrior's Return and Other Poems* (1808), £109.13.8 ¾ (2000 copies, last sold in 1815); for *Temper, or Domestic Scenes*, 3 vols. (1812), £612.9.2 (the last of the 3000 copies printed altogether were remaindered in 1838); for *Tales of Real Life*, 3 vols. (1813), £413.5.5 (2500 copies, last sold 1833); for *Valentine's Eve*, 2 vols. (1816), £365.9.11 (2000 copies, remaindered in 1833); for *Madeline*, 2 vols. (1822), £203.8.11 (1500 copies, remaindered in 1833); for *Illustrations of Lying, in All its Branches*, 2 vols. (1825), £214.0.5 (1500 copies, last sold in 1833); and for *Detraction Displayed* (1828), £19.15.2 (2000 copies, remaindered in 1833). Opie's last work, a book of poems entitled *Lays for the Dead* (1834), was printed in an edition of 1000 and remaindered in 1838; it realized a loss. She also printed her husband's *Lectures on Painting* in 1809, receiving 250 copies as her copyright fee (I/142/207).

31 For example, Opie's *Temper*, published in 1812, sold out all 2000 copies of the first and false second editions in twelve months. Opie may have received £432, her share of the profits, at that time or in the following June. A delay of two years was more common, as in the case of the fifth edition of *Father and Daughter*, published in 1806, but not profitable until 1808.

32 Earnings for 1813 were £448.18.5; for 1814, £311.13.11; for 1815, £134.5.6; and for 1816, £294.5.7. In addition, Opie received a gift of £100 from Longman in 1814.

33 A similar gift in 1816 to the poet James Montgomery was offered more directly. Rees called him one of their "successful & most esteemed authors" (I/99/173).

34 Magregor, 86. The Longman archives also make clear that Magregor is wrong to attribute *Self Delusion, or Adelaide d'H . . .* to Opie (85); Longman published this work and another, *Domestic Scenes*, for a Mrs. Blair (see I/3/174–175).

35 Austen's mother required £460 a year to support herself and her two daughters after her husband died in 1805, *Austen Papers, 1704–1856*, ed. R. A. Austen-Leigh ([London]: privately printed by Spottiswoode, Ballantyne, & Co. Ltd., 1942), 235. The genteel spinsters and widows of Elizabeth Gaskell's *Cranford* make do on considerably less, though with much recourse to the expedients of "elegant economy." Miss Matty Jenkyns' income before the failure of the Town and County Bank can be calculated at about £160 a year, and it served to support both her and her sister when Deborah Jenkyns was alive.

36 *Father and Daughter* ran through nine editions for a total printing of 6750 copies plus the first three editions (probably another 2750 copies); *Simple Tales* and *Temper* reached 3000 copies each. Opie's *Poems* (1802) were also popular: editions three through six totaled 5000 copies.

37 See the Longman Impression Books; 6000 copies of the *Elegant Extracts* in verse were printed in March 1796 and 6000 of the prose version were produced in the next year (I/140/7, 18). Subsequent orders—for example, of the verse extracts in 1801 and 1805—usually were for 5000 copies (I/141/4, 144).

38 Austen seems to have made £684.13.0, which represents, according to her own memorandum of her earnings, some £600 that she had invested in "Navy Fives,"

£13.7.0 (residue of profits on the first edition of *Mansfield Park*); £12.15.0, profits on the second edition of *Sense and Sensibility* received in March 1816; £38.18.0, the first profits on *Emma*, received in February 1817; and £19.13.0, further profits on the second edition of *Sense and Sensibility*, received in March 1817 (see Hodge, *Only a Novel*, 208).

We can only approximate Austen's likely earnings through profit-sharing because precise figures for the size of most of the editions printed in her lifetime are lacking. She earned £140 from the first edition of *Sense and Sensibility*; based on the figures in the Longman records for books of similar length and price (15s) printed in 1811, this profit from selling on commission means that the first edition probably consisted of 750 copies. The second edition, again judging by the Longman records, was unlikely to be larger. It was published in 1813, most likely in an edition of 750, and reached a break-even point in 1815, as Austen's memorandum makes clear. (The novel sold at 18s in boards and thus is somewhat comparable to Opie's "third" edition of *Temper* [3 vols., 1813], of which 1000 copies were printed; like the second edition of *Sense and Sensibility*, *Temper* sold slowly, and Opie received her first profits in 1816, just as Austen did.) Again, the Longman records suggest that the first edition of *Mansfield Park* probably consisted of 1500 copies; the John Murray archives indicate that the second edition of *Mansfield Park* and the sole edition of *Emma* consisted of 750 and 2000 copies respectively. The third edition of *Pride and Prejudice* appeared after Austen's death. Assuming that the first two editions amounted to 1000 and 750 copies respectively, then we can estimate that Austen would have made £780 (or 14 percent more) before her death if she had published all her novels by profit-sharing. This sum is very conservative. If the editions were in fact larger, she would have made more money.

39 10:2 (1794): 382.

40 Letter 1113, 30 August 1817, *The Journals and Letters of Fanny Burney (Madame D'Arblay)*, ed. Warren Derry (Oxford: Clarendon Press, 1982) 10:631–32.

41 This trend very soon reversed itself. Many nineteenth-century women took on male pseudonyms; by the 1861 census women outnumbered men in the professions of teaching and midwifery, but in the 1865 census only 145 women admitted to being authors, as compared to 1,528 men. W. J. Reader, *Professional Men* (London: Weidenfeld and Nicolson, 1966), 172–73.

The Ideological Implications
of Onomatopoeia
in the Eighteenth Century

R O Y   H A R R I S

Twentieth-century linguistics recognizes onomatopoetic words only as constituting a small, rather marginal and perhaps even dubious exception to the general principle that the linguistic sign is arbitrary.[1] The term *onomatopoeia* does not even appear among the entries listed in the most recent dictionary of linguistic terminology.[2] This omission would have struck many eighteenth-century writers about language as remarkable and perhaps inexplicable. It would doubtless have seemed so to the editors of what may be regarded as being, among its other claims to fame, Europe's first dictionary of linguistics, the *Encyclopédie*, which contains an important article *Onomatopée*, written by Beauzée. For the eighteenth century onomatopoesis was a phenomenon of considerable importance in the debate over how language began, and all participants in that debate took seriously the theory a later age was to ridicule under the derisive title of the "bow-wow" explanation of the origin of language.

It is always of interest to examine why an explanation once taken seriously comes to be dismissed as ridiculous or *vice versa*. The history of ideas provides many such examples, but the case of onomatopoeia is particularly instructive. *Onomatopoeia* itself—as the *Encyclopédie* article points out—is a term borrowed from the Greek and all it means etymologically is "word-making" or "name-making." Its very restriction to those examples of word-making which supposedly exemplify, to cite the *Encyclopédie* again, *vox repercussa naturae* already embodies a theory of the origin of the linguistic sign. What is particularly important about the idea of *vox repercussa naturae* is that it suggests something primitive, pre-

209

civilized, something which antedates the time when language and linguistic behaviour became subject to the rule of convention, or even to the emergence of social institutions at all. An echo is a natural phenomenon, not a social phenomenon. Hence, potentially, the onomatopoetic principle supplies the basis for an alternative account of the origin of the linguistic sign to that given by those Enlightenment theorists for whom the linguistic sign was essentially and inextricably social in origin; and perhaps more significantly still, an alternative account to that given in the Bible. Thus its ideological implications are of considerable moment.

In just the same way, and for exactly parallel reasons, a mimetic theory of song as propounded by Lucretius in *De rerum natura* (where human imitation of the chirping of birds is given as the explanation) posed a potential threat to the "orthodox" eighteenth-century theory of the divine origin of music, which held that Adam and Eve sang spontaneously in praise of their Creator in the Garden of Eden.[3] A conflict automatically arises between aetiological explanations based on "natural causes" and aetiological explanations based on appeal to mythology or divine intervention. (For musicologists, however, mimetic theories retained their plausibility longer, and were not derisively dismissed in the nineteenth century as "cheep-cheep" explanations of the origin of music.)

Already in 1680, Dalgarno, in a passage which Hans Aarsleff quotes in *From Locke to Saussure*, had claimed

> All languages guided by the instinct of nature, have more or less of Onomatopoeia in them, and I think our English as much as any. . . . Take for example, *wash, dash, plash, flash, clash, hash, lash, slash, trash, gash,* etc. So *grumble, tumble, crumble, jumble, fumble, stumble, bumble, mumble,* etc., of which kind of words, the learned and my worthy friend Dr. Wallis has given a good account in his English Grammar. In all these and in such like words there is something symbolizing, and analogous to the notions of the things, which makes them both more emphatic and easy to the memory. But in words literally written, and of a mere arbitrary institution, there can be nothing symbolical.[4]

The quotation from Dalgarno illustrates on what shaky empirical foundations claims about onomatopoeia were made at that time. There is no attempt to prove that the words Dalgarno cites actually have an onomatopoetic origin. They are simply presented in long rhyming lists, in the hope, presumably, that the reader who recognizes the possibility that some of them could be onomatopoetic will just accept that all of them are.

Again, when Leibniz makes use of onomatopoeia in order to argue against Locke, like Dalgarno, he makes no attempt to prove his assertions. In the *Nouveaux Essais*, it is simply assumed to be obvious to any intelligent person that, for example, the Latin *coaxare* and the German *quaken*, both verbs meaning "to croak," are quite independently derived from the oral imitation by human beings of the natural sounds made by frogs.[5] Similarly, the *Encyclopédie*, which quotes Leibniz with approval on the subject, seems to regard the facts of onomatopoeia as self-evident. This poses an initial question worth pondering: why did Enlightenment writers accept the onomatopoetic thesis so uncritically?

By the "onomatopoetic thesis" or "onomatopoetic principle" is meant here the proposition that all (or many) languages contain words which originated as vocal imitations of the things those words designate. This is the basic or simple form of the thesis. There is also a stronger or extended form of it, to be examined below: namely, that all words in all languages originally reflected in their phonetic composition the specific nature of the thing designated. Ideologically, the onomatopoetic principle was always potentially a two-edged weapon. One edge was that it could be used to argue, either overtly or by implication, against the Biblical account of linguistic origins.

The Bible says only two things of any importance on the subject of language. On the one hand there is the story of Adam giving names to the animals in the Garden of Eden; and on the other hand there is the story of the Tower of Babel, which allegedly explains the reason for the diversity of human languages. Nowhere does the Bible mention onomatopoeia in connection with either story. So the first thing that can be seen as suspect or contentious about onomatopoeia in the Enlightenment context is that it is something human beings have discovered about language on the basis of their own unaided observation. It is in no sense a revealed truth about language.

In the second place the onomatopoetic principle offers the basis for a naturalistic theory of the origin of names, which does not rely on divine prompting of the kind described in the Book of Genesis. In its logically simplest form, such an account might envisage three stages in the evolution of the linguistic sign. Stage 1: Prelinguistic. Imagine a primitive community which has no language and lives by hunting. It is essential for such a community to learn to distinguish the calls of different wild creatures, and to associate each particular call with the presence of a bird or animal of a particular species: for example, to recognize that a certain roar is the roar of a lion. So, in this prelinguistic state, nature already offers to the community a basic semiotic model. A certain audible sound means "lion," or, more explicitly, "there's a lion about." The community learns to rely on this model for the very best of practical reasons: namely, survival. Stage 2: Mimetic. The primitive community develops the practice of vocal imitation of natural animal calls. There is a whole range of possible motivations for this mimetic stage, ranging from idle amusement to magico-religious and purely informational purposes. Here the head "informational" would cover the fact that an obvious way of warning someone of the approach of a lion is to imitate the roar of a lion.

In primates there are good examples of mimetic vocalization used as warning calls to indicate the presence of predators: so Stage 2 of the theory has some empirical support. The importance of Stage 2 in the evolution of the linguistic sign is that here the natural semiotic model recognized in Stage 1 is extended. There is a new chain of association created, which links the mimetic vocalization back to the original animal call and hence back to the animal itself. Thus a primitive vocabulary of onomatopoetic signs becomes possible. Stage 3: Linguistic. This is the crucial stage, and involves a further extension of the model; namely, the realization that the model will work whether or not the correlation between vocalization and meaning is based on imitation. In other words, any vocal utterance will do to mean "lion" provided everyone understands that connection. Thus, by a two-step extension of the original semiotic model provided by nature, one progresses to conventional vocal signs. The motivation for this third stage is simple: it depends on the communicational utility of vocal signs, plus the fact that not every creature or object it would be communicationally useful to be able to designate provides the would-be designator with a natural call or sound to imitate. So in effect the human being has to use some imagination and invent one. But the semiotic matrix for this invention is already provided in advance by Stage 2.

An account along these lines requires only three basic assumptions. First, that the human being has a natural capacity for vocal mimicry. (This is the initial posit of Beauzée's *Encyclopédie* article.) Second, that it would have been socially useful to primitive man to use vocal signs for the purpose of communication. (This, presumably, no one doubts.) Third, that the human being is a sufficiently intelligent creature to be capable of the process of abstraction involved in isolating the semiotic relationship between sound and meaning from the mimetic relationship. Granted these three assumptions, the way is clear for explaining the origin of the linguistic sign without appeal to divine intervention. Furthermore, this is an account which does not assume the monogenesis of language, as the Biblical story does. It allows for the possibility of languages emerging independently in any human community where the appropriate conditions are present, and hence bypasses the Tower of Babel explanation of the diversity of languages.

Such a theory, being both plausible and internally coherent, would at the very least give grounds for the suspicion that the Bible does not tell the whole truth about language, language being an endowment which distinguishes the human being from the rest of Creation. If that much of the Creation story is challenged, then it must follow that the entire Creation story comes under suspicion; for exactly the same reason that in the nineteenth century it was recognized that if Darwin was right about even one species then the whole of Biblical biology crumbled. So why, it may be asked, did no Enlightenment rationalist see the ideological potential of the onomatopoetic principle and seize that opportunity? Many works of the period mention onomatopoeia, but they obscure the topic by dragging in red herrings. The worst red herring of all is the notion of what John Webster in the seventeenth century called "immediate sounds of the soul."[6] This is the "extended onomatopoetic principle."

One of the most interesting eighteenth-century treatments of this principle is the *Traité de la formation méchanique des langues* by Charles de Brosses, published in 1765. The presence of the word *méchanique* in the title is already an indication that the focus of interest is not upon any religious or supernatural account of the origins of language. According to de Brosses, the human vocal apparatus is naturally constructed in such a way that it can produce only a strictly limited number of basic speech sounds. These he calls the "germs" of language, and he describes the natural process of onomatopoetic word formation in the following passage.

> In this small number of germs or articulations, the choice of those to be utilised in the construction of a word, that is to say the name of a real object, is physically determined by the nature and quality of the object itself; in such a way as to depict, as far as possible, the object as it is; for otherwise the word would give no idea of it; so that any man who is in the position of imposing the first name on something that is rough will employ a rough sound and not a soft one; just as, from among the seven primary colours, a painter who wishes to depict grass is obliged to choose green, and not violet. . . .
>
> Thus the system of the original making of the human language and the imposition of names on things is not arbitrary and conventional, as is customarily imagined; but a genuine system of necessity determined by two causes. One is the construction of the vocal organs which can render only certain sounds analogous to their shape. The other is the necessity and property of the real things one wishes to name. . . .
>
> Thus . . . there exists a primitive, organic, physical and necessary language, which is known and practised by no people in the world in its pristine simplicity: but which all men none the less speak, and which constitutes the basis of language in all countries.[7]

Here we see the idea of onomatopoeia extended from the basic notion of vocalic imitation into something more complex and mystical. De Brosses believes that a natural affinity between different sensory qualities is involved: thus a rough sound is appropriate to a rough object. It is this—and not simple auditory identity—which is compared to the connection which makes the painter select green in preference to violet in order to paint the colour of grass. Furthermore de Brosses holds that although we do not realize it, this same recognition of sensory affinities operates in the languages we speak today. In other words, onomatopoeia of the "bow-wow" type is only the most superficially obvious form of a principle of similarity or analogy which constitutes the natural relation between form and meaning. This "extended onomatopoetic principle" long outlived the Enlightenment, and was still taken seriously even when the bow-wow theory in its crudest form was held up to ridicule. For example, it survives in the nineteenth century in Steinthal's so-called "pathognomic" principle, and it is essentially this idea which underlies Max Müller's theory of roots in the 1860s. It turns up in a more sophisticated form still in the 1980s: for example, in Marcel Toussaint's recent book *Contre l'arbitraire du signe*.[8] But it was by no means an original idea in the eighteenth century. In all probability de Brosses took the "rough/soft" example straight from St. Augustine's *De Dialectica*, where we find an exactly parallel argument concerning the extension of onomatopoeia.[9] And ultimately it is a notion which goes back to Plato's *Cratylus*, where Socrates first uses the analogy from painting which de Brosses revamps in the passage just quoted. By trying to weld together all this intellectual flotsam and jetsam of the centuries, de Brosses ends up with a naturalistic theory of the origin of the linguistic sign which strains credulity no less than the Biblical account. Why could the eighteenth century produce no more convincing theory of onomatopoetic origins than this?

Perhaps there will be a temptation to argue that the pass had already been sold by Leibniz. Leibniz had argued in the *Nouveaux Essais* that the extended onomatopoetic principle was precisely the principle Adam had used in naming the animals. There Théophile says: "I am inclined to believe that Adam did not impose names in any other fashion."[10] However, the fact remains that the Bible does not tell us what Adam's principle of nomenclature was. In Genesis, the Lord never says "Don't be silly Adam: how could an animal like that possibly be called a *camel*?"

In retrospect it is remarkable that at no point during the Enlightenment debate about the origin of language do we encounter an outright rejection of the onomatopoetic principle. This is surprising. For it is simply a *non sequitur*, as Max Müller, later followed by Saussure, realized, to suppose that because we recognize certain sound-sense correlations, as exemplified in a word like *cuckoo*, those correlations automatically support the onomatopoetic principle. On the contrary, onomatopoeia may well be a secondary phenomenon, which projects the contrasts of a particular phoneme system on to our perception of noises occurring in the world of nature. In other words, it may be not a case of *vox repercussa naturae* but of *natura repercussa vocis*.

It may be that the reason why the onomatopoetic principle managed to survive the intellectual scrutiny of the Enlightenment was that ever since antiquity an exactly parallel account had been accepted as explaining the origin of writing. Writing, according to traditional wisdom, developed from visually iconic representations of natural objects. Written characters, in other words, originated as simplified drawings.

As Joseph Priestley puts it in 1762, "both natural probability and history show that picture-writing, with the contraction of it in Hieroglyphics," preceded alphabetic writing. Priestley considers the question of whether alphabetic writing was given to mankind by God, and concludes that it has too many imperfections "to have been the product of divine skill." As to the origins of picture-writing and its subsequent evolution, nothing could be plainer in Priestley's estimation:

> To express a tree, or animal, they who first used this method would probably begin in the most simple manner, by drawing an actual sketch or outline of the tree or animal, and proceed in like manner to depict all other visible objects. . . . By degrees they would learn to contract these pictures, and only to draw so much of their first outline as was sufficient to distinguish one expression from another. Thus two swords, and then two cross-strokes would serve to express a battle: which was at first represented by the figures of men in a fighting posture; and to denote impossibility, a plain horizontal line might suffice for the water, and two upright strokes for feet. . . .[11]

Now this mimetic theory does not fall foul of anything the Bible says, for the simple reason that the Bible says nothing about the origin of writing. Adam was not taught how to draw in the Garden of Eden, nor invited by God to determine any pictorial conventions. Yet somehow mankind managed to acquire the art of graphic representation, as both ancient and modern civilisations amply demonstrate. It was perhaps this analogy that both enhanced the plausibility of the onomatopoetic principle and at the same time prevented the exploitation of its ideological potential to the full. If so, this is one more example of the endemic scriptism of the Western tradition imposing an interpretation of the facts of speech.[12]

NOTES

1 Ferdinand de Saussure, *Cours de linguistique générale*, 2nd ed. (Paris: Payot, 1922), 101–02.

2 D. Crystal, *A Dictionary of Linguistics and Phonetics*, 2nd ed. (Oxford, New York: B. Blackwell in association with A. Deutsch, 1985), x.

3 Warren D. Allen, *Philosophies of Music History* (New York: American Book Co., 1939), 50 ff.

4 George Dalgarno, "Didascalocophus" in *Works of George Dalgarno* (Edinburgh: Reprinted by Constable, 1834), 126.

5 Hans Aarsleff, *From Locke to Saussure* (London: Athlone Press; Minneapolis: University of Minnesota Press, 1982), 88–9.

6 Ibid., 60–61. The reference is to John Webster's *Academiarum Examen* (London: Printed for Giles Calvert, 1654).

7 Charles de Brosses, *Traité de la formation méchanique des langues et des principes physiques de l'étymologie* (Paris: Saillant, 1765), xi ff.

8 Maurice Toussaint, *Contre l'arbitraire du signe* (Paris: Didier, 1983).

9 Friedrich Max Müller, *Lectures on the Science of Language* (London: Green, Longman and Roberts, 1864) 2:348.

10 Aarsleff, op. cit., 661.

11 Joseph Priestley, *A Course of Lectures on the Theory of Language and Universal Grammar* (Warrington: W. Eyres, 1762), 32, 34.

12 Roy Harris, *The Language-Makers* (London: Duckworth; Ithaca, New York, Cornell University Press, 1980), 6 ff.

Hazlitt, the Novel, and the French Revolution

ROBERT W. UPHAUS

Two of the more influential approaches to the topic, the French Revolution and the English novel, are those by Gary Kelly and Ronald Paulson. Focusing on Thomas Holcroft's idea of "unity of design" as the distinctive impulse behind English Jacobin fiction, Kelly argues that such novelists as Bage, Inchbald, Holcroft, and Godwin "tried to show how their characters had been formed by circumstances, and how character and incident were linked together like parts of a syllogism."[1] Employing a "perfectibilian" technique that is the literary corollary of the basic millenarian philosophy of the French Revolution, these novelists used their fiction as "imaginative enactments of a philosophical argument" (Kelly, 16); the primary goal of their efforts was, as Kelly argues, to "effect a moral revolution in [their] readers" (Kelly, 19). Such a moral revolution, presumably, would function as the reader's surrogate experience of the transformation of philosophical and political values associated with the French Revolution.

In a similar fashion, though drawing on a more extensive range of materials, Ronald Paulson also deals with the subject of artistic technique and how it was accommodated to the fact (and aftermath) of the French Revolution. Paulson writes, "The 'figuration' of revolution could well have been my title."[2] As Paulson sees it, "The sheer novelty of the French Revolution required new forms of representation and even more basically raised the central aesthetic challenge: how to represent the unprecedented" (Paulson, 26). An example of how Paulson reads the representation of the unprecedented may be seen in his assertion that "I do not think there is any doubt that the popularity of gothic fiction in the 1790s and well into the nineteenth century was due in part to the widespread anxieties and fears in Europe aroused by the turmoil in France finding a kind of sublimation or catharsis in tales of darkness, confusion, blood, and horror" (Paulson, 221). Such a remark invites comparison with Hazlitt's aside regarding the contemporary historical context of Radcliffe's fiction: that is, "Mrs. Radcliffe's 'enchantments drear,' and mouldering castles, derived part of their interest, no doubt, from the supposed tottering state of all old structures at the time."[3]

I do not wish to dispute the views of either Kelly or Paulson; rather, I wish to extend their focus so that it falls as much on reading and readers as it does on technique or artistic representation. Through William Hazlitt we can witness the process of how one attentive and sympathetic reader read some of the principal texts that either directly or indirectly responded to the fact and consequences of the French Revolution. As a Dissenter, Hazlitt was bred a child of the French Revolution who, commenting on the revolution and its aftermath, asserted, "In the late quarrel about Liberty, upwards of five millions of men have been killed, and *one king*" (20:40), and who to his dying day celebrated Napoleon as "a thorn in the side of kings" (13:ix).

Hazlitt's criticism offers several important vantage points on the French Revolution and the novel: first, as a Dissenter he knew the key issues, key terms, and key English figures who were sympathetic to the French Revolution; second, he was a contemporary of that generation of writers (including Godwin, Scott, Coleridge, Wordsworth, Southey) who were initially enthusiastic about, and then subsequently appalled by, the revolution; third, Hazlitt was the best critic of the novel in his time. His best essays on the novel are collected in *Lectures on the English Comic Poets* (1819) and *The Spirit of the Age* (1825). Many of these essays show that Hazlitt, like so many of his contemporaries (whether for or against the revolution), knew how to read ideologically. That is, he realized that the literature of the late eighteenth and early nineteenth centuries was based on and expressed a system of interconnected literary, political, and philosophical values. Clearly, if William Blake could read Reynolds' *Discourses on Art* and conclude, somewhat astonishingly, "This Whole Book was Written to Serve Political Purposes,"[4] it is pretty obvious that the novels of Holcroft, Godwin, and Scott were far more likely to elicit ideological readings, especially during a time of rampant political hysteria.

I should emphasize that when I refer to ideological reading I have in mind, as Hazlitt does, both the surface and deeper structure of the fiction I shall consider. If, for example, we focus on Paulson's idea of how to represent the unprecedented, it will become clear that such novelists as

Holcroft, Godwin, and Scott responded to the effects of the revolution through a variety of strategies of indirection. However, I should note that at least some contemporary readers may not have found these strategies very indirect. For example, Hazlitt glances at Inchbald's *Nature and Art* (1796) and quickly concludes that the novel "would scarcely have had the same popularity, but that it fell in (as to its two main characters) with the prevailing prejudice of the moment, that judges and bishops were not invariably pure abstractions of justice and piety" (6:123). Somewhat like Inchbald, but far more methodically, Holcroft and Godwin basically internalized the philosophical premises of the revolution within their settings, plots, and characters, though it is surely true that Godwin explicitly and aggressively attacked concepts of property and class structure in *Caleb Williams*. Scott's method of indirection was to deflect the reader's contemporary fears within the context of the remote, and sometimes revolutionary, past, at the same time that he attempted, as Hazlitt notices, "to restore the spirit of loyalty, of passive obedience and non-resistance" (11:22)

To begin this examination of Hazlitt's ideological reading of fiction, I shall first look at his *Life of Thomas Holcroft* published in 1810. Of the revolutionary period and its philosophical premises, Hazlitt observes:

> Kind feelings and generous actions there always have been, and there always will be, while the intercourse of mankind shall endure: but the hope, that such feelings and actions might become universal, rose and set with the French Revolution. That light seems to have been extinguished for ever in this respect. The French Revolution was the only match that ever took place between philosophy and experience: and waking from the trance of theory to the sense of reality, we hear the words, *truth*, *reason*, *virtue*, *liberty*, with the same indifference or contempt, that the cynic who has married a jilt or a termagant, listens to the rhapsodies of lovers. (3:156)

Here Hazlitt suggests several avenues of entry both into the general subject of the French Revolution and the English novel and into the specific matter of how Holcroft's fiction expressed and internalized responses to the revolution. The idea that the revolution dramatized a "match" between philosophy and experience can be clearly seen in the fiction of both Holcroft and Godwin—indeed in all the Jacobin novelists. Both authors tested their philosophically conceived characters against the experience of contemporary events. Similarly, both authors established their plot situations on and generated their dialogues through the use of such key "perfectibilian" terms as reason, truth, virtue, liberty—the ostensible values embodied by the French Revolution. As for the rising and setting of the "sun" of the revolution, that was a matter, as we shall see, that was left for Scott to record in his fiction.

Hazlitt's commentary on Holcroft's *Anna St. Ives* (1792) provides a superb example of the ideological reading (and system) characteristic of the pro-revolutionary novel of the 1790s. To begin with, Hazlitt refuses to separate Holcroft's political views from his moral views. Arguing that Holcroft's politics "were never any thing more than an enlarged system of morality" (3:121) — the same would be true for Godwin — Hazlitt reads the principal characters of *Anna St. Ives* as "ideal beings" (3:128). They are ideal in at least two respects: first, they function as abstractions that are designed to appeal to the reader's understanding rather than sympathy; and second, as abstractions they stand for key principles of the enlarged system of morality that is itself a representation of the forces of revolution.

Looking at Frank Henley and Anna St. Ives, whom he reads as the "philosophical hero and heroine of the work" (3:129), Hazlitt remarks: "They are not so properly characters (that is, distinct individuals) as the vehicles of certain general sentiments, or machines put into action, as an experiment to shew how these general principles would operate in particular situations. . . . They are the organs through which the voice of *truth* and *reason* is to breathe, and whose every action is to be inspired by the pure love of *justice*" (3:129; my italics). Hazlitt obviously knows how to read ideologically; he easily translates the key terms, gestures, and plot devices. For example, on the use of duelling in *Anna St. Ives*, Hazlitt writes that Holcroft's purpose is to demonstrate how "persons convinced of the truths he wishes to express, both may and ought to act in the present state of society" (3:129). Hence Holcroft arranges for Frank Henley to refuse a duel with Coke Clifton (an act of apparent cowardice), only to have Henley save Coke Clifton from drowning; the purpose of this episode is to show, as Hazlitt says, "an act of true heroism rising superior to the prejudices of false honor" (3:129). Such an episode displays for a sympathetic English reader a paradigm of democratic virtues displacing aristocratic prejudices.

However, it is also true to say that Hazlitt reads such an ideological novel with critical reservations, mainly because the characters remain, as he says, "the pure creatures of the understanding, mere abstract essences, which cannot kindle too warm a glow of enthusiasm" (3:129). Hazlitt is, therefore, quite impatient with *Hugh Trevor* (1794/1797) — a sequel, as a "political work" (3:136), to *Anna St. Ives*. He realizes that the novel intends to depict "the vices and distresses, which are generated by the existing institutions of society," but he rejects Holcroft's ideological use of characters, arguing that "it certainly is not necessary, in order to expose the *imperfections* of existing institutions and manners, that the profligacy which he has ascribed to these characters [of a Lord and a Bishop] should be universal" (3:136).

Hazlitt realizes that this kind of novel is an "experiment," a bold attempt to make the novel an ideological vehicle of, and response to, the French Revolution. In the 1790s the novel advanced the revolutionary experiment in two general ways: it promoted the message that "truth had a natural superiority over error, if it could only be heard; that if once discovered, it must . . . soon spread and triumph" (3:132- 133). This is the philosophical basis of Godwin's *Enquiry Concerning Political Justice.* No less important, the novel as a print medium created the opportunity to spread the progress of revolutionary values. Hazlitt writes: "The art of printing would not only accelerate this effect, but would prevent these accidents, which had rendered the moral and intellectual progress of mankind hitherto so slow, irregular, and uncertain" (3:132). As a "speculative politician" (3:132), Holcroft integrated the novel as an art form with the revolutionary expectation that the 1790s heralded an "era of moral and political improvements" (3:133). Holcroft was, as Hazlitt contends, "among the foremost and most ardent of those who indulged their imaginations, in contemplating such an Utopian, or ideal state of society" (3:133).

This utopian impulse also appears in Godwin's fiction, but Hazlitt quite rightly turns to Godwin's *Enquiry Concerning Political Justice* to discern the utopian basis of the revolutionary novel. Hazlitt singles out Godwin's work as the strongest formulation—what Hazlitt calls the "*experimentum crucis*"—of the revolutionary ideology. Godwin himself referred to *Political Justice* as "the child of the French Revolution,"[5] and in *The Enquirer* he announced that "the cause of political reform, and the cause of intellectual and literary refinement, are inseparably connected."[6] Godwin hoped to establish a rational basis for the reforms brought about by the French Revolution. The key principles of what Hazlitt calls Godwin's "new perfectibility code" (11:21) are as follows: "Sound reasoning and truth, when adequately communicated, must always be victorious over error; Sound reasoning and truth are capable of being so communicated; Truth is omnipotent; The vices and moral weakness of man are not invincible; Man is perfectible, or in other words susceptible of perpetual improvement."[7] These five principles are the basis of the revolutionary ideology embedded in Holcroft's fiction, as they are the informing philosophical principles of all so-called Jacobin fiction. These principles translate, respectively, into the following key terms: reason, sincerity, the progress of truth, benevolence, and the improvement or perfectibility of man.

Hazlitt well knew that Godwin's perfectibility code was vulnerable to the abuse of both "the enthusiasts of the French Revolution" and the "madder enthusiasts, the advocates of Divine Right" (11:23). The attitudes of the latter sort are vividly displayed in the poetry of *The Anti-Jacobin*. There one finds such memorable responses to reform and revolution as: " 'And Lead through Discord's low'ring storm, | " 'To one grand RADICAL REFORM!' "; or "Till madding crowds around them storm | 'FOR ONE GRAND RADICAL REFORM' "; or "Whatever is in France is right, | Terror and blood are my delight." Fancying themselves men who "prize our Country, love our King, | Adore our Contitution," the writers of *The Anti-Jacobin* were fond of attacking Godwin and Holcroft as "creeping creatures, venomous and low, | 'Paine, Williams, Godwin, Holcroft; praise Lepaux!' "[8]

No reactionary himself, Hazlitt is keenly aware that Godwin's *Enquiry* delivered "such a blow to the philosophical mind" (11:17) as to unsettle the same "things as they are" that would appear in the title of his next work a year later. For Godwin, whose ethical system assumes the exercise of *"reason without passion"* (11:20), the hero—be he in society or in literature—must always be "the hero of duty," the practitioner, that is, of reason, justice, truth, benevolence, and sincerity. However, in Hazlitt's view *Political Justice* inadvertently becomes, as *Caleb Williams* later dramatizes, a *reductio ad absurdum* of the very ideology Holcroft promotes in his fiction. Hazlitt observes that Godwin's *Political Justice* "has done more than any thing else to overturn the sufficiency of this principle by abstracting, in a strict metaphysical process, the influence of reason or the understanding in moral questions and relations from that of habit, sense, association, local and personal attachment, natural affections, &c.; and by thus making it appear how necessary the latter are to our limited, imperfect, and mixed being, how impossible the former as an exclusive guide of action, unless man were, or were capable of becoming, a purely intellectual being" (6:132). Hazlitt here anticipates Godwin's shift away from the perfectibility code in his fiction, and his subsequent turn toward what Godwin later called the "empire of feeling" and the "culture of the heart."[9] These novels demonstrate Godwin's repudiation of what he describes as the "unqualified condemnation of the private affections" in *Political Justice*,[10] a repudiation as much of the terror in France that used the perfectibility code as its rationale.

Significantly, Hazlitt—unlike some recent readers—does not read *Caleb Williams* as an ideological novel. Rather, he is much more attentive to the novel's sense of psychological interplay and complicity. Hazlitt argues that *Caleb Williams* "owes everything to internal conception and contemplation of the possible workings of the human mind" (6:130). I do not wish to be understood to imply that *Caleb Williams* is not an ideological novel; it demonstrably is, from the preface to the title on through to the conclusion. However, Hazlitt's basically psychological reading squares well with the second and final conclusion Godwin wrote for the novel. In an apt analogy Hazlitt likens the interplay of Falkland and Caleb to the "reaction and play . . . [of] Othello and Iago" (6:131). Despite modern readings that have suggested that Falkland is an ideological surrogate for the figure of Edmund Burke, Hazlitt—who was one of the severest and shrewdest critics of Burke in his time—sees not a glimmer of Burke in the novel.[11]

Hazlitt's entire reading is governed by the idea that "Falkland is the hero of the story, Caleb Williams is only the instrument of it" (6:131). Each character personifies a force. Hazlitt writes that Caleb is "the very demon of curiosity personified," and Falkland embodies the "romantic and chivalrous principle of the love of personal fame" (11:24). Of Squire Falkland, Hazlitt comments: he is "a sort of apotheosis of the love of fame. The gay, the gallant Falkland lives only in the good opinion of good men; for this he adorns his soul with virtue, and tarnishes it with crime. . . . he dies a martyr to fame, but a confessor at the shrine of virtue!" (6:130–31). Still, the possibility of an ideological reading exists in the key words Hazlitt associates with Caleb and Falkland: that is, virtue, the love of fame, chivalry, crime, curiosity. In potential these words may signify the tug-of-war between classes (i.e., squire versus servant) and the conflict between opposed sets of values—Falkland's "pride" that is founded on what Hazlitt, in another context, calls "the prejudice of either wealth or ancestry" (3:117) and Caleb's "restless and inquisitive spirit" (11:24) that, like any number of revolutionary tracts, reveals the evil at the heart of artistocratic pride and prejudice.

However, if I read Hazlitt correctly, it is in Godwin's novel *St. Leon* that he sees the revolution's "proud Temple of Reason" (11:20)—the intellectual basis of Godwin's perfectibility code—come tumbling down. Through the character of St. Leon, who may well be the fictional prototype of Victor Frankenstein (himself a worshipper at the temple of reason), Godwin critiques the basic premise of *Political Justice* and thereby, at least tacitly, revises if not rejects the rational claims of the French Revolution. Like some of the revolutionaries, St. Leon—whom Hazlitt calls "the hermetic philosopher" (6:132)—shares "no common tie of sympathy or suffering" (6:131) with other men. One need only listen to Hazlitt's description of St. Leon to be reminded of some of the more prominent French Jacobins, especially Robespierre and his ideas of the Republic of Virtue and Cult of the Supreme Being. Comparing Falkland and St. Leon, Hazlitt writes: "As the ruling passion of the one was the love of fame, so in the other the sole business of life is thought" (6:131). He then continues, focusing on the rational indifference of the kind of mind that, during the revolution, could endorse terror as a virtuous act; of St. Leon he observes:

The races of men pass before him as in a *speculum*; He is thrown back into himself and his own thoughts. He lives in the solitude of his own breast. . . . His is the solitude of the soul . . . the desert of society, the waste and desolation of the heart. He is himself alone. His existence is purely contemplative, and is therefore intolerable to one who has felt the rapture of affection or the anguish of woe. The contrast between the enthusiastic eagerness of human pursuits and their blank disappointment, was never, perhaps, more finely pourtrayed than in this novel. (6:131)

One phrase alone—the contrast "between the enthusiastic eagerness of human pursuits and their blank disappointment"—returns us to Hazlitt's previous observation that "the French revolution was the only match that ever took place between philosophy and experience" (3:150). In Hazlitt's reading, both *St. Leon* and *Caleb Williams*, which employ characters of the "same exalted intellectual kind" (6:131), test the intellectual principles of the revolution and ultimately record their failure. The philosophy of the revolution, with its emphasis on reason, virtue, justice, and perfectibility fails; and Hazlitt attributes that failure to a mistaken estimate of human nature—specifically, to a false model of the relation between reason and feeling.

In this regard, Hazlitt draws a very interesting comparison between the novelistic technique of Godwin and Scott. Because Hazlitt's politics are more compatible with those of Holcroft and Godwin, he is politically unsympathetic to Scott; but he understands and argues that Scott's novels provide the missing human element lacking in both the French Revolution and the rational philosophy that at least initially supported it. Hazlitt comments that "If [Scott] owes almost every thing to external observation and traditional character, the other owes every thing to internal conception and contemplation of the possible workings of the human mind" (6:130). From this distinction Hazlitt develops an intriguing analogy that visualizes the mental landscape of, respectively, Godwin's early revolutionary expectations and the counterrevolutionary tendencies of Scott's novels. About Godwin's rational model Hazlitt writes: "Captain Parry would be thought to have rendered a service to navigation and his country, no less by proving that there is no North-West Passage, than if he had ascertained that there is one; so Mr. Godwin has rendered an essential service to moral science, by attempting (in vain) to pass the Arctic Circle and Frozen Regions, where the understanding is no longer warmed by the affections" (11:23).

If Godwin's mental landscape is cold and frozen—the very setting in which Mary Shelley also tests the intellectual principles of the revolution—Scott provides a different setting, for he is a writer who, in Hazlitt's words, "shudders at the shadow of innovation" (11:23). Scott is no explorer of a "perfectibilian" future. Rather, as Hazlitt notes,

> The land of pure reason is to his apprehension like *Van Dieman's Land*; — barren, miserable, distant, a place of exile. . . . Sir Walter would make a bad hand of a description of the *Millenium*, unless he could lay the scene in Scotland five hundred years ago, and then he would want facts and worm-eaten parchments to support his drooping style. Our historical novelist firmly thinks that nothing *is* but what *has* been — that the moral world stands still, as the material one was supposed to do of old — and that we can never go beyond the point where we actually are without utter destruction. (11:58)

Hazlitt clearly understands the counterrevolutionary ideology of Scott's fiction. He draws out the internal principles through which Scott has simultaneously rejected the French Revolution and its millenarian expectations, at the same time that he recognizes the effectiveness of Scott's nostalgic appeal, with its resistance to philosophical abstractions. Hazlitt credits Scott with the awareness that "there is no romance like the romance of real life; and that if we can but arrive at what men feel, do, and say in striking and singular situations, the result will be 'more lively' . . . than the fine-spun cobwebs of the brain" (11:62).

There is no question that Hazlitt, shrewd ideological reader that he was, grew tired of the rational "cobwebs" produced by the Jacobin novel. He clearly acknowledges that the "political bearing of the *Scotch Novels* . . . is a relief to the mind, rarefied as it has been with modern philosophy, and heated with ultra-radicalism" (11:64–65). And yet, in spite of his sense of relief and fond as he is of Scott's characters in particular, Hazlitt nevertheless blisters the implicit ideology of Scott's fiction. Hazlitt's list of charges against the "political bearing" of Scott's novels is lengthy, but it vividly displays Hazlitt's strength and insight as an ideological reader.

Basically, Hazlitt sees an internal contradiction in Scott's novels. That contradiction involves a disparity between the essential openness of Scott's literary imagination and his rigid political commitments. For example, Hazlitt wryly observes: "Through some odd process of *servile* logic, it should seem, that in restoring the claims of the Stuarts by the courtesy of romance, the House of Brunswick are more firmly seated in point of fact, and the Bourbons, by collateral reasoning, became legitimate!" (11:65). Having flushed out the tangled ideological logic of the novels, Hazlitt turns next to the tension, if not contradiction, between Scott's political intent and the actual tendency of what he depicts. Hazlitt remarks:

> [Scott's] loyalty is founded on *would-be* treason: he props the actual throne by the shadow of rebellion. Does he really think of making us enamoured of the 'good old times' by the faithful and harrowing portraits he has drawn of them?. . . Is he infatuated enough, or does he so dote and drivel over his own slothful and self-willed prejudices, as to believe that he will make a single convert to the beauty . . . of lawless power and savage bigotry, when he himself is obliged to apologise for the horrors he describes [?] (11:65)

Scott's intention may well have been, as Hazlitt says, "to put a spoke . . . in the wheel of upstart innovation. . . . [and make] us conceive a horror of all reform" (11:66); but Hazlitt believes that Scott is thoroughly "besotted as to the moral of his own story," for he inadvertently reveals the horrors of the past to be no less barbaric than the terrors of the revolution.

To conclude: in this brief examination of Hazlitt's readings of Holcroft, Godwin, and Scott, I have attempted to describe a spectrum of fictional responses to the French Revolution. These fictional responses vary considerably—with Holcroft strongly committed to the philosophical principles of the revolution, Godwin initially enthusiastic but subsequently more critical, and Scott greatly opposed but perhaps somewhat deluded about the tendency of his own fiction. Hazlitt's criticism enables us to attend to both the process of ideological reading and the fictional representation of the French Revolution. Through Hazlitt's criticism we get an insider's view of how the French Revolution and the English novel interacted. If there is, finally, a general truth to emerge from this brief examination of the French Revolution and the English novel, that truth may have been most succinctly summarized in Thomas Holcroft's diary entry dated 14 November 1798. There Holcroft records that "the only change of opinion I had undergone was, that political revolutions are not so well calculated to better man's condition, as during a certain period I, with almost all the thinking men in Europe, had been led to suppose" (3:202).

NOTES

1 Gary Kelly, *The English Jacobin Novel 1780–1805* (Oxford: Clarendon, 1976), 16. Hereafter cited in the text as Kelly.

2 Ronald Paulson, *Representations of Revolution (1789–1820)* (New Haven and London: Yale University Press, 1983), 4. Hereafter cited in the text as Paulson.

3 *The Complete Works of William Hazlitt*, 21 vols., ed. P. P. Howe (London and Toronto: J. M. Dent, 1930–1934), 6:123. All further references are cited by volume and page number in the text.

4 *Blake: Complete Works*, ed. Geoffrey Keynes (London: Oxford University Press, 1969), 451. For further discussion of Blake's ideological reading, see Robert W. Uphaus, "The Ideology of Reynolds' *Discourses on Art*," *ECS* 12 (Fall, 1978): 69–72.

5 William Godwin, *Uncollected Writings* (Gainsville: Scholars' Facsimiles, 1968) 284.

6 William Godwin, *The Enquirer* (New York: Augustus M. Kelley, 1965), x.

7 William Godwin, *Enquiry Concerning Political Justice*, ed. Isaac Kramnick (Baltimore: Penguin Books, 1976), 139–40. Kramnick's edition, like that of F. E. L. Priestley, is based on Godwin's final revised edition of 1798.

8 *Poetry of The Anti-Jacobin*, ed. L. Rice-Oxley (Oxford: Blackwell, 1924), 10, 51, 67, 84, 185.

9 See, respectively, C. Kegan Paul, *William Godwin: His Friends and Contemporaries*, 2 vols. (London: Henry King, 1876), 1:294, and the preface to *St. Leon* (1799).

10 This quotation comes from reel 4 of the Shelley-Godwin Collection of Lord Abinger. I am grateful to Professor Lewis Patton and the Duke University Library for permitting me to view reels 1–5 of the Collection.

11 See James T. Boulton, *The Language of Politics* (London: Routledge & Kegan Paul, 1963), 226–232; David McCracken, "Godwin's *Caleb Williams*: A Fictional Rebuttal of Burke," *Studies in Burke and His Time* 11 (1969–1970): 1142–52; and Gary Kelly's discussion of *Caleb Williams* in *The English Jacobin Novel*. For Hazlitt's reading and criticism of Burke, see Robert W. Uphaus, *William Hazlitt* (Boston: Twayne, 1985), 36–45.

Cowper, Hayley, and Samuel Johnson's "Republican" Milton

For Louis A. Landa

JAMES KING

> [William Cowper] was not British or enlightened or far-sighted or adapt-
> able. He was English, and most so when he forgot his nationality and
> took a country walk. He had his conscious patriotic gestures, and some
> of them were effective; but there is a stay-at-home air about them which
> makes them rather ludicrous in our eyes. . . .[1]

So E. M. Forster claimed in 1932. In some ways, he is right, but there
was an adventuresome side to Cowper's political beliefs. To use Forster's
terminology, Cowper was "British" as well as "English" in his "patriotic
gestures"—his beliefs went beyond the boundaries of narrow political issues to more universal sentiments of concern for the plight of the poor,
the oppressed, and the disenfranchised. Nevertheless, it must be acknowledged that Cowper and radicalism seem at first a strange congruence,
especially when one remembers that William Copwer was a life-long Whig,
who only occasionally quarreled with his cousin, Lady Hesketh, an ardent Tory. Indeed, his most unabashed statement on freedom and its use
is contained in a letter to her of 23 March 1793:

> You are as well convinced as any body, even as my patriotic self, that
> the people have certain rights and privileges which cannot be denied them
> but by an usurpation. But then I observe you think them always in the
> wrong when they demand them. Here seems to lie the difference between
> us. You approve all the measures of the Court, or of the Minister, and
> I am pleased with every struggle that is made against them when they

229

> infringe the birthright of the Commons. We both love the King, but I the King and every tittle of true and rational liberty. . . .[2]

Although, as this passage shows, Cowper's Whiggism was obviously one which was never narrow and bigoted, it did include admiration for monarchy and Parliament. John Milton, on the other hand, was, as Christopher Hill has asserted, "a propagandist of revolution, a defender of regicide and of the English republic."[3] At first glance, then, it would seem impossible that these two men could have similar political values. However, in order to come to a precise understanding of Milton's influence on Cowper in this matter, we must consider Cowper's relationship to two other men: Samuel Johnson and William Hayley. Cowper hated Johnson's *Life of Milton* and in 1792 he became a close friend of William Hayley, an advocate of many of Milton's republican sentiments. The influence of these two intermediary figures ultimately nudged Cowper in a more radical direction, and I shall show this by using Cowper's pencil annotations to his copy of Johnson's *Life of Milton*, by discussing his outrage at the suppression of William Hayley's *Life of Milton*, and, finally, by citing his eagerness to defend Richard Phillips, a publisher of seditious material. I begin with a sketch of the place of Milton in Cowper's life and poetry.

At the age of fourteen Cowper first encountered Milton's poetry. At that time he admired *Lycidas*, being especially taken with its "Liveliness of . . . Description . . . Sweetness of . . . Numbers" and the "Classical Spirit of Antiquity that prevail[ed] in it."[4] As an older man in the late 1770s and early 1780s, he saw Milton as the poet through whom he could escape the emasculating spectre of Alexander Pope, whose "oily smoothness"[5] he despised. Indeed, Cowper came to realize more and more as work progressed in 1781 on his first independent volume of verse, *Poems by William Cowper of the Inner Temple, Esqr.* (1782), that he lacked Pope's aphoristic complexity and delicacy in the couplet form. Subsequently, in his attempt to forge a literary career as if Pope had not existed, Cowper used Miltonic blank verse in *The Task* (1785) to write a late eighteenth century *Paradise Lost*. Cowper continued in much the same manner from 1786 to 1791 when he translated Homer into blank verse.

According to Cowper, Pope had perpetrated a fundamental distortion on the original: "The Iliad and the Odyssey, in his hands, have no more of the air of antiquity than if he had himself invented them."[6] The end result of Pope's desire to ornament Homer with rhyme, elegant diction and picturesque scenes had been to smother him. Cowper concluded his comments with the particularly cutting remark: "Pope resembles Homer just as Homer resembled himself when he was dead."[7] During all the five tedious, fretful years he spent on Homer, Cowper constantly had before him the example of Milton's blank verse. If one wished to capture the primitiveness of Homer, it was necessary to have roughness intrude itself into the verse line. However, even the loyal squad of supporters who surrounded Cowper felt that he sometimes went too far in this direction and to that charge he answered: "With respect to those lines, which are said to be prosaic, if indeed they be such, I will undertake to show no small number, that are equally such in the sublimest parts of the Paradise Lost."[8]

Since Cowper's career—as well as his ambition—had from 1781 to 1791 largely been devoted to Miltonic means through which to define a literary self as if Pope had not existed, it was perhaps natural that he agreed in the summer of 1791 to edit Milton's poetry for his publisher Joseph Johnson's proposed Milton gallery. However, at this time, a second spectre reared its head in the person of Samuel Johnson, who had died seven years before in 1784. Five years earlier, in 1779, Cowper had expressed his irritation at Johnson's treatment of Milton in his life of that poet. Cowper had been particularly dismayed by Johnson's lack of sympathy with blank verse. Johnson "talks something about the unfitness of the English Language for Blank Verse, & how apt it is, in the Mouth of Some Readers to degenerate into Declamation. Oh! I could thresh his old Jacket 'till I made his Pension Jingle in his Pocket."[9]

Irritation with Johnson gave way to a new anxiety of influence in 1791, when Cowper undertook to edit Milton, a poet with whom he had a strong sense of identification. For much of his life, Cowper viewed himself as a man disinherited by God, as a person crippled by an overwhelming sense of damnation. However, Milton's obvious disability—his blindness—had been transformed into a strength as in the invocations to "holy Light" in Book III and to Urania in Book VII of *Paradise Lost*, where Milton reminds his readers that although he is physically blind, he feels called upon to illuminate the spiritual condition of mankind. The irony is that he who has been robbed of sight becomes the appropriate person to discourse on inner light. Indeed, the poet seems to suggest that his disability has made him the most likely person to speak of such things. This aspect of Milton's existence obviously appealed to Cowper, and he hoped his experience, harrowing as it was, of spiritual darkness would enable him, in turn, to write of the possibility of spiritual rebirth. In imitating Milton, he hoped that what was dark in himself would be illuminated.

Cowper's reaction to Samuel Johnson's treatment of Milton was thus both literary and personal, and his anger comes boiling to the surface in the fifty notes he made about 1791–92 in his copy of Johnson's *Life of Milton*. For the purposes of this paper, I cite those notes in which Cowper comments on Johnson's treatment of Milton's politics. Where John-

son says, "Milton's republicanism was, I am afraid, founded in an envi-
ous hatred of greatness. . .," Cowper rejoins: "Good Doctor! tis a delicate and tender fear." Johnson claims: "[I]t seems not more reasonable
to leave the right of printing unrestrained because writers may be afterwards censured, than it would be to sleep with doors unbolted, because
by our laws we can hang a thief." Cowper remonstrates: "Would you therefore cut off a man's finger lest he steal?" Johnson asserts that "if every
murmurer at government may diffuse discontent, there can be no
peace. . . ." Cowper calmly replies, "The fact is against this, because in
this country those things have already been permitted."[10] Cowper's sympathy with Milton in these notes does not indicate radicalism, but it does
show a willingness on his part to expand his concept of freedom under
the influence of his mentor.

Soon after he began work on his Milton project, Cowper became discouraged and eventually was pleased to abandon it. If this venture brought
him a great deal of discomfort and frustration, it was also responsible
for a letter from William Hayley (dated 7 February 1792) which reached
him belatedly on 17 March. Since early 1792 Boydell and Nicol had been
planning a rival illustrated *édition de luxe* to Joseph Johnson's Milton
project. George Romney was to provide the illustrations, and Hayley had
agreed to write a life of Milton to accompany the engravings. A newspaper
report claiming that Cowper and Hayley were rivals in writing lives of
Milton prompted Hayley to write to Cowper, and thus began their
friendship.

Hayley, the Man of Sentiment par excellence, was, like Cowper, a great
admirer of Milton and, what is more significant for our purposes, he also
despised Samuel Johnson's life of Milton. On 1 May 1792—before they
had met—Cowper was anxious to discuss their mutual "idol" and to
castigate Samuel Johnson: "Oh That Johnson! How does every page of
his on the subject, ay, almost every paragraph kindle my indignation!"[11]
The friendship between these two men was thus forged in admiration of
Milton and hatred of Samuel Johnson. It is no wonder then that Cowper,
who had no intention of becoming Milton's biographer, became Hayley's
coadjutor in a literary biography which was intended as a riposte to Johnson. In turn, Hayley prodded Cowper to write a commentary on *Paradise Lost* which would overturn Johnson's grudging treatment of that epic.

As Joseph Anthony Wittreich, Jr. has observed, Hayley's biography
is crucial in its "perception of Milton's libertarianism and [in its being]
the first to present and celebrate him as the hero of political radicalism."[12]
The biography was certainly perceived as such by George Nicol, the King's
bookseller, who had commissioned the book, when he told Hayley he
would not publish it in the form submitted to him. Indeed, Nicol forced

Hayley to delete huge sections from the 1794 edition which bears the Boydell-Nicol imprint. The "uncensored" version of the biography did not appear until 1796. Wittreich has perceptively summarized the differences between the two versions: "The first edition explains that Milton's 'character as a man, has been recently misrepresented'; the second asserts emphatically that his 'character as a man' has 'been greatly mistaken.' The first edition is apologetic for Milton's views on divorce; the second espouses them. [Other] passages, without exception, either reveal the political motives and ideals of Milton or exhibit the revolutionary character of his religious philosophy."[13] Nevertheless, the uncensored 1796 *Life of Milton* does not really contain seriously inflammatory material—its publication certainly did not lead to a prosecution for sedition. Nicol was likely offended by the extent to which Hayley allowed Milton a speaking voice in his biography, a speaking voice in which "the poet . . . [could] become his own biographer."[14] He might also have been concerned with the extent to which regicide and divorce were highlighted in the manuscript submitted to him. However, the 1794 biography still contains much material on these two issues. The preponderance of radical ideas—not their substantive content—in the manuscript must have been the crucial factor in Nicol's decision not to publish without excisions.

Nicol's action might have been precipitated by the widespread fear of French (revolutionary) ideas in England in the 1790s and specifically by the declaration of war against France in 1793. The strength of Pitt's regime, as J. Steven Watson has said, "was one derived from crisis and which encouraged hysteria. There was a witch-hunt in the countryside. The opinions of a village might be checked by a house to house inquiry."[15] Nicol's actions must be seen within this context, and Cowper's actions in that same year must be weighed against this backdrop of national paranoia.

As one would expect, despite the intimidating climate of opinion, Hayley was mightily displeased by Nicol's action. Not surprisingly, so was Cowper. A year earlier, on 25 November 1792, he had rejoiced with Hayley in finding "a liberal bookseller"; late in the autumn of 1793, Hayley had told Cowper, who had perused and approved the manuscript (indeed Cowper had been concerned with Part 2, the portion of the work which displeased Nicol), that the biography was in trouble. Agitated by his friend's distress, Cowper wrote him on 8 December 1793:

> I want to know many things which only you can tell me, but especially
> I want to know what has been the issue of your conference with Nichols
> [sic]. Has he seen your work—is he satisfied that he may publish it without
> hazard to the honour and glory of his King's-booksellership, or must you
> after all publish it on your own account? I am impatient for the appear-

ance of it, because impatient to have the spotless credit of the great poet's character as a man and a citizen vindicated as it ought to be and as it never will be again.[16]

Cowper obviously sympathized with Hayley's plight and approved the Milton biography because it was the work of a friend. However, his use of the verb "vindicated" is crucial: Hayley was to be admired because he was justifying Milton in opposition to the critical tyranny of Johnson, who had despised the seventeenth-century poet's politics.

By 1792, then, Milton's politics and his poetry were held in esteem by Cowper. Is there any evidence, however, that Cowper's political opinions underwent any change after he met Hayley in 1792? To a limited extent, I think there is. However, it must be kept in mind that Cowper's admiration for Milton is almost always focused on poetical—rather than political—issues. He particularly esteemed Milton's technical freedom. This does not necessarily make him an admirer of his notions of political freedom. Nevertheless, as we have seen, Cowper's response to Johnson's *Life of Milton* was political as well as poetic.

Moreover, in a letter to Hayley of 17 December 1793 concerning Hayley's suppressed Milton, he makes a telling point when he mentions Hayley's treatment of John Bradshaw, who had presided at Charles I's trial and pronounced the sentence of execution:

> I know not whether to be glad or sorry that you conceded so much as you have to your bookseller. So far as the measure may prove a relief to your mind, I am glad, but sorry that your work is to be so garbled. A procedure for which I see no necessity but what is created by the excessive timidity of said bookseller. It comforts me however that your own edition will be entire, and in that I hope you will replace Milton's expunged but admirable character of Bradshaw.[17]

Despite the liberal sentiments found in this passage (Cowper is expressing admiration for a regicide), there are others, written at approximately the same time, where Cowper is deeply critical of and hostile to the National Assembly in France and Thomas Paine.[18] To a large extent, his political opinions, it must be acknowledged, were both ambivalent and ambiguous.

To discover more clearly Cowper's politics in 1793, one must finally turn to an incident which occurred after Cowper met Hayley but before the debacle with Nicol in late 1793. In January 1793, the twenty-six year old Richard Phillips was imprisoned in Leicester gaol for selling copies of Paine's *Rights of Man*. This intrepid young man, who was allowed to continue the editorship of the *Leicester Herald* from his cell, wrote Cowper on 12 June 1793, asking him to write a song or sonnet favoring his case, perhaps something that might be sung in the streets (Phillips might have known that Cowper had been an active proponent of abolition—a sympathy, however, which did not indicate radicalism). On 14 June, Cowper sent him a civil refusal:

> I see not . . . how it would be possible for me to write any thing that would satisfy the demands of your resentment, just perhaps, and the warmer for being so, and that would not expose me to the evils by which you are so great a sufferer. . . . A tame composition, in short, would not serve *you*, and a spirited and vehement one might ruin *me*.
> It is possible too that we may differ a little in our political sentiments.
>
> I see many evils in the administration of public affairs, which I heartily wish redressed, but am by no means an approver of the spirit in which that redress has been sought. And if government, insulted as it has been and not a little endanger'd, has lately exerted itself to impose some restraint on publications of a seditious kind, I am not the man to quarrel with it on that account.[19]

Undeterred, Phillips wrote a second letter and sent Cowper copies of the *Leicester Herald*. Cowper, who had been quite candid on 14 June, wrote a sonnet in which he depicted Phillips as an Eve betrayed by an evil "tempter" (one Jackson,[20] who had purchased the book insidiously to inform against the young publisher):

> Phillips—the Suff'rer less by Law than Pow'r,
>   Though prison'd in an adamantine hold,
>   Might bear a heart as free and uncontroll'd
> In his dark cell, as in a Summer's bow'r.
> The sly accuser, who at such an hour
>   When all suspicion sleeps, like Him of old,
>   Eve's tempter, wreath'd in many an artful fold
> Conceals his drift with purpose to devour—
> He is the pris'ner; and those bars within
>   That hoop his sorry vitals round about
> Dwells one, who never shall compassion win
>   From Just and Good, 'till Judgment calls him out.
> Thou, then, less deeply at thy wrongs repine;
> Scorn is his meed, Commiseration thine.[21]

As he told his lawyer friend Samuel Rose (who in 1803 would defend Blake at Chichester against the charge of sedition), Cowper wrote this poem because he had been "[t]ouched by the hardship [Phillips] seems to have suffer'd"; however, Cowper was well aware that "Government is so jealous and rigorous at present that I fear'd to send it till some wiser man than myself should assure me that I might do it safely."[22] Rose immediately cautioned Cowper that it would not be wise to put this poem — although it did not in any way mount a political defense of the young publisher's plight — into Phillips' hands. Following his receipt of Rose's letter, Cowper wrote to Phillips *without* telling him that he had indeed composed the requested song:

> After an attentive perusal of your printed case and of the two letters which you favour'd me, I felt myself disposed to render you such service as I could in my way, but thought it prudent first to consult a friend of mine in London, an able lawyer, and in party-matters a man of great moderation. I sent him accordingly the papers containing your representation, and asked him if I might safely comply with your request. — His answer is in the negative; he says, as in my letter to you I had said myself, that it is not possible I should assist you by such means, and that the attempt would certainly be inexpedient, perhaps even dangerous. — You will excuse me therefore if I abstain from all interference. . . .[23]

Thus ended Cowper's most extended excursus into radical politics — the poem to Phillips was not published until 1921.

Several observations can be offered on this incident. First, Cowper obviously sympathized with Richard Phillips' difficulty, being moved at the very least to write a poem on his behalf. After all, he considered moving from the safety of his study to the danger inherent in participating in the public defense of a proponent of Paine. This clearly shows that Cowper's support of Hayley later in 1793 was not merely polite rhetoric. Second, Cowper was well aware before late 1793 of the dangers of radical politics — he makes this abundantly clear in his letters to Rose and Phillips; he did not wish to be accused of having written seditious verse, realizing that his sonnet could be interpreted as going in that direction. Third, the sonnet to Phillips is infused with a goodly dose of Miltonic usages and incidents (the most overt borrowings being from *Paradise Lost* IV, 9–10, IX, 494–500, and X, 511–17). Fourth, Cowper often described himself as a prisoner, and Phillips' situation was thus one with which he could readily empathize.

This last observation is crucial. Did Cowper identify merely with this aspect of Phillips' plight and thus write the poem? There is obviously some truth in this. Nevertheless, it does not provide a full, adequate explanation. As I have shown, Cowper in his 1791–92 jottings was sympathetic to Milton's radicalism. In 1792–93, he became a close friend to a man much more deeply committed to such beliefs than he was. Cowper's sometimes complacent Whiggism was pushed aside late in 1793 when Hayley's biography of Milton was censored. In addition — despite his clearly stated disagreement on the matter of "redress" — his earlier espousal of Phillips in June 1793 shows that he flirted with the idea of publicly supporting a publisher of seditious material.

In my opinion, it would be difficult to overestimate the influence of the republican Milton upon the reclusive poet from 1791 to 1793, as his appearance to Cowper in a dream in February 1793 makes clear:

> He was very gravely but very neatly attired in the fashion of his day, and had a countenance which fill'd me with those feelings that an affectionate child has for a beloved father. . . . I spoke of his Paradise Lost as every man must who is worthy to speak of it at all, and told him a long story of the manner in which it affected me when I first discover'd it. . . . He answer'd me by a smile and a gentle inclination of his head. I told him we had poets in *our* days, and no mean ones, and that I was myself intimate with the best of them. He replied — I know Mr. Hayley very well by his writings. He then grasp'd my hand affectionately and with a smile that charm'd me said — Well — you, for your part, will do well also.[24]

This dream prodded Cowper to remember that his career as a writer had been largely evolved from his dedication to Miltonic ideals, which Hayley had buttressed and which, he knew full well, had been attacked by Johnson. Later that year, in June, he took, if ever so discreetly, his firmest steps in the direction of Milton's radical politics. In such matters, he was quite capable of being "enlightened" and "adaptable."

NOTES

1 E. M. Forster, "William Cowper, An Englishman," *The Spectator*, No 5403 (16 June 1932), 75. In this essay, I am applying the term "Whig" to Cowper beyond the context of his adherence to the aims of that political party. I am suggesting that Cowper's Whiggism was one which questioned the King's claim to unrestrained authority. Like many others of his persuasion, Cowper would have been influenced by Locke's views on civil government and toleration, and such tendencies were heightened — as I argue — in 1792–93. I wish to thank Irma Lustig for her perceptive criticism of an earlier draft of this essay.

2 *The Letters and Prose Writings of William Cowper*, 5 volumes, edited by James King and Charles Ryskamp (Oxford: The Clarendon Press, 1979–86), 4: 312. Hereafter cited as *Letters*.

3 *Milton and the English Revolution* (London: Faber and Faber, 1977), 1.

4 To William Unwin, 31 October 1779, *Letters* 1: 307.

5 Ibid., 433 (to Joseph Johnson, *c.* 15 January 1781). Cowper's dislike of Pope is treated at length in James King, *William Cowper: A Biography* (Durham: Duke University Press, 1986), 108–9, 192–95, 198–99, 202.

6 Cowper's "Alethes" letter in *The Gentleman's Magazine, Letters* 5: 54.

7 Ibid., 58.

8 To Joseph Johnson, 1 February 1786, *Letters* 2: 472–3.

9 To William Unwin, 31 October 1779, *Letters* 1: 307–8.

10 J. Copley, "Cowper on Johnson's *Life of Milton*," *Notes and Queries*, New Series 24 (July-August 1977): 314.

11 *Letters* 4: 70.

12 Joseph Anthony Wittreich, Jr. in his introduction to the facsimile reproduction of Hayley's 1796 *Life of Milton* (Gainesville: Scholars' Facsimiles & Reprints, 1970), v. According to his biographer, Hayley's brand of Whiggism made him "an ardent and romantic lover of liberty" (137); he had " 'ideas of the loftiest kind' concerning the destiny of France; and so, when Edmund Burke brought out his eloquent *Reflections on the French Revolution*, Hayley without a moment's hesitation began to compose a refutal of them." Morchard Bishop [Olive Stoner], *Blake's Hayley* (London: Victor Gollancz, 1951), 140.

13 Wittreich, xi–x.

14 *The Life of Milton* (London: Cadell and Davies, 1796), 2.

15 *The Reign of George III, 1760–1815* (Oxford: The Clarendon Press, 1960), 356.

16 *Letters* 4: 438–39.

17 Ibid., 442.

18 See, for example, this comment of 1 June 1793 to Lady Hesketh (*Letters* 4: 344–45): "I have carefully perused the account you sent me of the execution of Tom Pain [sic], and have several objections to it. In the first place I object to his being executed in effigy only, and not in reality. . . . In short, had I been Master of the Ceremonies on this occasion, I would have conducted the business in a different stile . . . and leave Tom Paine to bring himself to the gallows in his own time. . . ."

19 *Letters* 4: 352.

20 This information is provided by John D. Baird in his edition of Cowper's later poetry ("The Poetry of William Cowper, 1784–1800, An Edition," Ph.D. dissertation, Princeton University, 1970), 547. I am also indebted to Baird's analysis of the Miltonic strands in this sonnet.

21 *Poetical Works*, ed. H. S. Milford 4th edition, with corrections and additions by Norma Russell (London: Oxford University Press, 1967), 642.

22 18 June 1793, *Letters* 4: 355.

23 Ibid., 356–57 (23 June 1793).

24 Ibid., 297 (to Hayley, 24 February 1793).

Following the Stage-Itinerant: Perception, Doubt, and Death in Swift's Tale of a Tub

VERONICA KELLY

The "Apology" to the fifth edition of *A Tale of a Tub* has appeared to some of its readers to be a place of comparative certainty and rest, a stretch of prose where we can hear with greater confidence the voice of the *Tale's* author, and where we can begin to learn the rhythms of his speech and to uncover his intentions before setting off again into the verbal labyrinth of the *Tale* in search of Swift.[1] A later addition, the "Apology" holds before the exhausted reader of the *Tale* a vision of an outermost frame, the promise of an authorial voice that will speak through the text to still its indulgence in exuberant negation and finally turn that extravagance to a clear and positive purpose. Our expectation that any author will sacrifice the distant and sly artifice of the persona to come to the defense of his work because it is, finally, the offspring and reflection of himself makes the apologist seem categorically different from, and superior to, the mad narrator of the *Tale*: it makes him seem less like a piece of dramatic rhetoric and more like a piece of Swift.[2]

But if the "Apology" takes us any closer to Swift, it is only by taking us farther into the conditions of circumstance that dictate the mutations of person, personae, and impersonations in the 1704 *Tale*.[3] The apologist's apology dwells on the issue of represented persons: it contains an account of the *Tale's* parodic impersonations of Dryden and L'Estrange, a set of satires directed at the "Persons" of its detractors, reference to the theatrical decorum of impersonation, and a rebuff to the attempts of its critics to render the *Tale* itself into a text that impersonates an author. Thus while the apologist's language and concerns can be taken as evidence

239

about the artifice of the *Tale*, it must be recognized that the evidence has been planted. While the way the apologist uses the concepts of person and "personate" may be said to reveal more about the status of the *Tale's* personae, more about the nature of Swift's art and, perhaps, more about Swift than does the narrator of the *Tale* proper, it must be conceded at the same time that the apologist himself is the face of a Grub-Street occasion, a figure on the public stage.

We can look at the *Tale's* treatment of persons as dramatic personae within the context of Enlightenment considerations of persons as representations. In the "Apology," as in the *Tale*, a person occurs as the construct of a public and polemical occasion. The "Apology's" attention to the printed spectacle of authorial identity recalls Hobbes' definition of a person as a stage persona, a particular and transient conjunction of words and actions:

> A Person, is he *whose words or actions are considered, either as his own, or as representing the words or actions of an other man, or of any other thing to whom they are attributed, whether Truly or by Fiction.*
>
> The word Person is latine: insteed whereof the Greeks have πρόσωπον, which signifies the *Face*, as *Persona* in latine signifies the *disguise*, or *outward appearance* of a man, counterfeited on the Stage; and somtimes more particularly that part of it, which disguiseth the face, as a Mask or Visard: And from the Stage, hath been translated to any Representer of speech and action, as well in Tribunalls, as Theaters. So that a *Person*, is the same that an *Actor* is, both on the Stage and in common Conversation; and to *Personate*, is to *Act*, or *Represent* himselfe, or an other. . . .[4]

A person by this definition is not psychological but theatrical and occasional, the vehicle of a civic function. In Hobbes' definition, "each person is already a self-impersonator in a sense – a masked and mediated representation of himself."[5] This public act of self-representation is internalized and naturalized in Locke, where the civic definition of a person as "a Forensick Term appropriating Actions and their Merit" operates with respect to a hypothetical and interior center, a psychological continuity consisting of consciousness and a memory and "capable of a Law, and Happiness and Misery."[6] When Locke redefines the stage persona of the *Leviathan* as a self-regulating psychology, the theatricality of Hobbes' "person" is not lost but, reformulated in the terms of the perceptual origin of conscious identity, it recurs as the mental imagery that characterizes the representative theory of perception and knowledge.[7] Locke's descriptions of ideas, conveyed in the language of image and resemblance, of page and character, of archetype and ectype, suggest that consciousness is mediated by the mental "objects" of perception. The visual bias of Locke's rhetoric implies that consciousness is a mental semiotic: it is his description of the ideas of primary qualities as representions ("the *Ideas of Primary Qualities* of Bodies, *are Resemblances* of them, and their Patterns do really exist in the Bodies themselves" [II, viii, 15, p. 137]) that, by grounding that *semiosis* within a mimetic frame, turns the text of consciousness into a theatrical event. In the conscious mind, as Locke describes it, the semiotic codes that are perceived as secondary qualities (colors, sounds, tastes) are understood with reference to the mimetic representations that are primary qualities (solidity, extension, figure, number) just as, in the theater, the performance of a play occurs within the context of the representational forms of the actors themselves and of the mise en scène. Placed in this interior "Tribunall," perception becomes a theatrical spectacle and, like theater, is suspected of harboring illusion and skepticism.

Locke naturalizes the theatricality of identity, and clears away the skepticism that accompanies the possibility of representative perceptions, by applying the doctrine of accommodation to simple ideas. Accommodation, a tool of Reformation theological teaching and exegesis, holds that God reveals himself to man through a mediating or symbolic vocabulary that is suited (accommodated) both to man's limited comprehension and to his need for redemptive knowledge.[8] Raphael, describing the war in Heaven to Adam, explains that he will accommodate his language to Adam's understanding, that "what surmounts the reach | Of human sense, I shall delineate so, | By likening spiritual to corporal forms, | As may express them best."[9] Raphael's task is to discover a vocabulary that is intellectually literal and spiritually allusive, that can encourage belief in the transcendant and immaterial truth through a language that is proscribed by the range and terminology of man's comprehension. While Adam's human limitations require that Raphael reduce the "spiritual" truths of heaven to the "corporeal" forms of metaphor, that metaphor—underwritten by Raphael's angelic vision—is endowed with the promise of a divine tenor. This promise, which is received as faith, translates both literal and figurative language into truth. In *De Doctrina Christiana*, for example, Milton admits that accommodated knowledge is incomplete but he admonishes that it is nonetheless adequate:

> For granting both in the literal and figurative descriptions of God, he is exhibited not as he really is, but in such a manner as may be within the scope of our comprehensions, yet we ought to entertain such a conception of him, as he, in condescending to accommodate himself to our

capacities, has shown that he desires we should conceive. For it is on this very account that he has lowered himself to our level, lest in our flights above the reach of human understanding, and beyond the written word of Scripture, we should be tempted to indulge in vague cogitations and subtleties.[10]

In Book IV of the *Essay*, writing about the "Reality of Knowledge," Locke argues that in the language of simple ideas the "reality of Things" is accommodated to that "which our state requires":

> Simple *Ideas*, which since the Mind, as has been shewed, can by no means make to it self, must necessarily be the product of Things operating on the Mind in a natural way, and producing therein those Perceptions which by the Wisdom and Will of our Maker they are ordained and adapted to. From whence it follows, that *simple* Ideas *are not fictions* of our Fancies, but the natural and regular productions of Things without us, really operating upon us; and so carry with them all the conformity which is intended; or which our state requires: For they represent to us Things under those appearances which they are fitted to produce in us: whereby we are enabled to distinguish the sorts of particular Substances, to discern the states they are in, and so to take them for our Necessities, and apply them to our Uses. (IV, iv, 4, p. 564)

Locke, like Milton, uses the doctrine of accommodation to prevent the "vague cogitations and subtleties" that lead to doubt. When Locke defines simple ideas as productions of "Things under those appearances which they are fitted to produce in us," the suggestion that perception is representational — burdened as it is by a radical skepticism — is reconceived in terms of divinely ordered production. The subtleties of skepticism are averted by the practical and moral usefulness of accommodated perception:

> The certainty of Things existing in rerum Natura, when we have the testimony of our Senses for it, is not only as great as our frame can attain to, but as our Condition needs. For our Faculties being suited not to the full extent of Being, nor to a perfect, clear, comprehensive Knowledge of things free of all doubt and scruple; but to the preservation of us, in whom they are; and accommodated to the use of Life: they serve our purpose well enough, if they will but give us certain notice of those Things, which are convenient or inconvenient to us. (IV, xi, 8, p. 634)

By using an exegetical tool to naturalize the theatricality of a representative realism, Locke concedes — in the very act of denying it — that sense perceptions are representations. Like the words of Scripture, the images of perception are part of a divine text; it is their status as *divine* representations, as heavenly theater accommodated to a human audience, that naturalizes them. This method of naturalizing the theatricality of identity would be unproblematic if Locke's application of the theological doctrine of accommodation to simple ideas did not provide the foundation for secular discourse, for once perception is accommodated and validated by use, humanity possesses a cognitive self-suficiency; once perception is accommodated, we can know what we need to know.

Locke, then, uses an argument about the divine production of simple ideas to contain the metaphoric characteristics of perception safely within the tradition of accommodation. That this is an argument that simultaneously translates perception into the "natural" language of a secular epistemology is the objection that directs Swift's use of theatricality in a *Tale of a Tub*. Swift uses the dramatic personae of the *Tale* to unmask this naturalized, secular discourse and to expose it as theatrical and skeptical; he uses an exaggerated theatricality to un-accommodate perception.

By casting the *Tale's* narrator in the roles of various committed but transient public persons and by giving its readers the function of the perceiving and unifying consciousness, Swift manipulates the disjunction between two conceptions of person—the first of a person as a thing perceived, a visible function or representation, the second of a person as a continuous perception or moral entity. A style without a memory, the *Tale's* narrator enacts a finite but randomly repeating series of forensic persons, which—in keeping with the *Tale's* theatrical paradigm—we can call his *personae*.[11] The "harlequin inconsistencies"[12] of these personae disrupt any attempts by the reader to find in the interactions of memory and consciousness an organization for the carnival of discontinuity being read. The *Tale* thus sets the sheer theatricality of the dramatic personae of the text against any reader's desire to read persons as self-sufficient and continuous psychologies. The simple and shifting personae of the *Tale* reject the psychologizing projections of the reader by setting up a syntax that equates person with persona, meaning with text. In perhaps the most infamous passage of the *Tale*, which describes an instance of simple but hyperbolical justice, the prostitute whose public persona is proscribed by her society is quite simply stripped of her person; "Last Week," the narrator writes, "I saw a Woman *flay'd*, and you will hardly believe, how much it altered her Person for the worse" (*Tale*, 173). The horror of this passage arises in part from its assault on the reader's self-consciousness. It replaces the tropes of an interior psychology with the literalized surfaces of a person that exists only as a theatrical persona or a legal actor. The literalness of this description, conveyed through the narrator's affectless account of the prostitute's death, reduces the prostitute as a person to her civic persona and livelihood: her person, the justice she receives, and the language in which it is described flatly coincide. Through its unwritten description of the prostitute's exposed interior, the passage refuses our desire as readers to reaffirm our interior psychologies through the persons represented in the text.

The *Tale* then sets itself up as a theater of civic personae and sets its readers up as the adjudicating audience.[13] But adjudication turns out to be endless and hopeless, as the narrative's transient affiliations create an impenetrable surface. The narrator's assumption of a series of civic personae occurs within a system of forensic naming that characterizes the relation of the *Tale's* narrator to his world, a convention by which persons are addressed as the *dramatis personae* of the public stage. The narrator of the *Tale* situates himself in a world defined by the perimeters of collegial and civic persons, a world composed of "*Wits*," Criticks, "our *Modern Saints* in *Great Britain*," "the *Grub-Street* Brotherhood," Societies, Commonwealths and Empires. In his belated preface, the narrator addresses his effusive thanks

> to *His Majesty*, and both Houses of *Parliament*; To the *Lords* of the King's most honourable Privy-Council, to the Reverend *Judges*: To the *Clergy*, and *Gentry*, and *Yeomanry* of this Land: But in a more especial manner, to my worthy Brethren and Friends at *Will's Coffee-House*, and *Gresham College*, and *Warwick- Lane*, and *Moor-Fields*, and *Scotland-Yard*, and *Westminster-Hall*, and *Guild-Hall*; In short, to all Inhabitants and Retainers whatsoever, either in Court, or Church, or Camp, or City, or Country. . . . (*Tale*, 181)

Rather than breaking out of this expanding network of affiliations, the apologist calls attention to the narrator's method of civic address by extending it into an apparently less fictive context. At its simplest, the recurrence of this forensic decorum in the "Apology" merely records the necessary distance that exists between an anonymous author and his shadowy reading public: conditions require that the author be referred to as the "Author" and the reader as the "Reader." But Swift makes the occasion of anonymity one of the founding ironies of the *Tale*. Itself an occasion, Swift's anonymity not only exaggerates the *Tale's* functional identification of persons with polemical moments, but reduces those occasions and those persons to a set of intertextual relations. Thus Wotton appears in the paper politics of the "Apology" as "the Answerer" and "the Reflector," and Bentley, much to the purported mortification of "Sir W. T.," is dubbed "the Adversary." Even Sir William Temple, "that noble Writer" who apparently stands as the champion of traditional values, devolves into the sum of his published parts: he is "universally reverenced for every good

Quality that could possibly enter into the Composition of the most ac-
conplish'd Person" (*Tale*, 11). Reduced to print, the action of the public
stage is reduced to the drama of Grub-Street personations: the "Answerer,"
who has "neither the Shape, Mettle nor Speed of that nobler Animal he
would affect to personate," is advised that "The Part of Minellius or Farnby
would have fallen in with his Genius" (*Tale*, 15).

In the printed world of the *Tale*, which lacks the visible depth of dramatic action, the civic functions of persons are conducted in the intertextual relations between one occasion for words and another. Thus the *Tale's*
narrator wages his forensic battles through acts of personation. The *Tale*
is an eye-witness account of the kind of textual maneuvering that is histori-
cized in "The Battle of the Books." The Bookseller, who must find a person to suit the motto found on the manuscript of the *Tale*, becomes a
persona in a quasi-allegorical journey from literary accident to literary
occasion, from one description to another, from *DETUR DIGNISSIMO*
through the opinions of Curates and Poets to the "Dedication." Convinced,
after much questing, that he has found "the Person intended by the
Author," the Bookseller nonetheless performs a reverse literature check:
"I have made several Persons, dip here and there in those Papers, and
before they read three Lines, they have all assured me, plainly, that they
cannot possibly be applied to any Person besides your Lordship" (*Tale*,
25). That person, The Right Honourable John Lord Somers, exists, finally, as an equity between two descriptions. The apologist himself occurs
as the persona of the occasion that he names, an apology for the polemic
that has arisen in print around the *Tale's* use and misuse of persons.

The apologist's claim that the *Tale* is original is situated within the "Apology's" polemical focus on issues of second order representation: on issues
of plagiarism, parody, and authorial identity. The apologist defends the
author's use of parody on the grounds that it is a moral corrective; it is
impersonation intended to unmask a kind of banal plagiarism or generic
writing. Parody, he explains, is the pointed matching of styles: "Those
passages in this Discourse, which appear most liable to Objection are what
they call Parodies, where the Author personates the Style and Manner
of other Writers, whom he has a mind to expose" (*Tale*, 7). The apologist
sets the originality of the *Tale's* parody against the redundancy of other
authors. Dryden and L'Estrange are vulnerable to the narrator's parodic
personations not because they are idiosyncratic but because they are generic: because the styles that embody their civic personae as writers are whol-
ly institutional. As Writers, they are interchangeable with a number of
other "Persons": "the Reader," the apologist remarks of one of the *Tale's*
parodies, "may find more Persons to give that Passage an Application"
(*Tale*, 7).

The apologist vindicates the *Tale* from charges of "plagiary" by an assertion of its absolute originality: "The Author . . . insists upon it, that through the whole Book he has not borrowed one single Hint from any Writer in the World" (*Tale*, 13). Contrasting the *Tale* to the writings of Dryden and L'Estrange, the apologist says of it that "He conceived it was never disputed to be an Original, whatever Faults it might have" (*Tale*, 13). But because the *Tale*'s author remains anonymous, its originality manifests not its origin but its occasion. Unlike the writings (and persons) of Dryden and L'Estrange, which are generic and interchangeable, the *Tale* is truly occasional, and its originality is a function of that occasional anonymity: in it, the *Tale* contains all persons (as personations) and none (it is itself unpersonated). To protect that anonymity, the apologist resists the attempts of readers and critics to name the author of the *Tale* with an entirely situational logic — a logic that responds to the demands of the moment. Twice he wards off claims of critics and booksellers to have named the author of the *Tale*:

> He thinks it no fair Proceeding, that any Person should offer determinately to fix a name upon the Author of this Discourse, who hath all along concealed himself from most of his nearest Friends: Yet several have gone a farther Step, and pronounced another Book to have been the Work of the same Hand with this; which the Author directly affirms to be a thorough mistake; he having yet never so much as read that Discourse, a plain Instance how little Truth, there often is in general Surmises, or in Conjectures drawn from a Similitude of Style, or way of thinking. (*Tale*, 6)

In the "Postscript," a reversal in the apologist's logic reflects the demands of the polemical occasion. Whereas, in the "Apology," similitudes of style were not enough to allow critics to conclude "another Book to have been the Work of the same Hand with this," in the "Postscript" to the "Apology," such information is enough to assure "Readers of Judgment" that "the whole work is of the same Hand":

> Since the writing of this which was about a Year ago; a Prostitute Bookseller hath publish'd a foolish Paper, under the Name of Notes of the Tale of a Tub, with some Account of the Author, and with an Insolence which I suppose is punishable by Law, hath presumed to assign certain Names. It will be enough for the Author to assure the World, that the Writer of that Paper is utterly wrong in all his Conjectures upon that Affair. The Author farther asserts that the whole Work is entirely of one Hand, which every Reader of Judgment will easily discover. (*Tale*, 20)

In countering these attempts to name the person of the text, the apologist removes the threat posed by critics and commentators to reduce the protean originality of the *Tale* to a simple or "naturall" personation (*Leviathan*, 217) by fixing its personae to the stabilizing center of an authorial name.

The *Tale*, it has been argued here, produces a world of forensic persons, the personae of civic and polemical moments, out of its occasional anonymity. It uses its *dramatis personae*—the apologist, the narrator, the prostitute, the beau—to discover in the naturalized language of accommodated perception and in its secular self-sufficiency the conditions of theatrical isolation and momentary self-reference that give rise to skepticism. The *Tale* reduces the trope of the world stage to its prototype in the metaphoric structure that epistemology imposes on the "world" of perception. In *A Tale of a Tub*, the metaphor that the world is a stage is literalized and universalized: perceived meaning is embodied in the vehicle of perception. Much has been written about the importance of point of view and perspective in Gulliver's *Travels into Several Remote Nations of the World*.[14] Treating both *A Tale of a Tub* and *Gulliver's Travels* as works that "dramatize a putative author who shapes the materials of his narrative," Everett Zimmerman argues that, in these works, "the narrator's status is closely related to the hermeneutical and epistemological issues in Swift's satires."[15] In the *Tale*, the relation is one of absolute intimacy: the personae of the *Tale* dramatize as polemical occasion the conditions of representation and circumstances which, in the skeptical inevitabilities of a realist epistemology, define the perceptual stage. Its itinerant theatricality locates in the essential figurings of the senses the triumph of doubt.

The *Tale's* narrator is "a Writer of short Memory" (*Tale*, 134) and his forgetfulness, which is an internal corollary to the *Tale's* anonymity, insures his originality. Writing without memory, the narrator himself is an anonymous textual occasion, a reflection of the vagaries of circumstance that are the *Tale*. When he explains that invention not memory is the favorite topic of modern rhetoricians, his explanation parodies a form of discourse developed out of the epistemological categories of perceptual experience and accidental consensus:

> Because *Memory* being an Employment of the Mind upon things past, is a Faculty, for which the Learned, in our Illustrious Age, have no manner of Occasion, who deal entirely with *Invention*, and strike all Things out of themselves, or at least, by Collision, from each other: Upon which Account we think it highly Reasonable to produce our great Forgetfulness, as an Argument unanswerable for our great Wit. (*Tale*, 135)

In his forgetfulness, the narrator becomes an inane prophet, the mouth-piece of circumstance. His amnesia transforms him into a *superficie*: his verbal surface mimics the superficiality of a modern *"Invention"* that reflects without retaining and that reduces words and things to moments in a semiotic atomism that functions by "Collision." The characteristic conflictual dualities of the *Tale*—ancient vs. modern, container and contained, satire or panegyric—are continually generated out of and levelled by the circumstantial character of the narrator's perception, as are the various polities and factions named and subscribed to by each of his personae. The narrator's ceaseless production of opposed figures or bodies out of perceptions which are uniformly figural and uniformly circumstantial appears both in the scope of the *Tale*'s satire and in its proliferation of strings of interchangeable metaphors which can conclude only with the inevitability of duality itself:

> Whether a Tincture of Malice in our Natures, makes us fond of furnishing every bright Idea with its Reverse; Or, whether Reason reflecting upon the Sum of Things, can, like the Sun, serve only to enlighten one half of the Globe, leaving the other half, by Necessity, under Shade and Darkness: Or, whether Fancy, flying up to the imagination of what is Highest and Best, becomes over-shot, and spent, and weary, and suddenly falls like a dead Bird of Paradise, to the Ground. Or, whether after all these *Metaphysical* Conjectures, I have not entirely missed the true Reason; The Proposition, however, which hath stood me in so much Circumstance, is altogether true; That, as the most unciviliz'd Parts of Mankind, have some way or other, climbed up into the Conception of a *God*, or Supreme Power, so they have seldom forgot to provide their Fears with certain ghastly Notions, which instead of better, have served pretty tolerably for a *Devil*. (*Tale*, 158)

The narrator's isocolonic proliferation of metaphoric options ("or" . . ., "or" . . ., "or" . . .) is symptomatic of his status as an amnesiac mirror. His invention working without reference to memory runs like a machine, generating a string of insignificant possibilities that conclude only in exhaustion and binary redundancy. This pointless reproduction of figures which are, like bodies, generated out of the immediately anterior figure, indicates that the narrator's language is trapped within the present tense of circumstance. Metaphor in this context is severed from the possibility of revelatory reference and becomes "Metaphysical Conjecture." No single metaphor is appropriate because, in a circumstantial discourse, metaphor signifies only its own womb-like capacity for figural reproduction.

The generation of metaphoric options and factional corporations, which is the source of the *Tale*'s turbulent satire, constitutes, beyond that, the very action of the *Tale*. Dramatic action as such is impossible on the *stage-itinerant*, where all is in motion. Drama in the *Tale* thus takes the form of personification and the character of the narrator's personae. The momentary, mercurial affiliations of the *Tale*'s satire take shape in its narrator who, having written "Four-score and eleven Pamphlets" . . . "under three Reigns, and for the Service of six and thirty Factions" (*Tale*, 70) goes on to personify himself in the course of the *Tale* as, among others, "our Corporation of Poets" (33), "the spacious Commonwealth of Writers" (61), "the *Grub-street* Brotherhood" (64), "the Commonwealth of Learning" (94), and "the present universal Empire of Wit and Learning" (124). These rapid metamorphoses on the part of the *Tale*'s narrator deny its readers the pleasure of dramatic irony—of a superior or synthetic position—by forcing them into a position of accommodated consensus with the narrator. As readers of the *Tale*, we are asked to affiliate ourselves with each of the narrator's momentary persons. We are even instructed, in a parody of realism's principles of common sense and shared experience, to assume an identical figure and position:

> Whatever Reader desires to have a thorow Comprehension of an Author's Thoughts, cannot take a better Method, than by putting himself into the Circumstances and Postures of Life, that the Writer was in, upon every important Passage as it flow'd from his Pen; For this will introduce a Parity and strict Correspondence of Idea's between the Reader and the Author. (*Tale*, 44)

Within an accommodated, secular semiotic, "a strict Correspondence of Idea's" requires complete identity of circumstance and posture, of moment and figure.

The personae of the *Tale* fulfill exactly the modern ideal of circumstantial wit (the narrator, remember, has avowed of the moderns that "our great Forgetfulness [is] an Argument unanswerable for our great wit"). In the persona's susceptibility to factional affiliation, the *Tale* presents a parodic version of the tragic unities in which tragedy is replaced by *Wit* and the unity of action is replaced by the circumstance of persons. Where, in the works of the ancients, the unity of action dramatizes the tragedy of persons, in the works of the moderns the circumstance of persons dramatizes the transience of action:

> *Wit* has its walks and Purlieus, out of which it may not stray the breadth of a Hair, upon peril of being lost. The *Moderns* have artfully fixed the *Mercury*, and reduced it to the Circumstances of Time, Place, and Person. (*Tale*, 43)

In the *Tale*, circumstance becomes the occasion of the comic flaw, for "there is something Individual in human Minds, that easily kindles at the accidental Approach and Collision of certain Circumstances, which tho' of paltry and mean Appearance, do often flame out into the greatest Emergencies of Life" (*Tale*, 162). An eminent modern, the narrator suffers the comic fate: he reduces all to sense and reflects as persona every passing circumstance of perception. In the course of the *Tale*, he fields so many circumstances and takes on so many personae that he closes unable to distinguish a self from a world, pausing "till I find, by feeling the World's Pulse, and my own, that it will be of absolute Necessity for us both, to resume my Pen" (*Tale*, 210).

In the image of the *stage-itinerant*, the *Tale* figures the mechanism of its own dramatization of perceptual circumstance. Like the *Tale*, the *stage-itinerant* is occasional and anonymous; like the *Tale*, it produces out of that occasional anonymity a repertoire of personae. The *Tale* uses its narrator and his many personae to play out as a drama of skepticism and credulity, of knaves and fools, the perceptual theatricality that accommodation naturalizes within an economy of common sense and experience. It ironizes the structural doubt endemic to a system of discourse that is built on accommodated perceptions by placing a radically impressionable and exquisitely sincere narrator in a world governed by the conditions of skepticism, a world in which an itinerant theatricality is inherent to perception. The narrator, as he takes on persona after persona, personifies the *stage-itinerant*: he becomes the stage, the players, and the audience of that microcosmic theater that plays just at the perceptual threshold, whose stage could be either of the mind or of the world, whose players can distinguish neither among themselves not between their putative selves and the putative world, and whose audience enacts the most intimate and most hopeless struggle to distinguish truth from fiction.

The power of the *stage-itinerant* to originate all modern productions depends on its ability to exemplify the plight of the modern understanding contained by the semiotic circumstances of its perception. The *Tale* as hermeneutic may be said to take place on perception's threshold, and to take a theoretical awareness of that threshold as the locus of an originary chaos to be prerequisite to is own generation of a satiric excess of disorderly factions and dualities. The perceptual threshold is that region between cognition and sensation which in the terms of Enlightenment philosophy of mind becomes both the locus and the abyss of origin. When, in *The Leviathan*, Hobbes defines sense as "originary fancy," thus introducing the distance of representation into the relations between cognitive and material reality, spatial uncertainty becomes endemic to perception: "And though at some certain distance, the reall, and very object seem invested with the fancy it begets in us; Yet still the object is one thing, the image of fancy is another. So that Sense in all cases, is nothing els but original fancy . . ." (*Leviathan*, 8). Locke places at risk even the possibility that temporal continuity will establish analogy between the now disjunct cognitive and material worlds when he writes, in the *Essay*, that sensory knowledge "*extends as far as the present Testimony of our Senses*, employ'd about particular objects, that do then affect them, *and no farther*" (IV, xi, 9, p. 635). Defined, as it is here, in terms of semiotic distance and temporal occasion, perception itself becomes the *stage-itinerant*. The modern understanding is circumscribed by its perceptual semiotics, and the world it constructs out of that *semiosis* is grounded on the determining theatrics of its perception. Thus circumscribed by circumstance, Swift's modern is suspended between a credulous and a skeptical hermeneutic, between accommodated realism's illusion of semiotic transparency (things) and skepticism's specter of absolute theatricality (signs).

The pan-theatrical conditions which the "*Refiners* of Philosophy" create at the threshold of perception are dramatized on the moving scene which is the *Tale*. They are the conditions of distance and metamorphosis which make it right for the *Tale* to contain a confusion of personae, to address a disparity of audiences, to move randomly or willfully from topic to topic, from place to place. They are the conditions because of which the *Tale* has no visible or known author, and by virtue of which its backdrop, mutable and expanding, grows to include the entire perceptible world. The ultimate transport of artifice, the *stage-itinerant* expands the represented scene to take in the known world, allowing the illusions of the perceptual theater to be naturalized as common sense within the accommodated boundaries of knowledge. For those taken in by the "universal" artifice of perception, the "vehicle of delusion" creates a world out of the human understanding.

But while the figure of the *stage-itinerant* traverses and maps for the credulous a world that can be known and articulated, it unmasks the invisible mechanism of secular discourse by naming and dramatizing the theatricality that accommodation makes natural: for Swift, skepticism remains endemic to the discourse that has naturalized itself by universalizing its semiotic incapacity. What the figure of the *stage-itinerant* reveals is reality as construed by common sense transformed into the universalized theatricality of the perceptual stage: the imagined reference of common sense disappears behind the moving back-drop which is the perceived world, transforming inference into the play of images that cross the shifting and groundless stage of the senses. That such inference is without meaning is the point which one of the *Tale*'s personae presses home to Prince Posterity:

If I should venture in a Windy day, to affirm to *Your Highness*, that there is a large Cloud near the *Horizon* in the Form of a *Bear*, another in the *Zenith* with the Head of an Ass, a Third to the Westward with Claws like a *Dragon*; and Your Highness should in a few minutes think fit to examine the Truth, 'tis certain, they would all be changed in Figure and Position, new ones would arise, and all we could agree upon would be that Clouds there were, but that I was grossly mistaken in the *Zoography* and *Topography* of them. (*Tale*, 35)

The genus of all modern productions, the *stage-itinerant* refigures the naturalized, perceptual semiotics of modern epistemology as a universal theater where the binary structures of dramatic, polemical, and physical conflict flicker in and out of a uniform representationalism. In the *Tale's* parody of referential continuity, semiotic categories are levelled and reference reduces to an empty gesture. On the *stage-itinerant*, all distinctions become nominal. The modern's experience is entirely but indifferently semiotic, an epistemological scene composed of effects which are clearly signs ("all we could agree upon would be that Clouds there were") but which are of random or doubtful signification ("they would all be changed in Figure and Position.").[16] This epidemic of representation means both that the imagery of the *Tale*, which is now on a level with all of perception, is primarily physiological, and that the material circumstance of unfounded representation defines the modern condition. Far from applauding this situation, Swift describes it as a paradise of fools:

He that can with *Epicurus* content his Ideas with the *Films* and *Images* that fly off upon his Senses from the *Superficies* of Things; such a Man truly wise, creams off Nature, leaving the Sower and the Dregs, for Philosophy and Reason to lap up. This is the sublime and refined Point of Felicity, called the *Possession of being well Deceived*; the Serene Peaceful State of being a Fool among Knaves (*Tale*, 44).[17]

The modern, as Swift portrays him, can be either a fool or a knave, either a credulous (accidental) or a purposeful atheist. Skepticism, completed in the distance and metamorphosis of a perceptual theater, is endemic: its "wild correspondence . . . set the mind erring in a wilderness of doubt" (Traugott, 96). The quest through this undifferentiated hermeneutic wilderness is the jaunt which we, as readers of the *Tale*, are invited to join, and where "the Reader quickly finds, it is all *Pork*, with little variety of Sawce: For there is no inventing Terms of Art beyond our Idea's; and when Idea's are exhausted, Terms of Art must be so too" (*Tale*, 50).

The *stage-itinerant* creates a state of figural plenty but of metaphoric indifference. On the perceptual threshold, the distinction between things original and things mimetic has become a nominal distinction between different moments of representation as have distinctions among different kinds of figures; in the *Tale*, people and books are simply different forms of representation and metaphoric and literal descriptions are simply different methods of representation. The figures of the public stage reduce to an equivalence with the letters of the Grub-Street stage because both are images on the perceptual stage. Modern writers, indistinguishable from their productions, share their ignoble fate. Both appear on the moving "Scene" of the perceptual stage, where transience and delusion negate the differentiating functions of vision and memory: "Tis true indeed, that altho' their Numbers be vast, and their Productions numerous in proportion, yet are they hurried so hastily off the Scene, that they escape our Memory, and delude our Sight" (*Tale*, 34).

Brought home to the threshold of perception, the problem of skepticism becomes intimately physiological; not only is knowledge of the world cast into doubt but the vehicle of knowledge is itself doubted. Thus the body, the vehicle of the senses, which are themselves the "Vehicle of *Delusion*" (*Tale*, 172), becomes the center of the *Tale*'s parodic disorganization. Doubt settles at the skin. The boundary and medium of the skin represents the jurisdiction of realist discourse and epistemology; as the body and the senses become the vehicles of doubt, so does the discourse that defines itself through them. The *Tale*'s parody of accommodated knowledge is sometimes gentle, as when the narrator abstracts the productions of the "most eminent Members" of Grub-Street in order that "These Notices may serve to give the Learned Reader an Idea as well as a Taste of what the whole work is likely to Produce" (*Tale*, 69). But its corrective is more infamously brutal. It is a presumptuous reason that disrupts the decorous if superficial relation that has been established between the object world and the senses:

> The two Senses, to which all Objects first address themselves, are the Sight and Touch; These never examine farther than the Colour, the Shape, the Size and whatever other Qualities dwell, or are drawn by Art upon the Outward of Bodies; and then comes Reason officiously, with Tools for cutting, and opening, and mangling, and piercing, offering to demonstrate, that they are not of the same consistence quite thro'. . . . In such Conclusions as these, Reason is certainly in the Right; . . . in most Corporeal Beings, which have fallen under my Cognizance, the *Outside* hath been infinitely preferable to the *In*. . . . (*Tale*, 173)

The *Tale* associates a plentitude of represented form with the variety of vice, disease, and death. The "Bales of Paper" which hold the books of modern authors disappear because

> Books, like Men their Authors, have no more than one Way of coming into the World, but there are ten Thousand to go out of it, and return no more. (*Tale*, 36)

Praise is less various than blame:

> For, as Health is but one Thing, and has been always the same, whereas Diseases are by thousands, besides new and daily Additions; So, all the Virtues that have been ever in Mankind, are to be counted upon a few Fingers, but his Follies and Vices are innumerable, and Time adds hourly to the Heap. (*Tale*, 50)

The proliferation of vice and disease is occasioned by a pandemic figural equity. Within an accommodated semiotic, all bodies, physical and verbal, are finally "of the same consistency quite thro' ": they are merely the microcosmic vehicles that constitute the universal vehicle of the *stage-itinerant* that comprehends them. The expression of material circumstance and invention, these bodies are purely vehicular, principles of conveyance and contagion. What they do is reproduce and, as the narrator concludes, "Going *too long* is a Cause of Abortion as effectual, tho' not so frequent, as *Going too short*; and hold true especially in the *Labors* of the Brain" (*Tale*, 206). Their reproductive fiction continues until language remembers the grave, turning — as it will — against the preferences of the narrator and his readership for the conceptual fiction of the imagination:

> Nor is mankind so much to blame in his Choice [for fiction over truth], thus determining him, if we consider that the Debate meerly lies between *Things past* and *Things conceived*; and so the Question is only this; Whether Things that have Place in the *Imagination*, may not as properly be said to *Exist*, as those that are seated in the *Memory*; which may be justly held in the Affirmative, and very much to the Advantage of the former, since This is acknowledged to be the *Womb* of Things, and the other allowed to be no more that the *Grave*. (*Tale*, 172)

The narrator's body and the bodies that he describes are, like the body of accommodated discourse, vehicles that exhaust or spend themselves. In a mock martyrdom (the hack, his writing years spent, has indeed been bled to death), the narrator's body serves the same purpose as his pen; it circumscribes and exhausts matter, running down — like a machine — when it has spent itself:

> I do here give Public Notice, that my Resolutions are, to circumscribe within this Discourse, the whole Stock of Matter I have been so many

Years providing. Since my *Vein* is once opened, I am content to exhaust it all at a Running, for the peculiar Advantage of my dear Country, and for the universal Benefit of Mankind. (*Tale*, 184)

Swift's levelling of physical bodies and rhetorical figures creates an inverse catachresis, for what is startling about the narrator's rhetoric is the absence of implied metaphor where the order of common sense demands it. The ecstatic proliferation of metaphors ends in a vision of horrible death in which metaphor ceases to be merely a representation of death and becomes its cause. For example, the infants so incidentally destroyed in the *Tale*'s diatribe against Time die because of their involvement in metaphor. It is their doom to be likened to books even before they can speak.

His [Time's] inveterate Malice is such to the Writings of our Age, that of several Thousands produced yearly from this renowned City, before the next Revolution of the Sun, there is not one to be heard of; Unhappy Infants, many of them barbarously destroyed, before they have so much as learnt their *Mother-Tongue* to beg for Pity. Some he stifles in their Cradles, others he frights into convulsions, whereof they suddenly die; some he flays alive, others he tears Limb from Limb. Great numbers are offered to *Moloch*, and the rest tainted by his breath, die of a languishing consumption. (*Tale*, 33)

The morbidity of metaphor in the *Tale* suggests that within the context of a secular and accommodated semiotic, metaphor joins with sin as an index and cause of mortality.[18] The metaphors of the *Tale* are different because metaphor can only mean death. The itinerant figures that we perceive on the *Tale*'s stage reproduce in a kind of semiotic relay, passing signification from vehicle to vehicle until, "when Ideas are exhausted," meaning collapses into the grave. Both the language and the plots of the narrator's expansive pretensions inevitably discover "the Hangman's remedy for all Diseases by death":

We whom the World is pleased to honor with the Title of *Modern Authors*, should never have been able to compass our great Design of an everlasting Remembrance, and never-dying Fame, if our Endeavours had not been so highly serviceable to the general Good of Mankind. This, *O Universe*, is the Adventurous Attempt of me thy Secretary;

——— *Quemvis perferre laborem*
Suadet, & inducit noctes vigilare serenas

To this End, I have some Time since, with a World of Pains and Art, dissected the Carcass of *Humane Nature*, and read many useful Lectures upon the several Parts, both *Containing* and *Contained*; till at last it *smelt* so strong, I could preserve it no longer. (*Tale*, 123)

This collapse of the *Tale*'s verbal metaphor into description of mortified flesh alludes to the parallel collapse of the perceptual metaphors that found an accommodated discourse. The narrator's monumental anatomy of human nature ends in the reek of death, and that mortal whiff addresses the senses with their inherent mortality: the nose smells its death, the eye sees it, language signifies it. In the very act of perceiving itself, the mind decomposes:

> For, it is the Opinion of Choice *Virtuosi*, that the Brain is only a Crowd of little Animals, but with Teeth and Claws extremely sharp, and therefore, cling together in the Contexture we behold, like the Picture of *Hobbes' Leviathan*, or like Bees in perpendicular swarm upon a Tree, or like a Carrion corrupted into Vermin, still preserving the Shape and Figure of the Mother Animal. (*Tale*, 277)

This vision of mortality is Swift's response to the perceptual epistemology of the modern, secular world. Like "Carrion," the body of accommodated discourse "reserves the Shape and Figure of the Mother Animal," but its apparent signification is grotesquely false: within the secular discourse of the moderns and the virtuosi, meaning is a figure "corrupted into Vermin," and the human mind is mother to its own corpse.

NOTES

1 In *The Masks of Jonathan Swift*, William Ewald writes that "it [the Apology] is for the most part a sincere explanation of certain aspects of the *Tale*" (Oxford: Basil Blackwell, 1954), 14.

2 For an effective discussion of why readers of the *Tale* should not project themselves across the barrier of Swift's personae to a hypothetical "Swift," see Fredric V. Bogel, "Irony, Inference, and Critical Uncertainty," *The Yale Review* 69 (1980): 503–19: "I think it is a mistake to posit immediately the presence of an author "like you and me" whenever we encounter such a speaker, for by doing so we not only simplify the great augustan ironists, we domesticate and tame them as well. We refuse them, and ourselves, the freedom to imagine someone who displays a human form, and has mastered numerous conventions of human conduct, but who is in crucial way different from us . . ." (510).

3 The controversy over Swift's use of a persona (or personae) in *A Tale of a Tub* has been long. The major essays include Maynard Mack, "The Muse of Satire," *Yale Review* 51 (1951): 80–92; Robert C. Elliott, "Swift's 'I,'" *Yale*

Review 52 (1963): 372-91; Irvin Ehrenpreis, "Personae," in *Restoration and Eighteenth-Century Literature: Essays in Honor of Alan Dugald McKillop* (Chicago: University of Chicago Press, 1963), 25-27; Gardner Stout, "Speaker and Satiric vision in Swift's *Tale of a Tub, Eighteenth Century Studies* 3 (1969): 175-99; Kathleen Williams, *Swift and the Age of Compromise* (Lawrence: University of Kansas Press, 1958); Harold D. Kelling, "Reason in Madness: *A Tale of a Tub*," *PMLA* 69 (1954): 198-222; William B. Ewald, *The Masks of Jonathan Swift* (Oxford: Basil Blackwell, 1954); Fredric V. Bogel, "Irony, Inference, and Critical Uncertainty," *Yale Review* 69 (1980): 503-19; Ronald Paulson, *Theme and Structure in Swift's "Tale of a Tub"* (New Haven: Yale University Press, 1960) and its review by Herbert Davis in *Review of English Studies* N.S. 12 (1961): 300-2; John Traugott, "A Tale of a Tub," in *The Character of Swift's Satire* (Newark: University of Delaware Press, 1983); Everett Zimmerman, *Swift's Narrative Satires: Author and Authority* (Ithaca: Cornell University Press, 1983); Frederik N. Smith, *Language and Reality in Swift's "A Tale of a Tub"* (Columbus: Ohio State University Press, 1979). See Howard D. Weinbrot, "Masked Men and Satire and Pope," *ECS* 16 (1983) for citations relevant to Pope.

4 Thomas Hobbes, *Leviathan*, ed. C. B. Macpherson (Hammondsworth and London, 1968), 217. Subsequent reference to *Leviathan* will be to this edition and page numbers will be cited parenthetically in the text.

5 Christopher Pye, "The Sovereign, the Theatre, and the Kingdome of Darknesse" (Ph.D. diss., Cornell University, 1985), 66.

6 John Locke, *An Essay Concerning Human Understanding*, ed. Peter Nidditch (Oxford: The Clarendon Press, 1975) II, xxvii, 26, p. 346. All subsequent references to Locke's *Essay* will be to this edition and will be cited parenthetically in the text.

7 For discussions of representative realism, see Richard I. Aaron, *John Locke* (Oxford: Oxford Univ. Press, 1971); Jonathan Bennett, *Locke, Berkeley, Hume: Central Themes* (Oxford: Clarendon Press, 1971); Richard Rorty, *Philosophy and the Mirror of Nature* (Princeton: Princeton University Press, 1979). For a helpful critique of this view, see John W. Yolton, *Perceptual Acquaintance* (Minneapolis: University of Minnesota Press, 1984) especially 4-6, 203-23.

8 For illuminating discussions of accommodation, see H. R. MacCallum, "Milton and Figurative Interpretation of the Bible," *University of Toronto Quarterly* 31 (1962): 397-415; C. A. Patrides, "Paradise Lost and the Theory of Accommodation," *Texas Studies in Language and Literature* 5 (1963): 58-63; Kathleen M. Swaim, "The Mimesis of Accommodation in Book 3 of *Paradise Lost*," *Philogical Quarterly* 63 (1964): 461-75; Anne Williams, "Gracious Accommodations: Herbert's 'Love III,'" *Modern Philology* 82 (1984): 13-22.

9 John Milton, *Paradise Lost*, ed. Alastair Fowler (London: Longman Group Ltd., 1968): Book 5, lines 571-74.

10 John Milton, *De Doctrina Christiana* in *John Milton: Complete Poems and Major Prose*, ed. Merritt Y. Hughes (New York: Odyssey Press, 1957), 905.

11 Both Kathleen Williams in *Swift and the Age of Compromise* and Denis Donoghue in *Jonathan Swift: A Critical Introduction* describe the *Tale*'s author

as a "style." Williams writes that "in *A Tale of a Tub* all the opinions expressed appear equally ridiculous and are expressed in the same fantastic style; the Author is himself a style rather than a person" (136); Donoghue describes the author as "the anonymous slave of print" (8).

12 Robert Elliott, "Swift's 'I,'" *Yale Review* 62 (1971): 378.

13 Howard Weinbrot writes, "Many commentators still believed that the roots of satire lay in earlier comic drama, or at the least included dramatic conventions; they thus regarded satire as especially subject to the playing of roles." See "Masked Men and Satire and Pope," *ECS* 16 (1983): 272.

14 For a representative account of this view see Denis Donoghue, *Jonathan Swift: A Critical Introduction* (Cambridge: Cambridge University Press, 1969), especially chapter 2, "Perspective."

15 Everett Zimmerman, *Swift's Narrative Satires*, 12–13.

16 "Mists arise from the Earth, Steams from Dunghils, Exhalations from the Sea, and Smoak from Fire; yet all Clouds are the same in Compositions, as well as Consequences: and the Fumes issuing from a Jakes, will furnish as comely and useful a Vapor, as Incense from an Altar" (*Tale* 163).

17 The most important model here is *Paradise Lost*:

> ... at foot
> Of Heav'ns ascent they lift their Feet, when loe
> A violent cross wind from either coast
> Blows them transverse ten thousand Leagues away
> Into the devious Air: then might ye see
> Cowles, Hoods and Habits with their wearers tost
> And fluttered into Raggs, then Reliques, Beads,
> Indulgences, Dispenses, Pardons, Bulls,
> The Sport of Winds: all these upwhirld aloft
> Fly o'er the backside of the World farr off
> Into a *limbo* large and broad, since calld
> The Paradise of Fools. (Book 3, lines 485–96)

The narrator of the *Tale* hopes that "every accomplishd Person who has got into the Taste of Wit, calculated for this present Month of *August*, 1697, should descend to the very *bottom* of all the *Sublime* throughout this Treatise" (*Tale*, 44).

18 In *Paradise Lost*, Sin gives birth to Death and harbors him in her womb. See especially her speech to Satan, *PL* Book 2, lines 746–814.

Mourning as Reception
in Rousseau's Julie

PATRICK COLEMAN

The broader the audience Rousseau imagines for his book, the more he tends to mediate the reading of that book through a curious mixture of explicit advice and rhetorical indirection. Whereas the philosophical *Emile* and especially the *Contrat social* present themselves relatively unadorned, the *Confessions*, the *Lettre à d'Alembert*, and *Julie* all manifest an obtrusive concern for the work's reception. In the case of *Julie*, Rousseau has special reason for worry: as the stern moralist whose reputation in part rests on his exposure of fiction's corrupting influence, how can he endorse his own novel? Rousseau may believe that anyone who reads Julie's story to the end will not tax its author with contradiction.[1] Still, he dares not trust the tale itself. The teller's critical and mediating presence must be seen if the reader is to arrive at the proper perspective. Editorial footnotes will interrupt the lyrical flow of the lovers' letters, and a lengthy preface not only anticipates questions and objections but, through the use of dialogue, incorporates the reader's criticisms into the text while dramatizing the seductions and feints inherent in any literary transaction.

The importance of this kind of textual apparatus has been paid increasing attention in recent years as the relation between what is essential in a work of art and what is merely "ornamental" has become problematic. In this paper I want to address this problem through an examination of the novel's epigraph: two lines from Petrarch inscribed in an elaborate *cartouche* on the novel's title page. "Non la conobbe il mondo, mentre l'ebbe | Conobill'io ch'a pianger qui rimasi," or, in Rousseau's own later translation, "le monde la posséda sans la connaître, et moi je l'ai connue, je reste ici-bas à la pleurer."[2] Since, as we know from the correspondence with his publisher, Rousseau carefully considered everything the printer should or should not put on the title page, down to the author's own name,[3] there is good reason for supposing that the epigraph serves a serious purpose. Indeed, in the "entretien sur les romans" that forms the so-called second preface to *Julie*, we see Rousseau pointing to the epigraph in such an urgent yet elliptical way that we are spurred to reflect on what Petrarch's words tell us about the novel they introduce. One might say that they offer a kind of first "reading" of the novel by someone close to the story, a response intended as a model for the public's own response. But before any assessment of the epigraph's actual import, a few remarks need to be made about Rousseau's use of quotation in the novel as a whole.

The epigraph is the first of ten quotations from Petrarch to be found in *Julie*.[4] We know how important Italian poetry was for Rousseau, but perhaps because the contrast between French and Italian music figures so prominently in Rousseau's discussion of artistic expression, critics have often assumed that Rousseau uses Petrarch only for his lyrical prestige. Daniel Mornet and Bernard Guyon, who have given us the major critical editions of the novel, agree on the absence of any significant thematic connection between the poems Rousseau quotes and the lovers' letters. The quotations are there only to enhance the "climat poétique" of the book.[5] Such a view is surely too narrow to cover the complexities of what Rousseau means by "expression," and there is no reason to suppose that the only meaningful context for the quotations lies in what the characters explicitly say to each other. It is interesting to note that in the one passage where the author could plausibly allow his characters to gloss Petrarch's text he declines the opportunity: when Saint-Preux returns to Meillerie with *Julie* he merely points to verses he has carved into the rocks without quoting or interpreting them (519). Here, as elsewhere, it is the reader's task to supply the missing link, to translate between contexts: first literally, since Rousseau quotes in Italian, a decision that not only allows the musicality to come through but which also sets the quotation at a certain distance from the text (when he wants to abolish that distance, as in the Meillerie passage, he leaves out the quotation); then metaphorically, as in the case of the editorial footnotes, by exploring how and at what level they are to be included in the reader's own interpretation of the work as a whole.

That new interpretive possibilities are opened up by a closer look at the Petrarch quotations is also shown by Christie Vance's study of the lines from poem 10 ("Gloriosa columna. . .") included in Saint-Preux's letter on the Valais (Part I, letter 23). In an earlier study, Jean-Louis Bellenot had established a general analogy between Saint-Preux's journey and

Petrarch's ascent of Mont Ventoux, providing a clue to the allegorical significance of the letter. By pointing out that Rousseau *misquotes* Petrarch, Vance is able to show how, within that allegorical context, Rousseau defines a notion not only of experience but of writing itself over against his illustrious predecessor. Quotation here does not merely illustrate, it constitutes the novel's discourse.[6]

Another example of such critical or ironic revision may be found in letter 36 of part one, in which Julie proposes to meet her lover in a remote *chalet*. As she suggests the erotic charm of the rendezvous, she quotes a line from the famous *canzone* "Standomi un giorno solo a la fenestra" (poem 323),[7] which indeed paints lovely pictures, but only to undercut them by acknowledging at the end the vanity of earthly beauty and happiness. The reader who knows the poem is at first disconcerted by the twist given the quotation, but is better able to accept Julie's "conversion" later on in the novel. By anticipating the heroine's about-face with this initially discordant note, Rousseau forges a better link between what he fears readers will see as two morally incompatible tendencies in his book.[8]

Another kind of problematic articulation is signalled by the epigraph: the connection between author and book. The personal tone of Petrarch's words has been used by many readers as evidence of Rousseau's infatuation with his heroine, the ideal woman the *Confessions* tell us he created in happy delirium and from whom he could hardly bear to part.[9] I do not wish to deny the justice of the biographical reference, but just as the "lyricism" of Italian poetry is not an answer but a question in *Julie*, so too the subjective character of the fiction is itself, as we shall see from the preface, only the beginning of an interpretation. I shall argue that the epigraph, properly understood, contributes an essential element to any assessment of Rousseau's fictional enterprise.

The preface to *Julie* circles uneasily around two questions: Did the characters really exist? Is the novel a moral book? These are, of course, the chief concerns of eighteenth-century novel criticism, and Georges May has documented the ways writers tried to justify their works within the framework of aesthetic doctrines hostile to the new genre.[10] Rousseau's circuitous defense of *Julie* also testifies to the difficulty of replying to objections he himself makes elsewhere to the value claims of fiction. Rousseau's search for a new critical context is what leads him to include the lines from Petrarch rather than his recently-adopted motto from Juvenal on the title page. Two aspects of the quotation are relevant here: its theme, mourning, and its position on the threshold of a text Rousseau claims not to have written but only to have edited for the reader's benefit.

In the preface, N, a sympathetic reader, adduces the epigraph as evidence that the characters really existed. "Ne voyez-vous pas que votre épigraphe seule dit tout" (29). R, the presumed author, responds by pointing out the uncertain provenance of this piece of text. "Je vois qu'elle ne dit rien sur le fait en question: car qui peut savoir si j'ai trouvé cette épigraphe dans le manuscrit, ou si c'est moi qui l'y ai mise?" The effect of this reply is to leave the initial question open while raising another about the relationship of epigraph to text. Paul de Man, with his characteristic flair for unsettling detail, has seen the importance of this move. Rousseau's is for him a rhetorical question in the deepest sense, whose purpose is to mark the aporias of figurative language, such that "the very statement by which we assert that the narrative is rooted in reality can be an unreliable quotation." Doubly unreliable, for not only do we not know who first borrowed Petrarch's words, but these words are themselves adapted from the gospel of John (1:14) and transferred to a far from sacred context.[11]

While not wanting to contest de Man's interpretation as a whole, I wonder if Rousseau at this particular point is really concerned with the epigraph's referential value. The preface is clear enough about the irrelevance of such a consideration, for, given the slim evidence for Laura's real existence and the fact that John's gospel quite clearly speaks of the spiritual as opposed to the empirical identity of Jesus, we hardly need Rousseau's added complication to question the epigraph's value as evidence for Julie's having really lived. Rousseau must want to draw our attention to another point.

A few lines above the exchange I quoted from the preface we find a clue to what it might be. Of Julie and Claire, R says: "Eh! qu'importe qu'elles aient existé? Vous les chercheriez en vain sur la terre. Elles ne sont plus." N: "Elles ne sont plus? Elles furent donc?" R: "Cette conclusion est conditionnelle; si elles furent, elles ne sont plus." The logic of this passage is a little complicated, since the conclusion to which Rousseau refers does not, as seems at first sight, correspond to the second part of the sentence just quoted, i.e. "elles ne sont plus." The demonstrative "cette," although it could perhaps be taken as announcing the deduction R is about to make, grammatically and by the fact that it occurs in dialogue is in reality attached to what N has just said. "Elles ne sont plus" is the idea asserted without qualification, while "elles furent" is the conditional conclusion drawn to make sense of an otherwise implausible statement. For it is odd to say, "elles ne sont plus" of characters who never existed. Yet this is precisely Rousseau's point of departure. Unlike Voltaire's God, who if he did not exist would have to be invented, Rousseau's divine Julie must be held to have existed in order to turn her absence into something meaningful, and reassuring too, since her non-presence is felt as a loss.

Here Petrarch offers some help by suggesting that the problem of the beloved object's existence and disappearance can, from a poetic point of view, be subordinated to that of the knowledge one can acquire through reflection on absence and intimacy as subjective experiences. Rousseau chooses lines that emphasize by repetition (*conobbe, conobill'io*) that we are indeed dealing with knowledge and not just emotion, even though that knowledge is grounded in the poet's activity of grieving (the sonnet appears in the second part of the *Canzoniere,* "after Laura's death") rather than on the existential status of the object mourned. Not that the latter issue is unimportant, for there are moral questions raised by what might seem like the exploitation of another person (or her image) for one's own purposes. As we shall see, these questions recur in Rousseau, but the lasting fame of Petrarch's work must have given Rousseau some reassurance that his "conditional conclusion" did not run counter to the demands of acceptable meaning.

One reason for Petrarch's appeal, and also for our inclination to believe Laura really existed, is the intense psychological reality of the loss Petrarch laments. Indeed this poet may be said to have invented the category of "psychological reality" as something culture must reckon with, whatever suspicion that culture may cast on the phantasms of imagination. The constitution of an inner object-world through a complex process of internalization, defense, and ambivalent feeling may have been facilitated by the religious framework within which Petrarch wants to edify his poetic constructs, but it is now anchored in the self as an end as well as a means.[12] Laura, unlike Beatrice, is not finally absorbed into the religious allegorization of her mediating function.[13] For all the conventions that surround it, including the poetic conventions later called "Petrarchism" that have banalized the poetry, particularly in France, the knowledge Petrarch has of Laura possesses a specificity and an irreducibility to system that Rousseau calls upon to suggest that his fictional creation is itself not to be subsumed under the aesthetic categories of his time.

These categories are the ones N initially deploys to gauge Rousseau's intention. The figure of Julie, he says, may be a "portrait," representing a particular, empirical individual; or a "tableau," representing through an individual character some aspect of universal human nature that may never assume such specific form. N needs to know what Rousseau intended before deciding whether the book is a good one of its kind. His difficulty in making an easy judgment is what prompts him to question R, who refuses to give a clear answer. N remains perplexed, since his experience of the novel suggests that Julie is a portrait, while his doubts about her existence make him wonder if she is not a failed tableau. The third possibility, that she is a particular individual who never existed, he is reluctant to accept because within his aesthetic framework (which he shares with many contemporary critics) such a figure may be an agreeable phantom but never the object of genuine knowledge.

Rousseau wants to suggest, however, that precisely because Julie floats, as it were, between the empirical and the ideally rational, she can be a source of knowing. Through the interplay of presence and absence in the reader's apprehension of the figure, Julie leads to a new awareness of the nature of subjective experience. Since the gap left by her absence can be filled neither by an appeal to broader experience nor by a move to transcendent modes of thought, we are left to trace its boundaries through a personal effort of introspection and reality-testing. To borrow a helpful formula from Michael Bell, we are invited neither to "see" Julie nor to "see through" her, but rather to "see around" her[14] to a reality that defines her limits but whose limitations she reveals by the shadow she casts on that reality.

Rousseau's model of literary character contrasts so remarkably with the shopworn clichés we find in the criticism of his time that we can appreciate the author's desire to offer it in an elliptical and defensive way. But the indirection of the preface may also testify to some uncertainty about the novel's success in realizing the author's conception or even, more fundamentally and in line with Rousseau's general view of human enterprise, to some anxiety about what it would mean to have succeeded. Success here does not simply mean approximating what will become the dominant form of characterization in the later, "realist" novel; it also means creating the conditions for a process of mourning. For somewhere between "elles ne sont plus" and "elles furent" there must be a death.

I want to consider, very briefly, two aspects of the novel that will help us understand Rousseau's difficulty in coming to terms with novelistic success. The narrative strategy and the moral thrust of *Julie*, as Rousseau conceives them, have broad implications for the development of the form. They also are illuminated by the epigraph, to which they will make us return.

To begin with the problem of morality, there appears in the preface's complex analysis of fiction's effects an assertion as mystifying and as intriguing as the one about Julie's existence. Unable to defend his book as suitable fare for young people in need of guidance, worldly sophisticates looking for distraction, or "lecteurs sévères"—the familiar categories into which readers were then divided—Rousseau tells us that *Julie* is written for married couples living in the provinces(19). They, above all, will find amusement, instruction, and consolation in a novel that portrays their condition sympathetically.[15] Leaving aside the first two of these qualities, let us look at the third. The idea fits in well enough with the theme of mourning, but its role is problematic. What exactly are readers to be consoled for? Nothing, it seems, since such readers are supposed by Rousseau to possess everything necessary for a good life. If they are unhappy, it is only because they think they are, led astray by urban writers who talk of passion and excitement. It would seem more logical for Rousseau, therefore, to offer encouragement rather than solace. If the novel is to offer consolation, it must first grant some reality to losses experienced only in the imagination. Such, of course, is the "loss" of Julie, brought about by the novel itself. The moral status of the book is further complicated by the suggestions that the reader's reaction to *Julie* is connected to analogous experiences in the reader's own life, experiences the novel evokes even as it attempts to console the reader for the pain they cause. Among these experiences are the transience of passionate love and the sense of time's flight, both central to the thematics of *Julie* and both touched on in the preface. Most of us would not hesitate to call these experiences real or to console those who suffer them. But they present a problem for Rousseau, who in the *Discours* and the *Lettre à d'Alembert* scorned those who are troubled by such things. In the anthropology of the *Discours sur l'inégalité*, passion is mere illusion and alienation; in the pragmatic politics of the *Lettre*, the mere passing of time is nothing so long as it is not marked by neglect of virtue or duty. These considerations are in fact those underlying Rousseau's negative attitude toward fiction.

Yet even in these earlier works we can point to a moment when the constricting effect of Rousseau's assumptions is undone by a shift from practical principles to a reconsideration of epistemological issues based on an awareness of the ambiguities of language.[16] As is true for many eighteenth-century authors, the focus on how we know unsettles established moral and social categories, and if Rousseau appears not to accept that fact as serenely as, say, Diderot, his exploration of its consequences is no less profound. Even readers who find *Julie* a deeply flawed novel have generally appreciated Rousseau's treatment of human time in the work. We therefore tend to take for granted the means Rousseau uses to get to this "higher" level of discourse.

But *Julie* is not a treatise. For all the importance of its philosophical component, it remains a novel rooted in an affective interpersonal context from which, as the dialogue form of the preface shows, it does not seek to escape. To acknowledge the reality of the reader's "imaginary" losses may be a simple matter when considering the novel as an exploration based on the *awareness* of loss. But to offer the novel as consolation means first to recall the source of that awareness in pain, and in so doing to inflict that pain.

Rousseau, it should be noted, does not actually speak of pain here, but only of consolation. Just as the proposition "elles furent" was scandalous in the earlier context, so is the idea of inflicted or reawakened pain, to the point of being unmentionable. Rousseau circles around the gap as he describes the strategies he employs in the novel to mitigate the force of the narrative. He points with pride to his elimination of narrative suspense and indeed of all breaks or turning-points in the plot. *Julie* is to come across as a seamless "romance dont les couplets pris à part n'ont rien qui touche, mais dont la suite produit à la fin son effet" (18). Not by the aggressions of dramatic action but by the repetition and amplification of tender feeling present from the beginning is the story to work its magic. The harmony of the *romance* is exemplified in the novel by the harvest songs described by Saint-Preux (part V, letter 7). It banishes whatever pain it recalls by putting the hearer in touch with the general order of nature, which knows no loss.[17]

There exists, nevertheless, a considerable difference between a harvest song and a novel so much the product of advanced culture as *Julie* — the difference, in fact, between peasant harmony and the sophisticated melodies of a Petrarch. The epigraph shows Rousseau's recognition of this fact, for in Petrarch's poem the fruit of knowledge is discontinuity: the world did not know | *I* knew. Petrarch goes on to say in that poem that such reconciliation as can be found in nature now is the product of the poet's own song of pain: "e'l ciel che del mio pianto or si fa bello."[18] The beauty is linked to the way knowledge of Laura is worked through by the grieving subject, not to a nature standing outside the mourning process and its negative aspects.

How are we to interpret the curious juxtaposition in Rousseau's text of this recognition of pain and a determination to give consolation so much priority as to suggest it can be offered without any pain to precede it? It would not be the only instance in Rousseau in which the logical order of things needs to be reversed if the text is to operate. There is some resemblance between Rousseau's intervention as author in *Julie* and the legislator's action in the *Contrat social*, which is to make the "effect" become the "cause," so that "l'esprit social qui doit être l'ouvrage de l'institution présidât à l'institution même."[19] In *Julie*, where the author's concern is for private rather than public morale, one might say that Rousseau offers consolation not as a denial of pain, but as the only available way to it. In a world of deadened sensibility and fragile mind, acquaintance with grief may first come through others' efforts to console. Perverse as it may seem, this approach may be the only one compatible with the reader's defenses and, perhaps more important, with the author's anxiety.

We find the issue dramatized in the character of Saint-Preux. As Etienne Gilson was the first to observe, in a famous essay whose implications are still worth exploring, the efforts Wolmar makes to "cure" Saint-Preux of his passion are presented in a positive way, even though they lead the young hero to feel the loss of Julie more acutely.[20] Indeed, the novel suggests that this increase of pain is at least as great a value as the pretense of a cure. The problem is that Rousseau does no more than sketch the possibilities opened up by this move. In the last parts of the novel, they are not pursued, with the exception of a few hints, such as the premonitory dream at Sion.[21] The predominant response of the narrative is denial or silence. We hear nothing at all from Saint-Preux, for example, after Julie's accident. A prominent sign of the difficulty is the epigraph itself, which stands outside the text, even though the lines could appropriately have been voiced by Saint-Preux within the novel. That they are not, and that Saint-Preux fades from view, suggests that Rousseau could not incorporate the pain of mourning directly into the book, for fear of spoiling the harmony of consolation it had to embody.

But surely we do hear cries of pain in *Julie*, in the letter on suicide (Part III, letter 21) for example, or in the famous account of the return to Meillerie (Part IV, letter 7) referred to above. There is no doubt, too, that readers perceived and responded to the novel's plaintive side. What is missing, though, is the dramatized connection between the pain and the knowledge Rousseau pursues and tries to communicate. Not a passive connection established through a feeble hero or an elegiac tone, but one actively forged and acknowledged as a literary intention. The puzzle of Rousseau's characterization of Saint-Preux, as we compare it to that of Julie, leads us to conclude that the connection cannot be made because of the aggression and self-assertion it involves. There is, first of all, self-assertion on the part of the character, caught between Wolmar's empiricism and Julie's piety in such a way that he cannot successfully argue the philosophical or moral legitimacy of his psychological experience except by resisting attempts to cure him of himself. Perhaps no other solution was possible within the limits of French Enlightenment thought, although one could read *Emile* as in part Rousseau's effort to reshape the terms in which human development could be conceived. It is significant that Saint-Preux's background is given some validation (and Wolmar and Julie's philosophies some limitation) by his appointment as tutor to Julie's children. We never see the result of his vocation, however, in the novel itself.

Self-assertion, too, on the part of the author, who cannot bring himself to acknowledge that the sense of loss communicated by the novel is not just "there," but is produced, and that the knowledge the work brings may not be coterminous with the consolation it offers. Perhaps Rousseau did not have the confidence in his characterization of Saint-Preux that he had in Julie's power to override the ambiguities attendant on the novel's success.

We hear pride and self-assertion, however, in the words of the epigraph. Rousseau's hesitation as to whether to say he put it or found it in the text is symptomatic of the hesitation manifested in the novel itself; it expresses the author's problematic relation to his own intentions. The gesture by which he points to the epigraph from the preface reminds us of all we find unsatisfactory or evasive in *Julie*. On the other hand, the epigraph *is* there on the title page, the page on which Rousseau as "editor" denies the privilege of authorship while accepting its responsibilities (27). Rousseau's refusal to explain the epigraph away, to make it serve some false vision of integration, typifies the lucidity that we find most valuable in his writings. We may no longer find easy pleasure (or easy pain) in reading *Julie*, but we do gain from it today a sharper sense that our activity as readers involves responsibilities and ambiguous self-assertions of its own.

NOTES

1 Jean-Jacques Rousseau, *Oeuvres complètes* (Paris: Gallimard, 1959 to date), 2:6. All quotations from Rousseau, unless otherwise noted, are from this edition, henceforth indicated as *O.C.*. Page numbers for *Julie* itself will be included parenthetically in the text.

2 The poem quoted is number 338 of the *Canzoniere*, "Lasciato ài, Morte," ll. 12–13. I have used the edition of Robert M. Durling, *Petrarch's Lyric Poems* (Cambridge: Harvard University Press, 1966). Rousseau's translation appears in a copy of the 1764 edition of his novel, annotated in view of a new impression. See the editor's note in *O.C.* 2: 1338. There is a brief study of Rousseau's translation by Michel Launay, "Rousseau traducteur et utilisateur de Pétrarque dans *La Nouvelle Héloïse*," in *Index des Mélanges littéraires, contes et opuscules de Jean-Jacques Rousseau*, edited by the Groupe Rousseau (Geneva and Paris: Slatkine, 1984), 221–234. Launay considers only stylistic matters of translation, not the larger literary problem raised by the quotations.

3 *O.C.* 2: 1336. See also *Correspondence complète de Jean-Jacques Rousseau*, ed. R. A. Leigh (Geneva- Oxford: Institut et Musée Voltaire-Voltaire Foundation, 1965-1984), vol. 7, letters 969 (17 April 1760), 973 (24 April), 1037 (29 June), 1046 (6 July).

4 The others appear in the following letters: I, 2, 23, 36, 48; II, 11, 15; IV, 2; VI, 7.

5 The phrase is Jean-Louis Lecercle's in his *Rousseau et l'art du roman* (Paris: Armand Colin, 1969), 166. See also Jean-Jacques Rousseau, *Julie, ou la Nouvelle Héloise*, ed. Daniel Mornet (Paris: Hachette, 1925), 1: 110–11, and Bernard Guyon's remarks in *O.C.* 2: 1339.

6 Jean-Louis Bellenot, "Les Formes de l'amour dans *La Nouvelle Héloïse*," *Annales, Société J.J. Rousseau* 33 (1953–55): 149–207; Christie M. Vance, *The*

Extravagant Shepherd: a study of the pastoral vision in *Rousseau's Nouvelle Héloise*, published as vol. 105 of the *Studies on Voltaire and the Eighteenth Century* (Banbury: Voltaire Foundation, 1973), 66–67. The line Rousseau omits, "onde si scende poetando e poggia," indicates, Vance says, a "poetic descent" Rousseau finds impossible, since in the latter's world, "there is no descent — there is only fall."

7 Ll. 4–41, but mistakenly substituting "ne mai pastori appressan" for "ne pastori appressavan." On this sonnet see Kenelm Foster, *Petrarch* (Edinburgh: Edinburgh University Press, 1984), 85 and the other sources cited there.

8 Lanson's formula is well-known: "un rêve de volupté redressé en instruction morale." For a recent study showing how at an early stage Rousseau's writing moved away from such dualism, see Christopher Frayling, "The Composition of *La Nouvelle Héloise*," in *Reappraisals of Rousseau: Studies in Honour of R. A. Leigh*, ed. S. Harvey et al. (Manchester: Manchester University Press, 1980), 181–214.

9 See *O.C.* 1: 430 ff.

10 Georges May, *Le Dilemme du roman au XVIIIe siècle* (Paris: Presses universitaires de France, 1963), ch. 4.

11 Paul de Man, *Allegories of Reading* (New Haven: Yale University Press, 1979), 204.

12 For an example of this new tone in a poem located close to the one quoted in the epigraph, see number 336, "Tornami a mente." Let me add that the focus on psychological reality in no way entails a claim about the achievement of an integrated or "whole" self. The contrary is in fact true of Petrarch's "scattered rhymes." See Giuseppe Mazzotta, "The *Canzoniere* and the Language of the Self," *Studies in Philology* 75 (1978): 271–96. My point is that a new stage is created on which conflicts can be named and played out. The question in Rousseau is whether access to such a stage can be gained, or whether certain problems will remain unarticulated.

13 "Beatrice, developed from the symbol and the scholastic, has become Laura, with her definite woman's personality." Francesco de Sanctis, *History of Italian Literature*, trans. Joan Redfern (New York: Harcourt, Brace, 1931; rpt. New York: Barnes and Noble, 1968), 1: 270.

14 Michael Bell, *The Sentiment of Reality* (London: George Allen and Unwin, 1983), 11.

15 For an interesting account of a provincial reader's response to Rousseau's works, including *Julie*, see Robert Darnton, "Readers Respond to Rousseau," in his *The Great Cat Massacre And Other Episodes in French Cultural History* (New York: Basic Books, 1984), 215–56.

16 See especially Paul de Man's *Allegories of Reading*. For an interpretation of the *Lettre*, see Patrick Coleman, *Rousseau's Political Imagination: Rule and Representation in the Lettre à d'Alembert* (Geneva: Droz, 1984).

17 *O.C.* 2: 610: "La nature a tout fait le mieux qu'il étoit possible; mais nous voulons mieux faire encore, et nous gâtons tout." But note Rousseau's inclination to emphasize negative feelings in revisions made on p. 609, variants b and c.

On the *romance* form, see Rousseau's *Dictionnaire de musique* in Jean-Jacques Rousseau, *Oeuvres complètes* (Paris: Hachette, 1885), 7: 258.

18 In Durling's translation, "and Heaven, which now makes itself so beautiful by my weeping."

19 *Du Contrat social*, book 2, ch. 7; *O.C.* 2: 383.

20 Etienne Gilson, "La Méthode de M. de Wolmar," in *Les Idées et les lettres* (Paris: Vrin, 1932), 275–98.

21 Part V, letter 9, especially p. 615.

Redressing Passion: Sophie d'Houdetot and the Origins of Julie, ou la Nouvelle Héloïse

SUSAN KLEM JACKSON

Few critical judgments adhere more tightly to a literary work or hold greater sway over its public than Gustave Lanson's famous line on *Julie, ou la Nouvelle Héloïse*. Generations of readers have by now been predisposed to regard Rousseau's novel as "un rêve de volupté redressé en instruction morale."[1] Even encounters with *Julie* which do not take the formula's validity for granted tend to position themselves by taking exception to it. Widespread suspicions that the "redressing" remains inconclusive are confirmed by Paul de Man's deconstruction of a polarity which could easily have been named, in Lanson's terms, "rêve de volupté"/ "instruction morale." Rather than in a permanent awakening, Julie's pivotal conversion would result only in a displacement of the initial fantasy, in a failure of past errors to instruct effectively.[2]

It is sometimes forgotten in the elaboration of responses to Lanson that he claims to account, not for Julie's actions, but for Jean-Jacques', not for the definitive text of *Julie*, but for the process of its composition. "*La Nouvelle Héloïse est sortie* d'un rêve de volupté redressé en instruction morale" (my emphasis). Christopher Frayling further reminds us that the formula privileges a version of that process told, compellingly and in greater detail than is reserved for the genesis of any other work, in Book Nine of the *Confessions*.[3] As an eminently quotable summary, Lanson's formula sustains belief in the accuracy of that genetic narrative. In turn, the formula derives staying power from a pleasing capacity for reducing the novel as written and the writing of the novel to a single plot line. The heroine's conversion would replicate the author's, and thereby proclaim the primacy of the empirical self; the genetic narrative would escape redundancy by actualizing the epistolary novel's potential for storytelling in general and for telling a specific story of redressing. Lanson's line emerges from this referential confusion endowed with two mutually reinforcing truth claims: it is true to the novel because true to (Rousseau's) life, and vice versa.

If the adequacy of the formula to the novel is open to question, so too is the historical accuracy of the genetic narrative which it summarizes. In some quarters, faith in the narrative's essential truth remains unshaken, despite the discovery of discrepancies between the chronology of Rousseau's life and his rendering of that chronology in the *Confessions*. Bernard Guyon at one point taxes the autobiographer with confusing "deux moments différents de la genèse de son oeuvre," but still affirms, when commenting on the prefaces to *Julie*, that: "les *vraies* explications de la genèse de son oeuvre ne seront avouées que dans les *Confessions*" (my emphasis).[4] Frayling concludes, however, on the basis of manuscript study, that the *Confessions fundamentally* misrepresent the early accession to the novel of elements belonging to the category of "instruction morale": some measure of redressing would have been underway long before the erotic fantasy had run its course. "Not only Lanson's conclusion — that *La Nouvelle Héloïse* increasingly came to resemble a book of 'instruction morale' — but the conclusion of recent commentators — that the introduction of religious themes constituted an 'afterthought' on Rousseau's part — need to be reconsidered in the light of this previously unpublished *brouillon*," the draft in question being that of Julie's recapitulative letter on the occasion of her marriage (III, xviii).[5]

Extension of the field of inquiry in another direction challenges the authority of the *Confessions* on more theoretical grounds. Christie V. McDonald reads a cautionary tale into the interplay between the episodes of the genetic narrative and intervening materials recounting Jean-Jacques' relationship with Sophie d'Houdetot. Coming into his love life when much of *La Nouvelle Héloïse* had already been written, Sophie cannot by definition have served as an artist's model for Julie. On the contrary, the real woman is said, repeatedly, to have replaced the novel heroine as the object of Jean-Jacques' affections. This reversal of an expected and still suspected order of events becomes the paradigmatic reminder in the *Confessions* of textuality's freedom from referential constraints. Fully assimilated, the moral would apply not only to *Julie* but to the text in progress: by flatly denying the pertinence of that most obvious and attractive referential possibility, the *roman à clef*, the *Confessions* cannot help but raise doubts about their own truth to life. However unwittingly, they make Sophie and Jean-Jacques literary characters of no less unknowable origin than Julie.[6]

There can be no exaggerating the value of retelling this cautionary tale if, as would seem to be the case, the *Confessions* still threaten to monopolize "truth" in the Rousseau canon. But knowledge of its dubious referentiality does not preclude rereading the genetic narrative, at a lower level of abstraction, as a story among others. Or, rather, as part of a story which would, like McDonald's, embrace the interpolated materials on everyday life with and without Sophie, and make of those materials something more than the diacritical mark of Lanson's radical discontinuity. The forthcoming rereading takes seriously Rousseau's obvious efforts to discourage our isolating either narrative strand, and to name the locus of their intertwining. A sometimes belabored preamble to Book Nine systematically reviews Jean-Jacques' past relations with women, and discovers true passion's absence even from his otherwise inexplicable attachment to Thérèse Levasseur (1:414, 426). Silenced throughout the preceding period of Jean-Jacques' *réforme*, desire is thus programmed to re-emerge in its purest state as a second-degree "besoin d'aimer" (1:426), and to preoccupy the confessional text until further notice. In reaffirmation of this exclusive commitment to desire, Rousseau expressly defers narration of events from the same period which are adjudged to belong in that other story of the *complot* or plot against him (1:438). His eventual failure to control the polarity, insofar as *l'affaire* Houdetot mediates the two stories, concerns me less here than that the *affaire* and the *entirety* of the genetic narrative should fall together within the bounds of text explicitly generated in the name of passion. Whatever really happened, elaboration of this composite "rêve de volupté" *in the text* does not end with the kind of redressing or change in registers from the erotic to the religious which Lanson had in mind. Rather, the moment of that redressing is subsumed by an ongoing narrative where righting Julie's wrongs somehow serves the end of getting more right even than in *Julie* the story of a protagonist named, not Julie or Sophie or even Jean-Jacques, but passion per se. Otherwise felicitous, Lanson's phrase nonetheless intimates already to speakers of English that our story of passion will hinge on literal acts of re-dressing, that is, of changing clothes.[7]

Even if the genetic narrative is considered in isolation, it turns out to comprise, not two, but three discrete episodes, and a brief coda (1:426–28, 430–31, 434–36, 438). *Julie* teaches us to read each of those episodes as privileging one in particular of three possibilities for the representation of "passions" told to Julie and Claire by their nurse and Claire's surrogate mother, Chaillot. According to Claire's recollection of the nurse's teachings, passions are made manifest through their "signes," through their "effets," or through "l'art de les réprimer" (2:45). Thus, in an initial springtime of exalted, objectless reverie, Jean-Jacques, in love with love, is shown to betray the conventional signs of passion: loss of appetite, predilection for solitude, irritability—signs which are nevertheless subject to malicious misreading, given the already available referent of misanthropy. That summer, as Jean-Jacques' reveries crystallize, decisions are made about the eventual novel's characters and setting; passion accedes to textuality, leaves a trace, produces unmistakable effects: "Je jettai d'abord sur le papier quelques lettres éparses sans suite et sans liaison" (1:431). Reserved for the winter months of the third episode is the designing of an overall "plan" which will permit the "ouvrage" to be "en régle" (1:431), where the expression "en régle" is read to mean in conformity not only with novelistic conventions but with legal prescriptions. For the self-styled Citoyen de Genève and censor of novels, public representation of passion depends on its legalization, which, in turn, depends on the "plotting" of defenses against it. As practiced in the *Confessions*, "l'art de réprimer les passions" produces long-winded insistence on Julie's exemplary conversion to virtuous womanhood and on the contribution of Julie and Wolmar's religious differences to a public plea for tolerance. In this text of passion repressed almost beyond recognition, Julie's name is never written until it can be coupled with that of "Volmar" (1:436), none other than the chief practitioner of artful repression in the novel—Volmar, who paints over the love affair's illicit *tableaux vivants* by having Julie and Saint-Preux re-enact them chastely.

The account of Jean-Jacques' "besoin d'aimer" is thus, according to Chaillot's three-part outline, complete. In both the outline and its fleshing out, "artful" repression is acknowledged to participate directly and on equal footing with signs and effects in the story of passion. But where is it written that deployment of this art must necessarily be reserved for the story's final chapter? Claire's letter would seem to strengthen the case for the inevitability of the linear chronology sanctified by Lanson. Julie's anticipated fall follows directly from Chaillot's untimely death *before* she had a chance to elaborate on the third and final aspect of passions: "Nous connoissons assés bien leurs signes et leurs effets, il n'y a que l'art de les réprimer qui nous manque." Except that Claire hastens to add: "Dieu veuille que ton jeune philosophe connoisse mieux que toi cet art là" (2:45), and acknowledges that, should Saint-Preux prove to be no better versed than his pupils in the art of repression, the only other solution to Julie's unfinished education would consist in baring her soul to her mother: "Il est vrai que le préservatif est facile: deux mots à ta mere et tout est fini; mais je te comprends; tu ne veux point d'un expédient qui finit tout" (2:45).

There can be no exaggerating the difference in outcome between the two scenarios. Were Julie to place her fate in the hands of her mother, the love story would come to an abrupt halt, reduced not to devious expression but to silence. The more desirable dénouement, that passion should live on *through* repression, depends on God's having graced *un jeune philosophe* with a talent for which youth neither disqualifies him nor qualifies the cousins. But on what other basis, once the polarity of age has been rendered irrelevant, can this talent have been categorically withheld from Mme d'Etange, if not on the basis of her sex? Claire's letter assumes that the art of repression descends normally, not from mother to daughter, but through a paternal line; what remains to be seen is whether God will claim Saint-Preux as His son. It is as though Claire were prescribing a test of Saint-Preux's manhood and, at the same time, suggesting that the accident of Chaillot's death has less to do with Julie's fatal ignorance than does the sex of teacher and pupil. Gender, rather than timing, would seem to be of the essence. For each new generation of women, repression is a lost art, an art "qui nous manque." If Chaillot dies without leaving any written record of her purported knowledge, Mme d'Etange cannot deal with textual evidence of Julie's downfall otherwise than by taking to her own deathbed; the mother's sole bequest to her daughter consists in the terrifying spectacle of submission to passion's effects. That Saint-Preux also fails spectacularly to make love livable testifies to the androgyny of which his character emits so many other signs. The example of his protagonist is hardly calculated to reassure a novelist in the making in whose eyes "les livres efféminés qui respiroient l'amour et la molesse" (1:434) function primarily to hypostatize the association between passion and emasculation. "[P]ouvoit-on rien imaginer de plus inattendu, de plus choquant, que de me voir tout d'un coup m'inscrire de ma propre main parmi les auteurs de ces livres que j'avois si durement censurés?" (1:434–35). Rousseau seizes the occasion of his genetic narrative to conjure up the specter of a perverse auto-castration, and to put Jean-Jacques to Claire's test of artful repression.

Vague threats of alienation in the feminine are raised as early as the genetic narrative's second episode, where the author admits to having lost control over the creative process. Up until a certain point in the novel's elaboration, everything, he claims, had gone smoothly. Having decided to bring his dream-text into clearer focus, Jean-Jacques is portrayed as acting swiftly and efficiently. Each of six consecutive sentences by which the *Confessions* achieve, unproblematically, the characterization of the *inséparables* and their lover/friend begins with the pronoun "je," followed by an active verb in the simple past. Scrupulous premeditation likewise leads to decisive action in the matter of setting: "j'établis à Vevai mes jeunes pupilles" (1:430–31). By contrast, the novel's epistolarity just happens. Neither premeditated nor justified retrospectively, the random throwing of letters onto blank pages causes ongoing problems. "Aussi voit-on que

ces deux Parties [the novel's first two parts], formées après coup de matériaux qui n'ont pas été taillés pour la place qu'ils occupent, sont pleines
d'un remplissage verbeux qu'on ne trouve pas dans les autres" (1:431). According to an equation typical of Rousseau, more (verbiage) results in less
(artistic perfection). Unjustified epistolarity as formal excess doubles and
denotes the irrational excesses of passion. The mark of that double excess can still be read in the novel's subtitle, "Lettres de deux amans," which
Joan de Jean, for one, has remarked to be curiously inadequate to the
novel's overall design.[8]

Looking ahead already to the moment when it will have occurred to
Jean-Jacques to attempt an "ouvrage en régle," Rousseau evokes as follows the predicament of a writer constrained by already written love letters: "lorsque je m'avisai de les vouloir coudre, j'y fus souvent fort
embarrassé" (1:431). It bears asking whether the situation is not more
properly "embarrassing" than simply awkward, and whether the more
heartfelt embarrassment might lie, not in the passionate materials themselves, but in the fact of having, of wanting even, to *sew* them together.
How womanly to be embarrassed in the presence of passion; how embarrassing and irregular to experience writing as a womanly art, as one of
the so-called *ouvrages de dames*. That the metaphorical interchangeabili-
ty of writing and sewing is central, rather than peripheral, to the genetic
narrative is suggested by pains taken to extend the metaphor. Not only
do the terms *matériaux, taillés* and *remplissage* call the verb *coudre* into
play, but, as we shall see, its redeployment in the third episode provides
a measure of continuity and a basis for discussing difference. Beyond that,
the *complot* about which Rousseau keeps saying that for the moment he
has chosen not to speak is twice characterized, by contrast with the present
patchwork of desire, as a "tissu de malheurs," as a wholecloth always already so tightly woven that it neither breathes nor allows its victim to
breathe (1:438, 446).

Whatever threat to masculinity inheres in the sewing metaphor would
seem nonetheless to be shortlived. At the conclusion of the genetic narrative's third episode, Jean-Jacques is shown to derive "un plaisir inexprima-
ble" from sewing together the novel's notebooks with blue ribbon, and
from committing such other acts of outrageous femininity as "making up"
his book with gilt-edged paper and blue and silver blotting powder (1:436).
What can have happened in the interval to transform sewing into a pastime
in which the author indulges unabashedly? For one thing, Rousseau has
re-flexed his authorial muscle, and proven equal to the task of engineer-
ing a "plot" as straightforward and seamless as any his enemies might con-
coct. His résumé of *Julie* so effectively writes out the excess of epistolarity
that, to read the résumé in isolation, one would hardly suspect that the

novel is still composed of letters, much less that piecing them together might pose any sort of problem. Recasting *Julie* as an organic unity means that ribbons can replace rhetorical flourishes. With the passage from metaphorical to literal acts of sewing, sewing's power to signify the "feminine" is transferred from the sewer onto the newly available corpus which will wear the products of his labors. The Jean-Jacques who now spares no expense in fetishistically dressing up his book for (the love of) Claire and Julie, "ne trouvant rien d'assez galant, rien d'assez mignon pour les charmantes filles" (1:436), merits the title of *haut couturier*. Not so the Jean-Jacques who, seduced in a prior incarnation into sewing for no good reason and for no-body, risked, like any seamstress, having his sewing reflect back on his own sexual identity. For, as *Julie* itself makes explicit, it falls specifically to women to *wear* their work in progress; Julie's sewing figures as one article among others in Saint-Preux's catalogue of the clothing which alludes in veiled but no uncertain terms to her desirability: "Ta robe, ton ajustement, tes gands, ton éventail, *ton ouvrage*; tout ce qui frapoit autour de toi mes regards enchantoit mon coeur, et toi seule faisois tout l'enchantement" (2:115–16, my emphasis).

It is the sewing here qualified as a bona fide secondary sex characteristic which Jean-Jacques must avoid, or risk self-incrimination in the "effeminacy" of novel-writing. So long as he remains caught up in the same vicious sewing circle as Julie, the threat posed to his manhood is that of an implied cross-dressing whose implications must be taken seriously. Only when sewing has been differentiated from writing, can the writer extricate himself from the perception of sexual identification with and through his *ouvrage*. Only when that *ouvrage* has been cast off as a living, breathing Other, can Jean-Jacques revel in the masculine artistry of "un autre Pigmalion" (1:436). Secure and yet nowise cured of his "érotiques transports"—that would be beside the point—he then returns, in the genetic narrative's coda, to the unfinished business of writing individual letters (1:438).

But this symbolic rescue of sexual difference from the clutches of passion is only part of the story elaborated in response to Jean-Jacques' "besoin d'aimer." Rather than spell the end of sewn-together texts, the genetic narrative itself participates in a patchwork whose *remplissages* are constituted by periodic returns to extra-literary events. Emphatically discontinuous, the composition of *Julie* is thrice interrupted in terms which challenge the reader to undertake a plotting here left for the most part unfinished. Only the first interruption begins by telling us, not what happened, but how to read what happened, as a rude awakening from reverie: "Au plus fort de ma grande exaltation je fus retiré tout d'un coup par le cordon comme un Cerf-volant" (1:428). Details follow: Jean-Jacques had problems with his health, his mother-in-law, and his nemesis, Voltaire – details clearly meant to reinforce the already explicit opposition between reality and fantasy. Syntactic parallelism notwithstanding, the sentences introducing the second interruption: "Au plus fort de mes douces rêveries j'eus une visite de Mad^e de Houdetot" (1:431), and the third: "Précisément dans le même tems j'eus de Mad^e de Houdetot une seconde visite imprévue" (1:438), differ from the first in leaving strictly chronological the relationship between real and literary life. It remains to interpret events as written, to place them with respect to *Julie*, to rationalize the excess.

At first glance, the second interruption's internal heterogeneity makes it difficult to imagine what seamless narrative could be extrapolated from the disparate anecdotes which account for the year's delay between the two springtimes of love for Julie and for Sophie. If Summer is given over to Mme d'Houdetot's first surprise visit (1:431–32), Autumn finds Jean-Jacques preoccupied with M. d'Epinay's orchard (1:432–33), and Winter brings, fast on the heels of a liberating plot line for *Julie*, the receipt of unexpected gifts from Mme d'Epinay (1:436–37). In fact, it is redressing which propels the life story forward, linking its anecdotes one to the other and to the genetic narrative, such that the *Confessions* end up writing a chapter of passion's story left necessarily untold by *Julie*. However amply it illustrates the signs, effects, and artful repression of passion, the novel is ill-positioned to speak directly of what we might call passion's *données*, or structuring pre-conditions. Begun in mid-desiring, Julie and Saint-Preux's affair obeys Nancy K. Miller's apt distinction between fictional memoirs, which lay the groundwork for a central experience of desire, and the epistolary novel, which dispenses with desire's pre-history.[9] Emphasis is otherwise displaced onto that pre-history by the incursion into Rousseau's memoirs of a heroine, Sophie d'Houdetot, with whom the hero fails to fall in love at first sight. It here becomes of the essence to unblock the text of passion. Thus, however idiosyncratic in its later unfolding, *l'affaire* Houdetot, as inscribed in pages uniquely respectful of the passing seasons, makes good on the implicit promise of a certain universality. As a prerequisite to bringing lovers together as such, the *Confessions* discover the obstacle posed by sexual difference to the flourishing of hetero-eroticism. A delicate balance must somehow be struck between what a phallocentric social order supposes to be the conflicting claims of literal inequality and the metaphorical equality of desire. Where shared passion is the anticipated end, whatever the overlapping genetic narrative does to confirm the male partner in his singular and preeminent maleness must be offset, albeit only partially, by a situation-specific neutralization of differences between himself and the other.[10] Only when the conditions of a false start have been altered, only with reference to the Spring of Mme d'Houdetot's second visit, can there be talk of passionate talk between her and Jean-Jacques.

To hear Rousseau tell it, her first visit got the affair off, quite literally, on the wrong foot:

> Elle s'égara dans la route. Son cocher, quittant le chemin qui tournait, voulut traverser en droiture, du moulin de Clairvaux à l'Hermitage: son carosse s'embourba dans le fond du vallon; elle voulut descendre et faire le reste du trajet à pied. Sa mignonne chaussure fut bientôt percée, elle enfonçoit dans la crote; ses gens eurent toutes les peines du monde à la dégager, et enfin elle arriva à l'Hermitage en botes, et perçant l'air d'éclats de rire, auxquels je mêlai les miens en la voyant arriver: il fallut changer de tout; Therese y pourvût, et je l'engageai d'oublier la dignité pour faire une colation rustique dont elle se trouva fort bien. Il étoit tard, elle resta peu . . . (1:432).

To read through the account is to discover just how suggestively misleading is Rousseau's introductory hint that the visit "eut un peu l'air d'un début de roman" (1:432). Rather than for one literal beginning among others, this artist's rendering cries out to be taken for an exhaustive allegory of the eighteenth-century novel heroine's text, as explicated by Nancy Miller.[11] Translated into the symbolic register—how else, *Julie* reminds us, is the feminine to make itself known?—every detail exudes hyperbolic femininity. The trajectory traced concretely is that of female sexuality experienced as alienation ("Elle s'égara dans la route"), of seduction by male desire ("Son cocher, quittant le chemin qui tournait, voulut traverser en droiture"), of eventual complicity in that desire ("elle voulut descendre et faire le reste du trajet à pied"). Localized penetration expressed euphemistically ("Sa mignonne chaussure fut bientôt percée") is no less immediately and universally devastating in its consequences, to her ("elle enfonçoit dans la crote . . . il fallut changer de tout") and hers ("ses gens eurent toutes les peines du monde à la dégager"). That this text belongs to the heroine alone is overdetermined by introductory material specifying that the visit was the first to Jean-Jacques which Mme d'Houdetot made in *her* life, not the first which he received from her in his, and including a genealogy such as one might expect to read at the outset of a feminocentric novel: "La Comtesse de Houdetot étoit fille de feu M. de Bellegarde . . .," and so forth (1:431–32). This variant of the heroine's text ends happily enough: with the aid of Thérèse, the fallen heroine is completely redressed; the Ermitage community shares a "colation rustique" worthy of their Clarens counterparts. But all talk and specifically talk of passion has been foreclosed; this *voiture embourbée* generates no text, only laughter. As if to underscore the self-sufficiency of the heroine's text and the hero's exclusion from it, she whose "mignonne chaussure" was pierc-ed is first seen by him — it is already late — pierc-ing the air.

To be sure, Mme d'Houdetot's "botes" are only a makeshift solution. There remains an unsewn breach, an opening for desire, which remains unspoken or spoken only deviously. Insofar as this anecdote rehearses not only the materials of the heroine's text but the conditions for its telling by a male author, Rousseau reminds us that he has fabricated everything which "happened" before Mme d'Houdetot came into view. In the heroine's silence, he can only imagine the "accident" as an object of his own fascination, as a site of desiring for not so much for the coachman's role already claimed by Saint-Lambert as for access other than imaginary to a heroine's text defended against further incursions by its own excessive femininity.

If Mme d'Houdetot departs "disposée à revenir" (1:432), sexual difference continues in her absence to impose itself as an obstacle to the text of passion. A pendant to the preceding anecdote of hyperbolic femininity immediately casts Jean-Jacques against type in the role of ultra-masculine hero. "Je passai l'automne," writes Rousseau, "à une occupation dont on ne se douteroit pas, à la garde du fruit de M. d'Epinay" (1:432). No less "inconceivable" than the circumstances of Mme d'Houdetot's appearance at l'Ermitage are the lengths to which Jean-Jacques now goes to implement his stewardship of M. d'Epinay's orchard. Routine supervision turns into a full-scale military operation, once our hero discovers that the gardener has been helping himself to the harvest, and dismisses him. "Comme ce grand coquin rôdoit toutes les nuits autour de l'Hermitage, armé d'un gros bâton ferré qui avait l'air d'une massue, et suivi d'autres vauriens de son espéce," Jean-Jacques is "forced" into the extreme measures of acquiring a guard dog and a rifle, and arming the new gardener as a sentinel. "C'étoit assurément la moindre précaution que put prendre pour la sureté commune un homme incommodé" (1:433). Doubly defensive of Jean-Jacques' defenses and of his manhood, the hero's text inscribes him in an armed fortress against which at any moment an attack may be mounted, and demands that he play *le chef de famille* to his household's "deux femmes timides" (1:433). Mme Levasseur, the original castrating Mother — *timide*? It is indicative of the absolute priority which passion's story currently enjoys that recent characterizations of this "vieille madrée," this monster, this serpent can so conveniently be half-forgotten (1:418–20). Neither the male nor the females are cut out for their roles in this play of absolute sexual difference. The hero is finally recast as a mock hero, when the anecdote of excessive masculinity dissolves, like its pendant, into laughter. "De Leyre m'étant venu voir dans ce tems-là, je lui contai mon cas, et ris avec lui de mon appareil militaire" (1:433). Ultra-masculinity produces only a good-natured exchange of war stories among men. Jean-Jacques' "fusil" defends the hero's text, just as Mme d'Houdetot's "chaussure percée" stood guard over that of the heroine; together—even and especially insofar as the gun signifies more straightforwardly than the shoe—they carry sexual difference to parodic extremes, and get the story of true love off to a false start.

If Summer saw the confinement of the heroine to her text, and Autumn the confinement of the hero to his, Winter is dedicated to finding a way out of this impasse, to unblocking the text of passion. No less a feat than reforming Jean-Jacques in the image of a Roman consul, retransforming him into a lover will require a further act, not of will, but of grace, and from an unexpected quarter.[12] Moved to claim that never before that winter had Mme d'Epinay given him such precious tokens of her friendship, Rousseau proceeds to single out two such tokens as demanding public acknowledgment:

> Un jour qu'il geloit très fort, en ouvrant un paquet que [Mme d'Epinay] m'envoyoit de plusieurs commissions dont elle s'étoit chargée, j'y trouvai un petit jupon de dessous, de flanelle d'Angleterre qu'elle me marquoit avoir porté et dont elle vouloit que je me fisse faire un gilet. Le tour de son billet étoit charmant, plein de caresse et de naïveté (1:437).

Rousseau characterizes his reaction to this gift of a petticoat as "singular"; Thérèse is reported to have thought him gone mad. And with good reason: Jean-Jacques tearfully kisses the petticoat and the cover letter twenty times each. As so often happens in the *Confessions*, the emotion is excessive, disproportionate to the event as told; the gratitude attributed to Jean-Jacques can be rationalized only with reference to the text in progress. How reassuring to learn, as though for the first time, that a petticoat can be made over into a vest. How essential to this reassurance that the same material now designated for intimate contact with a man's body should once have draped a woman's. Rousseau *must* take issue with Mme d'Epinay's recollection that she never wore the petticoat;[13] he must now press her into service as a woman, despite previous assurances that he never thought of her "in that way" (1:412), if he is to know this intimate material as both perfectly transferable between the sexes, and transformable. The male redressed, but not cross-dressed, in his vest need not fear even the appearance of misplaced femininity. But, in other words, maleness and femaleness remain intact only as contingent forms transcended by the commonality of fabric. A heretofore unnamable equilibrium between sameness and difference has been reached which enables the terms "petticoats" and "waistcoats" to designate public restrooms in Colonial Williamsburg, where an oral version of this essay was first presented. In silhouette, some coats are seen to be worn above, others below the waist; in each instance, the portion of the anatomy signified through concealment is that which, uncovered, offers only an indirect view of sexuality to the imagination. That the sex characteristics left out of the metaphorical exchange are primary for the male and secondary for the female can only further reassure whoever would live and survive with his manhood intact the experience of passion. To write of Mme d'Epinay's gift as "more than friendly," as the most touching evidence ever received of her prodigality, even as the ultimate sacrifice makes sense in the context of an unrecognized need to liberate the text of passion by the unthreatening neutralization of sexual difference. Jean-Jacques need not "courir les jupons"; he has just been gifted with what I earlier called "les données de la passion," and with an intuitive understanding of their crucial importance. It is no wonder that when passion as the object of a desire long since confessed and channeled into artistic creation finally materializes, the desiring subject covers the material in question with kisses. However, lest we forget that what has been unblocked here is not passion per se but its text, Rousseau fails to tell us whether Mme d'Epinay's petticoat was ever altered, choosing instead to confess, "J'ai longtemps conservé son petit billet" (1:437). It is the cover letter, the trace of excessive epistolarity, and not the undergarment itself, which underwrites the long-awaited text of passion.

The pivotal function of this anecdote is confirmed when springtime brings the return of a redressed Mme d'Houdetot to l'Ermitage. "A ce voyage," writes Rousseau, "elle étoit à cheval et en homme" (1:439). Had he not acceded to a state of grace, Jean-Jacques might have been as put off, as excluded by this more-than-Amazonian version of womanhood as he had by the hyperbolic vulnerability of Mme d'Houdetot's prior incarnation. As a rule, Rousseau claims, "je n'aime guéres ces sortes de mascarades," except, perhaps—the wording remains inconclusive—insofar as they sustain belief in the feminine's incapacity to signify itself without borrowing signs from the masculine. In any case, the forms of dress having been rendered contingent, the riding habit does nothing to identify the wearer otherwise than as a masquerader— neither man nor woman but, better yet in the light of indignities so recently suffered in the sewing of letters, non-man. And yet, this same masquerade realizes the exciting new possibility proposed by Mme d'Epinay's letter of sharing material. With one all-embracing look, Jean-Jacques is "taken"; "et pour cette fois, ce fut de l'amour" (1:439).

Embroidering on the *coup de foudre* requires some ten pages and numerous reprises, which stand in garrulous contrast to the single self-contained paragraph of Mme d'Houdetot's first visit. Released from the confines of a hyperbolically feminine pre-history, the heroine can for the first time be apprehended immediately in a not entirely flattering portrait: "Mad^e la Comtesse de Houdetot approchoit de la trentaine et n'étoit point belle ..." (1:439). As for the hero, he can, with impunity, bequeath the remnants of his "appareil militaire" to absent soldiers MM. d'Houdetot and Saint-Lambert, and even to Mme d'Houdetot herself, whose activity is recounted in muted metaphors as that of laying siege to Jean-Jacques' heart (1:438). A history of exclusively masculine conquest is being rewritten as romance—not *Veni, vidi, vici*, but "Elle vint, je la vis. . . . Pour m'achever elle me parla de St. Lambert en amante passionnée" (1:440). Because the passion which each in turn confesses is shared but not mutual, it takes on a life of its own, acceding to ever greater, ever more autonomous materiality. "[T]oujours," writes Rousseau, "l'amour [était] en tiers entre elle et moi" (1:445), there to be caressed like some new *jupon/gilet*.

Or rather, as an accompanying *billet*. For as the story makes increasingly clear, what Jean-Jacques and Mme d'Houdetot are supposed to have shared was a jointly authored *text* of passion. If so, in what words did Mme d'Houdetot speak so devastatingly of Saint Lambert, or Jean-Jacques communicate his love by devious reference to its signs in him? For hundreds of pages, Rousseau has fostered our complicity in Jean-Jacques' longing for the miracle of expression adequate to its object. The miracle finally occurs: "Ce fut dans ce bosquet qu'assis avec elle sur un banc de gason sous un Acacia tout chargé de fleurs, je trouvai pour rendre les mouvements de mon coeur un langage vraiment digne d'eux. Ce fut la prémiére et l'unique fois de ma vie; mais je fus sublime" (1:444). But this perfectly transparent language of naked passion is accessible to us only through the mediation of effects: "Enfin, dans un transport involontaire, elle s'écria: Non, jamais homme ne fut si aimable, et jamais amant n'aima comme vous! mais votre ami St. Lambert nous écoute, et mon coeur ne sauroit aimer deux fois" (1:444). When Mme d'Houdetot finally speaks directly, it is only to declare an impossibility of passion, to invoke the Oedipal triangle as a strategy of repression, and to tease us with the fact that, unlike the supposedly omniscient Saint-Lambert, we have not overheard Jean-Jacques' sublime soliloquy. Objectified, fetishized passion does not speak; it is only said, over and over, to have spoken.

For all our plotting (against) Rousseau's sewn-together confessions, it is they which have the last exclusionary laugh. It is out of the question that we should satisfy any desire to know what, besides text, happened between the two lovers; there will be no advancing beyond the talking stage. By substituting the text of passion for passion itself as the object of his discourse, by placing his extra-textual reality at a double remove from ours, Rousseau frustrates that desire, exacerbating it all the while by his referentially ambiguous protestations of unwillingness to "avilir ma Sophie" (1:444).

A return visit to M. d'Epinay's orchard would seem to be indicated. For if an unblocked text about passion exults in the "force contagieuse" of retroactive and all-consuming metaphorization (1:440), Rousseau shows us the way back to those available anecdotal materials from the heroine's and hero's texts in which desire can now be dressed. That Jean-Jacques and Sophie should, at the outset of her second visit, drink from passion's cup reminds us that, at the close of her first visit, they had shared a "colation rustique." Likewise, the episode of "la garde du fruit" permits of a *post facto* translation whereby Jean-Jacques, as eunuch, would watch chastely over another man's, Saint-Lambert's fruits, his own criminal tendencies and heroic manhood safely projected onto the two figures of the larcenous gardener and the nightwatchman. Defensive excesses would be justified retrospectively by the enormity of the real danger. A final image, that of triumphant presentation of the harvest to its rightful owner, a presentation made in conjunction with the legitimate spouse, Thérèse, would seem to argue for a chaste relationship between Jean-Jacques and Sophie. Except that the harvest is reported to have been delivered not merely intact but three times more bountiful than that of any previous year (1:432–34). Are we to take the quantitative metaphor for an indication of qualitative change in the person of Mme d'Houdetot, become — but in what sense? — "ma Sophie"? It is impossible to know how to read the clues or even if clues have really been planted, so fruitless is this rereading which takes as its unverifiable hypothesis the artful repression of Rousseau's desire, but which refers finally to our own desire to know what fruits, if any, his desire has borne.

Unable to certify passion on the basis of extra-textual effects, we must turn our desiring elsewhere. The only unmistakable effects of passion to which we can hope to accede are scriptural. But on this score too we are frustrated by attention-getting acts of suppression: in every case, the actual words have been lost in translation or merely lost. The idyll at l'Ermitage culminates logically in a confession of failed epistolarity. Waiting for Mme d'Houdetot to arrive at their rendez-vous, Jean-Jacques attempts to commit his feelings to "billets," but never succeeds in finishing "un qui fut lisible" (1:445–46). These "billets" remain as literally illegible to us as to Mme d'Houdetot. Not so those of Saint-Preux and Julie, which, though long since cloaked in legitimizing rhetoric, cannot help but come back — unredressed, unreconstructed — to mind. Just prior to foreclosing the text of his own "désir d'aimer" and launching into that of the *complot*, Rousseau refocuses the desiring of his readers on a for once attainable object: a readable text of passion, extant but absent love letters authored by him.

What Rousseau's genetic narrative would originate, then, is not so much the "Lettres de deux amans" as a reading or rereading of them. This preface among others to *Julie* is plotted both to motivate that reading, to constitute it as an expression of desire, and to prepare us for the receipt of Saint-Preux's first *billet. En attendant* d'Houdetot, we will have to make do with Rousseau's own epistolary supplement of choice. But to the extent that shared passion in that supplement is a given, rather than a gift, the real lovers' story, in turn supplements that of their fictional counterparts. The *Confessions'* account of sexual difference metaphorically neutralized and effectively enforced informs the fragmentary representation of passion in the novel. How else are we to understand that both Julie and Saint-Preux can have fallen in love, or that only Julie will really *fall* in love? Redressing after that self-styled "redresseur de torts" (1:26), Jean-Jacques Rousseau, is always as much a matter of writing difference as of righting wrongs.

NOTES

1 Gustave Lanson, "L'Unité de la pensée de Rousseau," in *Essais de méthode, de critique et d'histoire littéraire* (Paris: Hachette, 1965), 35. The article first appeared in Vol. VIII of *Annales de la Société Jean-Jacques Rousseau* (1912), 11–31.

2 Paul de Man, "Allegory (*Julie*)," in *Allegories of Reading* (New Haven: Yale University Press, 1979), 188–220.

3 Christopher Frayling, "The Composition of *La Nouvelle Héloïse*," in *Reappraisals of Rousseau: Studies in Honor of R. A. Leigh*, ed. Simon Hawley et al. (Totowa, New Jersey: Barnes & Nobles Books, 1980), 181–82.

4 Bernard Guyon, Intro., *Oeuvres complètes*, by Jean-Jacques Rousseau, ed. Bernard Gagnebin and Marcel Raymond (Paris: Gallimard, 1961), 2:xl–xli & lxiii. All references to Rousseau's works will be taken from Volumes I (1959) and II of this Pléiade edition, and will be acknowledged parenthetically in the text. Eighteenth-century spelling as reproduced in this edition has been retained throughout.

5 Frayling, 205–6.

6 Christie V. McDonald, "Jean-Jacques Rousseau: The Biographfiend's False Friend," *Romanic Review* 66 (1975): 302.

7 Both *Julie* and the *Confessions* set precedents for staging such acts, and for investing them with the power to signify moral transformations. I have in mind, for example, that Jean-Jacques' *réforme*, to which his "désir d'aimer" responds antithetically as a "seconde révolution" (1:418), is exhaustively rendered by a narrative of undressing (1:361–64). What makes the discarding of certain items

of clothing morally significant and conclusive is their designation as luxury items. The renunciation of extravagance in the marketplace thus becomes interchangeable with the silencing of *whatever* private passions for the contingent (besides a contingent "passion du beau linge") the *berger extravagant* had indulged in less austere times.

Prophetically linked in much more devious ways to the revolution of Julie's fall from innocence is the letter where the exiled Saint-Preux promises to present her, on his return, with "un habit complet à la Valaisane," taken from "la plus jolie taille du pays" (2:82). The anticipated transfer from one body to another here bespeaks a common female destiny which transcends whatever distinctions Saint-Preux has just drawn between the shocking "ampleur" of the Valaisanes' "gorge," and the smaller, more desirable breasts of Julie. In short order, the equilibrium will really be disrupted which Julie's present "ajustement" has achieved between the repression and expression of desire. Redressed à la Valaisane, she too will make a voyage of no return into emphatic sexuality.

Whatever else remains to be said about these two redressings, they differ significantly in their degree of literality. Julie's figures only metaphorically in the plot economy of *La Nouvelle Héloïse*, since subsequent letters fail to record whether Saint-Preux ever delivered on his promise of a souvenir costume. It is to be expected that such redressing as the *Confessions* later do in the name of desire will more closely resemble the metaphorical model of Saint-Preux's letter than the preponderantly literal account of Jean-Jacques' reform. To the extent, however, that gender difference underwrites the varying emphases on metaphor and on metonymy and that Book Nine will make gender difference crucial to the dynamics of hetero-eroticism, we might also expect further interplay between metaphor and metonymy to condition that redressing.

8 Joan de Jean, *Literary Fortifications: Rousseau, Laclos, Sade* (Princeton: Princeton University Press, 1984), 121.

9 Nancy K. Miller, *The Heroine's Text: Readings in the French and English Novel, 1722–1782* (New York: Columbia University Press, 1980), 84.

10 These structuring conditions of hetero-eroticism are extensively elaborated with respect to the *Lettre à d'Alembert* by Peggy Kamuf, in "Rousseau's Politics of Visibility," *Diacritics* 5 (1975): 51–56.

11 In *The Heroine's Text*. See, in particular, 4–20.

12 It will be recalled that a similar act of grace puts the finishing touches on the undressing of reform. Reluctant to part willingly with the last remnants of his luxurious wardrobe, his "beau linge," the would-be reformer is rescued from moral limbo—significantly enough, on Christmas Eve—by a burglar who makes off with every last collar and handkerchief (1:364). Is this burglar to be viewed as a savior or as a scoundrel? The same question might be asked about Mme d'Epinay; the answer depends on the value assigned to extreme instances of redressing. This tendency to make the major turning points of the life story contingent on last-minute intervention by "outside" agents satisfies the conflicting demands of plot (that the story should be punctuated by dramatic reversals) and character (that any such reversal should be experienced as alienating of the "real" self constituted in the *Confessions'* opening pages by an irreducible

opposition of "courage" and "vertu" with "foiblesse" and "molesse"). See 1:12. Crucial to Rousseau's autobiographical project, the end of subordinating narration to self-portraiture is clear and just as clearly subverted in the workings of the metaphor of redressing.

13 In her pseudo-memoirs, *Histoire de Madame de Montbrillant*. The pertinent passage is cited in the editor's notes to the *Confessions* (1:1484).

The Meeting Place of Autobiography and Censorship: *Rousseau's* Lettres à Malesherbes

E. S. BURT

Je remarquerai seulement, avant d'entrer en matière, que M. de Malesherbes, motivant tous ces retranchements sur les idées des catholiques, ou même des réformés, et moi raisonnant uniquement sur les miennes, ce n'est pas merveille si nous nous rencontrons peu.
Rousseau. To Malesherbes, March 10, 1761. On some changes proposed in *Julie*.

All writing involves a selection of material from the undifferentiated mass of experiences, as well as the molding of that material into a finite form. An active operation like a censoring—a practical selecting, registering, and discarding of material—goes on in any literary work. But the selection process is particularly important for autobiography, for knowledge of the principles according to which some material is routed toward expression and other material toward oblivion is more revelatory with respect to the self's foundations and limits than the material selected itself. The autobiographer's search for self-knowledge invariably demands the investigation of what might be called a system of censorship, in which the paths regularly described in expressing and repressing are laid down and remain for study. Censor, from *censeo*, means to register, to write down; and, to assess, to give an opinion. Both meanings are at work here. The self-knowledge expressed is itself subject to a kind of secondary censoring, a self-conscious reassessment, that makes it an unreliable source for any positive action on the part of the autobiographer. But the secondary process is inventive as well, and provides autobiographer and reader alike with new material for analysis.

What is not clear is what relationship the inventive system operating to produce autobiography might have with the institution of book censorship which arrogates the right, in eighteenth-century France at least, to make pronouncements on a book's suitability for transmission and circulation in the public domain. In the letter quoted above, written in reply to some changes proposed by a French censor to *Julie*, Rousseau suggests that the two are very different. The institution, as personified by Chrétien-Guillaume de Lamoignon de Malesherbes, *Directeur de la Librairie* from 1750 to 1763, and consequently head of the censorship system, motivates its cuts in a manner opposed to his own reasoning process. It is evident from the context and the tone of his comment that Rousseau does not think that the difference between his editorial decisions and the excisions to *Julie*[1] proposed by way of Malesherbes can be ascribed to ill will or to insufficient understanding on either side. Rather, he appears to suggest that it is of the very nature of the institution to be doctrinal to its cuts, to reason according to an already-determined set of ideas whose transmission is in part its object. Received ideas concerning the kind of material to be censored, unanalyzed opinions or unacknowledged models shape the institution's choices. An author, on the other hand, reasons and represses according to his own rules, which only occasionally, and as it were, coincidentally, conform with those of the censor. In the case of the author is considered publishable whatever comes out of the reasoning process, whereas in the case of the institution, only what is deemed publishable makes it past the censor's scissors.

Now while the distinction posited by Rousseau between inventive and synthetic reasoning processes makes it seem easy to differentiate between institutional critics and authors, that distinction in fact very quickly breaks down. The institution tends to transgress its own rule and to excise not only what doctrine deems dangerous, but to make arbitrary inroads into the author's invention as well. One can easily understand how the distinction gets lost by thinking about the institution's representative, the censor. He cannot simply read a text as it presents itself to a given group of readers. His function is to determine whether to demand that certain statements be cut or replaced, in order to bring the work into line with orthodox doctrine. To do so, he must read suspiciously, imagining the various misinterpretations that can be given every word, and determining which words in the text must be changed to guard readers from error. The official reader has to give evidence of the very arbitrariness and imaginative inventiveness said to be the domain of authors. The loss of the distinction between author and censor is not an innocent one, politically speaking, but rather stands in need of analysis, since arbitrariness and inventiveness in administering the law can hardly be thought a good thing.

Autobiographers cannot hold strictly to the distinction either. Autobiographical texts must make use of conventional systems of signification within which interpretation gets played out. It has been argued, most convincingly by Starobinski,[2] that Rousseau's self is constituted as if in a fearful anticipation of an outside judgment, as a restricted domain that has excluded from its purview all positive knowledge, so that it cannot be said to invent anything but metaphors for itself. The fact that the *moi's* difference can only be communicated in a language shared by others means, furthermore, that the *moi* can always be interpreted as giving access to a universal rather than a particular self: the most conventional and unprovable opinion we may have is of our difference, as subjects, from one another.

In short, despite surface differences, stemming from their different relationships to meaning, autobiography sometimes shares a common ground with censorship in that it contains evidence of totalizing principles like the self as conventional as any other. On the other hand, the institution has in common with the autobiographer an occasional tendency to transgress the conventional bounds to which it ought—as administrative organ of the law—to adhere.

The exchange raises questions: can the institution be made to curb its transgressive tendencies? Does the autobiographical text end in a figure reconciling all its contradictions, or is the self only a strategic device, produced to allow the investigation of similar strategic devices, whose reliability it seeks to analyze? The crossing of functions—the self becoming an orthodoxy and the institution an inventor—means that, in agreement with a *de facto* principle of Rousseau criticism, a text like Malesherbes' *Mémoires sur la librairie et sur la liberté de la presse*[3] can be read for information on autobiography, and an autobiographical text like Rousseau's *Lettres à Malesherbes* can potentially illuminate political institutions. In the short space allotted here, I would like to offer a sketch of the kind of argument that would be involved.

The Institution as Borderguard

The difference Rousseau remarks in method of reasoning between author and censor corresponds to an officially-recognized difference in French law between their two products. A writer produces an invention, or, as we would say, a text, while a censor is engaged in the production of a reproducible entity, a book. The text as invention has a status independent of its context and of all the various economies into which it can be inserted. The government recognizes that independence at the very moment that it seeks to limit it in controlling the text's reproduction, in assigning profit-taking rights to authors, editors etc., in supervising its circulation—in a word, in turning it into a quantifiable, context-bound entity, a book. In the century-long struggle to determine the rights of authors and editors to profits, several definitions of the literary work were produced showing that the government recognized, at least in theory, the text's independence and its indeterminacy. A law passed in 1744, for example, called the text a gift translated, by way of publication into a need:

> La difficulté n'est pas de savoir si un ouvrage manuscrit appartient à son auteur. . .mais de décider si cet auteur ou le libraire qui le représente, lorsqu'il a *donné* son oeuvre au public et que, pour ainsi dire, *il en a fait un besoin*, a le droit d'empêcher ce même public d'en multiplier les copies (my emphasis).[4]

As a discovery or invention, the text belongs as much, and in the same way, to its public as it does to its inventor. It is only in compensation for the effort, the time, the candles that the author puts into his work, and in gratitude for his help in feeding the book industry, that society accords him a limited profit—in money and in glory—for his invention.

A law passed a century later formalized the various insights of earlier rulings and stated that the work ought to be considered as a relinquishing of property (*un dessaisissement*):

> La nature des choses n'a donc pas crée de propriété littéraire pour l'oeuvre une fois livrée au public. La nature des choses a crée le contraire: elle a crée un dessaisissement.[5]

While the government formally recognizes that the text once in the public domain has an indeterminable destiny, and that it indeed rules over the strange domain where domains are not claimed but relinquished, the admission of the text's indeterminacy in theory is simultaneously accompanied by a strong imperative to oversee the transmission of the work,[6] to determine its entry into the public context, in keeping with the government's own regulatory power. To the extent that the *Librairie* seeks to define texts and institutions as ruling over different spheres—one of determinate contexts, the other of indeterminate ones—a first selection process is already going on.

Malesherbes' *Mémoires* do not seek specifically to distinguish text and book, but the distinction is operative in his discussion of the domains of government and individuals with respect to the literary work. It is in keeping with the rule of good government, says Malesherbes, that the government confine its regulations to citizens' activities and not attempt to supervise their thought:

> Le gouvernement, fait pour prescrire aux citoyens des lois sur leurs actions, n'a point d'empire sur leurs pensées. Il est injuste et impossible de dominer sur les opinions, par conséquent de faire supprimer, tronquer ou corriger les livres dans lesquels elles sont exposées (257).

It is in the interests of the state to limit its own control over texts because only by way of free discussion can the truth become known and the progress stimulated by its search be made:

> La discussion publique des opinions est un moyen sûr de faire éclore la vérité et c'est peut-être le seul. Ainsi toutes les fois que le Gouvernement a sincèrement le noble projet de faire connaître le vérité il n'a d'autre parti à prendre que de permettre à tout le monde la discussion sans aucune réserve, par conséquent d'établir ce qu'on appelle *la liberté de la presse* (223).

Of course there are difficulties. Or rather, there is one obstacle, and one reserve, to the unlimited freedom Malesherbes wants to accord texts in principle. In determining its authority to be over actions, and that of texts to be over opinion, the government reserves for itself the right to strike out anything tending to unsettle that boundary.[7] The obstacle, of course, is that the very distinction aimed to protect the opinions expressed in texts from inroads by the government is a distinction inhabiting the texts themselves. We know from Austin that language can be constative, stating opinions about the world, and performative, acting to create contexts. The terms are not imported here. Malesherbes finds a similar distinction operative between works that testify and those that discuss: "Celui qui avance un fait dont il a connaissance personelle, est un témoin qui doit se nommer pour soutenir sa déposition; mais celui qui disserte, qui discute, doit en être dispensé, puisque son nom est indifférent à la thèse qu'il soutient" (301). The difficulty is that it is hard to distinguish when language is acting to create contexts, and when it is simply being used to state opinions about things. Indeed, theoretically, any and every sentence can be read as revealing, exposing an idea, and thus as acting, or as representing an idea, and thus as opining. From a practical perspective, then, Malesherbes' first attempt to limit the government's right to investigate texts must be a failure. Indeed, in thus attempting to restrict its sway to action, to the outside of texts, he is actually asserting the government's unrestricted right to make cuts inside the borders of texts.

Malesherbes suggests that the obstacle to freedom of opinion could be surmounted, however, and the government's reserve respected by a reasonable compromise if the government were willing to regulate only those elements that threaten the government's right to regulate action. Certain, and indeed, most performatives do not contest that right, but merely serve to create a discursive space within which opinion can be discussed. He becomes quite ironic over the case of a censor so foolish as to think that the philosophical fiction in Rousseau's *First Discourse* was actually proposed as a model of a state to which we ought to return (260–61). In most cases, and the case of a philosophical argument is the clearest one, performatives serve as aids in the presenting of arguments, and do not threaten the government at all.[8] In those cases in which performatives can be said to constitute the chief argument—and the clear case is that of fiction, whose figures are ornamental—there can be no bearing on the public domain, so that, at least in theory, excisions also need not be made.

Several remarks can be made here. First of all, the distinction Malesherbes is attempting to apply between texts that chiefly expose opinions and those so completely within the domain of persuasion as to pose no threat at all, is a distinction in line with Enlightenment doctrine. Any work which seeks to argue an opinion can only help in the "éclo[sion] de la vérité" (229) which it is in the government's interest to foster. And any work which, less usefully, presents a picture, a moral tableau, at the very least helps educate man toward moral law, and in no way interferes with a law based on reason.[9] Rousseau is correct to identify Malesherbes with the institutional method for rationalizing cuts, since he makes his decisions according to an orthodoxy, albeit the orthodoxy of Progress.[10]

In the second place, Malesherbes' attempts to bring reason and the institution into line with one another depend on an encounter between author and text, in which a determination as to what kind of text is at issue is made. Indeed, he comes very close to recommending a kind of reading pact in the reforms he proposes. The point requires a brief digression.

The major reform Malesherbes wants to institute is that of voluntary censorship. He proposes that authors be permitted to choose whether to submit or not their work to the censor. Cautious authors, those who fear the punishment of the law, will choose to be censored, he suggests. And those hotheads and enthusiasts who prefer freedom to censorship can publish their work untrammelled. Voluntary censorship will have the effect, Malesherbes argues, of exempting most authors from punishment. In the first place, any author who asks to be censored is saying, in effect, that he wants all dangerous excess to be cut from his work, wants it to be weighed and measured in conformity with the cool light of reason, wants his argument to be subject to all the tests to which arguments are subject.[11] He has signified as clearly as is possible that he has aimed his work at the exposing of truth in the progress of ideas. Says Malesherbes of such authors: "[Ils] cherchent à éclairer le public plutôt qu'à l'échauffer" (310). Even authors who do not choose to censor their works would benefit indirectly from the protection accorded reasonable men. In the fearful anticipation of what would happen to them if faced with judgment, authors who chose not to censor would be indicating in a word that their works were not destined to be read by light of reason, but were aimed at the imagination. By choosing not to censor, the author of a fiction absolves himself of any interest in the enlightenment of the public, and puts his money instead on the rewards given vanity by public admiration. Only figures found here, he declares. By signifying their choice to censor or not to censor, authors will determine the destination of their work before it leaves their study.

Now this is a very liberal proposal, and one that would mean that it would become possible for any text to be published in France. Still, the governmental sphere of inspection over texts has been enlarged. All texts published in France would bear a sign, in the presence or the absence of the approbation, that they had been judged by their authors to be arguments addressed to reason or fictions addressed to the imagination. That is as much as to say that the government would force authors to censor themselves.[12] Malesherbes' liberalism is compensated for in the unwarranted expansion into the very territory it wants to protect. The effects of his proposals would confirm Rousseau's assertion, in a letter written to Malesherbes on November 9, 1760, that the government cannot ever relinquish a control it has once seized: "[Le Gouvernement] ne sauroit, quand il le voudroit, adoucir [la riguer de la censure]; car un gouvernement qui peut tout ne peut pas s'ôter à lui-même les chaînes qu'il est forcé de se donner pour continuer de tout pouvoir."[13]

Malesherbes seeks to exempt from the reforms two kinds of hybrid texts: those whose arguments are dependent on cases—legal memoirs and the like—in which inadequacies of the system are being exposed; and those whose arguments are dependent on the author's word—autobiographical texts, for instance. The first should be given unlimited freedom; the second watched over with great care, and the authors punished when necessary. His reasoning makes sense, since libel would remain a crime under the new laws, and a personal accusation, unsupported by anything but the author's word, and doing no public good, ought not to be exempted from punishment.[14]

But at the same time, the exclusion of autobiography from the general policy of liberalism appears motivated by another reason as well. The author, in Malesherbes' utopia, must have privileged knowledge as to whether his work is reasonable or imaginative. But autobiography cannot help but present instances in which the author's judgments on self and work will appear unreliable, because in autobiography we can have only the author's word for what is advanced. Furthermore, because the autobiographer, when discussing his relation to his text, is himself just another reader, talking about a work already separated from him, autobiography can question the reliability of any and all attempts to determine the text's transmission. Thus, Rousseau's account in the *Confessions* of the publication and condemnation of *Emile* first pits an author, dubious that his work could appear in France without scandal, against several readers, chiefly, Mme. de Luxembourg and Malesherbes, both so certain in their judgment that the text is not dangerous that they work, against the author's express request, to have it published secretly in Paris. After publication, the author is entirely secure in his conscience that his work is useful, and certain that all precautions have been taken for its proper reception; the bitter reality — that a growing number of readers do not share his opinion (the work will be condemned across Europe) — takes him by surprise. Whose judgment is reliable? And when?[15] Malesherbes' hostility toward the autobiographical makes sense, then, since the cornerstone of his proposal is that an author has a privileged knowledge about his text that autobiography can question.[16]

By looking at an example of how the author's confrontation with his text takes place, we ought to be able to discover what makes the author's judgment every bit as unreliable as the censor's, and consequently what makes it impossible for Malesherbes' reform to work.

The Author Confronts his Text

Rousseau's *Lettres à Malesherbes* provide our example. The *Lettres* are at first sight devoid of traces of the paranoid Rousseau, the one we have come to associate with the working of the textual machine. A celebration of the *moi*'s "indomptable esprit de liberté" (1132) and of his imaginative flights, it is the only one of Rousseau's major works to remain silent both on the question of the censuring of the imagination by reason, about which Rousseau often wrote explicitly, and on the censorship system of the *Ancien Régime*, generally the topic of his letters to Malesherbes, and with which events in the publication of *Emile* and *Julie* around the time the *Lettres* were being written made Rousseau uncomfortably familiar. The letters constitute a self-portrait acclaimed as one of Rousseau's finest lyrical achievements: "l'admirable portrait lyrique" (XXII), "une sorte de rhapsodie s'organisant autour du thème du bonheur dans la solitude" (XXXII), as Raymond and Gagnebin characterize it.

But an absence of any reference to censorship of course does not mean that censorship is not operative. It does not mean either, as one might too hastily conclude, that Rousseau has repressed the whole issue of exclusions and inclusions, and its attendant specters of mutilation, in choosing to write a lyrical piece. The selection process at work in the subject's apprehensions of the world is very much the focal point of the *Lettres*. The products of that selection process considered in its inventive mode, are variously called "les êtres chimériques" (1131) and "les écrits que j'ai fait dans ma solitude" (1131). We should not let the appellation *être*, applied to written works, lead us astray here. The alternation in terms reflects the author's own vacillation, when confronted with his work, over whether the encounter is with a being like himself, another consciousness, or one very different from him. The *Lettres* propose various confrontations of this sort, and thus can be said to dramatize, as a problem of knowledge, the question of what consciousness can recognize, and what it must misunderstand, in its own productions.

Prompted by two letters in which Malesherbes diagnoses the source of Rousseau's fears in a disposition toward melancholia and authorial vanity,[17] Rousseau quickly seeks to leave behind the personal stakes involved, marking a separation from the pleasures and vexations of his daily existence, and turning his thoughts toward the inner man:

> J'aurois moins tardé Monsieur à vous remercier de la derniere lettre dont vous m'avez honnoré si j'avois mesuré ma diligence à répondre sur le plaisir qu'elle m'a fait. Mais outre qu'il m'en coute beaucoup d'écrire, j'ai pensé qu'il falloit donner quelques jours aux importunités de ces tems ci pour ne vous pas accabler des miennes. Quoique je ne me console point de ce qui vient de se passer, je suis trés content que vous en soyez instruit puisque cela ne m'a point ôté votre estime, elle en sera plus à moi quand vous ne me croirez pas meilleur que je ne suis (1130).

Rousseau sets aside the troubles about which he and Malesherbes have been exchanging letters together with all immediate pleasures, like the pleasure of keeping up a correspondence with Malesherbes. He invites Malesherbes to follow him instead in forgetting the present situation, and to return with him to enjoy a vision of the *moi* in his natural state, a description made in terms so general as to make the portrait contain a tableau, that is, in Rousseau's terms, a picture of man in general. Any understanding Malesherbes might have of the letters in terms of the immediate context, as documents pertaining to a referential being who once walked in Montmorency woods, is largely displaced by this turn to a reading of them as a fiction cut off from any present, having lost "ce qui vient de se passer." The text acts to create a fictional context within which the story of the *moi*'s developing consciousness can be read as an exemplary story, as precisely the kind of story that Malesherbes would welcome.

An often-quoted passage from the third letter summarizes and concludes a crucial stage in the exemplary passage on the imagination, namely, the stage during which the reverie becomes directed toward the beings imagined by the *moi* in his solitude, and a linguistic sign is produced.

> Bientôt de la surface de la terre j'elevois mes idées à tous les êtres de la nature, au systeme universel des choses, à l'etre incomprehensible qui embrasse tout. Alors l'esprit perdu *dans* cette immensité, je ne pensois pas, je ne raisonnois pas, je ne philosophois pas; je me sentois avec une sorte de volupté accablé du poids de cet univers, je me livrois avec ravissement à la confusion de ces grandes idées, j'aimois à me perdre en imagination *dans* l'espace, mon coeur resserré *dans* les bornes des etres s'y trouvoit trop à l'étroit, j'étouffois *dans* l'univers, j'aurois voulu m'élancer *dans* l'infini. Je crois que si j'eusse devoilé tous les mysteres de la nature, je me serois senti *dans* une situation moins délicieuse que cette etourdissante extase à laquelle mon esprit se livroit sans retenue, et qui *dans* l'agitation de mes transports me faisoit écrire quelquefois: O grand etre! ô grand etre, sans pouvoir dire ni penser rien de plus (my emphasis; 1141).

The passage contains a clue, in the tripartate division of ideas on which the *moi* reflects (ideas of natural being; ideas of universal system; ideas of an incomprehensible being embracing everything) that it can be read according to three different lights. It can be read by the light of the imagination, as giving access to the natural world; by the light of reason, as giving access to ideas of system, organized structures; and finally as giving access to ideas we get by reading texts of the sort this passage represents, that is, to ideas of an incomprehensible being able to embrace such incompatible things as ideas given by reason and ideas given by the imagination in the same place. Following Rousseau's hint that a climb (*j'elevois*) is necessary to get from one set of ideas to another, we will follow the order of their presentation.

The imagination's development can be divided into three movements, roughly corresponding to the three sentences of the paragraph: the imagination first expands outward to consider a world suspected to exist outside itself, then contracts to consider its own relation to the beings posited in the first stage, and then expands again in an act of creation producing a lyrical cry.[18] These movements can thus all be considered as stages in the process of creation. The *moi* starts by substituting for the natural world various abstract ideas of multiplicity (*tous les etres*), order (*le systeme universel*) and totality (*l'etre incomprehensible qui embrasse tout*), all of which are derived from its experience, but have lost all relation to it. The immensities the *moi* is trying to conceive entail a reflexive return to the seat of sensuous experience, the *moi*, in an attempt to give them concrete form. The return is discussed in passionate rather than intellectual terms: "je ne pensois pas, je ne raisonnois pas, je ne philosophois pas . . . je me sentois . . . je me livrois . . . j'aimois à me perdre . . . j'aurois voulu m'élancer . . ." In this second stage, the various abstract ideas about the universe the *moi* has derived from experience, are lent, by way of the imagination's power, properties of concrete, natural objects, such as weight (*le poids de cet univers*), undifferentiated mass (*la confusion de ces grandes idées*), and constriction (*trop à l'étroit*). During the expansive movement, the *moi* imagines abstract entities on its own model that it then re-endows with the properties it had forgotten in abstracting. The second stage gives the *moi*, now recognized as the seat of both movements, a desire for expansion past its own boundaries. A phrase like "j'étouffois dans l'univers, j'aurois voulu m'élancer dans l'infini" certainly expresses the *élan* of a self who, reaching his limits, feeling as it were, the edge of the container bounding him, the universe outside himself, seeks to expand beyond his spatial limits, and to imagine overcoming the limits of the imagination itself.

In the third part of the passage, the two movements of the imagination — creating abstractions and garbing them in sensuous form — are together called *l'agitation de mes transports*, and the vacillation between the two modes is considered to lead to the creative act, the birth of the lyrical cry.[19] The second stage had reached its ends in a desire for a new abstraction, representing an escape from the amorphous sensations felt as constricting with respect to the self's expansive wish. In the third stage, the dreaming of self subsumes the two trajectories into a single totality called being. The *moi* is seeking to name the source of his transports, and makes the mistake of locating that source in a being outside and greater than itself. In fact, of course, it is the vacillation between expansive and constrictive modes of the imaginative experience that is referred to by the term "being."

The expression itself is autonomous with respect to the *moi*'s original experience. It can be repeated (*O grand être! ô grand etre*) and invoked on various occasions (*quelquefois*). It takes on the value of a charm or talisman, and can truly be said to enjoy the autonomy of a literary creation, divorced from the conditions giving rise to it. The *moi* misunderstands the nature of the imaginative act, which he feels to be inspired by an outside force. But the misunderstanding is inventive; a work is produced that does not depend on the experience but can be used to recreate it, or can subsist to give it the lie, by comparison with periods of lesser exaltation.

The passage demands to be read as well in the light of the cooling off of the imagination presaged in the cry, and which has left its signs elsewhere. The narrating consciousness is not actually caught up in the celebration of the imaginative event signified. Instead, the passage is concerned with understanding the production of the cry, and with evaluating its worth with respect to the process it apparently summarizes. Rousseau does sometimes write passages invested in the reliving of an imaginative experience, but this is not one of those passages, which are invariably signalled by a move into the present tense.[20] Rather, the passage is written from the perspective of a reflective narrator, no longer caught up in the heat of creation, as the judgment rendered from the present on the past ecstasy ("*je crois* que si j'eusse devoilé . . . ") reminds us. The passage recalls an event from which it maintains a difference, and can thus better be read as demystifying the past ecstasy, as reflecting on the figure produced by it. If we read the phrase at the end of the second sentence in this light, for example, we find that it expresses as the real state of the *moi*, the state of feeling gagged or stifled: "*j'etouffois* dans l'univers"; and asserts its desire for infinite expansion to be unrealizable and illusory: "*j'aurois voulu* m'élancer dans l'infini.*" A mood of dejection prevails, in which a number of revelations are made about the series of transports leading to the lyrical production. One could emphasize here the circularity of the passage. The cry only returns us to the point of departure, by recalling the beings mentioned at the beginning, so that the self's wish to escape from the world, by means of the series of imaginative transports outward from its own confines into the infinite is revealed as leading it on a pointlessly circular and earth-bound path.

The lyrical cry at the culmination of the third movement is deemed a poor sort of language from the demystified perspective. To begin with, the narrator does not find it to have accomplished any revelation with respect to the mysteries of the universe: "si j'eusse devoilé tous les mysteres de la nature. . . ." He suggests that the failure to know the universe outside the *moi* may have been compensated for to some extent by the dreaming *moi*'s delicious feeling of ecstasy, but he nonetheless registers it as a failed recognition. The cry uttered cannot be considered to render a true account of the universe, which was, after all, one of the objects of its reflection. Furthermore, in choosing to express the vacillations as a natural figure like *being*, rather than seeking a narrative ordering them as a regulated series toward the work's production, the *moi* shows its incapacity for sustained reflection. The lyrical cry is a punctual invention, leading to no further thought, and having no further grammatical extension: *sans pouvoir dire ni penser rien de plus*. With respect to the infinite expansions aimed at then, the cry is also a failure. This second reading of the passage, undertaken from the perspective of the narrating consciousness, would confirm Malesherbes' suggestion that reasonable authors find figures to be deceptive with respect to the objective world, and insufficient to account for the order of their own propositions.

But a further question arises with respect to the passage concerning the worth of narrating consciousness' judgment, which we can best approach by asking what status we are to give the narrator's considered belief that the pleasures of ecstatic invention were greater than those that unveiling the mysteries of the universe would have provided, and that more truth would have been found had the path of system been chosen from the start. The narrator provides a convincing explanation of why dreaming consciousness should have overlooked its own part in the creative process, and never fully grasped either the objective nature of the universe outside it. The explanation is that greater pleasure was found in the chimerical creations than in understanding: "Je crois que si j'eusse devoilé tous les mysteres de la nature *je me serois senti* dans une situation *moins délicieuse. . . .*" The belief compensates for the original compensation by providing a reasonable explanation for it.

In substituting for the failed attempt to know the universe a present knowledge of the reasons for the failure, the narrator is engaged in the same kind of transports he deplores. The *moi* asserts that the pleasure of unveiling is less than that of producing a lyrical cry. The basis for the assertion appears to be that many ways of feeling have been associated with the second pleasure (*une sorte de volupté*; *ravissement*; *resserré*; *j'etouffois*), whereas only one, that of disrobing mysteries, is associated with the first. To measure pleasure as if it were quantifiable, susceptible of being counted or weighed in grams or ounces, is to apply attributes of order to what is asserted to be without them, and is equivalent to the imagination's applying the attributes of weight, boundaries, sizes, to the abstractions it has made.

The statement that invention is more fun than revelation, like the assertion that the study of literature is more fun, or less disciplined, than the study of science, is the kind of statement for which no reliable information is available. There is no reason to think that the narrating *moi* is not enjoying himself applying internal measures to the external world (*delicious situation, mysteries of the universe*) and external measures to the internal one (*less delicious, without thinking any more*).[21] To each the pleasures of his situation.

The gains made by saying one thing and doing another are considerable. The *moi* is conceived as a being whose truth can be revealed over time. The universe is determined as having an existence independent of the self, running according to laws that can be known. The discrepancy between word and deed, however, suggests that the distinction being operated here between a past reign of imaginative error and a present reign of truth hides an exception to the rule of telling the truth. The lie is tolerated for good reason, since it makes the distinction between truth and lie possible.

The fact that narrating consciousness recognizes itself as revealer of the mysteries of the universe rather than as producer of them, suggests that Rousseau agrees with Malesherbes' assumption that a reasonable man recognizes his intention in his work. But while Malesherbes would find that judgment to be reliable, Rousseau would note the discrepancy between what narrating consciousness asserts about the independence of reason from the imagination, and the imaginative exchanges he has to make to assert it. While narrating consciousness can see itself in its production, it can only do so by deliberately overlooking an exception to its rule. In the attempt to determine the intentional structure of his productions, reasonable man exhibits a tolerance for exceptions to the rule that may prove his undoing. Far from seeing an end in reason for the institution's inventive arbitrariness, Rousseau would be more inclined to find the institution to be a symptom of the arbitrariness of the former.

Since the passage in question is an autobiographical text where the terms being quantified are psychological, and where the *moi*'s capacity to achieve self-knowledge is always open to question, the discrepancy can easily be called self-delusion and attributed to Rousseau. But that Rousseau is able to distinguish the dubious value of the narrating *moi*'s concepts is evident from his use of the term *belief* (*je crois*), which at once expresses the *moi*'s adherence to the opinion, and gives the lie to the opinion as merely a matter of belief.

It is clear that each story—the story of the production of the lyrical cry, and the story of its undoing— at once includes and excludes the other. The narrating consciousness can include the production of a lyrical cry as an earlier mode of reflection, by making use of figures whose status as figure is denied. The dreaming consciousness can produce seductive figures like *l'agitation de mes transports* in which consciousness recognizes its vacillation between the modes of reflection and of imagination, by forgetting that order also produces meaning in texts.

But it is not yet apparent how we are to understand the relation between these two readings. Might a text contain two readings in a mode that does not necessarily signify their confluence in a single destiny like the one that being represents? That would seem to be the final question raised by the passage, in the third expression designating the object of reflection as the incomprehensible being who can grasp all things, including, we might suggest, readings that mutually condition and exclude one another.

The passage provides a key to the problem in the way it uses the preposition *dans*, repeated seven times in the paragraph quoted, and crucial in one of the phrases we have been examining: "J'etouffois *dans* l'univers, j'aurois voulu m'élancer *dans* l'infini." *Dans* in the first case indicates the space enclosed by the container, the contents of the universe or the *moi*, and means "inside, within." The meaning of the preposition explains the relations entertained between inside and outside, *moi* and universe: the *moi* is literally inside the universe while, in a familiar Pascalian reversal, the universe is being figuratively grasped by the *moi* over time. In the second case, however, the preposition no longer expresses a meaning but merely relates. It relates the self, as one kind of meaningful figure, to the infinite conceived as a trajectory out of all containers, in an ever-growing series of flights.[22] To the extent that it means anything, it means *out into*, but we can only give it that meaning by assuming infinity to be like a container at the very moment that it is asserted not to be like one at all.

Consciousness can read the second *dans* as marking the move from a spatially-organized sequence into a temporally-organized sequence, in which meaning can temporarily be deferred, because the history articulating the turn from the ephemeral experience to the prospect of an infinity of such experiences can also be thought of as a kind of inside. Consciousness understands the passage as including two readings in the sense that it includes two times for reading, one without any historical recognition, and the other outside that illusion, inside the history of the losses of such moments.

But in fact the second *dans* does not indicate a moment in the time (*dans une heure*), or even the inside of the time (*dans l'histoire*). Properly speaking, it has no meaning at all but is an indicator of pure extension: out into. Infinity is conceived as an infinity of extensions out into extension, that is, out into what has no inside, and is thus the very opposite of the anthropomorphic being conceived by the imaginative self. Only by a kind of prosthesis extending meaning past its legitimate bounds can the second *dans* be made to signify anything. It is an outreach, a pure signifier, and indicates language as extension, as exteriority in relation to consciousness. The second *dans* contests the opinion shaping consciousness' reflection throughout the passage that, in the end, it can know the rules of the system, and all will make sense.

What that means is that if the passage contains two readings, it is not because it is a closed context like a universe or a *moi*, or even, like a history of consciousness, an order articulated around a conversion. It is rather because it is a pure extension that it can be rationalized and read as containing a history of consciousness, or as a description of the imagination's vacillations. There is a conflict between consciousness' story, its rationalizing ability, and the text's capacity to embrace empty signifiers, sheer effects of order. It is the outside of language that consciousness wants to bring into its purview. But it cannot do so without making it into meaning, that is, routing to oblivion the very exteriority that it wants to grasp. The *moi*'s feeling of being stifled or gagged by a cloying too much of a muchness, by a steady stream of self-representations, can have no other source than its inability to bring the border that it crosses every time it extends itself into written language, back across the border into consciousness as anything but another representation of itself. At the same time, however, no grasp, however all encompassing, can fully exhaust a text's possible meanings, since meaning is not contained in the text, but rather the text, sheer extension, is read off in the confrontation with consciousness, as signifying. Whether a reader reads the second *dans* as an *à* (*j'aurois voulu m'élancer à l'infini*), suggesting either an infinite extension to, or repetition of the imagination's flight, or as a *vers* (*j'aurois voulu m'élancer vers l'infini*), designating the turn away from the imagination towards reflective consciousness, may be a matter of choice. But the passage asserts that its meaning cannot be restricted to those choices. It can mean only insofar as it is meaningless extension, unrelated to consciousness. But all attempts to make meaningful that extension must exclude from consideration its refusal to mean.

Rousseau would not foresee a very bright future for Malesherbes' proposal to liberalize censorship. He would be suggesting in the first place that the reasonable man who claims that persuasion can be excised from his text is lying, wilfully tolerating exceptions to his general rule, and, in the second place, that the imaginative man who claims to have closed off his fiction from all historical determination hasn't understood its mysteries at all. In the confrontation between author and his text, the author does not manage to know the nature of his text, and his word on its meaning is practically worthless. Only the assertion of the impossibility of knowing the incomprehensible being that is his text has any value at all.

Malesherbes' attempts to liberate censorship by separating literature from philosophy would censor precisely that message that Rousseau's text works hardest to make, namely, that no text can be constituted as an inside, as a meaning developed over time, except by virtue of its extension as sheer grammar. A rational man who wants to expose his opinions can only do so by writing, and writing is at once a rational system or grammar, and a system outside the reach of the law, equally capable of transmitting licit or illicit messages. The reasoning process at work in an autobiography does not deny that the text is extension, but instead persistently reinvents figures for the text that vacillate over their dependence on, or autonomy from, a recapitulative figure like the self. A rational system like Malesherbes', however, seeks to forget the necessity of excluding the text's exteriority from consideration every time one reads or writes; it consequently deliberately misunderstands the impossibility of mastering the effects of the system it legitimates. The censorship of censorship, Rousseau would suggest, is the aim of all rational, liberal systems like Malesherbes'.

NOTES

1 No pressing practical problem is being debated in Rousseau's letter. *Julie*, published by Marc-Michel Rey in Amsterdam and sold in France by Robin, had already been out for a month at the time the letter was written. The censoring of the work took place at Malesherbes' instigation; he hoped Rousseau would profit from the French publication. See the *Notices bibliographiques* in Rousseau, *Oeuvres complètes*, t. 1 (Paris: Gallimard, 1959). See also Pierre Grosclaude, *Jean-Jacques et Malesherbes* (Paris: Fischbacher, 1960), and Rousseau's *Correspondance complète*, t. VII, VIII, ed. R. A. Leigh (Geneva: Institut et Musée Voltaire, 1965–80).

2 See Jean Starobinski, *L'Oeil vivant* (Paris: Gallimard, 1960), 93–188; *La Transparence et l'obstacle*, 2nd ed. (Paris: Gallimard, 1971).

3 Chrétien-Guillaume de Lamoignon de Malesherbes, *Mémoires sur la librairie et sur la liberté de la presse*, ed. Graham Rodmell (Chapel Hill, N.C.: University of North Carolina Press, 1979). References to this work will henceforth appear in the text.

4 Henri Falk, *Les Privilèges de librairie sous l'ancien régime. Etude historique du conflit des droits sur l'oeuvre littéraire* (Geneva: Slatkine, 1970), 115–16.

5 Falk, 177. For a dissenting view, in which the literary work is deemed a property, see Diderot's *Lettres historiques et politiques sur le commerce de la librairie*, *Oeuvres complètes*, ed. Assézat and Tourneux, t. 18 (Paris: Garnier, 1876).

6 See Robert Shackleton, *Censure and Censorship: Impediments to Free Publication in the Age of the Enlightenment* (Austin: Humanities Research Center, University of Texas, 1975) for comments on the *Librairie* as preserver of the archive. His study makes the difference between prior censorship and censure by the law with particular force. For a more complete discussion of the *Librairie* under Malesherbes, see N. Herrmann-Mascard, *La Censure des livres à la fin de l'Ancien Régime (1750–1789)* (Paris: PUF, 1968); J. P. Bélin, *Le Commerce des libres prohibés à Paris de 1750 à 1789* (Paris: Bélin Frères, 1913); and F. Brunetière, "Etudes sur le XVIIIe siècle: La Direction de la *Librairie* sous M. de Malesherbes" in *Revue des Deux Mondes* 1 (1 fév., 1882): 567–612. See also

William Hanley's concise description, "The Policing of Thought: Censorship in Eighteenth-Century France" in *Studies on Voltaire and the Eighteenth Century*, 183 (Oxford: Voltaire Foundation, 1980), 265–95.

7 Respect for the law, protection for the individual are the twin motives behind the censorship laws. A difficult situation arises because French law, in Malesherbes' account at any rate, allows for the possibility of deciding that an action is criminal, even if no law prohibits it positively, so long as the intention can be shown to be criminal. The judges have to decide whether a proposition is an error or a crime, in order to decide the intention of its author, and can only decide whether a particular proposition is an error or a crime, if they have previously decided on the author's intention. They must rule arbitrarily. Under the circumstances, Malesherbes says, censorship is necessary both for the protection of the author, and for the protection of the law, which should not have to make decisions on undecidable cases in the courts. Censorship provides a kind of pre-determining of the status of the work and its intention, and ought to keep authors out of courts, for the sake of authors and the law alike. The reason for the government's reserve is operative behind the censorship laws that Malesherbes inherits, and in those that he proposes.

8 Cf. for example 224–5: "Je persistais dans mon sentiment, et je leur soutenais toujours que les erreurs n'auraient qu'un temps, et que, pourvu qu'un laissât la liberté de la discussion, ce serait à la longue la vérité qui prévaudrait." See also his discussion of the desirability of methodical exposition over persuasion, 238–9 and passim, as also his representation of the law as needing to conform to reason throughout the *Mémoires*.

9 Cf. 284–88 for Malesherbes' opinion on fictions.

10 One should be wary of equating philosophy with texts exposing opinion, however. In his own text, Malesherbes insists on avoiding the term *philosophy*. He does so because to use the term is to cause division of opinion that is not conducive to the kind of conviction he wants his argument to carry, namely, universal assent to an important truth. Malesherbes appears to consider his text to be philosophical, on condition that it not raise any hackles by mentioning philosophy.

"J'ai évité de prononcer le mot de *philosophie*, parce que l'âcreté des disputes élevées depuis quarante ans n'a pas laissé à ce mot de signification certaine. Suivant les uns, toute grande idée, toute vérité nouvelle est regardée comme apartenante à la *philosophie*. Suivant d'autres, *philosophie* est devenue synonyme d'*impiété*. Je crois qu'en Grèce, dans le beau siècle de la littérature, qui fut cependant celui de la persécution des philosophes, et à Rome, dans les différents siècles où les philosophes furent bannis, il y avait diversité d'opinions sur la signification qu'il faut donner à ce nom.

"Pour éviter les disputes autant qu'il est possible dans un mémoire où je cherche à réunir les opinions de tout le monde sur une vérité importante, j'ai dû éviter de nommer *la philosophie*" (281).

11 Cf. chap. 6 of the *Mémoire sur la liberté de la presse*.

12 Malesherbes suggests that financial pressure will be brought to bear on publishers, who will stand to lose their investment in case the work is judged libel-

lous or dangerous. Publishers will beome more cautious about accepting works for publication, and will take over some of the censor's functions.

13 p. 297, *C. c.* t. VII, (letter 1152, Nov. 5, 1760).

14 Cf. 301–07 for a discussion of anonymous publication and the libel laws with respect to memoirs, public denunciations, and autobiographical works.

15 Cf. Jean-Jacques Rousseau, *Oeuvres complètes,* ed. B. Gagnebin and M. Raymond (Paris: Gallimard, 1959), 1: 574–78. Page numbers referring to this edition will henceforth appear in the text.

16 Malesherbes' hostility toward autobiography makes itself felt in various anecdotal ways as well. One of the most interesting texts in this repect is transmitted to us by Grosclaude, 94–97. In a letter to Moultou, Malesherbes vacillates over the publication of Rousseau's autobiographical works, sometimes wishing, in the name of philosophy, that it not occur, sometimes wanting it, in order to expose the injustice of some of Rousseau's judgments:

"Mais les systèmes ou les principes du philosophe ne sont pas fondés sur l'authorité de son nom, comme les vérités historiques le sont sur le témoignage de celuy qui rapporte les faits qu'il a vus. C'est sa logique, c'est son éloquence qui fondent ses théories. . . .

"J.J. Rousseau est différent de tous les philosophes, en ce que ce ne sont pas seulement ses opinions qu'il a publiées. Il a produit en public son caractère et son ame tout entière, il ne parle point seulement de l'espirit à l'espirit, il parle du coeur au coeur. Sa grande ame est faite pour enflammer les lecteurs de son siècle et de la postérité et pour inspirer la plus grande confiance dans ses jugemens. Si cependant quelques uns de ces jugemens ont été injustes et dictés par cette violente passion qui l'aveugloit, il est nécessaire que ceux qui le liront et qui auront à juger son caractère et celuy des gens dont il parle soient avertis de ce qui doit les mettre en garde. . ." (94–95).

17 Cf. 335, *C. c.,* t. VII (Letter 1610, Dec. 25, 1760): "Pour moy, Monsieur, je vous diray avec toute la franchise qui vous et due que j'ay vu dans tous vos procédés une extreme sensibilité, un grand fond de melancholie et beaucoup de disposition à voir les objets du coté le plus noir, mais une disposition au moins égale à vous rendre à la justice et à la verité quand elle vous est présentée. La sensibilité de l'amour propre n'est etranger à aucun auteur. Ceux qui veulent la dissimuler cherchent à tromper ou se trompent eux mêmes. La sensibilité du coeur est imprimée dans vos ouvrages avec trop de force et trop de verité pour qu'on soit etonné de la retrouver dans votre conduite, ainsi à cet égard vous ne m'avés rien appris. . . ." Cf. also, p. 327, *C. c.,* t. VII (Letter 1591, Dec. 16, 1760).

18 See Jean Starobinski, "Espace du jour, espace du bonheur: Remarques sur la *Troiseme lettre à Malesherbes* de Jean-Jacques Rousseau" in *Studi Filosofici* (1978): 7–18 for a more extended reading of the passage in the light of the imagination.

19 The expression *étourdissante extase* is a particularly apt expression for the suspension in the imaginative creation of the two trajectories. The trajectory away from sensation towards the abstract idea is expressed by the term *étourdissante,* whose liberal meaning, "deafening," gets lost in its figurative meaning, "amaz-

ing," "astounding." And the trajectory of the ideal back toward its statement in sensuous form is suggested by the term *extase*, whose figurative meaning – a state in which one is *as if* outside the sensuous world reveals its roots in the sensuous world, since the inner state of being "outside" experience is attested to by no inner evidence, but by the external aspects of immobility, lack of response to stimuli, expression, and so forth.

20 See, for example, the famous episode of the stolen apples recounted in the first book of the *Confessions*:

"Le lendemain retrouvant l'occasion belle, je tente un nouvel essai. Je monte sur mes treteaux, j'alonge la broche, je l'ajuste, j'étois pret à piquer . . . malheureusement le dragon ne dormoit pas. Tout à coup la porte de la dépense s'ouvre; mon maitre en sort, croise les bras, me regarde, et me dit: courage . . . la plume me tombe des mains" (34).

21 The scene resembles in many respects the dramatic account Rousseau gives of the origin of language in the *Essais sur l'origine des langues*, as Paul de Man discusses it in his chapter on metaphor in *Allegories of Reading* (New Haven and New London: Yale University Press, 1979), 155. When reasonable man denounces the spontaneous metaphor "giant," which arises in his first meeting with another man, by means of a comparison between their sizes, the substitution of a language of measure for the spontaneous figure does not mean, says de Man, that his language has thereby lost all traces of figurality, but simply that it hides its figures by calling them concepts. The passion de Man analyzes is fear. *Amour de soi* is the passion generating the figures here.

22 We could call it a metonymy if it served to connect two contingent things. But it relates the self as locus of meaning, and infinity as a series of contingent moments, and there can be no way of knowing whether the relation between meaning and logical extension is contingent or not. The figure should more properly be called a catachresis, since it does not so much substitute for a literal term as function in the absence of one.

Rousseau and the Democratization of Language in the French Revolution

CAROL BLUM

Two separate but ultimately complementary manifestations of Rousseau's "democratization" of language appeared during the French Revolution: one forcing the admission of popular language into the preserves of "upper French," the other redefining fundamental political vocabulary in order to discredit the monarchy and to serve a new, wider-based polity.[1]

The French which the Académie française was founded to purify and protect was the language of an ascendant class; its nature hierarchical, its fortunes bound to those of an absolute monarchy. Behind this mandarin tongue stood another, still more rarified and difficult of access: Latin. A command of Latin and upper French bore witness to the essential superiority of the aristocrat and the existential achievements of the successful bourgeois. Upper French in the seventeenth and eighteenth centuries eschewed words that evoked "the village," the "old-fashioned," and the "lowly"; *le village, le vieux, et le bas*. Not only was the purity of language policed, its very utterance required royal permission. The *Comédie française* alone was privileged to present actors who spoke the French language on stage; the abundant popular theatrical performances of the Fairs, especially the Foire St. Germain, were officially denied the word although their mutism was infringed by ingenious subterfuges.[2]

Upper French for the upper classes, lowly French for the rabble: one language expressed the mind, the other gave voice to the body. Yet this neat distinction clearly reflected not reality but ideology. The French aristocrat or educated bourgeois was not ignorant of the plebs' pungent

309

monosyllabic vocabulary; he was, in fact, the possessor of two French languages, the upper, reserved for him and his peers in texts and discourse consonant with the official world, and the lower, which served him as amusement, as vehicle for the unseemly, as a play tongue in which he could momentarily suspend an onerous dignity.

At the great fair spectacles demos and elite were joyfully confounded. Nothing was better tone than a parodic mastery of lowly French by an exemplary upper Frenchman. Thus not long after her husband's solemn coronation as King of France and of Navarre by the Grace of God, Marie-Antoinette invited the market-women from Les Halles to come to Versailles so that she could imitate their accent for a part she was playing in a dialect comedy, *une pièce poissarde*.[3]

As in white America's long affection for black minstrel and "coon" songs, the lowly was delectable provided it remained below; the head called upon the body but reciprocal visits were discouraged. The great literary genres were insulated against the rising stink of the nether parts by a fine fabric of rules, conventions, and usages.

Edmund Burke held that the germinal events of France's Revolution were as much linguistic as political and social. The great "words" of Western civilization, as Burke described them, were being systematically emptied of their ancient, traditional meanings, and refilled with false and arbitrary ones. In what Steven Blakemore called "regicide and logocide," Burke linked the demise of the old sign with the physical death of the thing signified.[4] Burke's point is well illustrated by the word "souverain" as it was understood before Jean-Jacques Rousseau's political works, by the Encyclopedists, and after, by Revolutionaries.

The Encyclopedists, cognizant of and exploiting the phenomenon Burke signaled, had defined "souverain" in its traditional way, that is, as the *person* invested with power by the nation. Sovereigns were those individuals "à qui la volonté des peuples a conféré le pouvoir nécessaire pour gouverner la société. L'homme, dans la nature, ne connaît point de souverain; chaque individu est égal à un autre . . . il n'est pas dans cet état d'autre subordination que celle des enfans à leur père. Un souverain, quelque absolu qu'il soit, n'est point en droit de toucher aux loix constitutives."

The Encyclopedic definition of a constitutional patriarchal sovereign was underscored by an anecdote: "Le chevalier Temple disait à Charles II, qu'un roi d'Angleterre qui est l'homme de son peuple, est le plus grand roi du monde, mais s'il veut être davantage, il n'est plus rien. Je veux être homme de mon peuple, répondit-il."[5]

On the one hand the Encyclopédie followed tradition in equating the Sovereign with a human being, whether called King, or Empress, or Elector; on the other it urged enlightened reform by attributing the source of the Sovereign's power not to God but to the people and insisting it be employed for the people's benefit, not the ruler's. The King of England, it must be noted, was depicted as needing instruction as to the definition of his own being, and the chevalier produced a formula by which the British monarch could either be "the greatest king in the world" or "no longer anything." This method of pressing reform on individual sovereigns by means of condescending and sometimes menacing language was consistent in the *Encyclopédie* and its companion publication for crowned heads, Grimm's *Correspondance littéraire*. Nonetheless, it took Rousseau's audacity to de-humanize the sovereign altogether and to render him definitively "no longer anything." This he achieved not by homily but by fiat.

The total reformulation of the notion of "sovereign" by Rousseau in the *Contrat social* was truly radical in the sense that it up-rooted the past, it refused to bow to reality, it stated as axiomatic a moral definition of "sovereign" *not* as the human head of state, but rather as the whole body politic. "Le souverain" was not and could not be an individual human being. It was now defined as a collective sentimental mystery.[6]

The surrender of each individual to the group produced, Rousseau claimed in the *Contrat social*, "un corps moral et collectif composé d'autant de membres que l'assemblée a de voix, lequel reçoit de ce même acte son unité, son *moi* commun, sa vie et sa volonté." Having defined the state as a collective fusion of identity, Rousseau went on to reveal that a number of differing political entities were, correctly understood, but manifestations of a single phenomenon, the great body politic. Thus, "Cette personne publique qui se forme ainsi par l'union de toutes les autres prenait autrefois le nom de *Cité*, et prend maintenant celui de *République* ou de corps politique,. . . appellé par ses membres *Etat* quand il est passif, *Souverain* quand il est actif, *Puissance* en le comparant à ses semblables. A l'égard des associés ils prennent collectivement le nom de *peuple*, et s'appellent en particulier *Citoyens* comme participans à l'autorité souveraine, et *Sujets* comme soumis aux lois de l'Etat. Mais ces termes se confondent souvent et se prennent l'un pour l'autre; il suffit de les savoir distinguer quand ils sont employés dans toute leur précision." The whole science of government, then, resided in taxonomy, a linguistic political infallibilty Rousseau claimed and asserted he shared with few others. In all of France, for example, he allowed that only d'Alembert understood the word "Citoyen" correctly: "Nul autre auteur François, que je sache, n'a compris le vrai sens du mot" (*Oeuvres complètes*, 3:362).

Rousseau rendered null and void a king existing separate from his subjects. He accomplished this not through argument or demonstration but through investing old words with new meanings by magisterial pronouncement. "Republic," "State," "Sovereign," "people," "citizens," "subjects":

all of these terms which differentiated one thing from another under the Old Regime, were now to be understood correctly as a single being, the body politic, seen under varying light.

Much of the work of the French Revolution concerned the reordering of language, the invention of new signs for old referents, and, conversely, the transvaluation of old signs into the new code. "Everything," said François Deforgues, "even the language, must be regenerated according to the Republican system" (*Moniteur*, 30 frimaire, 12/20/1793). "Tu" became the obligatory form of address on 10 brumaire of 1793, thus abolishing a distinction long fraught with social and emotional nuance, and the Académie française itself was disbanded and many former academicians arrested.

Robespierre, perhaps Rousseau's most faithful Revolutionary disciple, insisted on the necessity of revising the old language: "Ce n'est point un vain mot que la République; c'est le caractère des citoyens, c'est la *vertu*, c'est-à-dire l'amour de la patrie." Republic, citizens' character, virtue, love of fatherland, these formerly distinct terms now were to be understood as synonymous. Of the seven volumes of his discourse covering a five year span, repeating new definitions of key words was perhaps the single most obsessive theme.[7]

At the trial of Louis XVI in the winter of 1792–93, Saint-Just made his mark upon the Convention by using Rousseau's definition of sovereign to condemn the King. As "sovereign" signified the state and the state was synonymous with the "people," Saint-Just demonstrated the necessity for executing Louis. "Depuis que le peuple français a montré sa volonté [by invading the Tuileries], tout ce qui l'oppose est hors le souverain, tout ce qui est hors le souverain est l'ennemi . . . entre le peuple et ses ennemis il n'y a rien de commun que le glaive."[8] The Kingship was semantically annihilated before Louis could be corporally beheaded.

For the generation making the Revolution, the new definitions of words like "sovereign," "state," and "people" had been underwritten by Rousseau's moral authority. Yet when Mme de Staël, daughter of Louis XVI's finance minister Jacques Necker, keenly aware of Revolutionary politics and herself an ardent disciple of Rousseau, wrote about his influence on that generation, she signalled another aspect. Not merely the reordering of abstract vocabulary, the cooptation of upper French for the purposes of lowly classes, but the opposite, the introduction of lowly French into upper French discourse. Mme de Staël said of Rousseau: "Il a le tort de se servir souvent d'expressions de mauvais goût . . . il se pique de forcer ses lecteurs à les approuver; et peut-être aussi que par une sorte d'esprit républicain, il ne veut point reconnaître qu'il existe des termes bas ou relevés."[9]

She was referring to the *Confessions* and *Emile*, serious works inscribed in an upper French openly, even provocatively smattered with "lowly" words in which the body and its effluences were resolutely committed to print. No reader could finish the *Confessions* and *Emile* unaware of Rousseau's preoccupation with tears, but his interest in urination, his concerns about lactation, his notions about ingestion, digestion, and ejaculation were equally unavoidable. A single example illustrates the point: Rousseau's description of the death of Mme de Vercelli, whom he had served as a lackey. The very notion of lackey as serious author was already a breach in the wall around upper French as stunning in its way as Figaro's venomous soliloquy; that the ex-servant should describe his aristocratic mistress's dying moments was acceptable in literature only if he displayed exemplary humility. The death-bed scene was a genre, a *morceau de bravoure* for the felicitous expression of appropriate sentiments. It was a genre, moreover, in which Rousseau excelled; Julie's last words in *La Nouvelle Héloïse* rivaled those of Richardson's Clarissa both in nobility and volume. Rousseau, mentioning his resentment at being treated as a "mere lackey" by Mme de Vercelli,[10] described her death in a few conventional sentences:

> Je la vis expirer. Sa vie avoit été celle d'une femme d'esprit et de sens; sa mort fut celle d'un sage.

A perfect brief obituary, demonstrating Rousseau's mastery of the genre. Next, however, the phrase which shocked his contemporaries:

> Enfin ne parlant plus, et déjà dans les combats de l'agonie, elle fit un gros pet. Bon, se dit-elle en se retournant, femme qui pette n'est pas morte. Ce furent les derniers mots qu'elle prononça (1:83).

To have entered the bedroom of a socially superior woman as a trusted servant, to have been witness to her private agony, to have exposed this woman's name, her body and its language in print when her head was no longer in control of her tongue, these were the verbal acts which Mme de Staël saw as "Republican" and provocative.

It is curious how Edmund Burke, too, seemed to feel that beneath or beyond the attack upon hallowed political words was an attack upon a woman. For Burke, the ultimate objective of Jacobin vocabulary was the "stripping of the Queen." A painful image of Marie-Antoinette reduced and humiliated adheres to Burke's preoccupation with "Revolutionary assaults upon traditional language." He spoke of the new order as one in which the "decent drapery of life is to be rudely torn off. All the superadded ideas, furnished from the wardrobe of a moral imagination, which the heart owns, and the understanding ratifies, as necessary to cover the defects of our naked, shivering nature, and to raise it to dignity in our own estimation, are to be exploded as a ridiculous, absurd, and antiquated fashion. On this scheme of things, a king is but a man, a queen is but a woman; a woman is but an animal, and an animal not of the highest order."[11]

Three journalists most intimately connected with Rousseau's name during the Revolution were Hébert, known as Le Père Duchesne, Marat, whose motto "vitam impendere vero" was Rousseau's own, and Camille Desmoulins. All three men, educated and from middle-class backgrounds, nonetheless made their influence felt through the systematic use of crude and violent language in reporting political events and associated this new linguistic mode with Rousseau. According to Camille, "Nous avons appris chez Jean-Jacques que . . . ce qui caractérise le républicain, ce n'est point le siècle, le gouvernement dans lequel il vit, c'est la franchise du langage."[12]

The trial of Marie-Antoinette, the same week that "tu" became obligatory, was a case in point. Her title was the first defense to be shattered, before her person could be attained. After the title, the name. No longer Reine, nor Marie-Antoinette, she was momentarily labelled "Citoyenne Capet." To objections that she was less than a citizen, she was sarcastically renamed Mme Veto. Finally, at the time of her trial, Père Duchesne, he of the mighty oaths, pronounced her animal:

> La tigresse autrichienne était regardée dans toutes les cours, comme la plus misérable prostituée de France. On l'accusait hautemen de se vautrer dans la fange avec ses valets, et on était embarrassé de distinguer quel était le goujat qui avait fabriqué les avortons éclopés, bossus, gangrenés, sortis de son ventre ridé à triple étage.[13]

A ceremonial degradation before an official execution. Although nameless and without title, the alien animal was *known* as the lowest prostitute in France. She whose *raison d'être* was blood, whose single essential capacity was that of reproducing a Bourbon Dauphin, was described rolling in the mud with her lackeys; her children no more "Les Enfants de France," but the diseased, crippled offspring of a dishonored creature, stripped and reviled.

The redefinition of "sovereign," which separated Louis from France, and the "stripping" of his Queen had not been easily accomplished; they were the arduous Revolutionary tasks of restructuring mentalities to admit a new polity. Rousseau's daring redefinition of abstract political vocabulary and his equally audacious introduction of "lowly" French into serious discourse served the Revolution by providing spokesmen with prestigious model texts. Rousseau, patron saint of *la franche parole*, had validated the language from below as the voice of the body politic.

NOTES

1 Albert Soboul discusses the change in language during the Revolution as the result rather than as the agent of emotional upheaval: "Le remuement formidable des passions que fut aussi la Révolution française, a soulevé les coeurs et les âmes. La langue s'en est ressentie, et donc les mots aussi. Plusieurs ont été emportés par une sorte de mystique, mystique d'amour ou mystique de haine, et ont été revêtus d'une valeur affective qu'ils n'avaient jamais eue. Certains, comme liberté, égalité ont été déifiés, et, par une sorte de mythe, ils sont devenus des idées forces, des forces vivantes dont l'action s'est fait sentir sur l'histoire elle-même." "Egalité du pouvoir et des dangers des mots," *AHRF* 217 (July–Sept. 1974).

2 In "The Speechless Tradition," Frederick Brown traces Boulevard theater to its origins in mute fair spectacle: "Extending back to the commercial fair from which it descended in a direct line, its history had been one of incessant guerrilla warfare against the *Comédie française*, of skirmishes with a censor determined that it should remain dumb and antic." *Theater and Revolution* (New York: Viking, 1980), 42.

3 Bernard Bray comments on the judgment of an eighteenth-century observer. "Dans ce siècle paradoxal où la pureté de la langue française irradie à travers l'Europe entière, les Parisiens se divertissent des jurements des poissardes. Sébastien Mercier, dans son *Tableau de Paris*, confirme cet engouement qui incite les grands encanaillés à copier le ton, imiter les inflexions de voix et les expressions de cette langue triviale: Marie-Antoinette a convoqué à Versailles les femmes de la Halle pour s'inspirer de leur accent avant de jouer elle-même une pièce poissarde." Introduction, *Romans d'amour par lettres* (Paris: Garnier-Flammarion, 1983), 40–41.

4 Steven Blakemore says of Burke's denunciation of the way in which French Revolutionaries reordered language to eliminate individuals: "Here language is used to reduce concrete people to 'nonpersons' by a bogus linguistic fiction which insists that these people are only linguistic abstractions — fictitious creations of the old European language." "Burke and the Fall of Language: The French Revolution as Linguistic Event," *ECS* 17 (1984): 284–307.

Gary Kelly, on the other hand, claims that Burke "dehumanized" the Revolutionaries by comparing them, for example, to savages. Savages, however, were not so much inhuman to Burke as foul and primitive, the attributes he imputed to the Revolutionaries. "Revolution, Crime and Madness: Edmund Burke and the Defense of the Gentry," *Eighteenth-Century Life* 9, n.s. 1 (1984): 16–32.

5 *Encyclopédie ou dictionnaire raisonné*, Ed. Diderot and d'Alembert (Lausanne: Sociétés typographiques, 1781), 21:541.

6 I discuss the question of whether the "body politic" constitutes an "organicist metaphor" underlying Rousseau's political writings in *Rousseau and the Republic of Virtue: The Language of Politics in the French Revolution* (Ithaca: Cornell University Press, 1986), 71–72. Debate over the same issue in Burke is discussed by Walter D. Love, " 'Meaning' in the History of Conflicting Interpretations of Burke," *Edmund Burke, the Enlightenment and the Modern World* (Detroit: University of Detroit Press, 1967), 117–129.

7 *Lettres de Robespierre à ses commettants* in *Oeuvres complètes*, 4:285.

8 Saint-Just, *Oeuvres complètes*, ed. Ch. Vellay (Paris: Charpentier et Fasquelle, 1908), 2:76.

9 Mme de Staël (Germaine Necker), *Lettres sur les écrits et le caractère de J.-J. Rousseau* (n.p.: 1788), 11–12. Robert J. Ellrich discusses the eighteenth-century's division of erotic language into a vulgar tongue for oral communication and pornographic literature, and an elevated "code of preterition" which, gauze-like, permitted the illicit to be glimpsed through its filmy texture. He comments that between the two modes of expression it was "Rousseau, the cultural out-sider who denounced the culture itself and refused to be part of it, [who] found himself denounced in turn and cast out by the representatives of both sides, officialdom and *philosophie*." *Eighteenth-Century Life* 9, n.s. 3 (1985): 217–228. The numerous public who did embrace Rousseau, however, went on in large measure to form the Revolutionary officialdom and intelligentsia. It was not exclusively erotic language that was at stake but the whole repressed plebian vocabulary of the physical.

10 Rousseau described the bitterness of the individual in command of the upper languages, condemned by circumstances to a humble station in life. "Quoi, toujours laquais? me dis-je en moi-même avec un dépit amer. . . . Je me sen-tois trop peu fait pour cette place pour craindre qu'on m'y laissât" (1:92–93).

His chance to advance finally presented itself when he displayed mastery of the ascendant language. He was serving a table at which the family motto, "Tel fiert qui ne tue pas" was being discussed. "Le vieux Comte de Gouvon . . . vit que je souriois sans oser rien dire: il m'ordonna de parler." At last ordered to speak by the head of the household, Rousseau informed the family of the meaning of its own words, demonstrating not his equality, but his superiority to them. "Tout le monde me regardoit et se regardoit sans rien dire. On ne vit de la vie un pareil étonnement . . . la louange qu'il me devoit, et qu'il me donna en effet si pleine et entière et d'un air si content que toute la table s'em-pressa de faire chorus . . . Ce fut un de ces momens trop rares qui replacent les choses dans leur ordre naturel et vengent le mérite avili des outrages de la fortune." The Abbé de Gouvon took Rousseau's education in hand, instruct-ing him in the other arcane tongue of the upper classes: "Trouvant sur tout que j'avois peu de latin, il entreprit de m'en enseigner davantage . . . en même tems au dessus et au dessous de mon état, j'étois disciple et valet dans la même maison, et dans ma servitude j'avois cependant un précepteur d'une naissance à ne l'être que des enfans des Rois." *Confessions, Oeuvres complètes* (Paris: Gallimard, 1961), 1:95–97.

11 *Reflections on the French Revolution* (New York: Dutton, 1955), 74. According to Steven Blakemore, "Burke sees his 'world' threatened by a new linguistic revolution in which old words are torn from their historical context and emptied of their historical meaning. These words are then 'filled' with the 'new Revolutionary meaning'. . . . In his *Preface to the address of M. Brissot to his Constituents*, Burke specifically connects this revolution in language with the Revolution in France. . . . In this new battle of the Books (texts) there is a linguistic battle over 'meaning ' in which Burke represents the ancients in his tradition and classical sources while the supporters of Revolution represent the moderns in their celebration of the new revolutionary literature" (284–6). Marilyn Butler discusses the political significance of radical language in England during the 1790s in her "Introductory Essay," *Burke, Paine, Godwin, and the Revolution Controversy* (Cambridge: Cambridge University Press, 1984).

12 Camille goes on to modernize Rousseau's critique of Molière's play by associating the virtuous, outspoken Alceste with Jacobinism and the moderate, polite Philinthe with reaction. "Molière, dans le *Misanthrope*, a peint en traits sublimes les caractères du républican et du royaliste. Alceste est un jacobin, Philinte, un feuillant achevé. Combien nous sommes loin de cette âpreté de critique, de cette rudesse sauvage des harangues et des moeurs . . . à laquelle on reconnaît une âme républicaine dans J.-J. Rousseau, comme dans le paysan du Danube; dans un Scythe, comme dans Marat! On trouvera parmi nous cette effroyable haine d'Alceste. J'aime mieux encore qu'on dénonce à tort et à travers, j'ai presque dit qu'on calomnie même, comme le Père Duchesne, mais avec cette énergie qui caractérise les âmes fortes et d'une trempe républicaine, que de voir que nous avons retenu cette politesse bourgeoise, cette civilité puérile et honnête, ces ménagements pusillanimes de la monarchie, cette circonspection, ce visage de caméléon et de l'antichambre, ce b. . . . .e, en un mot, pour les plus forts hommes en crédit ou en place." *Le Vieux Cordelier*, No. 7, quintidi, pluviôse, 2e décadi, An II, 133–39.

Burke was in basic accord with Camille's attribution of linguistic liberation to Rousseau, while reversing the value placed on the model. He commented that the Revolutionaries "dispute amongst their leaders, which of them is the best resemblance of Rousseau. In truth, they all resemble him. His blood they transfuse into their minds and into their manners. Him they study; him they meditate . . . To this man and this writer, as a pattern to authors and to Frenchmen, the founderies of Paris are now running for statues, with the kettles of their poor and the bells of their churches." *Reflections on the Revolution in France*, 262.

13 Jacques-René Hébert, *Le Père Duchesne*, 2nd series, vol. 4, no. 296 (Oct., 1793). Two numbers later (298) he expressed "la grande Joie du père Duchesne au sujet du raccourcissement de la louve autrichienne. . . ."

Jefferson's Music Library, His Catalogue of 1783, and A Revision of Lowens's Haydn in America

RONALD R. KIDD

It is by now well known that among Thomas Jefferson's bewildering assortment of talents, music also takes its place. While still a student in Williamsburg, he gained access to the highest rank of society. This access was due in part to his competence as an amateur violinist, capable of taking his place in informal chamber music. Music was always an important part of life at Monticello, first during his brief marriage and later with the Randolphs, his daughter's family. His carefully maintained account books inform us that he attended the theater and concerts whenever they were accessible to him in Williamsburg, Philadelphia, London, and Paris.[1]

Several articles on the subject of Jefferson and music have appeared in popular periodicals over the years, and there also exist single chapters within broader studies.[2] Only one book-length study has been published—that of Helen Cripe in 1974.[3] The contribution of that study lies in the compilation of references to various musical matters scattered throughout the family correspondence and other documents. Numerous questions, however, remain unanswered.

One area that has not received much attention is that of Jefferson as collector and bibliographer of music. This lack is unfortunate, because Jefferson's music library is undoubtedly the best documented private collection from that period of American life. On this basis alone Jefferson's music library merits a more thorough investigation than it has yet received.

The subject of "Jefferson and music bibliography" may be regarded as an extension of Jefferson's activities in the world of books and documents,

319

an area which *has* attracted much attention. In this field, the most weighty study is the recently reissued, five-volume descriptive catalogue of Sowerby,[4] which focuses on the second of Jefferson's four collections, the one sold to Congress in 1815. In addition to a catalogue of this collection printed for Congress, Sowerby's main guide was the manuscript catalogue made by Jefferson himself and completed in its earliest state by 1783.[5] (Despite subsequent expansion it is generally referred to as the 1783 catalogue.) Sowerby did not have access to Jefferson's enlarged catalogue of 1812, only recently recovered in a fair copy.[6]

Sowerby's investigation encompassed the chapter of the catalogue of 1783 which lists "music theory" books, as most of these were included in the sale to Congress and, in fact, are still preserved in the Rare Book Room. The ensuing chapters of musical scores she skipped over altogether, as these were not sold to Congress. These chapters then have never been subjected to the careful scrutiny and analysis which Sowerby brought to the rest of Jefferson's library. So far as we know the 1783 catalogue remained Jefferson's guide to his musical scores and was not replaced (as in all other subjects) by any later catalogue. It must therefore serve also as our chief reference in interpreting Jefferson's library of music.

In the original state of the 1783 catalogue these musical scores, including both owned items and desiderata, were laid out on four successive verso pages, three of which were quite full. Two pages were reserved for vocal works, two for instrumental. Items which were already in the library received a check mark; desiderata did not. With the exception of the penultimate opening, the music chapters of the catalogue are quite orderly, as they were not subjected to the extensive additions and emendations characteristic under other subject headings, such as law and agriculture. [Illustration I shows in skeletal outline the contents of the several openings of the music chapters, including that for music theory. In the original state of the catalogue, items would have appeared on the verso pages only.] The catalogue of musical scores documents possession — not in 1783, but at a later date — of roughly 130 printed collections, in addition to loose collections of sheet music, manuscript copies, and desiderata. Each collection would contain many songs, or, in the case of instrumental music, three, six, or twelve sonatas, concertos, duets, etc.

There is today a collection of music housed at the University of Virginia and Monticello, generally referred to as the Monticello music collection, which belonged to Jefferson and his descendants. The bulk of this material is connected with Jefferson's daughter Martha and her children. However, several of these volumes clearly come from Jefferson's private library, as recorded in the 1783 catalogue. Of Jefferson's original volumes,

Illus. 1. Catalogue of 1783:   Layout of music chapters.

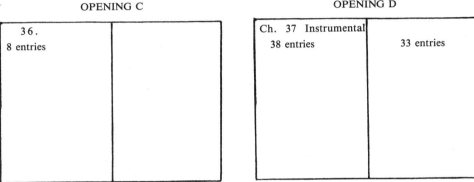

OPENING A

| Ch. 35. Theory 17 entries | 1 entry |

OPENING B

| Ch. 36. Vocal 29 entries | |

OPENING C

| 36. 8 entries | |

OPENING D

| Ch. 37 Instrumental 38 entries | 33 entries |

OPENING E

| 37. 30 entries | 1 entry |

(Also see Illus. 2.)

about fifty percent of the vocal music and less than ten percent of the instrumental survive.[7] The Jefferson music which has resurfaced in these collections has come from only two branches of descendants; whether other volumes are extant and still in private hands is not known. Jefferson marked his books by inserting his initials at signature I (J) and T. Since music was not printed in a similar fashion, no marks are generally included in his musical scores. We could identify such items only by their collation with Jefferson's own catalogue and the groupings into bindings sometimes indicated there by the addition of braces. If items came into the hands of a dealer and the Jefferson connection were unknown, they would likely be removed from their binding and sold as individual imprints. Identification would become impossible.

Just as in Jefferson's collecting of books, his music library was built up in several complementary ways. Account books register purchases of musical scores in Paris, Amsterdam, and Philadelphia. There can be little doubt that he purchased items also during the years in Williamsburg, as well as during a visit to London. From his father-in-law, John Wayles, Jefferson and his wife inherited some of the Wayles family collection. From John Randolph he acquired some music, along with a violin purchased by Jefferson when Randolph, a Loyalist, returned to England. One volume in the extant collection may reflect the Randolph purchase, as it has a more elegant binding than Jefferson normally required for his music volumes. From Baron von Geismer Jefferson was to have received a packet of music, although there is no record of its arrival at Monticello. Baron von Geismar was a German officer and prisoner of war who enjoyed chamber music sessions at Monticello during his "confinement" nearby: he repaid the hospitality when preparing to return to Europe by offering his music to Jefferson, knowing that he could readily replace it at home.

It was the custom of the Virginia plantation aristocracy to make gifts from their own libraries on special occasions, and some erasures in Jefferson's music catalogue may reflect such generosity. On the other hand, we find the name of Lady Byrd (of Charles City County) inscribed in one item in the extant Monticello music. This volume likely came into the collection from the Wayles inheritance and was probably a gift presented to one of the successive wives at the Wayles plantation, located in the same county. Another item in the collection contains the name of William Glen, an acquaintance of Jefferson and also from Charles City County.

All things considered, we cannot take Jefferson's collection as documented in his 1783 catalogue as a reliable index in every detail of his own tastes. Rather, it reflects the accidents of his collecting habits, his instinct for preservation, and his general bibliomania.

While Jefferson's organization of his catalogue was largely one of his own devising, based broadly on the divisions of human knowledge by Francis Bacon, the music chapters are influenced as well by music publishers' catalogues of his day.[8] These catalogues are generally organized according to genre with the classes of vocal music separate from those of instrumental. Often, for instance, the instrumental sections begin with full pieces (overtures and concertos), followed by trios, duets, and finally "solos." Such is precisely the order found in the first state of Jefferson's 1783 catalogue; Jefferson, however, does not waste space with subheadings.

Jefferson's first level of organization is outlined in a chart preceding his catalogue, in which music is divided into "theoretical"and "practical." In the catalogue itself the practical is further subdivided into vocal and instrumental, making three chapters in all: "35. Music Theory"; "36. Music Vocal"; "37. Music Instrumental." In the music theory chapter [Illustration 1, opening A], the only music chapter retained in the revised catalogue of 1812, Jefferson begins with the more speculative, philosophical books, follows with items of history and commentary, and concludes with popular didactic or "how-to" collections. The only theory title which was added to the collection while Jefferson was in Paris, is found on the recto page opposite the first group of titles; it was also later integrated into the revised 1812 catalogue.[9]

The vocal music chapter [opening B] begins with theater works — a single Italian opera, followed by others in English.[10] Sacred works follow — first the more ceremonial scores, such as Handel's Coronation Anthems, followed by practical collections of psalms and hymns. Finally, there are collections of English secular songs, continuing on the next verso [opening C] and at the end of his group, loose gatherings of single-sheet songs.

The instrumental chapter [opening D] starts with full pieces (concertos and overtures), proceeds to chamber sonatas for three or four strings, and concludes with duets. Passing by, for the moment, the list added later on the penultimate recto page, the final verso page [opening E] continues with solos (violin with figured bass), sonatas or "lessons" for keyboard, and finally, tune books for violin, flute, or keyboard. An item added to this instrumental group in Paris is positioned on the recto page opposite its class of violin "solos." As the like items were already in bindings, this added item was never bound in with other works and still exists today as a separate score, now missing its title page or any other form of identification.[11]

Before looking at the problematical long list on the penultimate recto page, it is worth pausing to stress the care and precision that went into this cataloguing effort. Not only in the general order, but in details as well, we come to trust Jefferson's annotations, the more we work with the cata-

Chap. 37   Instrumental.

✔. *Corelli's concertos in parts.*

✔. *Vivaldi's concertos in parts.*

✔. *12 Concertos chosen from the works of Vivaldi. 1ˢᵗ part.*

• *Vivaldi's Cuckow & Extravaganza.*

• *Hasse's grand Concerto.*

Pergolesi's overtures.

✔. *Handel's 60 overtures from all his Operas and Oratorios. 8. parts*

o ✔. *E. of Kelly's Overtures in 8. parts. Op. 1. [2ᵈ violin wanting]*

✔. *Arne's, Charke's Lampe's medley overtures in parts.*

• o ✔. *Abel's overtures in 8. parts. op. 1.*

✔. *Howard's Overtures in the amorous goddess. In parts.*

• ✔. *Corelli's Sonatas. 4 operas by Cooke. 4. parts.*

✔. *Corelli's Sonatas. op. 7ᵗʰ*

✔. *Lampugnani's Sonatas op. 1.* } *in 3. parts. 3. vols.*

✔. *Corelli's Sonatas. 4. operas*

✔. *Pasquali's 12 Sonatas in 2. sets.* } *in 4. vols.*

✔. *Humphries' Sonatas - - - - -*

• o ✔. *Corelli's 6 Sonatas. Op. 3   ✔ ✔ ✔*

✔. *Martini of Milan's Sonatas. Op. 1. 2. 3. 4.*

o ✔. *Abel Overtures Op. 1 in 3 parts*

✔. *Lampugnani's Sonatas.*

o ✔. *Giardini's 6. trios. op. 17.   ✔   ✔   ✔   ✔*

✔. *Campioni's Sonatas   Op 1. 2. 3. 4. 5. 6. 7.*

o ✔. *Humble's Sonatas   ✔ ✔*

✔. *Boccherini's Sonatas op. 2. 11.*

✔. *Gasparini's Sonatas.*

o ✔. *M. S. Sonatas by Kammel, Vanhall & Schwindel*

✔. *Campioni's 6. duets.*

o ✔. *Roeser's 6 duets. op. 2*

o ✔. *Godwin's 6 duets.*

✔. *Tessarini's duets. op. 2. - - - - -*

✔. *Bezozzi's duets.   ✔ ✔ ✔*

✔. *Martini of Milan's duets. op. 4. 7. 10.*

✔. *Battino's duets.* } *in 2 vols. folio.*

✔. *Figlio's nocturnals.*

✔. *Figlio's duets.*

✔. *Campioni's duets op. 8. ✔ ✔*

✔. *Degiardino's duets   op. 2. 13.*

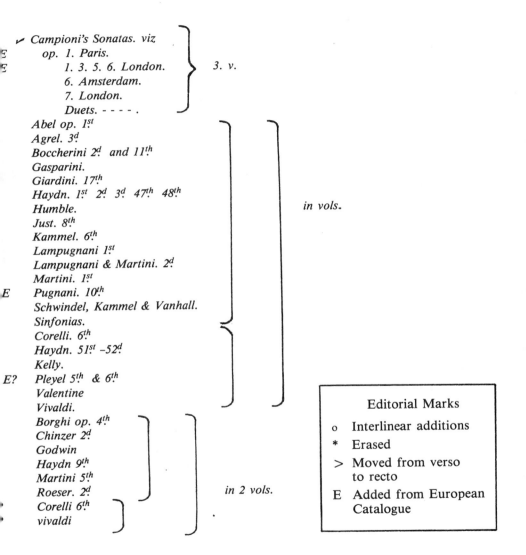

Campioni's Sonatas. viz
    op. 1. Paris.
      1. 3. 5. 6. London.
      6. Amsterdam.
      7. London.
      Duets. - - - - .
    3. v.

Abel op. 1st
Agrel. 3^d
Boccherini 2^d and 11th
Gasparini.
Giardini. 17th
Haydn. 1st 2^d 3^d 47th 48th
Humble.
Just. 8th
Kammel. 6th
Lampugnani 1st
Lampugnani & Martini. 2^d
Martini. 1st
Pugnani. 10th
Schwindel, Kammel & Vanhall.
Sinfonias.
Corelli. 6th
Haydn. 51st –52^d
Kelly.
Pleyel 5th & 6th
Valentine
Vivaldi.
    in vols.

Borghi op. 4th
Chinzer 2^d
Godwin
Haydn 9th
Martini 5th
Roeser. 2^d
Corelli 6th
vivaldi
    in 2 vols.

	Editorial Marks
o	Interlinear additions
*	Erased
>	Moved from verso to recto
E	Added from European Catalogue

logue. There are some minor slips such as a BLANK number of Vivaldi's volumes which Jefferson did not remember to supply. A large segment of the vocal chapter was at an unknown date bound into a single volume, but Jefferson did not indicate this by a brace added to his list, as he did elsewhere. Even this failure, however, reinforces his reliability. A brace added to the already ordered listing would have included items which were not in the newly bound volume but were only desiderata. Such an inexactitude must have gone against the grain of his orderly mind. Other problems or ambiguities generally result from factors outside the collection of which Jefferson could have had no knowledge—problems which face the modern scholar, such as variant issues of the same work.

The large listing on the penultimate recto page appears to have been added after the years in Paris, probably between 1790 and 1801. [See Illustration 2, a transcription in full of the penultimate opening.] As in other subjects in the catalogue, this verso page has become quite crowded by interlinear additions; yet it still does not include certain new works known to have been acquired. These are included in the "European catalogue," a long list of items procured while in Paris.[12] Jefferson's new acquisitions in these categories (full pieces, sonatas, and duets) could now only be added alongside on the recto page, as in other crowded chapters. However, before he came to do so, he had also decided to integrate these new works with others already listed on the verso and to make a new composite list. The only reasonable explanation for so doing is that he had decided to bind together both items from the original listing and the new acquisitions. The order of this new list departs from the original plan. Jefferson starts with his collection of Carl Antonio Campioni's music, a collection completed while in Paris. He was justifiably proud of this collection, having taken special pains with it. He then proceeds to other chamber works. Next, there are full pieces or "concertos," as he labels them, and, finally, more duets. Within each group the composers are listed in alphabetical order. It is hard to know why he did not retain his original order here. Again the only reasonable explanation for deviating from the established scheme is that he wished to reflect quite precisely the order planned for the bound volumes.

As the braces suggest [Illustration 2], the Campioni collection is indicated as bound separately from other sonatas or duets, in three volumes. The duets at the bottom of the list are in two. The chamber and full pieces are bracketed together, but again Jefferson neglected to fill in the number of volumes. This lacuna, the segregation of the Campioni, and other factors of the new listing also suggest that he was preparing the list for binding, but the volumes were not yet bound or at least not yet returned from the binder. If we believe Jefferson's annotations—and I am inclined to do so—all of the middle works, both sonatas and full pieces, were bound into a single set of instrumental parts (Violin I, Violin II, Viola, etc.). The first violin volume in such a case would be quite bulky, as would some others.

In 1801 Jefferson notated an order to John March, a Georgetown binder, for "1/2 Binding 17 vols. Demy folio Music Books letter'd &c."[13] It is tempting to believe that the order for binding refers to just this recto list, certainly the last major addition to the catalogue of music. As many of the items in the instrumental chapters were already bound together in 1783 or some time after and since Jefferson seems to have lost interest in vocal music, the connection of the binding with this particular page is especially attractive. In fact, I am convinced that the connection is valid, although proof could come only from rediscovery of one or more of the instrumental parts of the middle group. None of these volumes is now known to exist. There is one small challenge to this postulation. If we understand "Haydn 51-2," called both "sinfonias" and "concertos" in the list, to be the Paris symphonies, a minimum of thirteen volumes would be required to contain all of the instrumental parts, rather than the theoretical twelve now remaining (from the seventeen bound by March). However, the slight timpani part may have been bound and included by March as a "binder's doyen," or Jefferson could have had the timpani part tucked in loosely with the trumpet parts. Trumpet and timpani were often used together for a "military" effect. In other publications they are sometimes printed together in the same part.

In the transcription [Illustration 2] it is evident that some items of the new list were moved over from the verso, where they were usually then erased; others came from the "European catalogue." The remaining items, including all of Haydn, must have been transferred from another list of European purchases—perhaps including only music items—which is now lost.

The interpretation of Jefferson's music library that I hope to emend was set forth by Irving Lowens in a paper for the Haydn Conference, Washington, 1975. This study was followed by two published forms, the last as a monograph with full documentation.[14] Titled *Haydn in America*, the fuller study in general adds much to our understanding of music in the young republic. Lowens deals in some detail with the Jefferson matter, first with Jefferson's own library and second, with the family music extant in the Monticello collection. Lowens's prime revelation in the first category was that Jefferson himself owned no music of Haydn. While it is surprising that he arrived at that conclusion, there are several factors which may explain it.

Let us look once again at the problematical recto revision [Illustration 2]. Lowens must not have consulted the original manuscript catalogue, but a transcription in the published study by Cripe, where among other problems the arrangement and relationships in the original manuscript are not made clear.[15] Lowens, understanding this page to be like the other (i.e., verso) pages and subject to the same rules, points out that the Haydn items are left unchecked and are therefore only desiderata.[16] However, the check at the top, I believe, refers to the entire page. If one is not convinced on this point, there are still other supporting factors. We know that Jefferson had the Campioni items. We know that several items on the verso, items checked as owned, were moved over into this new list. Others known to have been purchased in Europe were added in as well. There is no question then that most items in the list were in Jefferson's library, yet they are recorded here *without* an individual check mark. Can we not assume that the pattern of check/unchecked simply was not relevant to Jefferson in this new list, and that all the items were owned, especially when he indicated all of them as bound together into volumes of instrumental parts?

Lowens does deal with the Haydn items listed, but as desiderata. "Jefferson wanted to acquire," Lowens tells us, "Haydn's 1st, 2nd, 3rd, 47th and 48th sonatas, his 51st and 52nd concertos, and his 9th duet." Lowens then throws in the towel with an exasperated parenthetical "whichever these may be." Although one can understand his frustration in identifying the listed items, the obstacle is mostly one of terminology—specifically the English terminology proper to the Virginia colony of Jefferson's youth. This terminology was, in fact, in the process of change during just that time, and Jefferson's years in Paris further confused the issue for him. It is not surprising then that Jefferson's nomenclature is ambiguous for the modern scholar.

In yet another place in his study Lowens tells us that an overture at the beginning of a program in early American concerts was only the *first* movement of a symphony. This he likely took from Oscar Sonneck. Sonneck advanced this theory in 1907, and it has been cropping up here and there for nearly eighty years.[17] But in England and in the parallel concert life of America, an "overture" was what we today call a symphony—in three or four movements. This did not mean that the leader of the band might not mutilate a work as expedient to his situation, but the term "overture" could as well represent a full symphony as it might a truncated one.

In Jefferson's catalogue, "sonata" represents string works for three or more instruments; this terminology would include string quartets. The contents of Haydn represented by the entries 1, 2, 3, 47, and 48 cannot be determined precisely because of variant issues in London, Paris, Vienna, and Amsterdam. But it certainly included Haydn's earliest string quartets, as well as some trios and the *Seven Last Words* in quartet arrangement. [In Illustration 3 the various possibilities are roughly sketched.] Next, the term "concerto" is used in the sense of "concerted," "for concerts," or "full piece," although Jefferson's Paris years are likely reflected by his use also of the term "sinfonias" to precede the identical grouping. In fact, the listing includes almost certainly Haydn's Paris symphonies of Op. 51-2, works which were the rage of Paris before Jefferson's departure. Only the duets in the last group are puzzling. There seems to be no trace of any duets opus (or number) "9." This item may be a publication of duets now lost — not that unusual — or a Parisian serial publication of Haydn's *Echo* as "9," also now lost.[18] In fact, the Godwin duets notated just above the Haydn listing are now also lost, but I have found advertising for them in catalogues of Samuel, Ann and Peter Thompson, London.

The misreading of this problematical recto page may be an understandable blunder, but Lowens carries it one step further and speculates that Jefferson's tastes ran toward the old-fashioned, transitional style of the 1760s. Certainly Jefferson's collecting slowed down after compiling the catalogue of 1783, but there also occurred after this time a burst of collecting while he was in Europe. The major support which Lowens claimed for his thesis is a carefully prepared thematic catalogue of the works of Campioni which Jefferson owned. The catalogue is still extant in the Monticello music. On these pages Jefferson indicated a desire to purchase additional string works of Campioni, and indeed he acquired three further collections while in Europe.[19] There can be no question that Jefferson was partial to Campioni's music, but one of the reasons for going to all this trouble must also have been the remarkable confusion — which has not been totally sorted out to this day — in the publication of Campioni's works in different cities of Europe.[20] Despite making this effort, Jefferson still had some duplication in his final collection.

Jefferson's period in Paris corresponded to the period of Haydn's greatest popularity there. Haydn's symphonies were performed at nearly every *concert spirituel* which Jefferson is known to have attended (as recorded in his account books). He likely heard Haydn's chamber music in the homes of the composer Krumpholz and other Parisian friends. Indeed, Jefferson did not leave the sound of Haydn's symphonies behind him in Paris, as they were popular in Philadelphia in the 1790s at Reinagle's concerts, to which Jefferson subscribed.[21]

On a more intuitive plane, it is hard to imagine that Jefferson would not be attracted to the orderliness, decorum, tunefulness, and wry humor of Haydn's instrumental style. According to my reading of the catalogue,

Illus. 3. Options for Haydn editions in Jefferson's library.

[Bracketed items with arrows indicate individual quartets or symphonies which *must* have been in the collection. Circled items with arrows are trios *likely* included.]

OP. "1" (all quartets)

PARIS   Chev/LeDuc = HOB III: | 1, 2, 3, 4, | 5, | 6 | (Trios)

↑↓

AMST.   Hummel = HOB II: 6; III: | 6, 1, 2, 3, 4 | (Quartets)

LONDON   Bremner = as Hummel
                Longman & Broderip = as Hummel

OP. "47"

VIENNA   Artaria   ⎫

LONDON   Longman ⎬
                                                       & Broderip ⎭

PARIS   Boyer Le Menu = HOB XV: 8, 6, 7
             (Strong trios arranged)

             Sieber = HOB XV: 9, 2, 10
             (keyboard trios)

OP. "2"

Chev/LeDuc = HOB V: F1, 19, D2, 18, 15, 16 (Quartets)

Hummel = HOB III: 7, 8, 9, 10, 11, 12 (St. trios)

Bremner = as Hummel

(KB trios)

OP. "3"

Chev/LeDuc = HOB II: 21, F5, 22

III: 10, 7, 8

Hummel = HOB V: F1, 19, D2, 18, 15, 16

Longman & Lukey = as Hummel

Bremner = HOB XV: 37, C1; XIV: 6; XV: 39, 1; XIV: 1

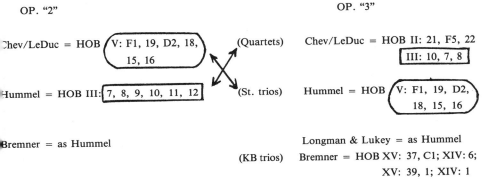

OP. "48"

quartet arrangement
7 Last Words
HOB XX-B

OP. "51–52"

Artaria 51 = HOB I: 82, 83, 84 ⎫ "Paris"
Artaria 52 = HOB I: 85, 86, 87 ⎭ Symphonies
Longman & Broderip = ↕ as Artaria
OR (unlikely)
Imbault 51 = HOB I: 83, 87, 85, 82, 86, 84
PLUS
Sieber 52 = HOB XX-A (7 Last Words for Orchestra)

Jefferson did indeed follow up the auditions of Haydn's music by seeking out and purchasing eight collections. Haydn then stands as Jefferson's second favorite composer, after Campioni, represented by ten collections.

One final point in Lowens's study which needs modification has to do with Haydn works now in the Monticello music, mostly keyboard reductions of symphonies. These pieces, Lowens claims, reflect not Jefferson's taste but that of the Frenchman Claude-Bénigne Balbastre, who taught harpsichord to the daughters while Jefferson was in Paris. In one extant volume, some of the pieces can be dated in the 1790s or just before; the binding of the volume has "Miss Jefferson" embossed on the cover.[22] As daughter Martha became Mrs. Randolph soon after the family returned from Paris in 1789, the volume must have belonged to Maria, the ill-fated younger daughter, who continued her musical studies in Philadelphia for a time. A second extant volume with Haydn transcriptions is bound but lacking the cover. Publication dates for some items in the volume of 1791 and 1792 suggest that it, too, belonged to Maria.[23] So the Haydn in the Monticello collection mostly reflects, not the instruction of Balbastre in Paris, but rather music available in Philadelphia in the 1790s and chosen for Maria by her father, or more likely, her teacher, J. C. Moller. The matter is, in fact, much more interesting as an indication of music-making in the young capital and for a study of "Haydn in America."

In conclusion, I am not trying to vindicate Jefferson. I do not presume that Jefferson's intellectual reputation would be severely blemished by any proven indifference to Haydn. But I do believe Lowens's premises to be patently false and hope only to set the record straight. It is not a matter of having to read between the lines of available sources, but one of approaching this documentation with appropriate confidence in Jefferson's bibliographical reliability.

NOTES

1 The account books, scattered among several repositories, are being prepared for publication in *The Papers of Thomas Jefferson*, Princeton University Press, edited by James A. Baer, Jr. and Lucia C. Stanton.

2 One of the more informative treatments is the chapter titled "The Musical Side of our first Presidents" in Oscar G. Sonneck, *Suum Cuique: Essays in Music* (New York: G. Schirmer, 1916).

3 Helen Cripe, *Thomas Jefferson and Music* (Charlottesville: University of Virginia Press, 1974). For additional bibliography on the subject of Jefferson and music consult this monograph.

4 E. Millicent Sowerby, *Catalogue of the Library of Thomas Jefferson* (Washington, D. C.: U. S. Government Printing Office, 1955; reprint, University of Virginia Press, 1983).

5 The manuscript volume is at the Massachusetts Historical Society, Boston. At the front of his catalogue Jefferson wrote the date "Mar. 6, 1783" and the number of volumes (2640) in his library on that date.

6 The copy of the 1812 catalogue, apparently in the hand of Nicholas Trist, is now in the Rare Book Room, Library of Congress. It will eventually be published by the Library of Congress, edited by Douglas L. Wilson and James Gilreath. For additional details on this document consult Douglas L. Wilson, "Sowerby Revisted: The Unfinished Catalogue of Thomas Jefferson's Library," *William and Mary Quarterly*, 41 (1984):615–28.

7 The Monticello music collection consists of various volumes deposited in the Manuscripts Division, Alderman Library, the University of Virginia; one large volume in the McGregor Rare Book Collection, also University of Virginia; and a few items at the Curator's Office, Monticello. Volumes which actually belonged in Jefferson's private library and are documented in the 1783 catalogue are found in the first two repositories.

8 While the precise progression varies, the principle of larger to smaller in instrumental lists is generally followed. This order can be found, among others, in the catalogues of both Robert Bremner and Peter Welcker; works published by both these London merchants can be traced in Jefferson's collection. Characteristically Jefferson made subtle changes to suit his own holdings and the guiding plan which he had set out for the catalogue.

9 The item purchased in Europe, Esteban Arteaga's *Rivoluzioni del teatro musicale Italiana*, was inserted near the top of the blank recto page. Jefferson's concept of "music theory" was, of course, much broader than the common usage today.

10 It is worth noting that the single Italian opera was Niccolo Piccini's *La buona figliuola*, based loosely on Richardson's *Pamela*. The publisher Robert Bremner undertook ca. 1770 to publish the opera in its entirety—an exceptional effort at that time. Jefferson was ever attracted to the curious and remarkable; I suspect that it was just this "complete" score which Jefferson proudly positioned at the head of the list of vocal music.

11 The untitled Pugnani score proved elusive at first, as it is in a relatively new format—a score for violin and "bass" (i.e., violoncello) without the usual figures in the bass. It appears very much like keyboard music and could indeed be played so, or by keyboard with a violin, the melody then being doubled. The writer made the identification in the course of investigating every title listed in Jefferson's catalogue.

12 The manuscript known as the "European Catalogue" is also at the Massachussetts Historical Society, Boston.

13 The item is in a list at the Huntington Library, San Marino, California (Catalogue # 5721). The binding described, although not distinctive, matches several of the extant volumes from Jefferson's library in the Monticello music. It is safe to assume that, at least in his mature years, this was his preferred binding for musical scores.

14 Irving Lowens, *Haydn in America with* [Otto E. Albrecht] *Haydn Autographs in the United States* (Bibliographies in American Music Number 5: Detroit, 1979). Unfortunately, much of the material on Jefferson was promulgated in the major review article by Jens Peter Larson, in *American Music* 2 (1984): 82.

15 Cripe, Appendix I.

16 Lowens, 19.

17 Oscar G. Sonneck, *Early Concert Life in America (1731–1800)* (Leipzig: Breit-kopf and Härtel, 1907; reprint, New York: Da Capo Press, 1978), 91.

18 One or possibly two sets of duets published by Gardom in London are lost. The *Echo* was issued in the series *Journal de violon* published by Porro in Paris. While a copy of the issue has not surfaced, a duet reduction is suggested by Porro's subsequent publication of duet arrangements of Haydn's *Echo*, independent of the *Journal*.

19 In Monticello music (University of Virginia, Alderman Library, Manuscripts Division) Acc. No. 3177, Box 6, Folder 34.

20 The Campioni list in the International Inventory of Musical Sources (RISM) is full of errors. Basically the problem revolves around the use of the same opus number for quite different works in Paris, London, and Amsterdam. Ironically Jefferson's carefully prepared thematic catalogue has provided a base from which to sort out the confusion — yet another (and unsuspected) contribution to the intellectual life in America!

21 Purchase of a subscription is noted in his account book in 1792 (see fn. 1). It is not known, however, which concerts he was able to attend. A favorite Haydn symphony was the "Queen of France" which, nevertheless, appears to have been dropped after Marie-Antoinette lost her head! (If played, the symphony was no longer so identified on programs). Cf. Sonneck, *Early Concert Life*, 87–96.

22 Monticello music (University of Virginia, Alderman Library, Manuscript Division): Acc. No. 3177, Box 5, Folder 24. The second volume containing Haydn transcriptions is Folder 12.

23 After Maria Jefferson's death in 1804 her harpsichord and music were stored in a cellar. Later these were offered to the music-loving family at Monticello, and the harpsichord was taken to Poplar Forest. The music eventually reentered the collection at Monticello. Some of the volumes in the extant Monticello music show stains from moisture damage, but aside from the two volumes containing the Haydn pieces, it is not altogether clear which items were Maria's.

24 Numerical identification are those of Anthony von Hoboken, *Joseph Haydn: Thematisch-bibliographisches Werkverzeichnis* (Mainz: Schott Söhne, 1957–   ).

The Enlightenment: What and Who?

LESTER G. CROCKER

The problem of interpreting the Enlightenment as a movement can serve as a classic example of the saw, "every man has his own history." When we compare the major interpretive works—those of Tocqueville, Taine, Mornet, Hazard, Becker, Frankel, Cassirer, Diaz, Ehrard, Cobban, Gay, Gusdorf, Venturi, Voegelin, Horkheimer and Adorno, and (if I may) my own—it is obvious that they add up to discord. We cannot put them together, even eclectically, and emerge with some general or unified result. Each historian is observing the same phenomenon and seeing different things. We cannot easily separate meaningful facts from the context of the mind that observes them. All sensation undergoes interpretation, and nowhere more so than in historiography.

It is not my purpose to examine and evaluate the above-mentioned studies, to specify their merits and shortcomings, both of which may be attributed to all of them. It is rather to discuss some basic or elementary problems of historiography which they make manifest by their vast divergences and which deserve careful scrutiny. As in mathematics, elementary problems are often the most difficult ones, sometimes indeed unsolvable. I should like, then, to inquire into two such problems and to propose some tentative, not final answers. One is the meaning of the word "Enlightenment" itself and how we should go about finding that meaning. To put it differently, who were the men of the Enlightenment? The second problem, on which I shall touch only briefly, is the influence and value of the historical movement the word denotes.

The first problem divides into two questions.

The first of these concerns the problem of defining the Enlightenment. "Enlightenment thought" and "eighteenth-century thought" are clearly not coextensive or covalent terms, or even chronologically coterminous.[1] Whatever broad segment of the latter one may choose to define, "Enlightenment" presents so many diversities, contradictions and conflicts that no definition appears adequate or completely valid; all involve arbitrary exclusions and inclusions that defy definition.[2]

For some reason, a compulsion to define has been an attribute of British and American scholars particularly. Gay, in the Preface to his second volume, announces that it "completes my attempt at defining the Enlightenment."[3] His definition may be summarized by his titles: "The Rise of Modern Paganism" and "The Science of Freedom." (I confess that I have never been able to attribute a meaning to the latter phrase.) Cobban is substantially close to Gay's second title. Franklin Ford, obviously vexed by the problem, has attempted a "Useful Redefinition," consisting of five items.[4]

Definitions are hard to maintain, especially in the writing of history, and we find "definitional" writers overflowing their definitions or straining to live within them. D'Alembert and Buffon had warned against definitions. As D'Alembert said, they do not explain the character of things as they are, but only enumerate "des idées simples renfermées dans la notion que nous formons de ces êtres."[5] According to Buffon, definitions are "imperfect representations," because they do not exhaust the phenomena or account for gradations. True knowlege, he says, cannot come from such arbitrary conventions, but only from descriptions.[6] Hegel later wrote, "Definitions should be stated in universal terms, while to use them immediately exposes in all its nakedness what contradicts them."[7] Definitions impose a restrictive order on phenomena, one with which historical reality usually does not coincide. History is recalcitrant to Linnaean classifications and clear distinctions that are satisfying because they help us to think. A certain stubbornness of the facts remains. We may apply to definitional approaches what Lawrence Stone says of "unilinear theories" of history: they ignore "the lack of uniformity of the directions of the trends," the failures of the various trends "to synchronize in the way they ought if the definition is to fit." They "reduce the enormous diversity . . . to a conformity which has never existed in real life."[8]

However, while we may not be able to *define* Enlightenment adequately, any more than Renaissance and Romanticism, we can, as Buffon suggested, *describe* them. Description displays, analyzes and organizes the phenomena—no more. About Romanticism, for instance, Hans Eichner has written that any definition that could encompass its diversity, its complicated and confused history, must be so broad as to be meaningless.

If we are to understand the phenomena, the proper question, according to Eichner, "is not, What is romanticism?" but, "What happened in the intellectual life of Europe in the period we now call Romantic?"[9] Not what it was, but what it did. This opinion is equally applicable to the Enlightenment, whether we call it a movement (as I do) or a period. In a description, the selected phenomena neither obey nor dictate categorical principles of inclusion or exclusion; they are only characteristic, and permit the flexibilities, shadings and contradictions that history requires and that definitions do not easily tolerate. Unlike the definitional approach, the descriptive is guided by the phenomena themselves and accepts the fact that the conceptual order that is reached may not be as convenient or decisive as we should wish it to be.

I should like to make these general observations more specific. A definition tells us what something *is*; in Scholastic terms, its essence or substance. A description, as I have said, displays the phenomena.

Question: define "liberty" in Enlightenment thought. Answers: (1) "Liberty is doing or being able to do what you want to do" — for your happiness, pleasure, self-realization (the radicals). (2) "Liberty is doing willingly what you ought to do" (Rousseau, Kant). (3) "Liberty is obedience to law" (Montesquieu, Voltaire, also Rousseau, who assumes that law and ought coincide in a true society). It is obvious that the three propositions conflict and are at least potentially contrary. What you want to do may not be what you ought to do. What you ought to do may not be what you want to do. To obey the law may be neither what you want to do nor what you ought to do. It is also obvious, then, that definitions are (by definition) exclusionary modes of thinking or of conceiving phenomena, historical or other. To define is to confine.

On the other hand, if one were to give a historical *description* of the notion, "liberty" in the Enlightenment, it would include *all three* and thus accurately account for the phenomena.

Question: define Enlightenment political thought. (1) It is "the science of freedom," or "modern liberal politics" (Gay). (2) It is the science of totalitarianism, or behavioral control (Voegelin). The definitions are exclusive of each other. Both deform the historical reality. A *description* of Enlightenment political thought would include both, and also what lay in between (enlightened despotism) and beyond (anarchism).

The second question, Who were the men of the Enlightenment? presents the concrete instance enclosed within the first. Is it correct to identify the two words, "Enlightenment" and *"philosophes"*? While some historians (Cassirer, Hazard, Ehrard, Gusdorf and I) refuse to make such an identification, others have done so, explicitly or implicitly. Gay, for instance, refers repeatedly and rather vaguely to "the little flock," and others make no distinction. This is to create artificial obstacles to a faithful historical account. Why, for instance, admit Shaftesbury and Lessing to the pantheon, as Gay does, and close the door on Morelly, La Mettrie and Dupont de Nemours? Franklin Ford, in his quest for a definition, is led to exclude other writers—Hume, Gibbon, and Adam Smith—to admit Walpole with reservations, but to include Priestley, Bentham and Godwin. No doubt Cobban and John Lough would have still different lists.

Suppose I were asked by you to draw up my list of who were men of the Enlightenment. I should be reluctant to undertake something so inherently difficult and elusive. If I had to, my list would be different from the ones I have mentioned (which differ among themselves). Those lists are based, with inevitable incongruities and inconsistencies (since no definition, as we saw, can account for the phenomena in a historical situation), on *what* the writers they choose to include—corresponding to a prior definition—thought; or on *some* of what they thought when, as these historians admit, some of it doesn't fit. My list would be based on *how* they thought; namely, on the use of emancipated critical reason, not on the particular, often contradictory conclusions to which their search for truth led them. In other words, since a description displays the phenomena, there would be no exclusions (as in the above definitions) based on philosophical positions reached by emancipated minds. Voltaire the deist, Diderot the atheist, Rousseau the pre-totalitarian, and yes, Sade the anarchist—all would be part of the historical reality we call the Enlightenment. All were using their emancipated reason to find new and better ways of conceiving the world and the world of men.

An objection possibly arises. Voegelin writes: "At last the right has been recognized to use one's reason as the sole criterion of truth."[10] Can this be a definition of the Enlightenment? I do not think so. If it is a definition at all, it is of method or attitude, not of the thing ("Enlightenment") itself, its content or substance, ideas, intentions, meanings. How one thinks is not what one thinks. The method is part of a description; but no one could write a history or interpretation of Enlightenment except on the basis of the diverse products of the method—the substance. These overflow any definition and can only be described, then analyzed and evaluated, if we are to see them in their complex, interacting reality.

Few historians evince a clear idea of the problem I have been discussing. It troubles Furio Diaz, but he refers to it only briefly.[11] At one point (215–16) he is disquieted because the philosophes, for whom religion was the focus of their attacks on the established order, excluded the marquis de Mirabeau from their *confrérie* (a necessary and justified consequence of their attitude). And yet, as Diaz points out, Mirabeau's economic theories were a significant contribution to new ways of thinking and an important impulsion to the reforms they wanted. The problem is even more acute when one considers the Physiocrats as a group, since the *philosophes* adopted many of their ideas, at least for a time, and claimed Turgot (who was associated with the "economists") as one of their own—though he was not anti-clerical or anti-religious.

Not unexpectedly, Diaz finds the question of Rousseau still more vexing. Rousseau was the Judas, a deserter and an enemy. Yet the *philosophes* could not help admiring his *Profession de foi*; and in contrast to what Diaz calls their "perplexities, weaknesses, and incoherences" in political thought, he set forth a coherent, revolutionary political theory in opposition to the existing order (264). Or again, we may take the case of La Beaumelle, scorned and rejected by the *confrérie*, especially by Voltaire. Yet La Beaumelle was the first to tie the pleas for religious toleration, which he made in tones as stirring as any *philosophe*, to an equally eloquent demand for political and civil liberties.[12] On the other side, we may well inquire to what extent Grimm was a *philosophe*. While present at the heart of the movement, he defined the only legitimate right as that of the strong, and defended monasticism; ten years later, Diderot was to realize that he, like Rousseau, had betrayed the cause.

Other cases could of course be cited, notably La Mettrie, whose influence on the political and ethical as well as scientific speculation of the materialists was profound though unacknowledged, and Mably— both of whom are excluded by the definitionists. No one has considered Dom Deschamps a *philosophe* (he was not), and few interpretations consider him as part of the Enlightenment. And yet, as Baczko has recently written, "L'oeuvre de Dom Deschamps ne doit plus être considérée comme un phénomène plus ou moins marginal pour l'interprétation des Lumières ... l'oeuvre de Dom Deschamps se voit déplacée de la périphérie à son centre."[13]

Sade, as we have seen, has been read out of the Enlightenment by a number of historians, notably by Gay, who sees him as "a caricature of the Enlightenment." (It is significant that Gay also calls Condorcet "a caricature of the Enlightenment.") Gusdorf, contrariwise, replaced Sade within the Enlightenment, in a stream that coexisted with the utilitarian, the naturalizing of the human domain, the intellectualist reductionism. Horkheimer and Adorno argue that Sade "mercilessly elicited the implications of the Enlightenment."[14] And Norman Hampson declares that "Sade's principles were already familiar to the writers of the previous generation."[15] In looking to the future as well as to the age I was treating, I may have gone too far in my emphasis on Sade. Yet the case of Sade illustrates the problem of trying to "define" the Enlightenment and of including or excluding writers in accordance with the definition. Gay himself comments that beneath reason the *philosophes* glimpsed a large undiscovered country, strange and terrifying. But he lets it go at that. His observation that the *philosophes* called for a disenchanted universe and an end to myth is acute. But as Sade illustrates, such a process could not be halted at a desired limit-point (one that would protect their own myths). In at least a few original minds, including Diderot's, it extended to a radical questioning of the bases of culture. We see that the definitional approach involves the danger of becoming a distorting application of a partly true, partly false preconception.

In other countries, too, many who were not *philosophes* and frequently did not share their intense, at times fanatical attitude toward religion, contributed to new modes of thought in every domain. The fact that Enlightenment was essentially, though by no means entirely anti-Christian in France does not mean that it had to be, or that it was so in other countries. It covers a spectrum from atheism to liberal Christianity. What does this signify, if not that religion itself, *qua* religion, was not the core of the Enlightenment? That core was embodied in the literal meaning of the word. Where Christianity's form and practice were inimical to the free search for "light," an obstacle to the goals of enhancing life and improving man and society, there rage against it waxed strong. Elsewhere, especially in Protestant countries, their coexistence, whether or not justifiable in terms of rigorous logic, was a fact, a comfortable *modus vivendi*. Even deists, who are always accepted as qualifying for the title of *philosophes*, were not entirely secular in their thinking, since to some extent they accepted supernatural explanations, a cosmos suffused by the Creator with value and even a "general providence." Frank Manuel has argued that it is possible to speak meaningfully of "the Christian deists."[16] Voltaire, Condillac, Rousseau, Turgot, many others, explained the natural order as ultimately connected with a rational divinity and consequently construed it as an order of final causes. For many "enlightened" men the function of deism was to preserve order and purpose in the universe, thus providing a sure ground for moral valuation.

The identification of "Enlightenment" with *philosophes*, even if we limit ourselves to France, therefore breaks down at every point. They were its most prominent and dynamic element, but it overflows them. Long ago, Lanson showed that the *esprit philosophique* was by no means their invention or monopoly. Margaret C. Jacob's *The Radical Enlightenment* (London, 1981) has reinforced and broadened that conclusion. The *esprit philosophique* was the sum of its multiple components, a cultural development of wider dimensions than is sometimes recognized. From false rules of classification engendered from such an identification derives the chaos of inclusion and exclusion.

It is possible to suggest a more accurate principle of classification that may serve as an aid to interpretation, a principle based not on subjective conceptualizations, but on an analysis of the data relating to the forces engaged in contention, whether as groups or as unassociated individuals.

The movement we are considering, with its imprecise beginning and ending, is characterized by a conflict between two large, inchoate groups. The one includes all those who groped for new ways of "thinking the world," based on the free play of critical reason and scientific progress. It must be kept in mind, however, that not every inquiring mind broke with the inherited *Weltanschauung* to an equal extent or in the same way. Thus in France and in the American colonies, but necessarily in every country, such a "rethinking" involved political and social changes or reforms, presaging revolution, but even there of varying degree and kind.[17]

The Enlightenment may be described, then, as a diverse intellectual movement whose general direction was to use free, critical reason, untrammeled (as far as one was consciously aware) by authority and tradition, in order to understand the universe, man's place in it, human nature and interaction, to improve the economic and political institutions of society and the conduct of individuals, to understand the proper uses of power and the proper relations between individuals and the community or state; and by so doing, to enhance human happiness and the quality of life. This description allows for the latitude that the diversity of historical facts necessitates. It does not stipulate conditions or doctrines, only a nebulous goal. It does not mean that critical reason could not justify authority and tradition after proper examination.

In France the situation was quite special, because of a widespread conviction that it was necessary first to *free* reason, and that existing authority and traditions were obscurantist, oppressive and intolerant. In Britain this was largely not the case, though dissenters and radicals agitated for greater power for the meritorious middle class. Nor was it the case in Germany, and only in a special sense in America. Therefore the most significant segment of the French Enlightenment, the *philosophes*, were aggressive in their aims and often radical in their theoretical conclusions and models. It is in France that we witness the birth of the malaise of alienation and a perception of what we now call the Absurd, as a feeling or even as a concept. Traces exist, to be sure, in other times and climes (e.g., John Gay in England). This experience, on the whole new for the modern world, led to another feeling or idea, that the individual is free to deny limit, to find authenticity by refusing what was taken to be the myths, illusions, frauds, and tyrannies of culture. However limited this phenomenon may have been, it was recognized in its own time and influenced later times. It was expressed in philosophical and novelistic forms; but an important part of the efforts of the *philosophes* was an explicit or implicit defense, on the political and moral fronts, of the validity of social norms — despite their "radicalism" — a defense that exhibits many configurations, including proposals for better or for new societies. It put them in an uncomfortable position. They, too, were myth-destroyers; but as I have suggested, they usually wanted to call a halt on this side of danger. This fact explains much: their compromises, sometimes intellectually dishonest; their loud aversion to La Mettrie, with whose brush they did not want to be spattered because that could too easily be done; and their political ineffectiveness, as Diaz has shown.

On the opposite side of the playing-field stood the traditionalists, those who resisted changing the old ways of "thinking the world." The "old ways" were usually Christian, but not necessarily coincidental with the institutional bounds of Christianity or circumscribed by it, even as the innovators were often but not necessarily anti-Christian or naturalistic. The traditionalists were not only the churchmen, but their allies, the court, the Parlements, much of the so-called "bourgeoisie" — people like Barbier, Hénault, Mme du Deffand, supporters of the inherited status quo in political and intellectual realms, those who feared novelty and change. They vented their strident polemics and used their power in all these fields.

The innovators, in turn, were not a block, but comprised at least two major components. In France, and in France alone (leaving aside the early Anglo-Dutch-Huguenot radical group described by Margaret Jacob), a number of important thinkers formed, for their contemporaries as well as for later history, a *confrérie* called *philosophes*. They felt themselves united (however disunited they were in most other respects) in a common struggle against a particular repressive régime which they wished to reform, not overthrow, and chose as its epitome the Church, whose power and doctrine, as the impediment to progress, had to be destroyed. Both Diderot and Rousseau foresaw the possibility of a revolution, but were not seriously preoccupied with it. The *philosophes*, wedded by a network of personal and professional interests to the régime, were not interested in bringing about an upheaval.[18] On the other hand, it can be argued that they were revolutionaries after all, *sans le savoir*, since in the existing institutional situation, with its system of vested interests, the reforms and changes in public attitudes they sought were not in point of fact realizable except through revolution, because they compromised the positions of those who possessed power — the ultimate source and intrinsic nature of all political structures; and further, because their writings helped to fashion a state of mind which, when circumstances reached a critical point, revolution became thinkable and, even more, conceptualized in a variety of shapes.

To achieve their goals, the *philosophes* mounted what was to some degree (an insufficient degree, Diaz shows) a concerted campaign. They were a spearhead, though non-*philosophes* like the curé Meslier and the Benedictine Dom Deschamps were even more radical, as was a Linguet on the other side. However, a vast area of the Enlightenment was peopled, in France as in other countries, by non-*philosophes*, men who supported progress and reform, who explored modern approaches to the eternal problems of morals, politics, aesthetics and economics. They, too, opposed repression by Church or state and advocated freedom of inquiry. Turgot, Jefferson, Price, Morelly, Paine, Adam Smith, and many others, including the Physiocratic group in general, were both enlightened men and men of the Enlightenment, but they were not *philosophes*.

Perhaps we can better understand who were "enlightened" men by describing those who were "unenlightened." The "unenlightened" accepted Scripture and dogma uncritically, believed in personal providence through supernatural intervention, and held to the authority of the magistrate, prince or state as superior to reason. The "enlightened" believed that men have the power, right, and exclusive privilege to forge their destiny, with whatever God or nature has provided them.

Yet even this principle of classification, like all classifications, has its inadequacies. To be sure, it would put an end to some long-standing and futile discussions, such as whether there was an Enlightenment in England or whether Buffon and Rousseau were *philosophes*. It would end the chaos we find in some histories concerning who belongs to the Enlightenment and/or its supposed equivalent, the group called *philosophes*. However, if it simplifies our problems it does not dissipate them. There were those, and they were not few who, like the economist Mirabeau, belonged to the Enlightenment in some ways and not in others. And there remains the problem of how to designate the members of the group or sub-group called *philosophes*. The simplest way to go about it would be to apply that term to the writers working around Voltaire at one end of an axis and Diderot-d'Holbach at the other. Although opposed to each other in important respects, and destined ultimately to split, they did work together, against religion and church, for toleration and freedom of thought, and for a role in political decisions. Their political action, it must be added, was quite different at each end of the axis in conception and effect.

Outside this axis of *philosophes*, thus rather narrowly but specifically designated, were many others, as I have said, who, spanning the spectrum from liberal Christianity to naturalism and atheism, from moralism to immoralism, preached and practiced the freedom of the mind to seek new explanations for speculative problems and new solutions to practical ones. They, too, were men of the Enlightenment, though sometimes they stood apart and might not have publicly accepted the title of *philosophes*.

This is not as neat as one would like; but perhaps it is more faithful to the realities of the past. At least it displays a problem which, for lack of recognition, has led to some confusion in historical writing. Montesquieu stressed the social necessity of religious institutions. Condillac was a non-subversive, liberal Christian, yet all accept his having played a key role in the Enlightenment. Was he a *philosophe* (he has been called "le philosophe des *philosophes*"), or an "enlightened Christian"—a phrase which itself, according to some "definitions," would be an oxymoron? What about Maupertuis? He was a committed Christian, but his writing came through with the color of deism or pantheism. He was not subversive, but he had an impact on subversive speculation. Surely, one would not classify such Christians with Bergier, Le Franc de Pompignan, and Nonnotte.

I would not deny that other modes of descriptive classification may be equally valid. It is possible, for instance, to divide the pro-Enlightenment forces in France into six groups: (1) the precursors (Bayle, Fontenelle, writers of clandestine manuscripts, etc.); (2) the first combatants to attempt an organization—the côterie of Boulvainvilliers, Dumarsais, Mirabaud, Fréret (largely in the 1730s); (3) "les solitaires": Montesquieu, Maupertuis, Buffon, La Mettrie, Morelly, Rousseau, Mably, etc.; (4) the Physiocrats, and Turgot; (5) "le parti philosophique," with its two axes or sub-groups; (6) the post-Enlightenment: Robert Darnton's "les ratés" (Brissot, Marat, etc.) and the Ideologues.

Coherence lay in the problems of the day, in the peculiar combination of rationalist and empirical methodology, in the objective of reforms and applications, or new ways of thought. In results, theories, proposals, there was relatively little coherence, when we view the scene as a whole, though to be sure, areas of agreement (religious toleration, abolition of judical torture) are easily found. The eighteenth century knew the fragility of classifications. They are based on consistency, either seeking it or imposing it. But the materials are more often than not rebellious, and almost always so when they are the work of human beings. Can we expect them to be consistent, and to lend themselves to our retrospective constructs? If the historian is to hold up a mirror to the past, as its loyal interpreter, he must not fear the complexities of which history is composed. The process of "ordering" the past can go only so far, never as far as we should like.

I have suggested that from the broader historical viewpoint the Enlightenment itself, strictly speaking, denotes not a "period concept" (to use a fashionable phrase), but a concept that is pertinent to a period which contained much else, contemporaneous and lasting. No historian has displayed this better than Gusdorf, though one may object to his personal slant. Samuel Johnson was perhaps the major influence in the English world of letters. The on-going argument as to whether or not he belongs in the Enlightenment is not fruitful. We recognize this if we recognize that the eighteenth century, like others, was a whole with inconsistent, conflicting and interacting parts. Nevertheless, the Enlightenment was so dominant a force, and from the lasting perspective of history so dominant, that it is doubtless admissible to use the period label, provided we understand it to have a limited heuristic value.

The second major problem—evaluation of the lasting import and influence of the Enlightenment—remains pretty much in limbo, at least as a subject of objective investigation, except for individual figures like Hegel and Stendhal. Such an investigation is scarcely possible when there is no consensus as to what Enlightenment means in historical terms. In fact, many have condemned or exalted very different images of it, or in some instances have denounced it without having a clear conception of it. Judgment has all too often stemmed from obvious prejudices, from intellectual *parti pris*, and emotional commitment. This is particularly true of those who vilified the Enlightenment in the nineteenth century, identifying it with the hated *philosophes*; but it is also true of some twentieth-century historians who have written as its apologists or bitter enemies. Some of the interpreters I have mentioned have judged it to have been a failure, some a success, others are not sure. Such judgments are, again, fruitless, or at least premature. Sound historiography does require an estimate of the influence and effects of the Enlightenment, so that its role in history can be interpreted, its relation to what came before and after it evaluated. It shuns approbation or disapprobation stemming from what in the eighteenth century would have been called "enthusiasms." It admits that Enlightenment had its light and its shadows, and does not banish "the dark side" as foreign to it. To mask one wing of a building is to destroy the architecture of the whole. I should argue—though some would disagree—that the historian who plays the role of attorney for the defense or the prosecution betrays his proper function as soon as he steps beyond the most objective judgment he can muster in the face of *all* the evidence.

Interpretation is the heart of historiography because we want human experience to make sense. The way each present sees its past is itself a part of history. No completely satisfactory account of the Enlightenment has been written. Probably it never will be; the openness of the past to the future frustrates the enterprise. Our inquiry has underscored an old lesson, that the interpretation of history, like history itself, is a living process, constantly renewing itself. Without that, the past would truly be dead; but it is not. History is not only the past; it is part of the thinker's present. Coleridge said that the historian's task is to "keep the past alive, in the present, for the future."

NOTES

1 "L'Europe des Lumières . . . ne représente qu'une appellation partielle sélectionnant certains aspects du devenir global." Georges Gusdorf, "L'Europe protestante," *Dix-huitième siècle* 17 (Paris, 1985).

2 A criticism of the definitional method was previously adumbrated by J. H. Brumfitt in his excellent *The French Enlightenment* (Cambridge, Mass., 1973), 12–13.

3 Peter Gay, *The Enlightenment: an Interpretation*, vol. II, *The Science of Freedom* (New York: Knopf., 1969), ix.

4 F. L. Ford, "The Enlightenment: Towards a Useful Redefinition," *Studies in the Eighteenth Century*, ed. Robert Brissenden (Toronto: University of Toronto Press, 1968), 17–29.

5 *Eléments de philosophie*, ed. R. N. Schwab (Hildesheim: G. Olms, 1965), 36.

6 *Oeuvres philosophiques*, ed. Jean Piveteau (Paris: Presses universitaires de France, 1954), 10–11, 14.

7 *Philosophy of Right*, tr. T. M. Knox (Oxford: Oxford Univ. Press, 1967), 14–15.

8 *The Family, Sex and Marriage in England 1550–1800* (New York: Harper, 1979), 416.

9 "The Rise of Modern Science and the Genesis of Romanticism," *PMLA* 97 (1982): 8.

10 *From Enlightenment to Revolution* (Durham, N.C.: Duke Univ. Press, 1975), 126.

11 *Filosofia e politica nel settesento francese* (Torino: Einaudi, 1962).

12 *L'Asiatique tolérant* (Amsterdam: Rey, 1748).

13 Bronislaw Baczko, review of André Robinet, *Dom Deschamps* (Paris: Seghers, 1974), in *RHLF* 75 (1975): 272.

14 *Dialectic of Enlightenment* (New York: Herder & Herder, 1972), xvi and Excursus II.

15 *The Enlightenment* (London: Penguin Books, 1977), 123.

16 *The Eighteenth Century Confronts the Gods* (Cambridge, Mass.: Harvard Univ. Press, 1959), 63.

17 It is well known that the French corpus contains works that describe socialist or communist types of society, but these are excluded by definitionist historians, who also resist totalitarian-type constructs as part of the Enlightenment. Some even consider Rousseau, strangely, as a precursor of liberal democracy. Hampson, a more "enlightened" historian, writes: "The escape from moral anar-

chy was already beginning to point towards a new totalitarian nightmare" (124). For the American experience, see *inter alia* Henry May, *The Enlightenment in America* (New York: Oxford Univ. Press, 1976), and D. H. Meyer, *The Democratic Enlightenment* (New York: Putnam, 1976).

18 See Charles Kors, *D'Holbach's Coterie* (Princeton: Princeton Univ. Press, 1976).

Contributors

REED BENHAMOU, whose paper was given at the ASECS meeting, teaches interior design at Indiana University. She is currently working on art and design education in eighteenth-century France.

CAROL BLUM's paper was presented at the NEASECS meeting in the fall of 1985. She is Professor of French at the State University of New York at Stony Brook. Her most recent book is *Rousseau and the Republic of Virtue* (1986).

JOHN L. BULLION, whose paper was presented at the meeting of ECASECS, is Associate Professor of History at the University of Missouri-Columbia. His 1982 book, *A Great and Necessary Measure: George Grenville and the Genesis of the Stamp Act, 1763–1765,* and his current project on *Empire and Taxation* (on George III and the origins of the American Revolution) are parts of a projected multivolume survey of British politicians and the American Revolution.

E. S. BURT of Yale University has just finished a book-length manuscript on Rousseau's autobiographies and is currently working on Diderot's pedagogical writings. The paper in this volume, first given at the NEASECS meeting, is a shortened version of a section in the former.

PATRICK COLEMAN is Associate Professor and Chairman of French at UCLA. He is currently working on a book on early French Romanticism. Professor Coleman's paper was originally presented to a meeting of ASECS in 1985.

LESTER G. CROCKER is William R. Kenan Professor Emeritus of French, University of Virginia. He was the first president of ASECS. He has been working recently on interpretations of the Enlightenment. His article, "Interpreting the Enlightenment: a Political Approach," appeared in the *Journal of the History of Ideas,* April–June 1985. His paper in this volume was presented at a Plenary Session of the SEASECS meeting in 1986.

JULIA B. CURTIS has a doctorate in history from Bryn Mawr College and has taught at the University of Massachusetts, Amherst, and Old Dominion University. She is writing a book on the seventeenth- and eighteenth-century Chinese export shards unearthed on colonial sites in Southern Virginia and has written articles on shipwrecks containing Chinese ceramics.

JAN FERGUS of Lehigh University has published articles on provincial readership in eighteenth-century England and a book on Jane Austen. She is engaged on a book-length study of the eighteenth-century reading public.

DAVID HAYTON, History of Parliament Trust, whose paper was read at the ASECS meeting, has published several articles on Anglo-Irish politics, 1689-c. 1750, the most recent being "Walpole and Ireland" in *Britain in the Age of Walpole* (1984, ed. by J. Black).

ROY HARRIS is Professor of General Linguistics in the University of Oxford. His most recent book is *The Origin of Writing* (London: Duckworth, 1986).

PAUL HOLDENGRÄBER, currently at Princeton University, is working on a full-length study of the impact of the museum, as institution and metaphor, on European literature from the middle of the eighteenth century to the present.

SUSAN KLEM JACKSON is Assistant Professor of French at Boston University. She has published articles on Rousseau and Isabelle de Charrière and is currently working on a book about Rousseau's occasional texts. Her paper was presented at the ASECS meeting.

VERONICA KELLY, Assistant Professor of English at Syracuse University, is writing a book on empiricism and literary form.

RONALD R. KIDD is Associate Professor of Music History at Purdue University, West Lafayette. He is currently completing a descriptive catalogue of Jefferson's library of music.

JAMES KING, Professor of English at McMaster University, is the author of the definitive biography of Cowper (Duke) and the co-editor of the standard five-volume edition (Clarendon) of the Cowper letters and prose writings. His newest book is *Interior Landscapes: A Life of Paul Nash* (Weidenfeld & Nicolson). His essay in this volume was presented at the ASECS meeting.

G. S. ROUSSEAU, UCLA, spent the academic year 1987 as a Senior Fellow of the National Endowment for the Humanities, and is most recently the author (with Roy Porter) of *Sexual Underworlds of the Enlightenment,* published by the Manchester University Press.

SIMON SCHAFFER lectures in history and philosophy of science at the University of Cambridge. He has published on the social history of experimental philosophy and astronomy in early modern Britain and France.

JEFFREY SMITTEN is Associate Professor and Interim Chairman of the Department of English at Texas Tech University. He is currently at work on a book tentatively titled "William Robertson: Modernism and History." His paper was presented to ASECS in Williamsburg.

JANICE THADDEUS of Harvard University has published articles on a variety of subjects, most recently on Swift in *SECC* and on Eva Maria Veigel, Mrs. Garrick, in *Eighteenth-Century Life.*

NORMAN J. W. THROWER is the Director of the William Andrews Clark Memorial Library, and Professor of Geography at the University of California, Los Angeles.

ROBERT W. UPHAUS, Professor of English at Michigan State University, is the author of *The Impossible Observer* (Kentucky, 1979), *Beyond Tragedy* (Kentucky, 1981), and *William Hazlitt* (G. K. Hall, 1985). His paper was originally presented at the Williamsburg meeting of ASECS.

KATHLEEN WELLMAN, Professor of History at Southern Methodist University, is working on connections between medicine and philosophy in eighteenth-century France, and completing a book on medicine in the philosophy of La Mettrie. Professor Wellman's essay in this volume was read at the ASECS meeting.

Executive Board, 1986–1987

Institutional Members

of the American Society

for Eighteenth-Century Studies

Arizona State University
University of Arkansas
National Library of
 Australia
University of Calgary
University of California,
 Davis
University of California,
 Irvine
University of California,
 Los Angeles/William Andrews
 Clark Memorial Library
University of California,
 San Diego
California State University,
 Long Beach
Carleton University
Case Western Reserve
 University
University of Cincinnati
City College, CUNY
Claremont Graduate
 School
Cleveland State University
Colonial Williamsburg
 Foundation
University of Colorado
 at Denver
University of Connecticut
Dalhousie University
Detroit Institute of Arts,
 Founders Society
Emory University
University of Evansville
Folger Institute of
 Renaissance and
 Eighteenth-Century Studies

Fordham University
Georgia Institute of
 Technology
Georgia State University
University of Georgia
Gettysburg College
Haverford College
Herzog August Bibliothek,
 Wolfenbüttel
University of Illinois at
 Chicago
Institute of Early American
 History and Culture
John Carter Brown Library
The Johns Hopkins
 University
University of Kansas
University of Kentucky
Kimbell Art Museum, Fort
 Worth
Lehigh University
Lehman College, CUNY
Los Angeles County
 Museum of Art
McMaster University/
 Association for 18th-
 Century Studies
University of Michigan,
 Ann Arbor
Michigan State University
University of Minnesota
Mount Saint Vincent
 University
State University of
 New York, Binghamton
State University of New
 York, Fredonia

353

University of North
    Carolina, Chapel Hill
Northern Illinois University
Northwestern University
The Ohio State University
University of Pennsylvania
University of Pittsburgh
Purdue University
University of Rochester
Rockford College
Rutgers University
Smith College
Smithsonian Institution
University of Southern
    California
University of Southern
    Mississippi
Swarthmore College
Sweet Briar College
University of Tennessee
University of Texas at
    Austin
Texas A&M University

Texas Tech University
Towson State University
Trinity College
Tulane University
University of Tulsa
University of Utrecht,
    Institute for
    Comparative and
    General Literature
University of Victoria
University of Virginia
The Voltaire Foundation
Washington University, St.
    Louis
Westfälische Wilhelms-
    Universität, Münster
The Henry Francis du Pont
    Winterthur Museum
University of Wisconsin,
    Milwaukee
Yale Center for British Art and
    British Studies
Yale University

Sponsoring Members

of the American Society
for Eighteenth-Century Studies

G. L. Anderson
Mark S. Auburn
Jeffrey Barnouw
Eric Bauer
Jerry C. Beasley
Emmett G. Bedford
Pamela J. Bennett
L. J. Bianchi
Carol Blum
Martha F. Bowden
George C. Branam
Leo Braudy
Elizabeth Brophy
Morris R. Brownell
Joseph A. Byrnes
Rosemary M. Canfield
Brigitte Carnochan
W. B. Carnochan
David W. Carrithers
Richard G. Carrott
Ellmore A. Champie
Henry S. Commager
Brian Corman
Howard J. Coughlin
Patricia B. Craddock
David W. Dangremond
Robert A. Day
John Dowling
A. C. Elias, Jr.
Lee Andrew Elioseff
Roger Emerson
Robert Enggass
Carol Houlihan Flynn
Jack Fruchtman, Jr.
Anne Barbeau Gardiner

Frank J. Garosi
Morris Golden
Peter B. Goldman
Josephine Grieder
Dustin H. Griffin
Walter Grossmann
Leon M. Guilhamet
Phyllis J. Guskin
H. George Hahn
Roger Hahn
Elizabeth Harries
Karsten Harries
Phillip Harth
Donald M. Hassler
Emita B. Hill
Stephen Holliday
Robert H. Hopkins
William C. Horne
Adrienne D. Hytier
Margaret C. Jacob
Thomas Jemielity
Frank A. Kafker
Deborah J. Knuth
Gwin J. Kolb
Carl R. Kropf
Colby H. Kullman
Catherine Lafarge
I. Leonard Leeb
J. A. Levine
Sidney J. Lewis
Herbert Livingston
Albert M. Lyles
Maynard Mack
E. Roger Mandle
Michael J. Marcuse

355

Geoffrey Marshall
Gita May
Temple J. Maynard
Donald C. Mell, Jr.
Paul H. Meyer
Earl Miner
Madeleine F. Morris
Nicolas H. Nelson
Melvyn New
Hal N. Opperman
B. A. B. Pasta
Harry C. Payne
Jean A. Perkins
Leland D. Peterson
Peter W. Petschauer
J. G. A. Pocock
John V. Price
Irwin Primer
Jules D. Prown
Richard E. Quaintance, Jr.
Ralph W. Rader
Clifford Earl Ramsey
Thomas J. Regan
Hugh Reid
James A. W. Rembert
Walter E. Rex
Danelle Rice
John Richetti
Jack Richtman
Betty Rizzo
E. L. Ruhe
Kathleen L. Russo
Peter Sabor
Mona Scheuermann

Rachel R. Schneider
Barbara Brandon
  Schnorrenberg
William C. Schrader
Richard B. Schwartz
Howard Serwer
Charles E. Shields, III
Frank Shuffelton
Oliver F. Sigworth
John E. Sitter
Henry L. Snyder
Patricia Meyer Spacks
Robert Donald Spector
Mary Margaret Stewart
Ann T. Straulman
Albrecht B. Strauss
Felicia Sturzer
Amie Tannenbaum
Madeleine Therrien
James Thompson
Edward Tomarken
Betty Perry Townsend
Daniel D. Townsend
John A. Vance
David M. Vieth
Tom Vitelli
Morris Wachs
Renée Waldinger
Howard D. Weinbrot
Joel C. Weinsheimer
David Wheeler
Roger L. Williams
Samuel H. Woods
John W. Yolton

Patrons

of the American Society
for Eighteenth-Century Studies

Index

Italicized page numbers indicate topics treated extensively.